BLACK POWER, BLACK LAWYER
My Audacious Quest For Justice

Memoir of
Nkechi Taifa

Published by
House of Songhay II
Washington, DC

WebSite – **www.blackpowerblacklawyer.com**

Copyright © 2020 • Nkechi Taifa
All Rights Reserved.

ISBN 978-1-7347693-1-9
Hardcover
ISBN 978-1-7347693-0-2
Paperback
ISBN 978-1-7347693-2-6
ebook

Library of Congress Control Number: 2020904848

Front Cover Image
Michael Anthony Brown/Kakonja
Design-n-Layout
Zama Cook • Sababu Filmworks
Back Cover Foto
Rodney Ladson

Manufactured in the United States of America

BLACK POWER, BLACK LAWYER
My Audacious Quest for Justice

Memoir of Nkechi Taifa, Esq.

Table Of Contents

Chapter Eight
"I Feel Good, Like I Knew That I Would"

Chapter Nine
"Fight the Power"

Chapter Ten
"Tears of a Clown"

Epilogue

~ Dedication ~

For My Brothers:
Rev. Ishakamusa Barashango, President Imari Abubakari Obadele,
former Mayor Attorney Chokwe Lumumba, Brother Kwame Afoh

For My Sisters:
Queen Mother Audley Moore, Dr. Frances Cress Welsing,
Dr. Jean Sindab, Sister Safiya Bukhari

I walked in your midst.
You inspired me.
You taught me.
You grounded me.
And now you are ancestors.
Rest in peace and power, knowing that
"The Struggle Continues…"

~ Acknowledgements ~

This book was decades in the making. First and foremost, thank you to all my family members in the ancestral realm, but particularly Mommy and Daddy for providing a nurturing and understanding atmosphere that allowed my dreams and aspirations to soar; to my Uncle James Ambrose McIntosh for his inspirations; and to my niece Tina Drake who departed far too soon, secreting within herself many exciting unwritten story threads.

To my sisters, Paula Drake and Roberta Kee – I appreciated your confidence in me, your constant support, and for always having my back. And to my miracle birth daughter Mariama, my barometer, who gave me frequent reality checks. Although I declined to follow all of her advice, I appreciated every opinion offered.

I am forever grateful to Paula Bernette Brooks – the first person I trusted to look at my manuscript in the rough, saw a diamond, and helped to smooth it out. Thank you Patrice Gaines, for picking up the mantle, further whipping my words into shape. And absolute love to Makini Nyanteh, who took my completed manuscript, tightened it up, and brought it across the finish line. My gratitude goes out to each of you. Thank you for helping me "birth this baby!"

I treasure my awesome and fierce Mastermind Team – Dr. Deborah Bernal/Mama Eshe and Sister Anuli Street, who in phone conference meetings each week for over a year, held my hand, kicked my behind, made me focus, served as a sounding board, and brilliantly helped guide me and light the path to success. I honestly could not have brought my memoir to fruition without your sage wisdom and indispensable advice.

I appreciate my beta readers who shared the gift of their time to plough through early drafts of my manuscript and provide valuable feedback, especially Edward Onaci, Carmen Crusoe, and Jasmine Mickens.

I am grateful to the amazing Marita Golden and the tremendous insight I gained from her writing workshops, especially the class with Tracy McGhee.

I am blessed for the awesome work of my spot-on production team – Zama Cook (layout and design), Paula Coleman (proofreading), Michael Brown (cover art), Oforiwa Idawa (web services), Willie "Yao" Brewer (videography).

Never underestimate the power of moral support. Thank you to my Solace Sistas' group – especially Angelyn Frazer-Giles, Trina Ramsey, Cynthia Roseberry, Subrina Wood, Keri Nash and Cynthia Robbins. I'm grateful for my Community Families, especially the Temple of Nyame, NationHouse, Roots, Ujamaa, Appeal, African Freedom Fund, N'COBRA, WPFW, Ausar Auset Society, National African American Reparations Commission, Institute of the Black World 21st Century, Black Family Summit, Institute for Karmic Guidance, Black Seeds, UNIA and the WO'SE Community. And I thank the Justice Roundtable coalition, especially my forever "ride or die" colleague, Jesselyn McCurdy.

Thank you to all the phenomenal members of the Taifa Memoir Power Team, which constantly expands. You know who you are. I'm indebted.

And I admire all those who could identify with my journey, encouraged me, or put up with my idiosyncrasies – particularly Dakarai Kearney, Khaleed and Makeda London, Khalid Abdur-Rasheed, Kamau Amin, Bomani Sekou, Tyehimba Peyton, Lydia Curtis, Teresa Price, Rasafik Weusi, Imamu Kuumba, Hanif Martin, Carla Potter, Venus Campbell, Ama Nyamekye, Donna Caldwell, Paul Coates, Kianga Cheryle Baptiste, Lawrence Kearney, Kibibi Tyehimba, Andrea James, Ebony Underwood, Alice Marie Johnson, Akinyele Umoja, Shushanna Shakur, Maynard Henry, Rosaline Preudhomme, Adwoa Carr, Roy Pearson and more.

And last but not least – I am humbled by the ancestors upon whose shoulders I stand, who impressed upon me to be absolutely authentic, to not be embarrassed, to tell it like it is, and to not hold back. I acknowledge their omniscient presence and contributions to the birthing of my book.

~ Foreword ~

When our sister Nkechi Taifa shared with me the manuscript for the book you now open, I drew a long, deep breath, triggered by an electric surge of anticipation, and exhaled a sigh of deep relief. We had, at last, her testimony. When she honored me by asking if I would write a foreword, I felt trapped under the weight of the task, freeing myself to write these few words only after serial reassurances from her that I was the one among her nation of comrades she felt best suited for the expected task. This is the spirit and technique of our Beloved Sister: She sets us all to work, expecting nothing more or less than that we match her example.

And what an example she is. Having watched Nkechi convene symposia, forums and working formations of human rights and social justice comrades for years, I know that she was/is a singularly unique connecting thread in a multiracial, multi-cultural and intergenerational tapestry of people committed to the best ideals of our common humanity. Having watched her convene and/or contribute to countless rituals of remembrance, reflection and renewal that joined elders to new generations of Pan African nationalists, I know that she was/is a Black pillar of consistent tactical and creative genius, anchored in an unapologetically African foundation.

I have watched Nkechi narrate the history of the centuries-long fight for reparations before audiences of lawyers, legal scholars and policymakers that left us all on our feet, reeducated and transformed. I have watched her stand next to the bodies of fallen elders and comrades and send forth their spirits with poetic conjure that left us all rising like Ra. I have sat next to her in strategy meetings and watched her carefully mediate, rip apart and lovingly re-direct often conflicting energies and agendas until we reached consensus in how to intervene on behalf of our political prisoners and other still-suffering movement soldiers.

You will now read the record to date of this remarkable woman's life and work. For years, those of us who know, love and have struggled alongside and learned from her have anticipated the day that so many more would grow from her experiences and insights. Far too many of our true warriors have joined our powerful band of ancestors without pausing to leave a testament, leaving the rest of us to keep their works and words alive from mouth to ear. The rest of us always turn to each other in the wake and promise not to be the next one to leave without speaking to readers in the future beyond the ones in living memory.

In this, as in so many other moments, Nkechi Taifa shows us the way to keep that promise. With this word before The Word, I assure you that the book you are about to read is one of the most important texts you will ever read. Though it is only a glimpse of one of those warrior lives spent in service to a people and to all people, it is a kaleidoscope of reflections narrated by one who walked and walks among the titans. By one who saw and sees it all and was at or near the center of a great deal of it. Nkechi has produced what the ancient Egyptians called a Sebayt, a teaching. It will endure. And you will be transformed.

Nkechi Taifa is, as the title of her memoir reflects, a Black lawyer. Those skills, to borrow from Gordon Parks' first memoir, were only her most public-facing set of weapons. She was driven to acquire the skill to pass the bar – quite literally – to represent the momentarily helpless among us before the legal apparatus that has, for two and a third centuries in this settler colony turned state, consistently stood between us and our liberation. And represent us she has, from birth at Howard University's Freedmen's Hospital to the front lines of the Black Power/Black Arts/Black Studies movements of the 1960s-70s to the front lines of Anti Apartheid, Anti War on Drugs and Anti COINTELPRO struggles of the 1970s-90s to the courtrooms, boardrooms and inner chambers of the White House in the years during, since and beyond.

Nkechi narrates her mastery of her chosen tools by detailing her grounding from childhood in the work of her fellow warriors of the last three generations of American and global African struggle. These giants, whose words and work educated, trained, often argued and stood shoulder to shoulder with and ultimately bequeathed to her the responsibility of duplicating their heroic feats, are for her not research subjects, trapped in the fragmented silences of scattered bits of archival material. Books and articles by too many non-combatant academics, writing in safety from ivy cloisters with privileges won for them by too-often sacrificed others, should be read only after reading the testaments and witnesses of those who lived and fought the battles. Nkechi has given us this gift and given her comrades a template for committing their own lives, memories and instructions to print.

Black Power/Black Lawyer is written in Nkechi's signature lyric and at once direct narrative style. For ten chapters, she anchors us in a journey through Black communities, with snapshots of remarkable Black people, beginning with her parents, whose most revolutionary acts are to be found in the love and sacrifice they poured into her. She is at turns blunt, uncompromising, vulnerable, triumphant and wounded, sometimes, in the words of Sister Sonia Sanchez, in the houses of friends. The entire text is soldered together with the tears and rage of an oppressed African nation, from enslavement to the bowels of today's indefensible prison system. It is also forged in the fire of revolutionary love, the type that never forgets but also forgives our people for doing what we have had to do to survive.

One of the many gifts of *Black Power/Black Lawyer* is that Nkechi sets a roadmap for searching out the lives and memories of now-Ancestors who trained her. Queen

Mother Audley Moore transitioned before she could leave a memoir. She is in these pages, as are Baba Imari Abubakari Obadele, Baba Chokwe Lumumba and Mama Frances Cress Welsing, among so many others. None of these giants left a written memoir for us to consider as a testament to their life and times. In gifting us with this text, Nkechi brings them and many others along with her, and sparks our memories of each person, demanding that we join her in an exercise of requiem, remembrance and recommitment to principled struggle.

Black Power/Black Lawyer joins watershed intellectual autobiographies/field manuals for African liberation such as Amy Jacques Garvey's *Garvey and Garveyism*, Ras Makonnen's *Pan Africanism From Within*, Angela Davis's *The Autobiography of Angela Davis*, Assata Shakur's *Assata*, Elbert "Big Man" Howard's *Panther on the Prowl*, Ron Walters's *Pan Africanism and the African Diaspora* and, more recently, Sarudzayi Sevanhu's *Pan African Revolutionary* and Ron Daniels's *Still on This Journey*. There are still far too few memoirs by our current generation of warriors birthed into the universe, and too fewer still of them written by our sister comrades. Nkechi has issued the challenge to her generation to rescue our stories from retelling by those who would blunt their revolutionary message. We will do well to honor her example by following it.

Nkechi Taifa will always be too young to have lived as many lifetimes as this book's pages of memory and conviction reflect. She begins this story with the execution of Emmett Till and carries it through the false promise of Barack Obama and the current crop of young revolutionaries for who she serves as a *Jegna*. As her comrade and brother of only slightly fewer years on earth, I am astonished at her capacity for remembering events and experiences. I am also grateful as a brother in the struggle to which she continues to give her life that she received a prodigious memory as one of her many gifts. There was a time when this book would've graced the shelves of her beloved Drum and Spear Bookstore, or New York's Liberation Bookstore. Today, you may be reading it on your electronic device. Only the technology has shifted: The struggle that Nkechi and the rest of us continue to wage remains the same. This book allows all of us who have walked with her to remember, to reflect, and to act in the living now. Asante Sana, Beloved Sister. And Asante Sana, Anticipating Reader: Enjoy this glimpse into the Souls of Free Black Folk.

Greg Carr, PhD, JD
Associate Professor and Chair, Department of Afro American Studies
Adjunct Professor of Law
Howard University
Washington, DC
July, 2020

~ Preface ~

"Mommy, did you get Rosa Parks out of jail?" quizzed my then five-year-old daughter, out of the blue, one warm evening. I started to burst out laughing, but caught myself after realizing the sincerity of her query. Suppressing a giggle, I carefully responded, "No baby, I was just a year old myself when Rosa Parks went to jail!"

Although unsure of what precipitated this question, I was honored all the same. My little girl made what I thought to be a quantum leap for a child so young – she associated her Mommy with Rosa Parks, a courageous woman who defied the laws of this land and was unjustly jailed. Filled with pride, I smiled brightly, gave her a big hug and added, "Sweetie, Rosa Parks went to jail a long time ago, but don't ever forget her story, because it is one of the reasons I always wanted to become a lawyer."

Later I lamented what I thought to be my inadequate response, but it was the best reply I could think of at the moment. In retrospect, I should have emphasized to my daughter the relativity of time. I should have impressed upon her young mind that although I was just a baby when Rosa Parks' protest catapulted the Montgomery Bus Boycott into the spotlight, within the context of time, the incident really was not that long ago.

Like my daughter, I was similar to most children and had a very limited perspective of the distance between myself and historical events when I was growing up. Slavery was 'way back in the old days,' which translated into a million years ago to my young mind. It only dawned on me in recent years that when Harriet Tubman died in 1913, my Uncle Ambrose was three years old. My father and mother were born shortly thereafter, only a scant seven and ten years later, respectively.

To this day I am convinced that my sensitivity to injustice emanates from the numbing shock I felt when I learned Black people were still being murdered for trying to exercise their right to vote during the early sixties, while I was in grade school. 'Way back in the old days' was actually not that long ago, yet young people today, including my daughter, view my childhood of the 1950s as far from their current reality as I did of my parents' time.

My story is, both solemn and spicy. It is part memoir, part textbook, part study guide, part exposeʹ *Black Power, Black Lawyer* teaches, preaches, rhapsodizes and tantalizes. It stitches suspense, calamity, humor and wit into a tapestry of history, politics, law, culture and romance. And it threads the needle connecting critical dots of the continuum for justice from yesteryear's freedom fighters to today's liberationists.

These pages encapsulate slices of my life narrative – the story of a little pumper-nickel-hued girl growing up in the eras of McCarthy, the Cold War and Civil Rights during the mid-20th century. The story of an impressionable young sister coming of age at the time of the Viet Nam War and the Black is Beautiful and Black Power Movements of the late 1960s and 1970s. The story of a maturing revolutionary finding her niche within the Cultural/Black Nationalist, Southern Africa freedom struggle, and reparations movements of the late 20th century. And the story of an indomitable woman-warrior-lawyer who helped transform criminal justice reform into a movement against mass incarceration in the new millennium.

These memories, whether serious, scandalous or sensational, helped shape my cultural identity and political consciousness, and all of these struggles were episodes during my life's quest for justice.

But be forewarned. My story does not encompass fairytales and lullabies. Thus, if you are seeking a book that will only envelope you with warm, fuzzy feelings of joy and happiness, or deliver nostalgia devoid of the pain of reality, this book is not for you. My audacious quest for justice is a gripping commentary on the realities of life, the perennial nature of human resistance against oppression, and my earnest embrace of what is fair and correct. Although sometimes raw, sometimes abrasive, sometimes passionate, I offer you my truth, unapologetically, and unfiltered, with honesty and authenticity.

Time and eras have always fascinated me, from the captivating tales of my childhood where a talisman catapults adventurers to centuries earlier, to the intriguing "teleportations" within the space-time continuum of Star Trek lore. My memoir chronicles episodes focused heavily on the time period I affectionately refer to as "The Struggle," spanning the first 50-plus years of my life. These eras are generally explored linearly, measuring sequential points along a horizontal line. I, however, embrace the exploration of these times more holistically – examining phenomena not limited to their chronological occurrences, but connecting dots to contemporary manifestations.

For what is time, I ponder, but a journey through the texture of a mosaic of experiences, layered with the painful sorrows and joyous hopes of mundane existence. Those who lived through the same times and events as me may have different interpretations of comparable experiences based on the contour and context of their own lives.

Some reading this book will readily identify with my journey, with a connected eye and ear. Others reading my story will eagerly grasp for understanding, soaking up the wonder of vicariously walking in another's footsteps. And there will be others who will peruse my memoir with something between disinterest and disbelief, politely skimming before resting this tome on cobwebbed shelves.

I have asked myself whether I should have made my book more universal, rather than one largely framed by race. I wondered whether I should have presented a more pacifist view to life, like the one immortalized by 1991 police brutality victim Rodney King in his quote: "Why can't we all just get along?"

Sure, I could have composed my memoirs around the birthday parties of my childhood when we played pin the tail on the donkey, swiveled to the limbo, and gleefully scrambled for candy after raucously busting open piñatas. Or the family summer vacations that I loved – traveling to Montreal, Canada for the 1967 World's Fair, the beautiful Catskill mountains in upstate New York, or the luscious beaches of Montego Bay, Jamaica. But those times, while happy and joyous, are not the centerpiece of my reflections when I think about what has framed my consciousness and the person I am today.

Instead, I am haunted by nightmares of chained dark-hued women aboard slave ships coping with the flow of their menstrual blood while gasping from the stench of vomit during dreadful voyages of the Middle Passage's maafa.[1]

I am traumatized by visions of that anonymous old White man who violated my body and my childhood at a beach somewhere up North sometime during the late fifties.

I am humiliated by being judged initially, not on the basis of my academic qualifications or expertise, but rather by the immutable color of my skin, the tongue-twisting ethnicity of my adopted name, and the cultural choice I made to not mutilate the natural coil in my hair.

I grew up during the fifties and sixties, matriculated through college during the seventies while evolving as a self-proclaimed revolutionary with thoughts and actions running counter to the mainstream. I spent much of the eighties trying not to get pregnant and, ironically, spent the early nineties trying to conceive. Simultaneously, I was striving to be a 'people's lawyer,' representing the indigent and those who fought for freedom.

After the turn of the 20th century and two failed marriages, I reflected on my life and career in justice advocacy and was determined to experience more. And thus I started the 21st century settling down and raising a miracle-birth daughter while tying the knot for a third time with an unlikely partner.

Mine is the story of a quest rarely told. The search for the resisters and the rebellious. The pursuit of issues on the cutting edge. There are memoirs chronicling icons striving for justice during the well-documented Civil Rights era, but not nearly enough has been said or written about the transformative journeys for self-realization of ordinary people growing up during the tumult of the Black Power era. This rich period of time between the late 1960s and 1970s through the early 1980s must be accurately acknowledged, embraced, and understood such that it may live and flourish in the hearts and minds of future generations.

Navigate this audacious quest with me as I bear witness to ancestors, people and episodes that swayed the shaping of my identity and consciousness. I want my pursuit for justice as a Black Power advocate and a Black Movement Lawyer to awaken, inform, provoke, move and, at its best, fire you up to either join, or continue, "The Struggle."

It's hard to know with which nostalgic memory to begin this journey with you. Sitting on the lap of that fine brother pulling security in the front office of the Black Panther Party? The "All-White-Girls-Catholic-High-School" in Maryland my parents made me attend? The piercing verses of my radical poetry? Dining with Minister Louis Farrakhan at Imari Obadele's mama's home in Philadelphia?

The African spirituality that prevailed over Western medicine that resulted in my pregnancy? The three times I have been arrested? The time I thought I had contracted AIDS? Being detained at an airport five months pregnant as an alleged enemy of the state? Accused of being an FBI agent?

Finding a husband through the classifieds? Winning a six figure settlement for my clients in a pivotal employment discrimination suit against a major news media network? Representing the lead defendant in the Capitol Bombing case? Being a catalyst which sparked the change to the infamous crack cocaine disparity? There are so, so many points of departure to choose from.

As a swirling, seemingly endless collage of disjointed, yet connected, life events race through my mind, an ancestral voice gently whispers, 'how about that reflection sitting in the Obama White House, when you realized no one there, other than perhaps the Secret Service at the entrance, likely knew anything about the real you.'

To the ancestors I respond: I hear you. Let's do this!

~ Prologue ~
"Judge Not"[2]

Section 1
Red Badge at the White House

It is November 30, 2016, and I am sitting in one of the reserved seats around the grand conference table in the prestigious and elegant Roosevelt Room, a meeting space in the West Wing of the White House and the principal workplace of the President of the United States. I am surrounded by the executives of a dozen or so social justice foundations and companies for a meeting with President Barack Obama's chief advisor, Valerie Jarrett. Although a bit miffed that I had to leave my cellphone in a cubbyhole outside the meeting room, I know that such protocols are par for the course for meetings in the West Wing.

As my slender brown fingers brush my right earlobe, I'm irritated that I had neglected to glance at a mirror before entering. 'Dang,' I silently mouthed to myself as I feel the space where a cowrie shell earring should have been nestled. 'Dang,' I echo as it becomes apparent that my locs[3] are askew. I see no other alternative in that instance but to discretely remove the sole edifice dangling prominently from my left lobe, and blindly smooth down the runaway wisps of my crinkly, coiled hair.

My eyes rotate toward my right to the bust of President Roosevelt situated on the cherry oak side table. My assigned seat is positioned in front of the locked door that someone whispered is the Oval Office, although its peephole is too high for 5-foot-me to peer into. There are scarcely two months left in the presidency of Barack Obama, and everyone in the room is still numb and reeling from the victory of controversial entrepreneur and TV reality star, Donald Trump, as President-Elect.

I am not really excited to be at the White House on this day. I have been on its grounds many times; in most cases attending meetings or events in the Old Executive Office Building, almost weekly, around issues of criminal justice reform. So the allure of these corridors of power wore off for me a long time ago. The West Wing, however, was not my stomping grounds, and certainly not the Roosevelt Room.

As I sat waiting for Valerie to enter, I reflected on one of my first times at the headquarters of arguably the most powerful person in the world. It was 2012 and I was a senior policy analyst for the Washington Office of billionaire George Soros' Open Society Foundations and Open Society Policy Center, working primarily on issues of criminal justice reform. I had organized a coalition meeting with a high-level Obama staffer, and had identified candidates from working groups of the coalition I convened, the Justice Roundtable, to brief the White House on our activities.

However, completely out of my control, I was late to the very meeting I called and was to chair. I couldn't believe it. While coalition member after coalition member, mostly White colleagues of mine, were whisked through the security entrance with the required green badge for unfettered entry, little Black me was stopped fast in my tracks, handed a red badge and ordered to wait for an escort.

"What?!" I stridently protested. "I organized this meeting. What's the problem?" I vociferously complained to the Secret Service gatekeeper, seething mad yet maintaining an appropriate amount of composure. It was embarrassing, being escorted like a child. Why would I be encumbered with a red badge? And from the Obama Administration?! I was livid.

I smile as I sit in the White House Roosevelt Room four years later after winning the fight for the coveted green badge, and ruminate on the confluence of circumstances over the past five decades that most likely resulted in me being singled out for strict security scrutiny. I marvel at just how little anyone in this room actually knows about me.

And then I remembered a pivotal phone call 28 years earlier.

Section 2
But They Are *White* Revolutionaries

It was 1988, and I had recently gone into the private practice of law. I was 33, a bit older than most new lawyers, having gone to law school at age 27 as opposed to right out of undergraduate school. I was representing indigent clients in fairly routine cases such as drug possession and simple assault, slowly building my law practice. I already had standing in the community as a revolutionary activist; my goal now was to gain a professional reputation in the legal arena. Then one day I received a consequential phone call.

"Sister Nkechi, this is Ahmed."

"Hey Brother, Free the Land!" I greeted him enthusiastically with the salutation of the New Afrikan Independence Movement.[4]

"Sis, you heard about the indictment?"

"Yes." I knew what he was talking about. The U.S. Capitol building had been bombed after the U.S. invasion of Grenada several years earlier and suspects had just been arrested. It was all over the news, but I had no details.

"Laura Whitehorn wants to talk to you."

"Who?" I quizzed, oblivious to the name.

"Laura. She's one of the defendants in the case."

I really only knew the name of one of the suspects, Marilyn Buck, who had just been convicted in the daring liberation of Sister Assata Shakur from prison years earlier. Talk about a modern-day Underground Railroad!

"Oh yes, Laura," I replied as if I knew exactly who she was. "She wants to talk to me?"

"Yes, she wants you to be her lawyer," he stated matter-of-factly.

How ridiculous can you get? I thought. A major RICO criminal conspiracy case in federal court?! The proposition sounded ludicrous. No way! Didn't I recently embarrass myself at my first jury trial? And quiet as it was kept, I was trying to balance my political work with my legal career. Quite frankly, I was apprehensive about meshing these two worlds this early in my career.

This was years before the internet, before Facebook, Twitter or Instagram. One could basically remain anonymous if one chose to, except of course from FBI surveillance. Despite my earlier years of Black Power salutes and revolutionary Black activism, I was trying to keep a low profile. I was a professional now, with an American Express card. I was trying to enter the legal mainstream; attempting to move away or at least downplay my presence in "The Movement." Of course, I revealed none of this to Brother Ahmed, who I considered the epitome of the "revolutionary's revolutionary."

But Ahmed's call made it clear that "The Struggle" was not going to let me go. And in my heart, I knew I was not ready to leave it either. Coming to terms with this, I realized I couldn't abandon the principles of righteousness I had believed in and fought for most of my life. I mean, wasn't this the reason I wanted to be a lawyer in the first place? Wasn't my dream to become a "people's lawyer," a "revolutionary lawyer?" Wasn't it my inspiration to defend political prisoners and prisoners of war?

But these are *White* political prisoners, a small voice inside me kept piping up. I took a deep breath. OK, White revolutionaries. Hell, I knew nothing about White people revolutionaries. I'd heard of the John Brown Anti-Klan Committee. I'd heard of the May 19th organization, the Weather Underground, Students for a Democratic Society, and the Prairie Fire Organizing Committee. But I had had no previous interactions or dealings with White supporters of the Black liberation movement, despite their whispered associations with "The Struggle." I was a D.C.– born and bred Black cultural revolutionary nationalist, organizing in the Black community, alongside other Black people, since my high school days.

"Nkechi!" Ahmed shouted impatiently into the phone, jolting me back to the conversation. "Laura Whitehorn's the lead defendant in the case," he added quickly. "She wants a conscious Black attorney. She wants a revolutionary Black attorney. She wants you!"

Lawd have mercy. Little ole new lawyer me. Me, who after years of being on the cutting edge of revolutionary action, was pathetically trying to be "a good Negro" and a "responsible" lawyer. But, despite the goosebumps, stomach gurgling, and a shitload of reservations, I told Ahmed yes.

"I'll talk to Laura," I said. I knew without a doubt I had to rise to the occasion. An ancestral voice inside my head said: Nkechi, you can do this. You must do this!

Chapter One
"O-o-h Child, Things Are Gonna Get Easier"[5]

Section 1
1954, and Before

Even though I entered Earth's physical plane on December 29th, just two days before the advent of 1955, I have wholeheartedly claimed 1954 as a sign of my destiny.

Nineteen fifty-four was an auspicious, historic marker: it was the very year of the Supreme Court's landmark *Brown v. Board of Education* decision, which ruled state-sanctioned segregation of public schools unconstitutional.

Nineteen fifty-four was two years before they hauled the inimitable Paul Robeson before the House Un-American Activities Committee, where he delivered brilliant testimony as a defense to scurrilous accusations.

Nineteen fifty-four was eight years before the indomitable Fannie Lou Hamer vowed to register to vote in Sunflower County, Mississippi, risking her livelihood and her life.

Nineteen fifty-four was two years before the newly enlightened Malcolm Little left prison a renewed and inspired man, and eventually became the fiery advocate for justice known as Malcolm X.

History was always my thing. It was my major in college and, as such, I tended to look at my life as it correlated to prominent historical events. I was born 29 years after the Honorable Marcus Mosiah Garvey's spectacular, military-style parades marched through the streets of Harlem. My birth took place 103 years after anti-slavery orator Sojourner Truth seized the platform of a tumultuous women's rights convention, incensed that the rights of Black women were being crassly ignored, and tersely demanded, "And ain't I a woman?" My life began 126 years after Denmark Vesey's ingenious, yet tragic, effort to free enslaved Africans in the South ultimately resulted in his assassination. I could go on, but suffice it to say I was born at a time when struggles for justice and liberation were both the pretext and context of my very existence.

Even the history of the hospital where I was born offered a hint of the pre-ordained journey I would undertake. I was born in Washington, D.C.'s Freedmen's Hospital, which later became Howard University Hospital. I get nostalgic every time I pass by the original red brick building that now proudly houses the Howard University Cathy Hughes School of Communications.

The very name "Freedmen" brings to my mind images of newly freed Black people lined up at the door of a modest hospital with their bodies, once bound in shackles, weary and infirmed, but eager for gentle care. With pride they waited to enter, seeking a modicum of treatment in a facility relegated solely to their lot. How could they have ever known that this hospital would go on to train some of the finest medical geniuses in the world?

The litany of medical pioneers associated with this historic institution are legion. There was Dr. Charles Drew, who revolutionized medicine by discovering that blood plasma could be stored, preserved and used in an emergency. There was Dr. Daniel Hale Williams, who performed the first open heart surgery and revolutionized the advancement of medical practices for generations to come. And there were so many others who walked those hallowed halls, whose brilliance and tenacity catapulted medical advancement, even in the face of the racism and discrimination they experienced in their time.

Of course I didn't know all of this when I was born, and sadly I didn't learn it later in school. However, Freedmen's Hospital was there for Black folk when segregated White medical centers systematically denied admission based on race. People were not refused medical treatment because they were elderly. They were not refused treatment because they were gay. They were not refused treatment because of a disability. And White women were definitely not refused. Black men and women were categorically denied medical care at White medical centers solely based on the color of their skin, following the dictates of the apartheid practices of the day.

My parents met as students at Howard University in 1941. Daddy's sister, my Auntie Willa, also went to Howard, majoring in medicine. Her roommate, Josephine, was a beautiful debutante who later became my mother. World War II separated the young couple, but letters kept the flame of love alive. Married in 1948, they spent 52 fabulous years together until my father's transition to the ancestral realm in 2000.

Mommy was a mathematical wizard. Unfortunately, those genes must have been recessive when I was born, failing to transmit to my DNA. My mother was the seventh and youngest product of two proud families – Queley and McIntosh – from the isle of St. Kitts in the Caribbean. It's a very popular family rumor that reggae star Peter Tosh from Jamaica is a relative, his birth name being McIntosh. It's certainly plausible, as my grandfather, James Albert McIntosh, was one of seven brothers scattered throughout the islands, bearing the same last name. Unfortunately, I only know the illustrious names of two of the brothers – Obadiah and Hezekiah.

My great grandmother, Harriet Holder, was a midwife who wanted my grandmother to be a nurse. There is another family rumor circulating that there is a possible family connection to President Obama's Attorney General, Eric Holder, whose roots also hail from the islands, and who is the spitting image of my late cousin Teddy.

When great-grandmother Harriet Holder discovered that James Albert McIntosh was coming around to court, she spirited her daughter, Clarice Georgina Queley (my maternal grandmother), off to Bermuda for nursing studies. James, however, caught the next thing smoking, or in his case, sailing, and followed his heart. Great-grandmother immediately sent my grandmother to New York and again, my grandfather followed. So I suppose it was destined they would marry and have my mother, Josephine Evangeline McIntosh, so she could marry my father, St. Elmo Caldwell, and eventually have me.

My grandfather, or Poppa as my mom called him, was a master craftsman. He could construct anything using his skills of carpentry, masonry, and glazing. He was also a 33rd degree Mason, although my mother doesn't have much memory of that. He was not a part of Marcus Garvey's Universal Negro Improvement Association,[6] but he believed in the Garvey movement and contributed heavily to the cause. His carpentry shop at 59th Street and Columbus Circle was close to the New York office where I would eventually work nearly 100 years later. Poppa eked out enough of a living to provide for his household, so that my grandmother did not have to work outside of the home until it became absolutely necessary. Her primary job was to raise seven children, and she did that well.

Although a homemaker much of her life raising children, my grandmother also worked for the Department of the Navy in Brooklyn during the Depression. Her job was clipping the threads from sailors' uniforms. The work – long, tedious and monotonous – was performed using a crude type of clipper. Family oral tradition has it that my grandmother took the initiative to design her own clipper that was much faster and more efficient than the one provided to the workers. Noticing the increase in productivity after Grandma began using her thread clipper, the department manager "borrowed" her invention and produced one for everyone in the unit.

I am clueless whether my grandmother actually invented this special clipper as alleged, but historically, the rights to so many inventions by African Americans were stolen, with no credit or compensation given. The axiom, "necessity is the mother of invention," most likely explains the ingenuity of inventions by Black folk during the enslavement, reconstruction and Jim Crow eras. Sadly, even today it is not widely known that Blacks invented some of the most essential components of American life, from refrigeration on a truck to the electric traffic light.

Whenever my daughter was required to do research for school, she knew to look for "the Black connection," for invariably there always was one. For instance, in her elementary school book report on Thomas Edison, I made sure her research included references on Lewis Latimer, a Black man who invented the electric light bulb and worked closely with both Edison and Alexander Graham Bell.

Latimer was one of the lucky African Americans who got patents and at least a smidgen of recognition. But there were countless others, buried in the annals of time, who received no acknowledgement or compensation for their contributions. So although Grandma's ingenuity went unnoticed in the world of trademarks, she nevertheless left her mark on society, as well as on me.

My mom, Josephine McIntosh, attended public schools in New York City, graduating from Washington Irving High School with high honors. Mommy received a perfect 100 score in the Geometry Regents, which was unprecedented for any student, Black or White. She was unequivocally brilliant. She received a tuition scholarship to Cornell University but was informed that she would be unable to find work in Ithaca because of her race. Unemployment in upstate New York would make it impossible for her to afford room and board. Thus, she moved to Washington, D.C., and attended Howard University on a full tuition scholarship. After graduating magna cum laude from Howard, she received a full tuition scholarship to D.C. Teacher's College to complete her master's degree.

Before I was born, Mommy taught at Margaret Mary Washington Vocational High School in Baltimore and Howard University in Washington, D.C. She then began an illustrious career with the D.C. Public School System, first as a teacher and then as an assistant principal at Roosevelt Senior High, until her retirement in 1985.

My father, St. Elmo Caldwell, was originally from North Carolina. He entered Howard on a football scholarship from Philadelphia's Roxbury High School. Daddy, born in Gastonia, N.C., to John Caldwell and Georgia Etta McKinney, grew up in the Manayunk area of Philadelphia. To my chagrin, I learned during my teenage years that he was actually not born to John Caldwell. Caldwell was his stepfather, which meant that Caldwell was not really his last name, meaning that it was not really my last name.

I grew up knowing that at a very young age Daddy suffered a serious illness and doctors swore he would die. Luckily for me and my sisters, he miraculously survived. Then doctors swore he would never walk. By the grace of God, although he stayed in the hospital for three years, he recovered and not only walked, but later tried out for the Olympics! Although small in stature, Daddy was endowed with exceptional speed and strength. All types of sports, including boxing, mesmerized him. He taught me to 'jab, cross and hook' almost from the time I could swing my arms. He was expert at baseball, softball, football, track, archery, and unquestionably his favorite: the martial arts.

Despite entering Howard, Daddy was intent on fighting in World War II, so he interrupted his studies, enlisted, and joined the Army. After watching the very sentimental play directed by Douglas Turner Ward, *A Soldier's Story*, it was always hard for me to fathom why my father would risk his life to fight for a country that sought to guarantee freedom and independence for people in foreign lands, yet denied it to those at home. The play poignantly brought home the humiliation and degradation confronting Black soldiers in 1944.

Discrimination notwithstanding, Daddy served with distinction in Italy with the 92nd Infantry (Buffalo) Division. He was wounded in action and finally came home with the Purple Heart Medal and several decorations and citations. He often related stories about the frontlines with pride – wallowing in muddy fox holes, not sleeping for days, and what it meant to always be "on point."

Daddy also told tales of being underestimated academically in high school by White teachers. He would tell me his teachers told him things like, "Boy, you couldn't have written that!" But Daddy loved literature and poetry, from Shakespeare to Invictus – and frequently enthralled us with legends of the Greek gods and goddesses. He even named our beloved family dog Achilles, after the mythic character invulnerable on every spot of his body save his heel.

Daddy hadn't been exposed to the teachings of John G. Jackson's *Introduction to African Civilizations*; Dr. Yosef Ben-Jochannan's *African Origins of Major Western*

Religions; *Stolen Legacy*, by George G.M. James; or, *Civilization or Barbarism*, by Cheikh Anta Diop. If he had, I know he would have made the connection that the Greco-Roman pantheon of gods and goddesses were copied from the ancient Kemetians[7] and co-opted with adulterated names and deeds.

But Daddy had not been exposed to the works available for me to read decades later. The extent of his ancient African cultural awareness was limited to Dr. Frank Snowden's text, *Blacks in Antiquity*, which he read while a student in Dr. Snowden's class at Howard University. Incidentally, I took the same course as my father, from the same professor, some 25 years later while I was a student at Howard. Later in life Daddy was enthralled with the West African Dogon cosmology. He was particularly fond of the star Sirius, often gazing up into the heavens with wonderment on star-filled nights.

Receiving a Bachelor of Science in health and physical education from Howard and, later, a master's degree from George Washington University in Urban Studies, Daddy also went to work for the D.C. Public School System in 1962, earning the distinction of serving for 27 years without missing a single day from work.

Daddy's passion, second only to his love for my mother, was the martial art of Kodokan Judo. He began his formal training in 1957, working out in the gym at the old 12th Street YMCA in D.C. It is now the Thurgood Marshall Center, a beautifully restored historical site. Equipped with a black belt, my father founded the Albright Judo Club in the early 60s, one of the first martial arts schools teaching Kodokan Judo in the Nation's Capital and the only one led by a Black man. He taught the class from the early 60s until he passed in the year 2000. Mommy swears that from its inception my Daddy never missed teaching his judo class every Tuesday night.

Perseverance was a word my father used constantly, and it was ever-present in my life for as long as I can remember. I did not make the connection until after he passed that perseverance was one of the cardinal principles of Daddy's treasured fraternity, Omega Psi Phi, Incorporated, and that it was a quality that every "Omega Man" must possess. The term was my father's trademark, and I'm positive I inherited this important value from him. He surely passed it on to me, and I credit the principle of never giving up as a major reason for success throughout my life.

Chapter One, Section 2
White Flight and Gentrification

My mother told me the physician that delivered me at Freedmen's Hospital, Dr. Walter Combs, was part of her Howard University undergraduate class of 1945. As a practicing physician, she described him as a superb doctor with an excellent reputation. She told me that when I was a little tot, one evening I became very sick. This was during the 1950s when doctors sometimes made house calls. Mommy told me she telephoned Dr. Combs, and he rushed straight over to the apartment, scooped up her tiny little pumpernickel-toned baby, positioned me in his car, and sped to the majority White Children's Hospital. With pride my mother recollected, "They let him right in, without a word." Relieved that he was not denied access, Mommy chuckled, "My Negro doctor must have saved some White child's life!" My mom grew up during the traumatizing Jim Crow era. I often peppered her with questions about what discrimination was like back then. Each time, however, my line of inquiry was met with indignation. This always perplexed me.

"What was it like to have to ride in the back of the bus?" I quizzed repetitively as a child.

"I never rode in the back of the bus!" Mommy always retorted indignantly. "You see, Needi, we were from New York," she would say. "That stuff didn't happen up there."

I was suspicious of the answer. I thought she was exaggerating about the lack of discrimination "up North." After all, she always affirmed that the reason she preferred shopping at the old Woodward & Lothrop Department Store in D.C. was because they treated her with more respect than its competitor, Hecht's. Whether or not her treatment was based on race, I really can't say, but Mommy always vowed, "I'm not going to spend my money in an establishment that doesn't appreciate it."

When I was around two years old, my parents moved from the far Northeast section of Washington, D.C. to upper Northwest, a predominantly White neighborhood. Over 50 years later, I was on a panel coordinated by the ACLU of Maryland. Before the forum I was casually chatting with one of the panelists, Mark Elrich, an elected official, about growing up in D.C., as we were both native Washingtonians. It surprised me when I discovered he grew up in the same upper Northwest neighborhood that I did.

Musing about the discriminatory times, he matter-of-factly confided to me that a real estate agent cautioned his family that they'd "better sell their Northwest home soon because the neighborhood was going to turn all black." My parents moved to that same upper Northwest neighborhood in Washington, D.C. in 1956, and true to the agent's prediction, by the early 1960s, it essentially had become all Black.

Upon hearing Elrich's remembrance, my mind traveled back to my own memories of the neighborhood: tree-lined streets with semi-detached houses and wide, clean alleys where we delighted in endless games of kickball, hop-scotch, double-dutch, and tag. There were no soccer teams in our schools in those days, no cross-country, no track, no crew. The most girls could aspire to at Whittier Elementary School was the esteemed "girl aide" position in the auditorium-turned-lunchroom where we sat and ate our meal on our laps. We could also hope to be promoted to the status of "patrol girl," helping students safely cross the street.

I was not allowed to be either a girl aide or a patrol girl, because it was said I was too short. This made me feel bad, but I accepted that this was just the way it was. Little did I know I would spend my career fighting against discriminatory policies. Although in retrospect there were so many opportunities I missed out on that either my school or community did not provide, I felt no lack. I joyously participated in the Brownies and Girl Scouts at Albright United Methodist Church, tennis and swimming at the Takoma Recreation Center, and the D.C. Youth Orchestra where I played the violin.

I loved the game of kickball in the spacious and tidy alley near the side of my house. The alley was also the perfect setting for my childhood activities of jump rope and tag. This was during the early 1960s, which is why it was hard for me to believe that as late as 1950, four years before my birth, D.C. alleyways once housed entire families of Black people.

Today, most people are clueless about these "alley dwellers" who proliferated in the Nation's Capital, an icon of Western civilization shielding yet another shameful secret. In 1950, these alley tenements were bulldozed and razed. Despite being a native Washingtonian, I was never exposed to this information, despite it being disturbingly close to my own lifetime and in my own city. The large immaculate alley we played in behind my home, however, was thankfully far removed from that grim reality.

In this new neighborhood my parents moved our family to, our next-door neighbors were an elderly White couple. Their house was filthy, filled with cats, old newspapers and tons of junk. But they were very sweet and quite hospitable. The wife died during the time I was in grade school, and the surviving relatives quickly spirited the husband away. They had been one of the last White "holdouts" in the neighborhood for years, a trend that was also reflected in my elementary school.

I remember a little White boy named Timmy, and maybe two or three other White classmates. But even that meager number diminished as the flavor of the neighborhood shifted rapidly from vanilla to chocolate.

"All White" schools became "all Black" schools – the product of White flight from the city to the suburbs. I vividly remember my kindergarten, first and second grade teachers were White; but, from third grade on up, my teachers were all Black.

I am witnessing the same phenomena – the shift in the "color" of the city – in reverse today. Not only in Washington, D.C., but across the country, once African American neighborhoods are rapidly shifting to Caucasian. Mortgages and rents are rising astronomically, increasing the number of Black foreclosures, easing the path for gentrification.

I remember the turning point in D.C. One afternoon during the late 90s I was riding in the car with my boyfriend down 13th Street Northwest in the inner city of Washington. It was an area that had been hit hard by the urban uprisings[8] of 1968 in the aftermath of the assassination of Dr. Martin Luther King. It was then that I first noticed the signature of change. White couples leisurely pushing babies in strollers with dogs of all type and pedigree on leashes. These new city dwellers casually occupied areas not long before characterized as ghettos.

"Dakarai, aren't they scared to walk around here?" I asked the man who would later become my husband. "Aren't they apprehensive about sitting out on their porches?"

"Naw, they ain't scared," he laughed. "They know all we do is shoot up and kill our own. When was the last time you saw a headline that read, 'Black gang kills White couple strolling baby and dogs in gentrified community?'"

He was right. *What did they have to be scared of?*

Today, my hometown is a very different place than it was when I was young. These newly converted, city dwelling White folk are the trailblazers on the frontier of change. It is astonishing that a once-dilapidated row house in the inner city is now exquisitely renovated and renamed a "townhouse," sporting an astronomical price tag. Gentrification is becoming a "new Jim Crow," as the majority of Blacks are being systematically priced out of inner-city housing markets.

In many instances Black residents are selling or turning over ownership of well-built brick homes in the inner city and moving into huge, pretty-but-cheaply-built wooden houses outside of the city that, in the words of my boyfriend that day, amount to nothing more than 'giant shacks.'

Chapter One, Section 3
Hair, Skin & Other Crude Experiments

There is one vision from growing up I will never forget. I don't recall exactly what year it was, but I know it was in the early to mid-60s, before the Afro hairstyle became popular. My big sister Paula and I had just entered D.C.'s Takoma Branch Public Library. I saw a Negro man (we all used the term "Negro" in those days) with hair that I couldn't stop staring at because I had never seen that much nappy hair, sticking up all over around one's head. All I could do was stare in puzzled amazement. Most Black boys and men kept their hair cut short during this time. My first thought was that this man needed a haircut in the worst kind of way, and I felt embarrassed and sorry for him.

Why was it that I equated nappiness with weirdness and something out of the ordinary? And why would I retain this innocuous memory, of all things, to this day?

Decades later, I deem it a grave indictment on our society that a young child of any race judges it strange when a member of her own race wears his hair the way it spirals naturally from his scalp. It was strange because at the time the Afro hairstyle was not the norm of Black cultural identity. It was strange because, in defiance of the dominant culture, and likely even criticism from members of his own race, this man was wearing his nappy hair boldly and proudly. And it was strange because the contradiction between what was natural and what was not natural never even entered my consciousness.

Around this same time, my grade school girlfriends and I used to take interesting tests. I'm not referring to math or spelling tests administered by teachers; rather, I'm referring to an examination administered amongst ourselves. I'm referring to what I called, "skin tests" wherein we, as children, internalized our own self-hatred to the extent that we created our own caste system.

We would thrust our little hands in front of our little bodies to compare whose complexion was lightest. It was quite scientific to our juvenile minds, yet the psychological impact was devastating. Why I even took part in such idiotic games is beyond my comprehension. Ironically, I was complicit in setting myself up for ridicule, since it was infrequent that a classmate's arm was darker than my own deep brown hue.

These "tests" instituted a cruel social status system, because they reinforced a false concept of superiority and privilege amongst the lighter ones who "passed" the test. Conversely, a sense of inferiority and disfavor was induced amongst those of us who flunked. Essentially, this was a test of life based solely on birth characteristics. The results were immutable and, for the darker-complected like me, one that could never be passed.

While some Black people succumbed to the damaging imprints left on their minds with a negative self-image, as I matured I dispelled the negativity provoked by such "skin tests" and unapologetically embraced Black culture and pride.

Memories like these are nevertheless painful. Despite my African-inspired name, cultural attire, and natural locked hair of today, I still remember and sometimes cringe at humiliations in my past. And sadly, because I grew up in a segregated environment, people who looked like me were the ones perpetuating the indignities.

There is one episode I will never forget that involved a crude, hand-drawn picture purporting to be grade-school aged me, sketched by a light-skinned neighborhood child, captioned, "you're black." I ran into my house and into the bathroom and cried and cried. I cried because to be called "black" at that time was one of the lowest humiliations that could be hurled against a person.

Another incident occurred around age 13 when a boy from my church boldly told me, "My mother said she would not want me to marry you when we grow up, because you are too dark and your hair is too short."

Such interactions deny schoolchildren the innocence of what it is to be young and carefree. They are such intensely painful experiences that they sear into your memory and last a lifetime. Today, respected and renowned Africentric psychiatrists such as the late Dr. Frances Cress Welsing, Dr. Aminifu Harvey, the late Dr. Amos Wilson, Dr. Na'im Akbar and Dr. Nana Pat Newton all offer theories and illumination based on their research on the myth of White supremacy, White world domination, and racism. As I grew older, these works profoundly impacted my thinking and the way in which I approached my work.

This "dark skin/light skin" dichotomy was prevalent and "in your face" during my formative years. I must have been about 10 or 11 when I conducted my first independent experiment, testing a theory that had been haunting me. Using empirical evidence (although I did not know what empirical evidence was at the time) as I rode through the community over a series of weeks, I observed trash collectors. I literally could not find any trash man, not one, with a light or even medium complexion. They were all dark-skinned, without exception.

The trash truck drivers were invariably White, but the laborers were not only Black, they were always dark-skinned. I then scrutinized other lines of work. My findings were that the more prestigious the profession, the lighter the hue of the workers hired for the job. Are these the types of experiments young people should have to conduct? Even at that young age, I knew White children were not saddled with this type of complexity in their lives.

I don't remember every hurtful detail or incident, but self-hate was a constant, collective feature of African American life and it colored nearly everything we did. For instance, there were countless numbers of times when young Black girls, including myself, did not go swimming because we did not want our pressed hair to "go back" to its natural nappiness.

D.C. author Marita Golden in her book, *Don't Stay Out in the Sun*, aptly depicts this sad phenomenon. I can't tell you how many times I heard that advice given to me – "Needi, don't stay out in the sun." I also remember spending half the summer in Ohio with my cousins, frolicking out in the sun most of the time, and then upon my return to D.C., overhearing disapproving whispers, "Needi is sooo much darker than when she left."

Although I proudly affirm that I have never put any chemically altering substance in my hair, I embarrassingly admit that I watched my then grade-school aged daughter gaze longingly at the pretty girl images on kiddie perm packages in the store. My now-deceased friend and ancestor spirit, Damu Smith, has a daughter two years older than mine. He once confided in me, "I will be satisfied if I can just get my daughter through high school without mutilation of her natural hair." He and I both agreed that hair styled naturally should not be mandated as the only option for Black women and girls, but rather affirmed as a legitimate and, I might add, preferred choice.

That's not to say that I always wore my natural hair with pride and admiration. I can't honestly say that the constant presence of my towering headwrap during the 70s, (the type later adopted by Neo Soul singer Erykah Badu) was solely the result of my cultural pride and identity. The adornment was also a beautiful cover for my laziness, allowing me the freedom to not have to periodically groom my hair.

One thing I have noticed today is that many women who wore their hair natural throughout the 70s and 80s now wear their hair in locs. Indeed, "locs" appear to be a natural progression of hair consciousness for many Black women who shunned the perm, disdained the Jheri Curl, and never felt comfortable with blow-dried, straightened hair. A prime example is my friend Denise Rolark, one of my classmates at both Rabaut Jr. High School and Howard University. Now she is Denise Rolark Barnes, the dynamic editor of the *Washington Informer* newspaper and host of cable TV's *Reporter's Roundtable*. Denise had the perfect Afro hairstyle back in the day. Today, she is adorned with beautifully enviable locs.

Chapter One, Section 4
Media Images and Race

As a young child, my big sister Paula related a story to me so many times that it is ingrained in my memory. During a 1950s television show, host Pick Temple asked a little Black child, "What do you want to be when you grow up?" The child responded loudly, "I want to be a white man!"

"Why?" the befuddled showman questioned, making the classic mistake lawyers do of asking the one question too many.

"Because my mother said 'n------ ain't s---!" the boy adamantly proclaimed. Tragically, many Black children of the Fifties reflected the legacy of self-hate drummed into their minds. Constantly, if not consciously, the message was reinforced by fairytales, grocery product containers, textbooks, television, newspapers and magazines. That child, and countless others like him, simply regurgitated learned values and responses, transmitted intergenerationally.

In the words of author Haki Madhubuti, we were all, by and large, ignorant of our "identity, purpose, and direction." Psychologist Joy DeGreuy contends that we were all traumatized, the victims of acute "post-traumatic slavery disorder." She describes this condition as a special debilitating stress produced by the horrors of the enslavement era, which continued with overt and covert racial discrimination.

To prepare for the *Brown v. Board of Education* trial on school desegregation, renowned psychiatrist Dr. Kenneth Clark performed the infamous study that revealed that when presented with a Black doll and a White doll, Black children preferred to play with the White one. Despite the fact that the darker-hued image closely resembled them, Black children consistently chose the White doll as clean, happy and nice over the Black doll which they saw as angry, sad and dirty. Fifty-three years later, a Harlem high school student conducted a similar study and, regrettably, the results remained the same.[9]

But this self-hatred does not have to be passed down from one generation to another. Personally, I was thrilled when my two-year-old daughter exemplified the reversal of Clark's conclusions. It was one of those mommy moments I will never forget.

While rushing through the grocery store to purchase some Pull Ups, the toddler diaper for use during potty training, my daughter Mariama was sitting in the front of the shopping cart. Without any provocation she furiously pitched onto the floor the bag of diapers I had hurriedly tossed into the shopping cart. She motioned dramatically toward another bag of diapers on the shelf. Astonished, I realized that the bag she wanted was the one with the little girl on it that, I swear, looked exactly like her.

I was thrilled! Yes, my daughter had shunned the diapers with the image of the little White girl that her harried and unobservant mommy had placed in the shopping cart. Mariama made it clear that she favored the box graced by the image of a beautiful little brown-complexioned girl.

Unable to conceal my beaming pride and enthusiasm, I triumphantly thrust the bag of pampers up in the air and babbled to a complete stranger in the aisle, "My daughter wanted the diapers with the little girl on the package that looked just like her!" Well, the woman on the receiving end of my exaltation just looked at me and then at my daughter, as if I had lost my mind and curtly stated, "Well, what did you expect?"

I didn't know what she was talking about until I noticed how the woman appeared fixated on how my daughter and I were attired. Mariama, in cute little African-style clothes and me, wearing a multi-colored head wrap and a Malian bogolan (more popularly known as "mud cloth") coat. Presuming what she was thinking, I tried to get this White woman to understand that I did not consciously persuade my baby to pick out the diapers graced with the image of a Black child.

"She's just two years old. I've never even talked to her about race," I added, still proud.

And then it dawned on me. Media images are everywhere in our environment, whether or not we are conscious of them. True, in our household she played with Black dolls or other dolls of color; most of her books contained images of people of African descent, as did the children's videos I purchased for her. She also attended an Africentric pre-school. Since birth (and before) she had accompanied me to cultural programs, meetings and political demonstrations. From the womb, I'd like to believe that the rhythm and energy of her environment had buoyed her sense of self and esteem.

However, living in the United States, negative and stereotypical images bombarded her childhood environment. Looking back on the animated children's movies of my daughter's generation, I see Disney favorites such as Aladdin where Jafar, the evil one, is portrayed as dark; and the Lion King where Scar, the wicked uncle, has a black mane; or Hercules, where the villain is portrayed as Black. It's no wonder Black children are adversely affected by exposure to subliminal media messages.

The predominantly White media and culture spoon-feed us the images we readily gobble up. They indoctrinate us with a mistaken identity, provide us with a misguided purpose, and steer us to a myopic destiny. This is why it is critical that we document and internalize our own history, controlling the images that characterize and define our existence.

Most Blacks in this country have been indoctrinated with a non-African mis-education that has whitewashed our minds with lies and distortions to make us hate ourselves. Even today, many Blacks don't know we come from a strong and mighty people; that our ancestors in Africa built the pyramids, temples and monuments which still stand firm today. The school history books of my generation failed to mention that it was African people who taught mathematics to the Greeks, originated the weaving of cloth, and were masters in astronomy, astrology, chemistry, physics, medicine, dentistry, and navigation. They made no mention of the fact that we built great civilizations and kingdoms such as Kemet, Nubia, Kush, Ghana, Mali, Songhay, Carthage, and ancient Zimbabwe.

I learned all of this piecemeal on my own, before entering high school. One great resource I relished was a small, beautifully illustrated pamphlet on African history that I devoured until it became tattered. It was at that moment that I vowed to do what I could to ensure other young people would not have to stumble upon their history; that they would have books that taught them history and education and culture. A seed was planted in me at an early age to help make a difference. And over the years, I did.

In 1977, I co-authored a children's workbook with Brother Imamu Kuumba entitled, *New Afrikan Children of the Sun*. It included games and puzzles, intertwined with lessons. In 1983, I authored *Shining Legacy: StoryPoems and Tales for the Young, So Black Heroes Forever Will be Sung*. Although a "kitchen tabletop" publication, the book was nevertheless professional by the grassroots standards of the day, and chock full of information weaved into moving stories accentuated with rhyme.

In *Shining Legacy* I featured freedom fighters who were under-represented in books for young people at the time, such as Denmark Vesey, who master-minded an elaborate rebellion to free enslaved people, and Joseph Cinque, who led a rebellion on the slave ship, Amistad. I published this book 15 years before the Amistad revolt became popular as a motion picture.

I highlighted in *Shining Legacy* Paul Robeson and Marcus Garvey, and featured the military genius, Toussaint L'Ouverture. L'Ouverture's strategies defeated the English, French and Spanish armies. This forced Napoleon to sell France's holdings in the "New World" to the United States, which doubled its land mass with the Louisiana Purchase and resulted in Haiti being the first Black Republic in the Western Hemisphere.

Shining Legacy also included enlightening storypoems highlighting freedom fighting women – Harriet Tubman, Sojourner Truth, Fannie Lou Hamer and Rosa Parks. And I included the story of the hero pivotal to my consciousness, Malcolm X. Through *Shining Legacy* I sought to provide identity, purpose and direction through original epics, ballads, sagas and tales depicting historical and cultural wealth, and the poignant illustrations of Mary Greer brought these freedom fighters of the past to life.

I authored a third book, *The Adventures of Kojo and Ama*, in 1992. It comprised seven wisdom-filled adventures combining excitement, fun and suspense with lessons in pride and heritage. The heroic black cat Sheba brought the children good luck as they found themselves in challenging settings ranging from an inner-city park to the deep South, and from the island of Jamaica to ancient Egypt. For this book, I partnered with Afia Akoto who illuminated these characters and stories through rich visuals.

Weaved into the *Kojo and Ama* adventure stories I created were actual historical figures such as Benjamin Banneker, who made the first clock in this country; Garrett Morgan's invention of the electric stop light; Jan Matzeliger, who revolutionized the shoe industry by inventing a method to bind the top part of the shoe to the bottom; and, Frederick McKinley Jones, who revolutionized the commercial food industry with refrigeration on a truck, thus allowing the transportation of food over long distances without spoiling.

The list of achievements of Blacks who persevered despite incredible odds is endless. I was thrilled to have the support of luminaries of the day who penned endorsements for my books, including former D.C. Poet Laureate Sterling Brown, Brother Haki Madhubuti of the Independent Black School Movement, the great poet Sonia Sanchez, and educator Jawanza Kunjufu.

My books were a mainstay in Black bookstores nationwide from the early 80s through the 90s, during a time when Black children's books were scarce. Thankfully, today, a look down the aisle of bookstores, both Black and mainstream establishment bookstores, reveals a wide array of literature for children and young people written by and about Black people, and I'm proud to have been one of the early pioneers who sought to make a difference, even though my books for young people no longer grace those shelves.

However, the paucity of books and material about Black history for children during my formative years still astounds me. I am reminded of this when I recall having to prepare to make an oral presentation before my 5th grade class. It was 1965 and I was 10 years old. The occasion was Negro History Week, which was in February.

Back then, Black folk had just one week, not a full month, for an official recognition of our contributions to American society.

The teacher assigned students to present oral reports on a famous Negro person in history. I was assigned to report on a great singer, Marian Anderson. We had no books about her, so Mommy had me look her name up in the encyclopedia. I wrote the report and practiced reciting it. My mother was so proud of me. She loved the way I enunciated each word and spoke with energy and passion – traits I would incorporate in every single formal speaking engagement since then.

Despite my stellar oratory uplifting vocalist Marian Anderson before my class, I simply could not understand why this prolific Black opera singer was barred from performing at the Daughters of the American Revolution's Constitution Hall. What was all the hoopla about? And who the hell were the "Daughters of the American Revolution" anyway?

I was young and clueless about societal and world affairs, even though pivotal events were unfolding daily on the world stage. For instance, during the early 1960s the public schools in D.C. had air raid drills. I remember being required to line up and walk quietly into the hallways to the lowest level of my elementary school building. Then we would sit cross-legged on the floor with our fidgety little arms placed over our small heads. We were then instructed to tuck our chins tightly on our chests.

During the early Sixties I knew nothing of the Cuban Missile Crisis or even the president, John F. Kennedy. I recall hearing a lot about the term, "Iron Curtain," even though it made absolutely no sense to me. Likewise, I recall hearing the term, "Malcolm X," on the radio and on the black and white television in the living room. But that also made no sense to me. I didn't even know then that Malcolm X was a person – I thought the term denoted some type of missile or robot – the Malcolm Ten, I thought.

By the mid-late Sixties, however, seeds of understanding germinated, largely because of my excitement thumbing through the encyclopedia and myriad other books in my family's home library. Being in the school system, my parents made sure that books were plentiful, even if they largely were devoid of affirming images for Black children.

Chapter One, Section 5
The Pony Incident and Emmett Till

There are many events I witnessed that shaped me – even as a child – into a woman who thirsts for justice. The pony incident was among them.

When I was a little girl, Daddy used to work at the Archives Federal Records Center in rural Springfield, VA before joining the D.C. Public School System in 1962. This would have been in the late 50s or very early 60s. One day he took me and my sister with him to a bank near his job. It delighted Paula and me to see a mini carnival in a lot near the bank. What captured my imagination almost immediately was the sight of several ponies, and I started chanting to anyone who would listen, "I want to ride the pony. I want to ride the pony!"

But no one seemed to be listening.

Not to be deterred, I repeated, "I want to ride the pony! Daddy, I want to ride the pony!"

It was sweltering hot that day, which in retrospect makes me think of the "dog days" D.C.'s first poet laureate Sterling Brown once movingly described in "The Ballad of Joe Meek."

> It was late in August what dey calls dog days; would make even beetle hounds get bulldog ways. Would make a pet bunny chase a bad blood hound; make a newborn baby slap his grandpa down ... The air it was muggy, and heavy with heat. The people all sizzled like frying meat. The icehouse was heaven; the pavements was hell, even Joe didn't feel too agreeable.

As a child, of course, I hadn't yet read Sterling Brown. But when I did, I recognized that kind of hot. That's exactly how it was that day as we stood in this long line waiting to ride the pony — me and Paula with Daddy, the only Black people among a throng of White faces.

I was hot and uncomfortable, but I wanted to ride that pony so badly. While we waited in line, sweating, a little White boy with a deep country accent pointed at us and scowled, "Y'all cain't ride." Then he turned and pointed to the White children behind us – "but y'all can."

My father argued indignantly, ignoring restrictions dictated by history to Black men during the 50s. Instead of acquiescing and allowing a kid to disrespect him, my Daddy spoke up, sternly asking, "Why can't my girls ride?"

Hesitating for a moment, the little White boy retorted, "My pappy said, y'all cain't do it."

"Well, you just go and get your pappy!" my Daddy demanded.

At my tender age and having been shielded from overt discrimination, it never crossed my mind that my father could lose his life for speaking back to a White person, even if that person was a child like me. It would be years before I read the bloodcurdling statistics outlined in the book, *One Hundred Years of Lynchings*. I was young and ignorant of the protocols of White-Black interaction. On that "dog day" in rural Virginia, all that mattered to my childish mind was that I could not ride that pretty pony.

"My pappy ain't here!" the impudent little White boy hollered defiantly.

I could tell my father was fuming. Without hesitation, he abruptly steered us from the line, went right back to the Franconia Branch bank, withdrew all his money, and never returned. He didn't explain why he closed his account, but I imagine my father didn't want to ever return to the site of the mini carnival.

I often think about the pony incident, but it wasn't until many years later that I understood why I was denied that pony ride. I felt wounded by the unfairness of discrimination based solely on the color of one's skin. And this unfairness fed my growing passion for justice, so that decades later I determined to devote my life to making changes that insure no other child would be subject to the kind of injustice I experienced that day.

For as long as I can remember, my parents – being educators – filled our home with books. Curled up in our den library, I spent hours with one particular book, published in 1956, *A Pictorial History of the Negro in America*, by Langston Hughes and Milton Meltzer. I was fascinated by the book's images.

Then one day I turned a page and saw the horrific image of young Emmett Till. It was at that moment that I really understood not only why I could not ride that pony years earlier, but also just how lucky my father had been that day. Unfortunately, Emmett Till had not been so lucky. Thankfully, Daddy was not charged with the offense that fourteen-year-old Emmett Till was accused of – addressing a White woman.

In 1955, any provocation against a White person could prove fatal. That is why when Chicago mother Mamie Till put her adolescent son Emmett on a train to Mississippi to visit his southern relatives, she cautioned him in advance to willingly get down on his knees and literally bow to a White person if necessary.

I will never forget the image of Emmett's horribly disfigured face. Indeed, I was always intrigued when I read about events happening during the 1950s, because it was the decade of my birth. But Emmett Till's case in particular unearthed the unending questions about race relations in my 10-year-old mind.

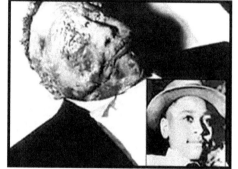

I read and researched, trying to understand how a boy could be killed for something that seemed so trivial. I found out that Emmett died in August 1955, 15 months after the *Brown vs. Board of Education* decision outlawed segregation in the nation's public schools. It was also just four months before Rosa Parks defiantly took a seat designated for a White person on an Alabama bus, and eight months after I was born. But for young Emmett Till, a self-assured, confident teen from fast-paced Chicago, it was just another hot summer day in the town of Money, Mississippi.

Young Emmett proudly displayed a photo of White friends from Chicago to his country cousins in Mississippi. Attempting to impress them with his familiarity with Whites 'up North,' he boasted that the girl in the picture was his girlfriend. They dared him to get familiar with a White female 'down South.' Emmett, despite his mother's warnings, did not heed the severity of the racial customs of Southern culture. Reportedly, he entered a country store, purchased some candy and, on the way out, said "Bye baby," to Carolyn Bryant, the wife of the White store owner.

Varying rumors rapidly circulated throughout the town about the occurrence: some claimed he wolf-whistled at her while others insisted he asked her for a date. Regardless of the exact words or sounds that may have passed from his lips, Roy Bryant, the store owner, was incensed that a Black male had approached his wife in any fashion.

Later, in the middle of that night, Bryant and his half-brother, J.W. Milam, entered the property of Till's great uncle, 64-year-old Mose Wright. They abducted the terrified boy, despite the vigorous protestations of the patriarch. Wright was sternly warned to not cause any trouble or he'd "never live to be 65."

Three days later Emmett Till's body was finally discovered tied to an iron cotton-gin wheel and floating in Mississippi's Tallahatchie River. One side of his forehead was crushed in, a bullet was lodged in his skull, an eye was gorged out, and an ear amputated. The boy's face was completely unrecognizable. The only way the bloated, bloody body could be identified was because a finger bore his deceased father's signet ring inscribed with his initials, L.T.

Mamie Till demanded her son's body be transported back to Chicago, and stead-fastly insisted the undertaker do nothing to groom the body.

"Open up the casket!" the distraught mother wailed. "I want the world to see what they did to my boy."

Although suffering in anguish, Mamie Till's decision was strategic. Her son's corpse would be displayed in an open casket so that the world could see what racism and hatred had done to her only child. Thousands of people attended the funeral and the photos of Emmett's brutally mutilated body was a key catalyst in helping to in-vigorate a nascent civil rights movement. Today, the brutality of murders by White police officers of unarmed Blacks captured on mobile phones has likewise garnered massive public attention and been pivotal in intensifying the movement for justice.

Bryant and Milam, charged with murder, were acquitted. It took the all-White jury about an hour to reach the verdict in what amounted to a mockery of a trial. Al-though admitting they kidnapped and beat Emmett Till, the two incredulously tes-tified they had left him alive. Mose Wright, Emmett's great uncle, heroically identi-fied the perpetrators at trial. Risking his life to testify against the two White men in a courtroom jammed with hostile White spectators, Emmett's elderly great uncle courageously pointed his finger at Bryant and Milam, stating simply, "thar them."

Two months after the trial, a White journalist paid the acquitted men $4,000 to tell what actually happened. Milam stated he and Bryant pistol-whipped Till, shot him in the head, wired a 75-pound cotton gin fan to his neck, and dumped his body in the river. Furious that the boy refused to beg for mercy or show remorse, and that he had flaunted a picture of his White girlfriend in Chicago, Milam shockingly ar-gued, "What else could we do? He thought he was as good as any White man."

It would be some years before I would understand the colossal impact of Mamie Till Mobley's undoubtedly difficult decision. The open casket prompted unparal-leled public attention to the brutal murder of young Emmett Till and helped people around the world become more proximate to racial injustice in America. I often use the "open up the casket" theme today during public speeches to demonstrate the importance of not sugarcoating injustice or sweeping it under the rug.

Till's murder resulted from pure racial terrorism, a cornerstone of the Jim Crow South. Everything about his story stuck with me and remains a key part of my ever-present quest for justice. Back then, I was not the kind of youngster who could shake off even the slightest injustice, and most certainly not the knowledge of something as horrific as a young boy being brutally killed because he said something to a White woman. I was a young person whose heart was broken when she found out that the lives of children born Black were considered worth less than the lives of children born White. And I was a girl who grew into a woman who was determined to right societal wrongs and find a way to repair historical injustices.

Chapter One, Section 6
Open Up the Casket!

My daughter once asked me, "Mommy, just what is lynching?"

My first thought was the legal definition. "Lynching is the practice of putting one to death by mob action without legal sanction or due process of law." But of course I didn't respond that way. I simply said, "Princess, lynching is killing and murdering people without letting them go to court."

I don't know what prompted her question. It made me wonder whether White kids questioned their parents about lynchings. But I should not have been surprised at my child. A poster-sized photograph of the burned and charred body of a lynched Black man propped on a pyre surrounded by a sea of grinning White faces has always been on a wall in our home. Such images, along with facsimiles of actual signs from the Jim Crow era, have been part of her living environment all her life.

I saw no need to sugarcoat history or pretend cruel injustices did not exist. I have always felt there is not enough education about such periods in history, and Till's terrorist-style murder was but the tip of the lynching iceberg. Once I knew about this traumatic part of U.S. history, it was important to me that my daughter never forget that history.

Among the many shameful episodes in the annals of American history, the practice of lynching arguably stands unparalleled as the most barbaric. Designed to instill terror in the newly freed Black people, lynching was a sadistic ritual that incorporated flagrant disregard for the law and the highest level of violence and cruelty. The sight of a dismembered Black man hanging from a tree was intended to horrify and strike fear into the hearts of Blacks and those sympathetic to their cause.

According to the book, *100 Years of Lynching*, at least 4,743 people were victims of lynchings between the beginning of reliable data collection in 1882 up to its relative demise in 1968. 73% of these acts were inflicted upon Blacks in the Southern states.

Although rape of a White woman by a Black man was the South's most often purported rationale for the epidemic of lynchings, these murders often served as a subterfuge to mask the real sources of White rage. One such factor was fear and jealousy of the political and economic ascendancy by Blacks. Blacks were also frequently blamed for crimes committed by Whites.

Moreover, there were cases of interracial relationships between consenting adults. Investigative journalist Ida B. Wells-Barnett argued that economic competition and racial hatred caused the mob lynching of three of her colleagues in 1892 following the successful opening of their grocery store, as opposed to an affront to a White woman, as alleged. As the result of an expose about these lynchings in her Memphis newspaper, *The Free Speech*, Wells' offices were demolished, and she was threatened with death if she returned to the state.

Launching an international crusade against lynchings, Wells lectured passionately in the United States and Great Britain for the arrest and punishment of lynchers. Her pamphlet, *The Red Record: Tabulated Statistics and Alleged Causes of Lynching in the United States*, was published in 1895. It proved statistically, from data generated by Whites themselves, that the "protection of white womanhood" was not the basis for lynchings. To the contrary, the evidence revealed that in no given year had even half the Black folk who were lynched been charged with rape or attempted rape. It also stated that in 1900, less than 15 percent of those lynched had been suspected of rape.

"Lynching," Wells forcefully contended, "was a form of intimidation to preserve the plantation economy and the white ballot box of the South."

Everything I know about Ida B. Wells-Barnett I learned on my own as an adult. I was taught nothing about this intellectually astute, courageous Black woman in school. Did my grade school teachers, Black or White, know anything at all about her? Likely not, as far as I could tell. Affectionately described as the "Princess of the Press," Ida B. Wells-Barnett courageously used her pen to detail to the world the depravity of the atrocious practice of lynching.

One hundred and twenty-six years after the mob lynching of Wells' friends, which led her to launch an international crusade against lynching, brilliant attorney Bryan Stevenson and his organization, the Equal Justice Initiative, opened the National Memorial for Peace and Justice and Legacy Museum in 2016 in Montgomery, AL. These phenomenal exhibitions were in honor and remembrance of the thousands of victims of lynchings, and underscored the uninterrupted connection between the enslavement era of yesterday and mass incarceration today.

One evening after touring the colossal monuments and the historic data and interactive exhibits within the museum, I went to dinner with two of my elders, Baba Leonard Dunston and Rosaline "Roz" Preudhomme, at a popular restaurant across the street from the museum. While waiting to be seated, my colleagues Queen Roz and Baba Lenny, who worked together during the 1980's when Dunston was Director of the New York State Division for Youth, were engaged in deep conversation with an articulate Black youth.

True to his nature, Baba Lenny kept up a drumbeat, accentuating the historic accolades of Queen Roz, focusing upon her direct and pivotal involvement in the Civil Rights Movement of the 1960s. After listening in awe to the tributes Baba Lenny was showering upon his friend and colleague, the youth looked at Queen Roz with the utmost of admiration, spontaneously blurting out, "You should be in the museum!" pointing excitedly to Stevenson's Legacy Museum across the street. Taking a moment to recapture her composure after we all cracked up laughing, Roz responded emphatically, "Yes, we should all be in museums!"

Although still chuckling, I remembered that I actually am in a museum–the National Civil Rights Museum in Memphis, TN, partially housed inside the Lorraine Motel, site of the 1968 assassination of Dr. Martin Luther King, Jr. As part of a 2016 renovation and expansion of the museum, filmmaker Malkia Lydia produced an exhibit to highlight issues of Black Power. I was thrilled and honored to be interviewed and filmed as part of the museum's inaugural exhibit on the Black Power era.

It is critical that the history of eras that have been swept under the rug are opened up and memorialized, and Bryan Stevenson's memorial in Montgomery to the lynching era and the nascent Black Power exhibit in Memphis are momentous steps.

Stay with me as I open up the grotesque casket of lynchings, memorializing material I learned on my own, many decades before the Equal Justice Institute shared its findings with the world.

Generally speaking, the close to 5,000 ritualistic murders described as lynchings involved one or more of the following elements: 1) The charge that a Black man raped a White woman; 2) A frenzied mob terrorizing a Black area and kidnapping one or more suspects from home, work or state custody; 3) Hanging the naked victim from a tree or to a pyre of wood; 4) Torturing the victim; 5) Riddling the lifeless body with bullets; 6) Dismembering the body (before or after death) and seizing choice parts as souvenirs; 7) Burning the body until it was unrecognizable; 8) Complicity and probable participation of law enforcement in the act and subsequent cover-up; and 9) Immunity from punishment for the perpetrators.

In many cases, the mob, ostensibly in an attempt to justify its actions, often held a mock trial or attempted to torture a "confession" out of the victim during the course of being burned alive and dismembered. Lynchings were often participatory events with all the trappings of a carnival atmosphere. Special trains transported families to the spectacle; children were excused from schools, and employees released from work to join in the "festive" occasion.

In *100 Years of Lynchings*, published in 1962, author Ralph Ginzberg offers this excerpt from the Springfield, Massachusetts Weekly Republican newspaper, illustrating the April 23, 1899 lynching of Sam Holt:

> Newman, Ga, April 23 – Sam Holt, the murderer of Alfred Cranford and the ravisher of the latter's wife, was burned at the stake, near Newman, Ga., this afternoon, in the presence of 2000 people. The black man was first tortured before being covered with oil and burned ... Before the torch was applied to the pyre, the negro was deprived of his ears, fingers and genital parts of his body. He pleaded pitifully for his life while the mutilation was going on, but stood the ordeal of fire with surprising fortitude. Before the body was cool, it was cut to pieces, the bones were crushed into small bits, and even the tree upon which the wretch met his fate was torn up and disposed of as 'souvenirs.' The negro's heart was cut into several pieces, as was also his liver. Those unable to obtain the ghastly relics direct paid their more fortunate possessors extravagant sums for them. Small pieces of bones went for 25 cents, and a bit of the liver crisply cooked sold for 10 cents.

An eyewitness account from a *Washington Eagle* correspondent details "indescribable tortures" inflicted on another Black man in a lynching in 1921. When I realized my father had been born by then and was one year old, it made the account more personal for me. It horrified me that this was the grim world that Daddy, an innocent Black baby, had been born into:

> They tore the Negro's clothing off before he was placed in a waiting automobile ... The Negro was unsexed and made to eat a portion of his anatomy which had been cut away. Another portion was sent by parcel post to Governor Dorsey, whom the people of this section hate bitterly ... The Negro was chained to a stump and asked if he had anything to say. Castrated and in indescribable torture, the Negro asked for a cigarette, lit it and blew the smoke in the face of his tormentors. The pyre was lit and a hundred men and women, old and young, grandmothers among them, joined hands and danced around while the Negro burned. A big dance was held in the barn nearby that evening in celebration of the burning, many people coming by automobile from nearby cities to the gala event.

How can I sleep with both eyes closed in a world where shocking headlines such as these were blasted in countless newspapers across the country during the early years of the 20th century? How can I not seek justice, even today?

These newspaper headlines are but a small sampling of the monstrosity:

"Roasted Alive"
"Negro Tortured to Death by Mob of 4000"
"Blood-Curdling Lynching Witnessed by 2,000 Persons"
"Lots Drawn for Souvenirs of Lynched Negro's Anatomy"
"Crowd Cheered and Laughed at Negro's Horrible Death"
"Negro Preacher is Found Swinging from a Limb"
"Negro Veteran Lynched for Refusing to Doff Uniform"
"15-Year old is Lynched; Wolf-Whistled at White Woman"

The callous demeanor of the executioners was ruthless:

"Lynched for Remark which may have been 'Hello'"
"15,000 Witness Burning of Negro in Public Square"
"Lynch Leaders Declare Lynching was 'Humane'"
"[Prominent White Farmer] Attempted to Shift Blame to 'Lecherous Looking Black'"
"Lynched After Refusing to Dance on White's Command"
"Thwarted Mob Lynches Brother of Intended Victim"

Most egregious was the tragedy of frequency admitted error:

"Texans Lynch Wrong Negro"
"An Innocent Man Lynched"
"Two Blacks Strung Up; Grave Doubt of Their Guilt"
"Believes Wrong Man Lynched"
"Lynch Mob May Have Erred"
"Wrong Man Lynched as Rapist"
"All Five Negroes Lynched Were Guiltless, says Keith"
"Negro Lynched at Roxboro was Wrong Man, says Boss"
"Prison Warden Doubts Guilt of Negro Lynched in GA"

And there was also flagrant disregard for the legal process:

"Lynched Before Trial"
"Negro Dragged from Trial and Lynched by Miss. Mob"
"Lynched Negro who Testified for Another Negro"

"Harvard Professor Favors Legalizing Lynchings"
"Negro Freed, then Lynched"
"Negro Dragged from Cell and Tortured to Death"
"Lynched after Receiving Supreme Court Reprieve"
"Governor Commends Lynchers"
"Lynched After Acquittal"
"Lynched Negro Cleared"
"Unable to Blast into Jail, Mob Burns it to Kill Negro"
"Cleared by Jury, then Lynched"

Was the tragedy of lynchings limited to Black men? Absolutely not. It often extended to Black women, who were also forced to suffer brutal gang rape as a prelude to tortuous murder. Consider these heartwrenching headlines:

"Rape, Lynch Negro Mother"
"Powerless to Aid Sister who was Raped and Lynched"
"Negro Suspect Eludes Mob; Sister Lynched Instead"
"Woman Pleading Innocence Lynched as Child Poisoner"
"Lynched Negro and Wife Were First Mutilated"
"Negro Mother and Child Killed"
"Negress Taken From Jail and Riddled with Bullets"

Not all White folk were conspirators in the horrific ritual of lynching. Although in most instances public officials either acted in collusion with lynchers, were sympathetic, or looked the other way, there were also Whites who refused to participate in mob violence. There were even some who courageously attempted to thwart lynch mobs and protect Blacks:

"Sheriff Rescues Negro After Holding Back Mob"
"White Women Seek Clemency for Negro Slated to Die"
"Lynched Despite Protests of Rape Victim's Parents"
"Sheriff Nearly Lynched"
"Mayor of Omaha is Dead of Lynch Mob Injuries"
"She Denies Rapist was Black"
"White Attempts in Vain to Rescue Victims"
"Sheriff and Negro Killed, 6 Deputies Wounded by Mob"

However, despite notable exceptions, lynch mob violence was embraced by the White populace and politicians alike. Because of the festive and supportive spectator atmosphere, most perpetrators made no effort to conceal their identities. However, investigations that followed lynchings were frequently fruitless, and indictments failed to be returned against known murderers because of "insufficient evidence." Pleas from those opposing mob violence to 'let the law take its course' often resulted in hangings immediately following guilty verdicts by all-White juries. The trials were often hasty and absent of evidence showing guilt.

Lynchings continued through Reconstruction, the process of the reorganization and reestablishment of the Southern states that seceded from the Union after the Civil War. The government during this period failed in its promise to protect the rights of the newly-freed Blacks. The foreseeable consequence of the withdrawal of federal troops from the former Confederacy resulted in the ascendancy of anti-Black terrorist organizations, such as the White Brotherhood and the Knights of the Ku Klux Klan (KKK). Such vigilante groups, often with the complicity of local government, sought, in the words of Black historian John Hope Franklin, "to exercise absolute control over the Negro, drive him and his fellows from power, and establish White supremacy."

Politicians frequently ran for office on platforms that they would loosen or decline to enforce state anti-lynching laws, ensuring blanket protection to murderers. For example, Governor James Vardaman of Mississippi declared that "every Negro in Mississippi would be lynched if necessary to maintain White supremacy." Governor Cole Blease of South Carolina received the finger of a lynched Black man in the mail and planted it in his garden. Senator William Van Amberg of Mississippi bragged of personally leading a lynch mob.

Distinguished African American scholar W.E.B. Dubois characterized mob violence and lynchings as "a sort of permissible Roman holiday for the entertainment of vicious whites." However, anti-slavery orator Frederick Douglass cautioned in 1892 that the South was not solely responsible for the shameful practice of lynching. He stated, "The sin against the Negro is both sectional and national; and until the voice of the North shall be heard in emphatic condemnation and withering reproach against these continued ruthless mob law murders, it will remain equally involved with the South in this common crime."

The creation of the National Association for the Advancement of Colored People (NAACP) in 1909 was, in part, a response to widespread lynchings and mob violence. Its mission statement included as one of its main principles, "to prevent lynchings, burnings and torture of black people." During its early decades, its primary goal was to achieve the passage of a federal anti-lynching law – as state anti-lynching legislation went largely unenforced.

Despite the organization's tireless lobbying efforts and the work of liberal Congressmen in introducing such legislation, a federal anti-lynching law never passed both Houses of Congress to become law.[10] Anti-lynching legislation did pass the

House of Representatives in 1922, 1937 and 1940, yet repeated Senate filibusters made such a bill impossible to become enacted. Despite assertions that it was the province of the states to prosecute lynchers under the states' rights doctrine, fewer than one percent of the perpetrators were ever tried in state courts.

Virtual anarchy and the lack of protection made the epidemic of lynching a prominent reason (besides economic incentives and better education) for the mass exodus of Blacks from the South. Many migrated to the West in the late 1800s and then to Northern cities after the turn of the century. Isabel Wilkerson's *The Warmth of Other Suns* poignantly narrates this migration.

Geographical relocation, however, provided little sanctuary. At the conclusion of World War I, Black soldiers returned from overseas expecting fair treatment and justice, but were met with an escalation of violence and oppression. In fact, the summer of 1919 was so filled with lynchings and mob violence that it became known as the Red Summer. As a result, 26 uprisings exploded across the country, in both the North and the South.

Violent racist mobs of White people decimated entire communities. Some better-known incidents include the 1873 Colfax Massacre where over 100 Blacks were killed in a KKK attack on a Louisiana courthouse. There was also the 1923 Rosewood slaughter, occurring the year my mother was born, where bloodthirsty lynch mobs destroyed an entire flourishing Black Florida town. Probably the most well-known was the 1921 bombing in Tulsa, OK of an affluent all-Black business district known as "Black Wall Street," which left over 300 Blacks dead and over 600 successful Black-owned businesses destroyed.

I have always felt that the injustices perpetrated against Black people during this period of history, through lynchings and destruction of Black communities, have been ignored. There is a maxim within the Jewish community in studying the Holocaust, "Never forget!" However, within the African American community, the opposite appears to be the practice. Not only do Black people forget, but the country chastises, ostracizes and vilifies those who seek to discover some of the roots of current day behavior, remember the injustices endured by our ancestors, and seek redress.

We forget why there is such a range of hues among Black people today. Most often the variation of skin tones emanated from the exercise of White male privilege—formally known as rape. It has been stated that the average age of Black females giving birth during the enslavement era was 13 years old. That means girls as young as ten years old were being sexually terrorized. If White men were systematically lynched for the widespread rape of Black women and girls during the era of enslavement, there would most likely not be very many White men left in the United States today.

Also not disclosed or discussed were the crude gynecological medical experiments performed on Black women and girls. Devoid of anesthesia, such cruel practices laid the basis for much of the modern medical procedures of today. Black folk should be angry. My burning question has always been: Why aren't more Black folk angry?

The institution of lynching was rooted in my mind early on by a history book that did not minimize the murder of Emmett Till. And everything I have read since then about the history of lynchings and the deliberate destruction of Black families and communities, has fueled my desire to open up the casket and help right both historic and contemporary wrongs inflicted on Black people.

Chapter One, Section 7
Me Too, Long Before #MeToo

Why is it I only confided in my big sister, Paula? I could have been no older than six. My baby sister Roberta had not yet been born.

I knew that something was wrong – because I was really embarrassed. I was even embarrassed – too embarrassed – to tell the whitestrangerman 'No.' I didn't know what to do. So I just kept on splashing and laughing in the beach water like all the other children.

But he was really hurting me. There were sharp pains between my legs where he kept trying to stick his finger. I stiffened and tried to squirm out of his grip. I giggled so that no one would know what was happening to me.

Should I have screamed, "Stop!"?

I was just a kid. He was an adult, a grown-up. What adults do is okay, even though you may not understand the reason why.

So I kept splashing, stiffening, giggling, splashing, stiffening so no one would suspect the awful reality of what he was trying to do with his finger.

Finally, I squirmed and escaped from the "yucky" grip of the whitestrangerman, still giggling nervously so he wouldn't think that I did not like what he was doing. Because he was an adult, and I was a child. And he gradually moved on to another little girl.

My mother taught me at an early age the anatomically correct language for private parts, so sobbingly I blurted out to my sister, "Th-that White man tried to put his finger in my vulva and it really hurt!"

"But don't tell Mommy and Daddy," I quickly pleaded.

I don't recall Paula's response. She was just two years my senior and I imagine my confession was quite a burden for her. Today, I feel so ashamed for not protesting. For not shouting, "Stop!" For not telling my parents.

There were just certain things that one did not talk about in those days. I never knew the name of the beach where we were, and I don't even recall the city, but it was definitely up North. Over the years I often wondered, Who was that White man? How many other little girls did he violate with his finger or even worse, some other part of his anatomy? Did he murder any of them? Did he go to jail? Is he now a judge or a government official? A priest? What caused him to do the things he did? Was he abused as a child?

Both my father and mother went to their graves never knowing of this incident. Heck, I didn't understand until years later that this was sexual abuse.

But why am I still embarrassed about it today? Perhaps it's because that single incident left a psychological scar on my soul for decades. As a young adult, I had flashbacks of it whenever someone's finger got too close to what I called my 'heavenly portal,' causing me to gently push their hand away. I actually felt physical pain just from the thought of it. This phobia was very specific. Never had a problem with a tampon. Never even had a problem with a penis when that was a consideration. But a finger – absolutely not! Ironically, the fear caused by this childhood flashback served a great purpose. It is probably what kept me a virgin through the end of high school.

* * *

As a young adult woman, I have been raped the way a countless number of women have been. I said "No!" to a particular young man's sexual advances; he ignored me and forced his body into mine. Yes, he was cute and 'conscious' and all that, but I simply was not interested in the brother. Yes, we went on a date and he came back to my apartment afterward. I made him some herbal tea with honey. He kissed me and whispered, "Do you want to do something?" And when I replied, "No," he ignored me. I said it again, more emphatically, and once more he pretended that I had no voice. He ignored my additional cries of "No!" until I found myself exhausted by my resistance and acutely aware of my physical inability to free myself of my current circumstances. Ultimately, I acquiesced and just laid there motionless. This was definitely not consent.

Did I classify it as rape at the time? No. The notion barely crossed my mind; this was the late 70s. The strange thing is that I still run into this guy occasionally, maybe once every five or so years. Have I ever told him he violated me? Nope. Did I even ever tell him how hurt I was? Again, no. I did not want to reopen the door to that memory.

Although I was silent then and after the beach incident as a child, I was not always mute when it came to protecting my body. I remember two times when my vocal advocacy saved me.

In one incident, I was at a casual friend's grandmother's apartment. We were kissing and hugging, but I did not want to have sex with him. At the time I was a virgin and envisioned my first time would be during a perfect romantic rendezvous. But I physically could not get the dude off of me, and I knew that unless I did some fast talking to convince him to stop, I was going to lose that battle. I started talking fast, tapping into the skills I would one day use to make a living as a lawyer.

"My brother, how can you do this? I'm a sister, a queen. This is what the White man does. How can you call yourself a brother?"

And on and on and on I ranted. Then finally, probably just to shut me up, he said, "Just go on and get out of here, girl." And I did.

I had no idea where I was, but it was very close to some hospital in the now-gentrified area of Capitol Hill. Luckily, I had some money in my pocket and caught a cab to about a block from my home, since I still lived with my parents. I was still shaking when I walked into the house. Did I tell my parents about this? Did I tell my sister? Did I tell my best girlfriend? The answer for each was: Hell no! And along that vein, I never sought any type of help or support. This is what happens to countless numbers of girls and women. It may never be known how many of us have endured sexual abuse or rape, or any violation of our bodies and minds. That which is not confronted, however, cannot be healed.

The second incident was several years later, while I was in college. This guy's apartment was down the street from Howard University's Meridian Hill dormitory, where I lived. He was from the continent of Africa. I said "No!" several times, but he completely ignored me, disrespecting my wishes. Still, somehow I got away from him before his conquest was successful and managed to get myself out of that apartment and fast.

I immediately called my revolutionary brothers, and they came. Tyehimba, and 6'5" foot, 250-lb. Brother Lee who came with his revolver. I don't know what they said or did, but they assured me that this dude would never ignore the word "no" again.

Over the years I have been sexually abused by an unknown White man at a beach up North, an ordinary Black dude, a so-called brother in "The Struggle," and a "brother" from the African continent. My experiences showed me you cannot stereotype sexual abusers. They come in all colors and creeds, and from all walks of life. And sexual abuse is a horrific crime that spans generations.

Today, the reckoning with men who use their power to sexually abuse women and girls has been momentous. But this scrutiny comes centuries late for this country's original victims of sexual exploitation – Black women and girls, who agonized horribly, often in forced silence, during the enslavement era and beyond.

The White men of that day faced no consequences; Black females were victim to the sexual whims and wishes of every White male, and Black men were not allowed to respond in defense of them in manners befitting of a human being. As a result, today's "Me Too" movement should be expanded to reach back, not just 10, 20, or 30 years, but to the beginnings of our forced sojourn in this country as victims of the enslavement era.

Indeed, no matter how hard I try, and no matter how egregious the harm, it has been difficult for me to divorce the sexual harassment allegations against Black men of today from the historical reality that confronted them yesteryear. And it has been difficult for me to separate the rightful indignation of today's White women accusers against Black males, from the sordid, privileged and complicit past of their White female predecessors. I loathe the racist criminal punishment system and believe in the elimination of mass incarceration. As such, I don't see how the incarceration of the disgraced Bill Cosby, at age 80, or the removal of the iconic John Conyers from Congress, will make women feel any safer.

As society today reconciles with the accusations and disclosures of the indefensible personal flaws of individuals, we must begin the necessary process of national healing by acknowledging the historic harm of enslavement and White privilege which led to colossal and commonplace sexual violations and depravity against enslaved women and girls, as well as enslaved men and boys. The trauma from this unacknowledged past still exists today.

The reasons for sexual violence are myriad. It may be partially because of a sense of entitlement and power, mental health issues, or a lack of respect. Whatever the reason, we as women must use our voices to stop attacks on our bodies and the bodies of others, and be brave enough to speak out against the perpetrators. But we must also recognize that despite deplorable, yet human frailties, it is incumbent that we unapologetically lift up lifetime legacies of steadfastness on issues of justice and civil and human rights. Besides exposing the sexual transgressions of powerful people in politics, entertainment and media, accountability movements must also challenge "the powers that be" to take up the mantle of historic justice.

From my birth at the end of 1954 to my sixth-grade school year in 1966, I would say my experiences were within the normal range of African American children growing up within the middle-class socio-economic status my family enjoyed. The experiences of those first 12 years, however, would pale in comparison to the tur-bulance of my teenage years. As an idealist within the circle of militant protestors of the Black Power era, I would become a young sista in "The Struggle."

Chapter Two
"Say It Loud, I'm Black and I'm Proud"[11]

Section 1
My All-Black-Neighborhood-Junior-High-School

The early years of my consciousness shaping were 1967 to 1969. I was very excited to learn I would attend Rabaut Jr. High School. Rabaut was newly built and opened its doors the year before my 1967 enrollment. We lived around the corner and several blocks up the street from the school. The school was new, pretty, clean and, to me, a welcome change from the bleakness of the aged Whittier Elementary. I would be in Rabaut's second graduating class; my sister, Paula, was in its first.

I was in Beta 7. That seventh grade designation was a manifestation of the school's tracking system at the time. The first few categories, patterned after the Greek alphabet, were Alpha, Beta, Gamma, and Delta. Classmates Joyce and Marian were in Alpha 7 and they were indeed smart, both later becoming physicians. My best friend Kathy and I were both in Beta 7. I don't know if that meant we weren't as smart, because we actually got A's and B's. Ultimately, I would feel this was a cruel and unscientific way of categorizing children.

At Rabaut, I believe the system was soon eliminated because I recall no more overt labels after seventh grade. For many years my colleague, attorney Faya Rose Sanders of Alabama, was on the frontlines of decoding the tracking debacle in places where it still existed and was part of the movement to eliminate this discriminatory practice.

Songstress Roberta Flack was a music teacher at Rabaut. This was before her hit single, *Killing Me Softly*, catapulted her into national fame. My sister was in her class, but unfortunately I was not. However, I had several other teachers at Rabaut who received neither fame nor fortune, but left lasting impressions upon me.

There was Mr. Lang, the teacher most catalytic to my developing a political consciousness. I have no recollection of his first name, but I remember him looking like a combination of younger versions of the academician Cornel West and the poet Amiri Baraka. When I think of Mr. Lang I recall a brown-skinned man with a beard and big Afro. The class he taught was either called Black Studies or Afro American History. Whatever it was called, I couldn't wait to take it. Still, the only memory I have of that class is meeting Huey.

I met Huey P. Newton on a huge poster tacked to the bulletin board of Mr. Lang's eighth grade Black Studies classroom. The image on that poster was one of a proud, determined Black man with a black beret cocked on his head, a rifle gripped in one hand and a spear nestled in the other. Brother Huey posed majestically in a grand slam wicker peacock chair. I was mesmerized.

"Ooohwee he's soooo cute," one girl nearly swooned.

"I wish he was my main squeeze," another mused.

Yes, all the teenage girls in my class were giggling over how fine they thought Huey Newton was. But I was mesmerized, not because of his looks, but his circumstances.

Why is he in jail? I pondered. And why are his lawyers White?

These were the questions that kept turning over and over in my mind. The question that gnawed at my soul most was, *Where are the Black lawyers to represent the Black people?*

After seeing that poster and entertaining that question, I knew right then that I wanted to be a lawyer. My rationale was quite elementary. I looked around and saw members of the Black Panther Party getting shot up and thrown in jail. I was shocked that, for the most part, White lawyers were representing them. Progressive lawyers, yes. Radical lawyers, yes. But did I see anyone who looked like me representing them? I did not.

Actually, in my family's network of friends and acquaintances, I met no lawyers, other than my Aunt Clarice in New York, who never actually practiced law, but excelled in real estate. In fact, the only profession I was really familiar with was teaching. Mommy and Daddy were both educators. I saw and admired teachers. And somehow there seemed to be no other choices that presented themselves to me of what I should aspire to be professionally other than a doctor, a lawyer or a teacher.

"Needi," my father explained, "You have to be good with numbers to be a doctor, and good with words to be a lawyer or a teacher." With that criteria in mind, the choice was an easy one for me and I ended up being both of the latter.

In junior high school, I became aware of the Black Panthers because they were controversial and made front page news. Still, I lacked the tapestry of history in which to set the organization.

I didn't know about the 1857 Dred Scott case where a Supreme Court Justice pronounced unequivocally in a U.S. court of law that a Black person in America had no rights that a White man was bound to respect. I was oblivious to the 1822 trial of Denmark Vesey, who mobilized over 9,000 Blacks and masterminded a slave uprising in South Carolina. I had not a clue about the Amistad slave ship rebellion in 1841, when international law was applied in a domestic court in the U.S. The judicial ruling served as a springboard for the release of kidnapped Africans destined for a life of enslavement.

I had no knowledge of the governmental sabotage of one of the largest African-descended movements in the U.S. – Marcus Garvey and the Universal Negro Improvement Association (UNIA). I didn't even know about the four little Black girls who had been bombed while attending Sunday school in Birmingham, AL, when I was in third grade.

I can't say that Mr. Lang and the Black Studies class educated me to any of these Black history facts. But I can say that the class he taught helped ignite a lifelong thirst for knowledge of Black history and once ignited, I dug for the truth and found books and research that fanned my passion into a burning flame.

Mrs. Gregory and Mrs. Taylor are two other junior high school teachers that I will never forget. Mrs. Gregory was young and pretty with a big, bodacious Afro that would have put both revolutionary Angela Davis and poet Sonia Sanchez to shame. She was my science teacher and taught us how to determine blood types, which I found fascinating. However, the only substantive thing I really remember from that science class did not involve test tubes or dissecting frogs. What really amazed me was how Mrs. Gregory majestically transformed my classmate Beverly.

I think I was in the eighth grade, during the time when we girls were experimenting with our hair in its natural state. Beverly came to school one day with her best attempt at the hairstyle known as an Afro. However, something was not quite right about it. Her hair stuck out in all the wrong places. Young people can be so cruel and the kids in our school were no different, taunting that her hair looked "kinda 'flicted.'" They mercilessly teased Beverly until she was in tears. I felt so bad for her.

Then Mrs. Gregory strode into that room, took only one moment to assess the situation, and saved the day. Words can never express how proud I was of my teacher at that moment. Mrs. Gregory whisked Beverly out of the main classroom and into the backroom that housed test tubes and flasks. I don't know what went on while they were back there, but when they emerged Beverly had a gorgeous Afro that could rival any on the front cover of *Ebony* Magazine back in the day.

Mrs. Gregory was awesome. My Black teachers were more than academicians. They were life-shapers. I don't think the deleterious impact of segregated schools on the continuity of Black culture can be ignored, glossed over, or appropriately measured. For instance, could Beverly's hair transformation have occurred in a majority White school? Would a Caucasian teacher have been inclined to, or have even been able to, rescue Beverly with her hair? I think not.

Yes, I was born during the time when school segregation was struck down by the Supreme Court. But should that period be classified as famous or infamous? To my way of thinking, the verdict was hypocritical and infamous. I have always thought it plausible that there was an ulterior motive behind the Supreme Court ruling for the plaintiffs in *Brown vs. Board of Education*. I believe the "powers that be" feared the effects that a well-documented claim of genocide against the United States could have.

In 1947, Black leaders including W.E.B. DuBois, William Patterson, Mary Church Terrell and 94 other members of the National Negro Congress delivered a statement on racial discrimination to the Secretary General of the United Nations. DuBois later presented to the United Nations a 100-page petition and appeal for help prepared by the NAACP. The petition swelled to 237 pages and became a documented indictment of hundreds of wrongful executions and lynchings. It was noted that these murders amounted to nothing short of genocide. The petition also cited 10,000 undocumented cases, as well as evidence that Southern states had unlawfully used poll taxes and literacy tests to prevent Blacks from exercising their right to vote.

The eyes of the world were on the United States, watching in disapproval as these practices were systematically carried out. Wouldn't it have been easier to simply let Black children sit next to White children in the nation's public schools, rather than risk the condemnation of the world community? I submit that for the above reasons, the decision was made and the die cast to desegregate the nation's schools with the now laughable "all deliberate speed" clause in the *Brown* Supreme Court decision. The proviso that Black children board buses leaving predominately Black neighborhoods to be integrated with those Whites who, for whatever reason, were unable to escape to the suburbs or to enroll their children in private schools, inflicted further trauma on Black students.

So as the Black Studies movement of the Sixties and early Seventies made its debut, and the "Black is Beautiful" and "Black Power" eras began, Black youth began picking up books en masse and rejecting the exclusionary teachings of so-called White supremacy. It was not uncommon during the 1970s to be standing at the bus stop and see a brother or a sister reading a copy of *The Miseducation of the Negro* by Carter G. Woodson, the *Autobiography of Malcolm X*, the *Wretched of the Earth* by Franz Fanon, or don l. lee's poetry compilation, *Don't Cry, Scream*.

The movement for Black pride and the quest for Black history were responsible for helping me and many others of my generation formulate a sense of cultural identity. Yet there were and are so many Blacks who remain oblivious to their formidable ancestry. They remain unaware of the many notable contributions of our African forbearers to mathematics, science, spirituality, literature, art, and virtually every important discipline. The knowledge of their cultural roots remains shallow or non-existent. I believe this is the reason many Black people continue to lack identity, purpose and direction.

For example, if the mythical character, Tyrone, in my speeches knew that his ancestors in Africa performed intricate surgical eye operations, would he feel he has nothing to contribute and be contented to waste away on the corner with his homies in the hood? If Sharmeka knew that people who looked like her performed the first open heart surgery, engineered blood banks and made the first clock in this country, would she feel she has no potential? If Bay Bay knew, despite being subjected to enslavement and subsequent discrimination, that his ancestors invented telegraphic and electrical devices and excelled against all odds, I believe his self-esteem would be elevated enough to prohibit him from engaging in activities destructive to himself and his community. With such knowledge, Bay Bay, Tyrone, Sharmeka and count-less others like them would strive to reach whatever heights their thoughts could conceive and their actions could manifest.

It is impossible for me to tell you who Nkechi Taifa is without also dispensing a Black history lesson. When I look in the mirror, I see Queen Nzingha. When I look at a Black teenage boy on a Northeast street corner in D.C., I see Shaka Zulu. When I watch the news of the day, I view it through the lens of my personal history as a Black person in America.

I was fortunate to start my education in a nurturing, melanin-enriched environment. I will never forget the teachers who placed me on the right path. Besides Mr. Lang and Mrs. Gregory, there was also my English teacher, Mrs. Taylor. She was a ded-icated, stern, older woman – a matronly type who donned gloves during blackboard instruction, as years of chalk dust had caused irritation to her fingers. We teased and giggled unmercifully about this behind her back and out of earshot. But what made Mrs. Taylor memorable to me were not her gloves or subject-verb agreement drills. Rather, it was her requirement that the class write a poem during a lesson on the styles of writing. I don't recall ever being asked to write a poem before, and I was excited.

"Anita, what are you going to write about?" my classmate Kathy asked.

"I think I'm going to write about Martin Luther King," I responded.

The underlying circumstances that provided the background for that first poem still stick out in my mind.

"Roll up your window Needi," Mommy sharply admonished as our 1962 green Chevy ambled cautiously down Washington, D.C.'s 14th Street in Northwest.

Why? It's stuffy in here. This is what I wanted to reply, but something in the tone of my mother's voice warned me to not question but immediately obey.

I peered out the closed car window. "Oh, my God," I exclaimed in disbelief. Right there on 14th Street was the Army. In the community. My community. With guns. Machine guns!

We kept the windows up, even though the weather was mild. Dr. King had been assassinated and people, hurt and angry, had taken to the streets, transforming the community into what appeared to be a war zone. As we drove down 14th Street, one of the hardest hit corridors, I was stunned. The scene appeared to have come straight from the battlefields of Vietnam. D.C. appeared war-torn.

I stared at smashed store windows as the car drove by. Trash from looted goods littered the streets and sidewalks. But most memorable to me were the signs scrawled hastily across store windows that read, "Soul Brother." Even Jewish and Asian businesses proclaimed, "Soul Brother!" Why this designation? The terrified store owners appeared to hope that just like the story in the Bible where houses were passed over if blood was posted at entrances, businesses owned by Black people would likewise be spared by the insignia "Soul Brother." And, for the most part, they were.

That explosive, racially charged background was a prelude to the inspiration for my first poem. A simple rhyme, it was the genesis of a multitude of poems that would become increasingly angry verse, an acceptable channel for centuries of pent-up anger within my DNA.

I feverishly began writing the poem:

There once was a man
He was King of our land
But they shot him down
And took off his crown
And said 'what y'all gonna do now?'

Well, we went down 14th Street
And scared off the pig beat
And everyone was told
That anything without soul
Would be burned and looted for keep.

Then the funeral came
for the man who had won fame.
He had preached non-violence
But when he died, there was no silence.

I will go on to say
He will be back one day
With victory in his hands
And we are so proud
That he was our man.

In junior high school, I read everything I could get my hands on. Most of the informative literature I devoured could be found in the den-turned-library of my family's home, where I spent hours intently pouring through pages upon pages. I was mesmerized by Sammy Davis Jr.'s autobiography *Yes I Can*; Claude Brown's *Manchild in the Promised Land*; and Langston Hughes', *A Pictorial History of the Negro in America*. I wanted desperately to feel good about my people, my history, my culture, my ancestry and myself.

What I read about poverty and oppression filled my thoughts as I fell asleep at night. My life seemed so sheltered. I came to understand from television and magazines that my middle-class life differed from the middle-class lives of White people. And on the pages of the books I perused, I saw that my life was also far removed from the lives of the Black people I read about who were economically deprived.

Chapter 2, Section 2
African Name, Cultural Attire, and Unconditional Love

"Atina Llewdlac." This is the name that preceded "Nkechi Taifa." At first glance it may appear confusing, but on second glance you'll easily notice that it is simply my birth name, "Anita Caldwell," spelled backwards. Me and my girlfriend Kathy (Yhtak) playfully inverted our names during our junior high school years as part of our adolescent spirit. Although it would be several years before I knew anything about African names, there seemed to be some type of power propelling me to address the issue of self-determination at a time when other young girls were thinking about boyfriends or pimples.

This name thing was quite a trip for me. First was the realization around age 15 that Caldwell was not my paternal grandfather's last name. Then came the realization that even if it was, it was simply "massa's" name, a slave name, appended as one's surname.

Oh no, I contemptuously decided. I want no parts of that! And so it was that at the age of 15, I went on a quest to adopt an African-inspired name. I chose my first name, "Nkechi," from the first African names book I ever bought. It was one of the treasures I purchased from D.C.'s Drum and Spear Bookstore, which was then located at 14th and Fairmont Streets, N.W.

Kojo N'namdi, who later became a noted television and radio anchor, was working at the bookstore, and rang up my purchase. I found out later that Ralph Featherstone, a Student National Coordinating Committee (SNCC) organizer, owned the store. Featherstone and his colleague, Herman "Che" Payne, were tragically killed March

7, 1970 when the car they were riding in was bombed outside of D.C., in Bel Air, MD.

The two were on their way from assisting with the trial of H. Rap Brown, later to be known as Imam Jamil Al-Amin. At one time, Brown had been Chairman of SNCC,[12] as well as Minister of Justice for the Black Panther Party; and named as Minister of Defense for the Republic of New Afrika. To my understanding, the car bombing deaths of Featherstone and Che were never investigated, and popular media reported that they were carrying dynamite and blew themselves up.

The book I bought at Featherstone's store indicated that the name, Nkechi, means "loyalty." I repeated the name slowly and carefully and pondered the meaning. I decided the name fit me perfectly. I told myself: Yes, I'm loyal to "The Struggle." (Strangely, however, every African names book I've seen since then defines my name as "God's gift"). Luckily, that appellation was right on time as well, and I accepted and adopted it.

Unfortunately, there was no pronunciation guide in that first book, and it did not even dawn on me that the way I pronounced the name may not have been correct. "Na-kee-chee," sounded somewhat like "Keisha" to me, a name for Black girls that had grown in popularity during that time period, so that was how I pronounced the "ke" part. It wasn't until I was in college that I realized that "N kay chee," as opposed to "Nah kee chee" was the correct pronunciation. However, by that time the name's vibration of "Nah kee chee" was firmly entrenched in my psyche.

I rationalized royally whenever confronted about my inaccurate pronunciation. "Well, my brothers and sisters, you know, our tongues have been colonized. We are an African people, but have been stripped of our language, our culture, our history, and our names. Our culture has been adulterated and, anyway, I'm a New Afrikan."

Incidentally, my name has gone through several metamorphoses. I have also used Nkechi Ajanaku, which I stopped using after discovering there was a family in Tennessee with that surname that practiced polygamy, and I did not wish to be mistaken for one of the wives. I first chose the middle name "Nzingha," after the great Queen Nzingha of Angola. Then I adopted "Malika" – which means "queen" in the Kiswahili language. Finally, I settled on just a first and last name – Nkechi Taifa. "Taifa" resonated with me because it means "nationhood" or "nationality." It was a name I grew into even more deeply as I became engaged in the Black Nationalist movement.

I have never been sensitive about people mispronouncing my name. Some enunciate it exactly as the Ibos in Nigeria pronounce it: "N' kay chee." Others pronounce it, "N' kee chee." Still, others articulate it the way I do, "Nah kee chee." It's not something I get uptight about.

While in college I always admired Sister Imani Kazana, who worked for D.C. City Councilmember John Ray and simultaneously headed up the Wilmington 10 Defense Committee. I often supported the Defense Committee by passing out flyers and participating in rallies and demonstrations.

Professionally, Sister Imani was referred to as Ms. Kazana because it became acceptable to use Ms. instead of Mrs. after the advent of the Women's Liberation Movement. I thought Ms. Kazana sounded so cool. I wanted to be like her and vowed that I, too, would use my African name professionally when I grew up – and I did. Upon graduation from law school nearly 20 years after I first starting using "Nkechi," I made my adopted name official "by the White man's law."

I was always incredulous when people asked, "Who gave you your name?" I didn't know back then it was customary for some esteemed person to "give" you an African name.

"Shoot, I picked it out myself!" I would snap. Did that make my name any less legitimate?

"No, I didn't have a ceremony," I constantly found myself explaining. "I simply looked through a names book and chose it myself."

But perhaps the most important charm to me was my family's unconditional love and acceptance of my new identity. Some parents have disowned or ostracized their children for adopting an African or Muslim name. To the contrary, Mommy and Daddy kept their minds and hearts open, and always accepted and respected my choices in life. I am eternally grateful for the exceptional support I had from my family in all of my undertakings, and that I was raised by parents that supported me in my self-expression.

It was not just my parents who valued the direction my life was taking without ever one ounce of negativity toward me, but my sisters were also supportive. Paula is two-and-a-half years older than me, and my sister Roberta is six years my junior. Neither were really around the house by the time I was coming into my own as a teenager. Paula was off to college, and Roberta was only around nine. As such, they were not involved in my day-to-day activities, but did know their sister had an African name. Although no family member ever abandoned my childhood nickname, Needi, they all willingly called me Nkechi.

Regarding my baby sister, I was both shocked and thrilled to discover that decades later Roberta still remembered and treasured the African name I bestowed upon her when she was a child.

"You gave me the name, 'Asali,'" Roberta recalled joyfully.

"Oh my goodness," I laughed. "Yes, I did. I had forgotten all about that!"

"You said Asali meant sweetness or honey," she added.

I smiled from ear to ear. When she was born I nicknamed my baby sister "Kissy," because she was so sweet I wanted to kiss her all the time. And she became Kissy to everyone in the family. While the sweetness of "Asali" seemed quite fitting to me, I don't think she ever really used her African name. Nonetheless, it made me feel so good and proud that she remembered the name throughout the decades.

It's the little things like that, that mean so much to me. I'm still amazed at my family's tolerance of me. They stomached me reciting the section about Thanksgiving every November after grace at the dinner table from the book, *African People and European Holidays, A Mental Genocide*. They politely listened as I reenacted Frederick Douglass' speech at summer cookouts, "What to the American Slave is Your 4th of July?"

They smiled while receiving Kwanzaa rather than Christmas gifts from me at the end of each year, and often accompanied me to citywide cultural celebrations. My parents took Tai Chi classes from the Ausar Auset Society, one of the groups I frequented. They even joined the Black rifle club I became a part of and went to the range with our group.

My family has been so supportive of me throughout my life – they were the fuel that allowed my engine to roll through all its twists, turns, challenges and triumphs. I doubt I would have felt comfortable cultivating the unconventional path I chose if they had protested. They gave me the space I needed to grow and develop and become the person I am today.

In addition to choosing an African name, it was also around age 15 that I purchased my first dashiki, at Rev. Doug Moore's African shop on Georgia Avenue. Moore was also a D.C. City Councilman. Later during his Council tenure he wrote a stinging indictment of city government entitled *Buying and Selling of the D.C. City Council*. Many dismissed him as a lunatic after he reportedly bit someone after an argument, but my fond memory of him, besides his being a no-nonsense Councilman, is that he opened a store that made it possible for me to fall in love with and purchase my first cultural garb.

The attire from his shop included my first dashiki and African headwrap fabric, as well as the blue and white African print fabric I used to make the first real dress I ever sewed on a sewing machine. Designing a dress was a requirement in the sewing class I was taking at Rabaut. Actually, the dress I designed was quite hip. It was a long African print dress, sleeveless, with a halter-top and matching gele, and I looked good in it.

It was also during this same time period that I delighted in dragging the heavy black telephone into my tiny bedroom at night, as there were no cordless or cell phones back then. I would close the door and call up the radio station WOL 1450 AM to listen to *The Dewey Hughes Show*. Dewey was current media mogul Cathy Hughes' husband in those days.

Each week he featured different, enthusiastic, well-spoken guests on his *Speak Up* show, discussing some type of social justice or political issue. I would carefully craft a question or response, and call in. Those were the days of rotary phones, where each number was dialed on a circular disc that took what seemed like forever to come back to its original position so that you could dial the next number. I had mastered the art of calling the number very slowly and waiting before dialing the last number until the previous call had just hung up. I then quickly turned the dial to the last digit and voila, I was on the line.

At the time, I never understood why Dewey and his guests always made such a big fuss whenever I called in. "Little sista, how old are you?" often questioned Petey Greene, one of the commentators who frequented the show. It annoyed me greatly when they asked my age, and what grade I was in. I knew they thought I was too young to be calling in or too young to raise politically and socially conscious questions. Although I was only in junior high school, I really did not consider myself young.

It never dawned on me that I may have been politically advanced for my age. In fact, many of the discussions I listened to on *Speak Up*, and the community lectures I later attended, went in one ear and out the other. I just knew that what I heard made my adrenaline rise. And when I mustered the courage to comment or ask questions, I could not do so unless I first carefully wrote out my words. This preparation allowed me to feel and sound confident. If I were not prepared, my hands got clammy, my body became tense and anxious, and a funny sensation would settle in my stomach.

Unfortunately, these symptoms would continue through most of my life, making me apprehensive to speak extemporaneously. But I ultimately grew to love public speaking and became quite proficient at it, or so I've been told.

And as long as I was prepared with my notes, I was always fine.

Chapter Two, Section 3
Good Gurl, Bad Boyz and The Struggle

I got stuck on the soulful songs of the Seventies.

"Don't mess with Bill, no no no no, don't mess with Bill." Or, "I heard it through the grapevine, yes I heard it through the grapevine."

I couldn't sing a lick, but I could be heard all through the house, wailing away. I used to go to the house parties that were popular during the 70s with my girlfriends Kathy, Michelle, Donna and Susan. Although I did the dances of the day such as The Jerk, The Funky Chicken, The Tighten-Up, The Funky Broadway and The Bump, for some strange reason I never learned what is today lauded as D.C.'s signature oldies style: hand-dancing.[13]

Like most Black young people of my era, I watched Soul Train religiously. Teen-a-Rama was also a popular TV show that was filmed in D.C. and starred many of today's hand-dance masters in their youth – Doc Barnett, who became a well-known drummer; Lawrence Bradford, who is credited with transforming D.C.'s hand-dance into a fine art; and, Tippi Mavrette. However, to this day I could kick myself for not learning how to hand-dance as a teen. I always thought it was because I spent so much time with the books and in "The Struggle" that I never really learned that dance. The truth of the matter, however, is that I really never had much rhythm, and I still don't today, despite the stereotype that all Black folk can dance.

As a teen, I was square in so many ways. I couldn't sing or dance, and I didn't do drugs. But, like most of the girls, I turned my attention to boys. I was the classic example of the proverbial "good girl" who liked "bad boys." In fact, one brother named Kent, who used to live in Virginia, recently told me his memory of me was as "the only virgin he knew that didn't want to be a virgin."

When we were teenagers, he told me stories of how he and his homies went into D.C. and burglarized houses. The first time he told me this, he saw the horrified look on my face and quickly added, "But don't worry Anita. They was all White folk's houses, across the park." I gave a sigh of relief. I could not have a boyfriend that stole from Black people. It didn't dawn on me at the time that he didn't know for sure they were "all White folk's houses." It also never dawned on me that one day one of those houses could be mine.

Of course Kent ended up landing himself in jail. He kept talking about how he was going to contact his lawyer, and he seemed proud that he had a White lawyer. It perplexed me, How could this dude afford a lawyer who was on call? And a White lawyer at that? I wasn't aware of the Sixth Amendment. I knew nothing about court-appointed lawyers either, although one day I would be one. All I knew was that Kent had his own personal White lawyer that he called whenever he got in trouble. I bumped into Kent recently, after not having seen him in over 30 years.

"What do you remember about me?" I asked him, explaining that I was writing a book.

"You was strange, Anita," he immediately volunteered. "You was a virgin that didn't want to be a virgin. You wanted your cake and eat it too. You always sent me home with a case of blue balls."

"Yeah, something else Anita," he continued.

I cut him off. "Remember, my name is Nkechi now, and has been so for over 40 years."

"Oh yeah right, Nke... Nke...," he stammered, attempting to pronounce my African name before giving up, saying, "Anyway girl, you almost got me killed."

"What you talking 'bout?" I asked curiously.

"You know I was a thief," he continued. "You know it's hard to catch a burglar, it's something like chasing a ghost. But I finally got caught."

Good, I'm thinking, before you burglarize my Chevy Chase home with its pretty manicured lawn.

"So how did I almost get you killed?" I had become quite curious now.

Well I was at Southhampton Prison in Virginia. I was 18 years old. I was down there where Nat Turner kilt all them folk. The area was like KKK ... You used to write me crazy letters and they was reading my mail, you know. They censored everybody's mail. You always ended your letters with Lasimatuashindbilashaka. Lasimatuashindbilashaka.

I really thought Kent had gone off the deep end.

"Slow down, dude, I can't understand what you're saying!"

He repeated the word, but emphasizing different syllables. "Lasimatu SHINDBILASHAKA."

"Oh, my goodness! Are you trying to say 'Lazima Tutashinda Mbili Shaka?'" I asked in amazement.

Kent nodded in relief.

"We will conquer without a doubt!," we both burst out excitedly, laughing in unison.

"Dag, I haven't said that in years," I mused nostalgically. "No, decades. I remember I used to end all my letters back then with that Kiswahili phrase."

"They used to call me the young militant," Kent continued. "I told them, 'Hey look y'all trying to break me, but it ain't happening.' I got into a fight with a White guy at the time. It almost turned into a mini riot."

"I had court-appointed lawyers," Kent continued. "But once they asked about any prior criminal history, I was ruined."

"I know what you mean," I added. "It's so easy for Black folk to have priors, due to the way policing is carried out in Black communities."

Kent, however, didn't seem interested in my analysis. He continued:

"If it were not for Second Genesis, I would have been in prison for a very long time. It literally saved my life. I didn't expect to live to be 25. But the director, Barry Francis, took time with me. It was a drug program, and I wasn't addicted. But going through the program was a quick way to keep from going to prison forever."

I was somewhat familiar with Second Genesis. It was an alternative to incarceration, before drug courts. However, to be eligible for the Second Genesis program, one had to be drug-addicted. Kent had not been addicted, but asserted he was in order to partake in the program as a way to side-step imprisonment.

The same situation existed to be eligible for housing services; one had to be deemed homeless to qualify. Apparently, folk in dire circumstances sometimes find it necessary to pretend to fit a certain profile in order to be eligible for much-needed assistance, often reserved for what's deemed to be the most desperate cases. But should one have to pretend to have a drug problem to get out of going to prison, or be considered homeless to receive housing services? Policies such as these were woefully misguided, in my opinion, and my desire to support reentry services for people convicted of crimes would punctuate my work in the future.

Chapter Two, Section 4
My All-White-Girls-Catholic-High-School

Mommy and Daddy forced me, the consummate militant and self-described revolutionary, to go to Regina High School, a predominately White, Catholic school for girls in Maryland. I considered myself Ms. Black Power, yet here I was stuck in whiteness, and I was not even Catholic. What would Che Guevara have felt? What would Patrice Lumumba have said? What about Harriet Tubman?! I felt I was betraying my ancestry. I also understood, realistically, that both of my parents' professional careers had been with the failing D.C. Public School System – Mommy as a teacher, counselor and assistant principal; and, Daddy as a teacher. They chose Regina for me. That was the end of the discussion.

Dutifully, I put on the prim and proper brown and tan uniform with the required saddle shoes, put my hair up in my characteristic Afro-puff bush ball, which is how I wore my hair when I wasn't wearing an African gele[14] on my head, and off to Regina High School I went. It was 1970.

I entered Regina in the 10th grade, although Catholic schools traditionally began with the 9th grade. I spent the 9th grade at my beloved Rabaut Jr. High. There were exactly three other Black girls in my high school class. My new friends included the African American girls from all the classes, a Filipino girl who hung with the Sistas, and a White girl who had a Black boyfriend and was the only White member of our Black Student Union. My segregated lifestyle ended, and I had my first real introduction to White people at Regina.

"I can't believe she didn't wash her hands," I exclaimed to one of my Black classmates after witnessing a Caucasian student bypass the sink as she left the bathroom.

"Girl, don't you know that's how White folk are?" she responded.

Clearly, I didn't know anything at all about White folk, except what I saw on TV and in the movies and magazines. My only personal experience was that they all seemed to have big, pretty houses with lush green lawns. I had seen this with my own eyes when I visited a White family's home in Chevy Chase when we had a Girl Scout Troop exchange with a troop west of Park. In D.C., the phrase west of Rock Creek Park was the equivalent to the phrase, "across the tracks," words understood by Blacks nationwide. Little did I know that one day I would live in one of those Chevy Chase houses with a landscaped lawn.

At Regina, my parents thought I would get a good education and be protected from the vices of bad boys and drugs. Ironically, however, my first introduction to drugs was at Regina. The first time I ever saw marijuana, some of my White classmates were lighting up joints while lounging in the grass rotunda in front of the school. I thought, *Whoa, Mommy and Daddy thought they were trying to save me from such inner city vices, and now here it is right in front of my nose in the suburbs.*

Out of curiosity, I must confess that I took a puff.

"Uggh!" Although I had succumbed to peer pressure, I instantly knew it was not for me. In retrospect, what was most unnerving was that not one of my White teenaged classmates gave a second thought to the fact that marijuana was illegal at the time. I dare say this was true for the other drugs they indulged in. They were privileged and accustomed to being able to do whatever they wanted. I would think of them years later when I realized that there are people actually serving life sentences for marijuana possession. And, of course, a disproportionate number of them are Black.

Daddy drove me to school every day, and I caught the bus home. At least, most of the time I caught the bus home. There were many occasions when the bus just took too long. I then stuck out my thumb and hitchhiked from New Hampshire Avenue in White Oak, MD, to 3rd Street and New Hampshire Avenue, N.W. in D.C., several blocks from my home. Today I am shocked when I think back to my naïve behavior. But for the grace of God and the benevolence of the ancestors, I was not kidnapped or murdered.

I only had one troubling incident. A grown man who looked like a construction worker in his 20s gave me a ride one afternoon and kept harassing me. They say the Lord looks after fools and babies, and I must have had elements of both. I hopped out of his truck with lightning bolt speed once he reached my destination and dashed home as best as I could in my hard saddle shoes.

Chapter Two, Section 5
Lil Militant Me

My relationship with Regina High School is difficult to convey. It was rather bizarre, but keep in mind this was the early 1970s and no matter the subject, militancy and my growing political consciousness seeped into my classroom discussions and writings, yet had no negative impact on my grades. Relentless, I took every opportunity to inject relevancy into take-home assignments. I raised thought-provoking questions, investigated cultural dissonance, and challenged legitimacies. I was, so to speak, 'in your face' and no one – not a single nun – sought to pull in my reins. Who knows if it was liberalism, fear, or guilt. Whatever the reason, I had the complete freedom to express myself without fear of sanction.

I always made sure to connect whatever I was writing to the situation confronting Black people in this country or in the diaspora. For example, I wrote "Revolution Throughout the Centuries as Compared to Our Present Day Situation" for my term paper in the required course, Modern European History. I got an A.

For my French class report I wrote about France in 1958, facing the threat of civil war over the question of Algerian independence. Even an essay I had to write on the importance of Russian History was not spared. In my paper I explained that "The history books in America have been used as a weapon against us. We need to study, research and rewrite the false images in the textbooks, which serve only to maintain the erroneous notion that the European is the only power on earth…"

I then went on to compare the "similar derogatory images" in U.S. history books regarding Russian history. I concluded by stating that "especially for Black people in this decade of the 70s, not to know Russian history is bad; not to wish to have this knowledge is worse, especially in light of the situation presently evolving in Angola on the African continent. It is a must that we study, broaden our perspectives and deal with the entire world, for everyday we are affected by it."

While at Regina I composed a sort of manifesto, a document accompanied with images I cut out of magazines and pasted in my handmade, stapled booklet. I did not share it in school; I did not show it to friends. It was my special creed – something I instilled within myself. In essence, this high school musing was a vision of an alternate society in the U.S. and how it would be governed:

> The country will be sectioned off – either north/south or east/west. All people owning property or anyone who does not wish to distribute his wealth equally – 'from each according to his ability to each according to his needs' will live in one section of the country. All oppressed people who

wish to advance humanity and the system of Ujamaa will live in the other section. There will not be discrimination as to race, although the majority of Ujamaa citizens will be Blacks, Indians or Chicanos for those are the most oppressed and more willing to try something new. There shall be two persons responsible for the survival of the society in its initial stages, male and female. They will be called 'Responsibles' for that is their job – to be responsible for the society.

It will be a communal way of life under the motto, "Do unto others as you would have others do unto you." Community survival programs will be implemented such as free food, health and clothing. The revolution will not be violent, but rather the radical change in the way of thinking of the people. We must begin to think in terms of community rather than individuals, cooperation as opposed to competitiveness, and love as opposed to exploitation. To fully achieve this goal, the primary focus will be on re-education.

Children just born must reap the full benefit of these changed values. They will be taught from the cradle not to think only of themselves, but the good of the community as a while. If for some reason one reverts back towards the inhumanity of the oppressor culture, he shall be punished by having to leave the Ujamaa territory and go back to the oppressors, who have been functioning as before, but rapidly decaying as the majority of the people have departed. In the future the whole country will be united under Ujamaa when the oppressors see how much progress we would have made.

Portions of this idealistic concept are likely what primed me for later rebellious beliefs, setting the stage for a future philosophy I would promote for many years.

***

For reasons totally inexplicable to me, I was one of two students selected by Regina to attend the prestigious Maryland Girls' State, housed at the University of Maryland, Baltimore Campus, in 1972. It was sponsored by the American Legion Auxiliary and billed as "a thrilling adventure into the realm of Government in Action." However, I really would rather have been at the National Black Political Assembly in Gary, IN held that same year.

"You will learn what it means to be a citizen of the United States," the Girls' State notice read. I thought to myself. Shucks, I could have been chanting "It's Nation Time!" in Gary. I could have been one of the 3,000 official delegates, one of the elected officials or perhaps one of the many revolutionaries in attendance. I fantasized as I continued my reverie. I could have been helping to draft the National Black Political Agenda, sketching out the goals of the election, which included a proportionate number of Black representatives to Congress, community control of schools, national health insurance and the elimination of capital punishment.

Instead, I found myself parading around all week with White girls, running for mock political office and campaigning for the passage of imaginary legislation while being inundated with American patriotism. Then I was struck by a nagging suspicion. *Patriotism. Maybe that's why Regina High School sent me to Girls' State – to drum out my militancy!*

Little did I know that decades later my career would center on advocacy before Congress for real legislation. Little did I know that I would lead campaigns to enact legislation against discriminatory sentencing and racial profiling; and in support of societal re-entry of formerly incarcerated people, statehood for the District of Columbia and many other hot-button issues.

Talent Night was one bright spot in that grueling week of Girls' State. During auditions they selected me to perform my dramatic poem, "Slavery 1970." The poem, which would have been labeled "spoken word" today, centered on the connection between drug abuse and enslavement and let me tell you, the Girls' State policy-makers-to-be were completely mesmerized with both the content of my poem as well as my forceful delivery.

I adored Sister Denise's creative writing class at Regina High School. She required us to maintain a journal, and it was my constant companion throughout high school. If per chance you were to ever stumble upon and read this journal, please be forewarned: it may give you the impression that I was a ghetto-dwelling, dope-smoking person who hated all White people. Not one element of that description, however, characterized the real me.

The first entry in my journal was my satire on the U.S. Constitution's Preamble:

Fourscore and seven years ago, them pigs brought forth upon this continent us slaves, conceived in slavery and dedicated to the proposition that all men are not created equal. Now we are engaged in a great race war, testing, whether this nation or any nation so conceived and so dedicated can long endure…

Interestingly, despite my satiric rendition, I remember the original Preamble verbatim to this day, due to compulsory indoctrinated recitation during grade school. Wouldn't it be great if today's children were required to memorize the Nguzo

Saba,[15] or the New Afrikan Creed[16] as part of their standard public school education? A five-line technique I learned in my high school creative writing class fascinated me. I have no idea what it is called, but using my own content, the structure shaped like a diamond was as follows:

Africa

Black   Hot

Diamonds   Gold   Ivory

Genesis of Civilization

Home

Empire

Imperialistic   Racist

Conquering   Murdering   Bombing

War Never Ceases

USA

Black Woman

Courage   Beauty

Fine Fearless Faithful

Mother of Civilization

Queen

I used this succinct technique with creative five line content throughout my precious journal.

Sister Denise encouraged us to write, write, write. I wrote what I felt, and what I felt were the passions and struggles of the day. During several classes we had to demonstrate emotion and "point of view" in our writings. I wrote from the point of view of a North Vietnamese man confronting and then communing with a Black soldier. I wrote from the point of view of a Black man sitting in a prison's solitary confinement cell. I wrote about the majesty of Black women and the strength of Black men. I wrote about Black misery and described police officers as "pigs" and White people as "devils." I wonder what Sister Denise thought of my many diatribes against society, the Viet Nam War, racism and poverty. I felt no shame. My classmates nicknamed me "Lil Black" and I was militant to the core.

Chapter Two, Section 6
Flirting with the Black Panther Party

Every summer throughout my teenage years my family traveled to New York to visit my Uncle Ambrose, who lived at 123rd and St. Nicholas Avenue in Harlem. The only thing I didn't like about visiting were the smells when I walked into his apartment building. The tenements had an odor to them, which I always attributed to rat poison as I hop-scotched over the white powder strewn on the common staircase. Uncle's apartment, however, was always spotless, odor-free, immaculate and clean. These New York visits gave me the opportunity to be closer to my Uncle, who lived to be just months shy of his 100th birthday, and who had carried on the trade of his father, a master carpenter.

Uncle's carpentry shop was located on 125th Street, around the corner from his apartment. I relished visiting him at his shop, as it gave me the opportunity to leisurely amble through the colorfully vibrant Harlem community. I strolled past the vendors hawking incense, bootleg goods, tee shirts and African clothes. I often stopped to gaze at the huge array of my favorite  item – Afrocentric earrings. My signature style as a teen featured tight bell-bottom jeans that hugged my behind, a form-fitting body shirt or mid-riff top tied seductively beneath my youthful breasts, my ever-present gele headwrap, and platform shoes. Long, dangling, imitation-gold hoop earrings completed my teenage fashion statement.

"Hey lil Sista," the brothers hanging out on the corner of 125th and Lenox Avenue always flirted as I walked by. "Hey, my Brothers," I replied teasingly, waving my hand and switching my little round teenage butt down the street. I had no fear and did not feel disrespected. I had love for my people and the guys hanging on the corner were my brothers.

That same carefree nature manifested in D.C. as well. I often caught the bus adorned in my away-from Catholic-school bell-bottom jeans, complete with the characteristic towering, multi-colored, African gele circling my head. The bus swerved down Georgia Avenue, past the campus of Howard University, to the Black Panther Party office. At that time it was located at 1610 7th Street, N.W., next to the then Southern Dining Room. The brothers and sisters held informative PE (political education) classes in the larger back area. However, I usually loitered around the front office with the cute brother named Tee who was pulling security.

"Sista, come sit on my lap," Tee would coax. Unhesitatingly, I always complied.

I remember one day looking longingly at his copy of Chinese Chairman Mao Tse Tung's *Little Red Book*, which the Panthers were distributing and marketing wholesale. This book was a veritable bible during the Chinese Cultural Revolution, and it was the most printed book in the world at the time.

"Brother Tee, can I borrow Chairman Mao's book?" I asked boldly.

"Of course, My Sista," he replied, smiling majestically.

Gushing with the utmost appreciation, I asked, "When do I need to give it back?"

"My Sista, when you have internalized his teachings," he magnanimously replied.

Well, that just made my day. He couldn't have said anything more political or revolutionary than that. I was awestruck.

Every Saturday, I used to meet Tee and the other Panthers downtown to sell Black Panther papers. My main spot was in front of an earring store at 13th and H Street, N.W. Sometimes I also sold papers in front of the Soul Shack record store on F Street. The police, in marked and unmarked cars, rode by constantly.

"There go the pigs again," Tee pointed out, schooling me.

I put on my meanest scrawl and sold papers even more exuberantly than before.

Tee was a short, slim, nice-looking brother with light eyes that looked green. He donned a distinctive hat as opposed to the characteristic Panther beret cocked to one side. I was in luvvv! "Coffee, Tee, and Me" I used to scribble in my high school journal, and doodle little hearts around the words.

Of course he never knew any of this, and no, he was not my boyfriend. But I sho nuff had a crush on this dude. I wasn't so blind, however, that I was ready to give

up my virginity. As a testament to the gentleman he was, despite all the rhetoric you may have heard about the Panthers sexing up the sisters, once my position was made plain, he respected my wishes. I think he was 19 and I was probably 16. We kissed, hugged and squeezed but he never got in my cootchie!

Although no other Panthers paid much attention to me, the Panther office was also where I first met Anita and Wesley. Shortly thereafter, she would change her name to Nkenge Toure. Years later she'd become a champion of women's issues and the host of the famed WPFW radio show, "*In Our Voices*." The man who was her husband during the Panther days would later become one of my political comrades, Patrice Toure. Nkenge always stood out in my mind because her birth name was Anita, just like mine, and because she was an example of the strong Sista I strived to be. My Panther world revolved around Tee, selling papers, and taking political education classes. Today, I'm embarrassed to say that I have little memory of those political discussions other than the occasional "Right On!" and "Power to the People!" slogans. I think I must have suffered from a mild form of Attention Deficit Disorder at political lectures in my teen years. Mainly, my teenage hormones enjoyed profiling and gawking at the cute dudes.

I was, however, mesmerized by the Panther's 10-point program found in the mid-section of *The Black Panther* newspaper every single week.

October 1966 Black Panther Party Platform and Program. What We Want; What We Believe:

1. WE WANT FREEDOM. WE WANT POWER TO DETERMINE THE DESTINY OF OUR BLACK COMMUNITY. We believe that Black people will not be free until we are able to determine our destiny.

2. WE WANT FULL EMPLOYMENT FOR OUR PEOPLE. We believe that the federal government is responsible and obligated to give every man employment or a guaranteed income. We believe that if the white American businessmen will not give full employment, then the means of production should be taken from the businessmen and placed in the community so that the people of the community can organize and employ all of its people and give a high standard of living.

3. WE WANT AN END TO THE ROBBERY BY THE CAPITALIST OF OUR BLACK COMMUNITY. We believe that this racist government has robbed us and now we are demanding the overdue debt of forty acres and two mules. Forty acres and two mules were promised 100 years ago as restitution for slave labor and mass murder of Black people. We will accept

the payment in currency which will be distributed to our many communities. The Germans are now aiding the Jews in Israel for the genocide of the Jewish people. The Germans murdered six million Jews. The American racist has taken part in the slaughter of over fifty million Black people. Therefore, we feel this is a modest demand that we make.

4. WE WANT DECENT HOUSING, FIT FOR THE SHELTER OF HUMAN BEINGS. We believe that if the white landlords will not give decent housing to our Black and oppressed communities, the housing and the land should be made into cooperatives so that our communities, with government aid, can build and make decent housing for the people.

5. WE WANT EDUCATION FOR OUR PEOPLE THAT EXPOSES THE TRUE NATURE OF THIS DECADENT AMERICAN SOCIETY. WE WANT EDUCATION THAT TEACHES US OUR TRUE HISTORY AND OUR ROLE IN THE PRESENT-DAY SOCIETY. We believe in an educational system that will give to our people a knowledge of self. If you do not have knowledge of yourself and your position in the society and the world, then you will have little chance to relate to anything else.

6. WE WANT ALL BLACK MEN TO BE EXEMPT FROM MILITARY SERVICE. We believe that Black people should not be forced to fight in the military service to defend a racist government that does not protect us. We will not fight and kill other people of color in the world who, like Black people, are being victimized by the white racist government of America. We will protect ourselves from the force and violence of the racist police and the racist military, by whatever means necessary.

7. WE WANT AN IMMEDIATE END TO POLICE BRUTALITY AND MURDER OF BLACK PEOPLE. We believe we can end police brutality in our Black community by organizing Black self-defense groups that are dedicated to defending our Black community from racist police oppression and brutality. The Second Amendment to the Constitution of the United States gives a right to bear arms. We therefore believe that all Black people should arm themselves for self-defense.

8. WE WANT FREEDOM FOR ALL BLACK MEN HELD IN FEDERAL, STATE, COUNTY AND CITY PRISONS AND JAILS. We believe that all Black people should be released from the many jails and prisons because they have not received a fair and impartial trial.

9. WE WANT ALL BLACK PEOPLE WHEN BROUGHT TO TRIAL

TO BE TRIED IN COURT BY A JURY OF THEIR PEER GROUP OR PEOPLE FROM THEIR BLACK COMMUNITIES, AS DEFINED BY THE CONSTITUTION OF THE UNITED STATES. We believe that the courts should follow the United States Constitution so that Black people will receive fair trials. The 14th Amendment of the U.S. Constitution gives a man a right to be tried by his peer group. A peer is a person from a similar economic, social, religious, geographical, environmental, historical and racial background. To do this the court will be forced to select a jury from the Black community from which the Black defendant came.We have been, and are being, tried by all-white juries that have no understanding to the average reasonable man of the Black community.

10. WE WANT LAND, BREAD, HOUSING, EDUCATION, CLOTHING, JUSTICE, AND PEACE. And as our major political objective a United Nations-supervised plebiscite to be held throughout the Black colony in which only Black colonial subjects will be allowed to participate, for the purpose of determining the will of Black people as to their national destiny.

The Panther office was not my only political hangout. During the early 70s, I also sat through intriguing lectures at the Topographical Research and Information Center (the TOP Center). It was located upstairs in what was once the People's Involvement Corporation (PIC) building, an auspicious warehouse-looking edifice on Georgia Avenue. The third floor of the building also housed Melvin Deal's African Heritage Dancers and Drummers and facilitated other cultural and political activities and forums. I also frequented a house on 18th and Kilbourne Street, N.W., which regularly featured stimulating lectures with notable historians such as C. L. R. James and other luminaries.

I don't know if I remember any of the philosophies, teachings or lectures at any of these hangouts. Perhaps some type of osmosis was going on and I internalized knowledge subconsciously. I do know that I characterized everything I heard as very revolutionary, and all were part of my introduction to "The Struggle."

I really shouldn't beat up on myself, though. High school girls my age were not out running the streets like I was with radical intellectuals many years their senior. Most girls my age were content to read dreamy romance novels or Nancy Drew mysteries. My best friend Kathy always said that I preferred living on the edge, being the daring one, and taking risks. At the time however, my "escapades," as she classified them, seemed quite ordinary and normal to me.

One day while riding the bus on my way to the Panther office, I ran into the assistant minister at my church. He initially seemed quite surprised to see me, and then deduced out loud, without actually questioning me, where I was headed. With certainty he surmised, "Anita, you must be in this neighborhood visiting a church."

The statement was plausible. In the Black community there is usually a church on one corner and a liquor store on the other, and D.C. fit that schematic as well as any majority-Black area. By process of elimination, to the pastor, a church was the most logical reason for my travel that evening. I thought it would be polite to just smile, rather than go into a long explanation of the fact that I was actually on my way to a PE class at the Panther office up the street from the church. I played with the idea of inviting him to join me to learn about why we must struggle to be free. But I decided it was best to just smile angelically until he reached his destination, or I reached mine.

Chapter Two, Section 7
Brothers From "the Nam"

I also hung out with Sister Evalina and Brother Popps, Spade de Mau Mau, Brother Vicious (not sure how he got that name as he always seemed tame to me), and Brother Raqeeb, through whom I met this eclectic crew.

I met Brother Raqeeb in the Anacostia section of D.C., on Good Hope Road S.E. He was working at a community organization that featured a drug awareness program. I was there gathering information for a high school paper on drug abuse. I gave him my phone number, and later it was through him that I met the brothers who served in the Viet Nam War, colloquially shortened to "the Nam." They taught me the "dap" greeting. The dap was the signature handshake of the brothers from "the Nam," and those close to them. It signified affinity and solidarity. The bond I felt for those rebellious spirits during my last year in high school is probably one of the reasons I never felt the need to join a sorority in college. I became even more enthralled with "The Struggle."

To this day I am amazed at my utter lack of fear during those high school years. I would jump on the bus and travel everywhere around the D.C. area – Northwest, Northeast, Southeast, Southwest, Maryland, the projects – you name it. Again, I must emphasize that I didn't smoke, drink or use drugs. I was a virgin until I was almost 18. I was really a goody two-shoes girl that happened to like "bad boys."

So just what is a bad boy? To me, a bad boy was worldly and daring. He had no fear. Raqeeb, tall and dark, and my first real boyfriend, fit all the criteria. He was a bad boy who had been in "the Nam," one of the thousands of Black youth who were politicized by the horrors and injustice of that controversial war. Some years later I read Wallace Terry's bestseller, *Bloods: An Oral History of the Viet Nam War by Black Veterans*. The book, with its riveting personal narratives of the experiences of 20 Black men who fought in Viet Nam, opened my eyes even more. I later became friends with Brother Ari Merretezon, one of the book's contributors, then known as Haywood Kirkland, who co-founded the Incarcerated Veterans Assistance Organization. Hollywood used the exploits that sent him to prison after "the Nam" as the prototype for the bank robbery in the blockbuster movie *Dead Presidents*, which starred Larenz Tate as Brother Ari.

Raqeeb made me a black-braided band, put it on my wrist and burned the ends together. Conscious brothers from "the Nam" wore similar bands.

"Don't ever remove it," Raqeeb solemnly instructed. I honored that directive for several years, long after we parted, until a smelly infection grew on my wrist. But during the time it adorned my arm, it made me feel so connected to the movement. When we, the kindred souls sporting these braided bands, saw one another, we offered a silent nod or a clenched fist. If we were close, we dapped. I so loved the comradery.

Raqeeb, Evalina, Popps and I, along with the others, would go up Northwest to Dingane's Den on 18th Street and listen to jazz or the group Plunky and the Oneness of Ju Ju and get something to drink. My drink of choice was always just apple juice. After the show we sat on the wall outside and, as always, rapped about "The Struggle."

On a typical Saturday I might sell Panther papers downtown, go back to the Panther office, and then drop by the Community Fabric and Gift Shop. The shop was located at the corner of 7th and Florida Avenue, N.W., next door to the office of the *Third World News Magazine*.

Community Fabrics was managed by a brother I called Ollie, whose name I later found out may have been Ali. The shop is long gone, but I spent many a Saturday just hanging out there, or shopping for African fabric, earrings, bracelets, bangles, incense and other Africentric items. Ollie also played his saxophone right there in the shop, and I loved to just sit there and listen to his wailing horn.

I spent my high school weekends hanging out in the hood with what my father called "the bad boys." I attended Regina High School during the week, but I was never interested in socializing with my friends from Regina. I did, however, attend my 11th grade junior prom, accompanied by parentally acceptable Larry Brown.

I must have been going with Raqeeb at the time, but I couldn't ask him to my prom. After all, in the eyes of my father, he was a bad boy. After surveying my options, I chose Larry, a good, clean-cut boy who had joined Daddy's fraternity, Omega Psi

Phi Incorporated, also known as the Omegas. I knew he would be acceptable as a prom date to my parents. And, he was. He brought me the requisite corsage, drove me to the prom, and brought me back home, all while being a perfect gentleman.

Over four decades later, I ran into Larry at a hand-dancing club. I was excited to see him, and ours was a nostalgic reunion. He later mailed me the prom picture he had kept all those years. He was always a nice and kind guy, which unfortunately worked against him in our youth. I simply could not help that I was attracted to bad boys.

Every summer during high school I had a job, thanks to my mom's connections while working for the D.C. Public School system. I would characterize these early 1970s jobs as paid internships today. I worked as a clerk/typist at the Department of Housing and Urban Development (HUD), the Department of Vocational Rehabilitation, and the classified advertisement department at the *Washington Post*. They all paid me the minimum wage and I learned how to save money. Although my personal high school employment pre-dated the mayoral tenure of Marion Barry by several years, the summer youth employment program he initiated as Mayor opened the door to productive work experiences for countless D.C. youth and is one of the positive lasting memories I have of him.

While at Regina, I also did a lot of volunteer work and community service for academic credit. One assignment was as a candy striper at D.C. General Hospital in the Crippled Children's Ward. There was no Metro subway at the time, so I caught several buses and traveled all the way across town to volunteer. The recreational therapist, Eileen, was a nice young White woman. She was my supervisor in the Ward and was most appreciative of my efforts to cheer the children. I read my own poems and stories by Black authors to the children, dramatically pouring my heart out in prose and in rhyme. I enjoyed reading them the story in the coloring book, *Children of Africa*. I acted out scenes for them from Aesop's Fables. I read them *A Sound Investment*, by Sonia Sanchez, and recited to them the poem *Ego Tripping* by Nikki Giovanni.

Interacting with the children in the hospital was really painful for me, but I had to be strong and try not to let my heartbreak about their conditions show. I saw children who couldn't walk, and some who were terminally ill. I am reminded of them today when I see children impacted by war in foreign hospitals, with limbs blown off by bombs, or bodies otherwise decimated. My high school summer employment and volunteer experiences, coupled with my intellectual curiosity and militancy, helped set the stage for my future work ethic and the empathy I have for the downtrodden, the disenfranchised and those with societal disabilities.

Chapter Two, Section 8
The Red, Black and Green Patch

I grew up with Judo and the martial arts, a testament to Daddy being a black belt Sensei (instructor) in Judo. We went to Judo class at Edwin Takemori's studio every week until Daddy opened up his own club. It was the only Black Judo club in the Washington, D.C. metropolitan area at the time. In fact, today I can't go into the Albright United Methodist Church social hall, where Daddy's Judo classes were held for almost thirty years, without giving a little respectful bow at the entrance, as it was the club's official dojo. Daddy held his Judo class at the church, every Tuesday night. It used to embarrass me that he always ended a conversation with one of my friends or even a complete stranger with the salutation, "See you Tuesday night." That translated into, "Come to my judo class on Tuesday."

Although I advanced to the level of brown belt under my father's tutelage, I think Daddy feels I betrayed him by also taking a Tae Kwon Do karate class at the church on Wednesdays. But I met Jerry at karate, and he always came adorned with a red, black and green patch sewn on his gi.[17] I think I fell in love at first sight. It wasn't just Jerry though. It was that red, black and green patch and everything those colors[18] stood for. And so naturally, I sewed a red, black and green patch on my karate gi as well. I thought Jerry was absolutely fine! However, my father saw him simply as a bad boy.

Jerry was my prince in shining armor, a revolutionary easily spotted by his red, black and green patch. He also happened to love Wild Irish Rose wine, which I thought made him sound philosophical. So what if he came from the projects? I saw him as my "Man-child in the Promised Land," to borrow the term made famous from the memoir by Claude Brown I was reading at the time. So what that he had dropped out of school? To my mind that was because the White man's educational system only serves to brainwash us.

In hindsight, however, I understand why my parents freaked. I remember the first time Jerry walked me home and came in.

"Do you have a job?" my father queried forcefully. "And just what are your intentions, young man?" he grilled.

"I'm a body man," Jerry replied proudly.

"What!?" my father alarmingly snapped.

"A body man," Jerry repeated. "You know, an auto body man."

I could see my father sigh with relief.

"And your intentions, young man?" my father repeated as he rapidly composed himself.

"Well, Mr. Caldwell. I don't have any intentions. I just want to go out with your daughter."

"Humph," my father responded, turning to walk upstairs. "See you Tuesday night," he muttered as he left.

And that was that. So on Tuesdays, Jerry came to judo and on Wednesdays, karate. He and I were inseparable.

You see, Mommy and Daddy never knew anything about Black Panther Tee – they barely knew about Viet Nam vet Raqeeb. But here Jerry was, in their face, at their church, every Tuesday and Wednesday night.

Forty years later, I don't blame them. But back then, to my infatuated nearly 18-year-old mind, they just didn't understand. One night I decided I was going to spend the night at Jerry's house. I couldn't believe my parents actually came all the way to the Kenilworth Projects in Northeast to fetch me after I called them at midnight (out of courtesy, mind you), to inform them I was "grown" and would be home the next day. To my chagrin, I had to give up the address. An hour later we rode home in silence and have never discussed it since. But rest assured, never again did I make the mistake of informing my parents of my "independence."

I was head over heels in love with Jerry. I tried to give him the African name, Bomani, but he chose Ode, which meant "born along the road," which I thought was ridiculous. Who wants someone just born along the road? Bomani, on the other hand, means "warrior," and that's what I wanted my man's name to be. WARRIOR! I capitulated, however, and said, "Okay, your African name will be 'Bomani Ode.'"

However, for some reason, the name Jerry was always fixated in my mind, and I rarely called him either Bomani or Ode. In fact, even today I sometimes call out the name, Jerry, unconsciously. Trust me, not in bed, but sometimes in the shower, or mindlessly doing housework. Calling out Jerry's name was not the reason my later marriages broke up, but I did seek therapy for this baffling habit of calling out the name of some old boyfriend from thirty years earlier. The conversation with the shrink went like this:

"Do you drink?" the therapist asked.

"No," I responded.

"Do you smoke?"

"No."

"Do you use drugs?"

"No."

"Well, if calling out an old boyfriend's name is the only vice you have, you have nothing to worry about."

Whew, I'm thinking. What a relief. I'm not crazy after all. I guess there are worse problems I could have had!

Chapter Two, Section 9
Strolling Down Memory Lane

I met Jerry through an older brother, Bill Street, who was also in the karate class and brought Jerry with him. Bill was tall and brown-skinned with a large Afro. Bill was the president of a locally based organization called Black Land Movement (BLM), which operated in the Shaw area of Washington, D.C.

As of 1971, the District of Columbia had a 60 percent Black population. Bill said it was no accident that the city probably had more urban renewal projects either in planning or execution than any other city of comparable size. The 675-acre Shaw Urban Renewal Project was the largest single urban renewal program in the city at the time, and among the largest urban renewal projects in the United States.

Plagued by the typical ills of any urban Black community, the Shaw area had about three times as many fires, and an average income of under $4,800 a year. Roughly one-third of the population made less than $2,950 a year. Education in the area, and the city in general, was extremely inadequate. Approximately one-half of Shaw's then 50,000 residents had an eighth-grade education or less. It was from this socio-economic, geographic base that Black Land Movement originated in 1968.

Black Land Movement was based on the belief that control of our communities could only be realistically analyzed in terms of the political acquisition, development, and dispersal of land.

Bill would state: "We feel that all the opportunities and benefits available under Urban Renewal Law should be developed in Shaw by and for its residents." He added, "Some organizations and agencies will assure you that the opportunities and benefits are in the interests of Shaw residents, but we know through our experiences with these and other institutions in our community that this is simply not true."

BLM was divided into five areas: Housing, Economic Development, Youth, Food, and Communications. By the time I met Bill, the primary programmatic area still operational was Communications, which published *Black Land News/Magazine* (BLNM). Bill was the editor of the publication, and its pantheon of columnists included Brother Preston, operator of Your Natural Food Market; Brother Claude of the community organization Black Umoja; and, Charles "Selrach" Ford whose focus was photography/sports. At age 17, I enthusiastically joined the paper's staff as administrative assistant.

I did not know it at the time, but through the pages of BLNM I met people who would in the future become mentors or play other instrumental roles in my life. They included community activists such as Edell Lydia, who later became known as Kwame Afoh and one of my comrades with both the Republic of New Afrika and the National Coalition of Blacks for Reparations in America. Kojo Bill Jones, who later published a book, *Red, White, Black and Blue*, was also influential to me. Otis Daniels, who became Brother Rasafik Weusi, in later years asked me to be the godmother for his first son. The BLNM paper included articles written by Rev. Ishakamusa Barashango, prime minister of the Temple of the Black Messiah; as well as ads from the cultural shop Zaro's House of Africa, founded by Nana Kwabena Brown. Both Rev. Ishakamusa and Nana Kwabena would contribute to my future spiritual development.

Sister Anuli Street was Bill's wife at the time. When I met her, we immediately clicked. Her headwrap during those days would rival mine. She was tall, queenly and light-skinned, and I was a petite, dark-hued, "queen-in-training." Anuli hired me as the official babysitter for her three children, as well as a file clerk and administrative assistant for the News/Magazine. When you are in the midst of life's events, you often don't realize the future impact and lifelong associations of people you encounter. And so was the case with Anuli.

Anuli was my first Black female inspiration and role model, and I wanted to be just like her. She was not only a mother but also an activist, a creative visionary and, I would later find out, a consummate entrepreneur. I would follow in her footsteps to also become an activist, an entrepreneur, a visionary and, finally, one day into the future, a mother.

***

One day during that future time, while in the basement of my own home, filing my own papers from the past, I was amazed to stumble upon many of the old papers I had always cherished and saved throughout the decades. As I strolled down Black Land News/Magazine's memory lane, it brought both smiles and tears to my face, and underscored within me the realization that the more things change, the more they remain the same. Strumming through the crumbling, tattered yellowed pages today reveals nostalgic headlines, articles and columns that chronicled the struggles of the late 60s and early 70s.

One particularly memorable column to me was labeled, The Spook, described as the only man "who sees all the funny stuff goin' down. One who saw the shit the way it really happened."

> *The Spook can't help but shudder at the thought of Wally Washington (your mayor) asking (and getting) $75,000 to study a lottery for D.C ... all he needs to do is ask some of the bloods on the street and they'll tell him how to play numbers.*

That tidbit was hilarious. Even my schoolteacher daddy, who definitely was not a "street blood," could have told the Mayor how to play the numbers.

> *The Spook strongly believes that there does exist in Anacostia a man who could run for mayor and surprise a lot of folks by an upset victory over the present crew...*

The Spook was correct. That man turned out to be Marion Barry, former organizer for the Student National Coordinating Committee (SNCC) and later to be affectionately known in Black D.C. communities as our "Mayor for Life."

People outside of D.C. and many Whites who live west of the Park are often perplexed with the adoration that the Chocolate City had for Barry. He won election after election, despite many vices that included drugs and womanizing, and despite being sent to prison. But he was popular and connected comfortably with both youth and elders. Marion Barry is also credited with the growth of the Black middle class in Washington, D.C., through provision of government jobs and access to minority contracts. He was also successful in getting youth out of trouble and off the streets with his Summer Youth Program.

*The Spook must say to all who hear – I told you so. Frank Wills, the al-
leged Black discoverer of Watergate, is unemployed because the money is
not rolling in on his "fame." Somebody ought to explain to the brother and
his advisors that, to the American people, the real hero of Watergate is
Richard Nixon...*

It is, indeed, tragic about Frank Wills. He was a 24-year-old private security guard
at the Watergate Hotel Office Complex in Washington, D.C., on June 17, 1972 when
he discovered that locks to a room had been tampered with. The arrests of the five
burglars inside who had planned to bug the headquarters of the Democratic National
Convention triggered the infamous Watergate scandal and, eventually, the resignation of President Richard Nixon in 1974. History might have turned out quite differently had Frank Wills not been so vigilant at the Watergate Hotel that fateful
night. He should have died a famed hero's death, rather than unemployed, destitute
and penniless at age 52.

As my fingers turned the frayed pages and more headlines whizzed past my eyes
like a motion picture, I mesmerized over other memorable *Black Land News/Mag-
azine* headlines: "Ruchell, the State Didn't Prove its Case," "Who Controls D.C.
Politics," "Redevelopment Land Agency-PawnBrokers of Deceit," "Dick Jones and
Others Bring Big Suit Against City," "Behind Bars: Brutal Experiments on Prisoners," "Has RNA Been Shackled?" and "The SouthWest Freeway Project." Each
of these had a story behind it, and my thirsty young mind eagerly soaked up knowledge and information from the rich historical tapestry within the *Black Land
News/Magazine.*

While pouring over the decades-worn papers during the late nineties in my own
home, I reminisced on my days as a teenager in Bill and Anuli's basement, absor-
bing their treasure trove of valuable archives while fulfilling my filing duties as
Black Land's administrative assistant. Yes, I sold national Black Panther newspapers earlier, but the BLNM was legendary because much of the information was
local, homegrown. While filing, if there were two copies of an issue of any publication, I had permission to take one, adding to my own collection.

The BLNM file in the Black Land Movement basement office included not just
BLNM papers, but also Black Panther Party papers from the late sixties, *Third
World News Magazine, Muhammad Speaks, The New Afrikan, Finally Got the
News, The Guardian, The Black Scholar*, and more, and I eagerly devoured them
all. From the time I became captivated as a young girl by the horrifying account of
Emmett Till that I stumbled upon in the *Pictorial History of the Negro in America,*

I had been on a powerful quest to discover my destiny.

It was at that time sitting in the BLNM's basement office amidst rebellious news-papers hammering the revolutionary spirit and fervor of the times that it became crystal clear – how could I not be a militant? How could I not be a revolutionary? How could I not be part of the movement? My quest, I surmised, was to find my place in this burgeoning struggle.

I was so engrossed in nostalgia sitting cross-legged on my basement floor flipping through the now-ragged files I had saved decades earlier as a teenaged admin-istrative assistant for Sister Anuli, that I did not notice my 6-year-old daughter, Ma-riama, saunter in.

"Oh sweetie, look! *Third World News Magazine.* This is history. You see, they called Europe the 'First World' and America the 'Second World,' and the 'Third World' denotes the underdeveloped nations, which actually sweetie, should be classified as the 'First World' because as you know everything began in Africa."

As I dreamily browsed through the pages, I failed to notice that my daughter had long departed. She obviously was not as thrilled as I was with either my archaic discoveries or my convoluted ramblings.

"Ama, Ama look," I crooned, still trying to elicit her curiosity. "Here's an article about Ujamaa School, before they moved to the big building." Captivated, I con-tinued my historical reverie without noticing that Ama was no longer in earshot.

"See, there's an ad with Rosemary Reed Miller advertising her new baby back car-rier with her baby strapped to her back. She had a chic upscale shop called Toast and Strawberries for a long time, in the trendy DuPont Circle at that. She's been to parties at our house!" My voice rose excitedly. "OMG, there's a column on Black Christian Nationalism, by Rev. Ishakamusa of the Temple of the Black Messiah! He was my mentor," I babbled elatedly. Although I knew none of these luminaries when I was the organization's file clerk, many would later become powerful in my life.

I then happened to pick up the December 31, 1971 issue of *Muhammad Speaks.* An issue characteristic of millions of issues before and after – an issue inundated with principles of upliftment, self-help, buying Black, and articles and editorials that in-form, teach and inspire.

One caption caught my eye, "Messenger's Program is the Best Cure for Drug Abuse, Addiction and Crime." There is no question that the Nation of Islam was the frontrunner of effective programs to combat drug abuse, keep Black youth off the streets, and put something positive on their minds.

Digging through the 1971 end of the year issue from *Muhammad Speaks*, I was proud to come across "Diggs Quits U.N.," an article by Charles Simmons. An excerpt read:

> *United Nations – On December 17, Detroit Congressman Charles C. Diggs, Jr. called a special press conference and read an eleven-page statement condemning the U.S. government policy toward Africa. He emphasized the United States' alliance with South Africa, Rhodesia and Portugal, including both economic trade assistance and military deals.*

Little did I know that years later I would work for an organization protesting U.S. policy towards Southern Africa. And I did not know it at the time, but within the next decade Congressman Charles Diggs would agree to join a defense committee in support of political prisoners that I would lead.

In concluding, Rep. Diggs said,

> *As a member of the U.S. delegation to the United Nations, I have tried in vain to get underway a real consultative process on United States positions here at the United Nation... After much thought I have decided that considerations of integrity and of the now desperate need to turn United States policy around from the perilous course on which it has embarked require that I completely disassociate myself from this administration on African policy.*

I continued browsing through *Muhammad Speaks*:

> *"The trial of Angela Yvonne Davis is scheduled to begin on January 31, 1972 in San Jose, California..."*

"Mariama!" I loudly implored, trying to summon her from her bedroom haven upstairs. "Please come back. You've got to see this. This is history, sweetie, I was in the twelfth grade when this was happening!"

> *Angela is in her second year of pre-trial solitary confinement. Chief Defense Counsel Howard Moore Jr. has argued that prejudice against Black militants and Communists is greater in Santa Clara County... than in Marin County.*

Another taste from the same issue of *Muhammad Speaks*:

> *Rev. Jesse Jackson's Operation Push (People United to Save Humanity)*
> *held its first meeting, Saturday, December 18, at Metropolitan Theatre*
> *on Chicago's South Side.*

"Ama! This was Jesse Jackson's first meeting!"

> *'Central thrust of new group will be economic,' Rev. Jackson said. In his*
> *speech, Rev. Jackson praised The Honorable Elijah Muhammad, remarking*
> *'Nobody has done more to aid the dope-addict than Mr. Muhammad – with-*
> *out the use of methadone, but by giving the individual a belief in Self.' But*
> *he failed to mention the Muslim economic program...*

Poor Jesse, I mused. He gets dissed from all sides – always seemed to be in a no-win situation. "Look, sweetie, here's one about H. Rap Brown."

> *H.Rap Brown appeared in Manhattan Supreme Court December 13*
> *personally to plead 'not guilty' to a 24 count indictment charging him with*
> *attempted murder and robbery in a shootout outside the Red Carpet Lounge*
> *on West 85th Street last October. Suffering from several gunshot wounds,*
> *Brown is still hospitalized since his arrest and looked thin and ill in court.*
> *He returned to Bellevue immediately after his court appearance...*

"Ama," I continued yelling upstairs. "You need to research H. Rap Brown. His Muslim name is Jamil Al Amin and, appallingly, he's back in prison today."

By this time my husband at the time has come downstairs to find out why I'm talking so loudly and in such an excited voice.

"Dakarai, look at this article about the Wonder Bread Company." I thrust the frayed pages in his face. "I had no idea!" Dakarai perused the paper and recited:

> *A boycott has been called against Wonder Bread by the Women Strike for*
> *Peace. The peace group exposed the firm as one owned by the producer of*
> *equipment which guides bombers.*

"What?" he reacted as he held the paper up high. We used to go on schooltours to the Wonder Bread Company, one of the few factories in D.C. from back in the day.

"We did too," I added wistfully.

"Now listen to this morsel," I jeered. "Sounds like the precursor to drones!"

The remote bomber guides are used so that no human pilots are needed to direct them to their targets.

"And here's the critical call to action," I proclaimed, directing Dakarai's eyesight to the now faded words on the page:

Pointing out that the owner of Continental Baking Co. is also International Telephone and Telegraph Co., the women urged shoppers to write to the president of I.T.& T., H.S. Geneen. The women also promised that the boycott would continue 'until I.T.& T stops making products that support the war.'

Speaking volumes today, my jaw dropped as I read more illuminating news from last century's *Muhammad Speaks* newspaper:

John Mitchell, U.S. attorney general told delegates here attending the National Conference on Corrections that they would soon have the 'opportunity' to practice their new correction 'techniques' on a target number of prisoners as a result of local and national 'improved' law and order systems...

At the time I was filing the papers as a teen in Anuli's basement, I did not know that criminal punishment reform would become my career's major niche area of expertise. I somberly continued perusing:

Mitchell took advantage of the opportunity to brag about the administration's successful law-and-order stance... The Attorney General spoke for 20 minutes with characteristic arrogance. He never mentioned prison rebellions at Attica or Rahway where the administration's so-called prison reform and correctional techniques were in grand display. Nor did he mention that Nixon publicly approved of the air-ground police attack and "massacre" of the Attica inmates...

I flashed on that memory and was suddenly 16 years old, glued to the six o'clock news on the black and white television screen in my family's living room, watching in horror the images of powerless Black men paraded naked through a prison yard after Attica, a prison in upstate New York, is needlessly stormed. I remember vividly how hard it was to hear the TV, as torrential rains were beating against the front windows of my family's home, rains that had pummeled the east coast that week of September 9 through 13, 1971.

Yes, the invasion to take back a prison from prisoners who had been protesting the refusal of the state to provide them with basic human needs, was unnecessary. The imprisoned men had been in control of the institution for four days, but it was raining and had been raining consistently. Everything was muddy. They would likely have given in.

But again, the lies.

New York state officials took license with the truth in its retaking of Attica. This was similar to the 1969 Illinois state fabrication that nails tacking posters to walls were actually bullet holes and used as justification for the unprovoked murders of Chicago Black Panther Party leader Fred Hampton and Mark Clark while sleeping in their beds. New York insisted that prisoners slit the throats of the hostage guards when the evidence clearly revealed the guards died from the state's gunfire. With the exception of the massacres of Native peoples of the late 19th century, the 1971 New York State Special Commission on Attica characterized the assault to take back the prison as "the bloodiest one-day encounter between Americans since the Civil War."

But glued to the TV as a teenager in 1971, I envisioned myself one day being part of a negotiating team that would be summoned by prisoners to mediate a prison takeover. Throughout my career that never happened, but it might perhaps explain why I later made the choice to work for the National Prison Project. You see, Attica helped to inform the person I would later become. I was an idealistic girl who wanted to be a part of changing the world, and help others change it as well.

The article ended wistfully, declaring that despite the Attorney General's boasts of public safety, "business as usual" was the order of the day:

> Unwarranted arrests of Blacks, kangaroo court trials, unjustified convictions and long-term sentencing – followed by cruel, inhumane punishment, poor health and unsanitary prison conditions – continued as the law and order tactics of Nixon's cops, judges, and prison wardens.

But oh, if we knew then what we know now, that Nixon's criminal justice policies in general and the War on Drugs in particular were, in actuality, a racially motivated crusade to criminalize Blacks and the anti-war left, we might have been able to abate the repressive policies before they took hold. Nixon's domestic policy advisor, John Ehrlichman, revealed in a 1994 interview with journalist Dan Baum, that:

> We knew we couldn't make it illegal to be either against the war or blacks, but by getting the public to associate the hippies with marijuana and blacks

with heroin and then criminalizing both heavily, we could disrupt those communities. We could arrest their leaders, raid their homes, break up their meetings, and vilify them night after night in the evening news. Did we know we were lying about the drugs? Of course we did.[19]

The *Muhammad Speaks* newspaper capped with "The Muslim Program, What the Muslims Want, What the Muslims Believe:"

1. We want freedom. We want a full and complete freedom.

2. We want justice. Equal justice under the law. We want justice applied equally to all, regardless of creed or class or color.

3. We want equality of opportunity. We want equal membership in society with the best in civilized society.

4. We want our people in America whose parents or grandparents were descendants from slaves, to be allowed to establish a separate state or territory of their own – either on this continent or elsewhere. We believe that our former slave masters are obligated to provide such land and that the area must be fertile and minerally rich. We believe that our former slave masters are obligated to maintain and supply our needs in this separate territory for the next 20 to 25 years – until we are able to produce and supply our own needs. Since we cannot get along with them in peace and equality, after giving them 400 years of our sweat and blood and receiving in return some of the worst treatment human beings have ever experienced, we believe our contributions to this land and the suffering forced upon us by white America, justifies our demand for complete separation in a state or territory of our own.

5. We want freedom for all Believers of Islam now held in federal prisons. We want freedom for all black men and women now under death sentence in innumerable prisons in the North as well as the South. We want every black man and woman to have the freedom to accept or reject being separated from the slave master's children and establish a land of their own. We know that the above plan for the solution of the black and white conflict is the best and only answer to the problem between two people.

6. We want an immediate end to the police brutality and mob attacks against the so-called Negro throughout the United States. We believe that the Federal government should intercede to see that black men and women

tried in white courts receive justice in accordance with the laws of the land – or allow us to build a new nation for ourselves, dedicated to justice, freedom and liberty.

7. As long as we are not allowed to establish a state or territory of our own, we demand not only equal justice under the laws of the United States, but equal employment opportunities – NOW! We do not believe that after 400 years of free or nearly free labor, sweat and blood, which has helped America become rich and powerful, that so many thousands of black people should have to subsist on relief, charity or live in poor houses.

8. We want the government of the United States to exempt our people from ALL taxation as long as we are deprived of equal justice under the laws of the land.

9. We want equal education – but separate schools up to 16 for boys and 18 FOR GIRLS ON THE CONDITION THAT THE GIRLS BE SENT TO WOMEN'S COLLEGES AND UNIVERSITIES. We want all black children educated, taught and trained by their own teachers. Under such schooling system we believe we will make a better nation of people. The United States government should provide, free, all necessary textbooks and equipment, schools and college buildings. The Muslim teachers shall be left free to teach and train their people in the way of righteousness, decency and self-respect.

10. We believe that intermarriage or race mixing should be prohibited. We want the religion of Islam taught without hindrance or suppress. These are some of the things that we, the Muslims, want for our people in North America.

Problematic issues of sexism and gender roles notwithstanding, there were overarching themes in the platforms of most of the Black Power newspapers of the day that spoke volumes to me. Themes of freedom, justice, equality, and education. Themes of police brutality, self-defense, separation and land. Themes of reparatory justice. Themes that will remain near and dear to me throughout my life, and themes I would end up working on throughout my career as part of my quest for justice.

Chapter Two, Section 10
Artistically Prophetic

I think it was during my last year in high school that I met Brother Kwasi. We met at an African Liberation Day organizing meeting in a 15th Street apartment across the street from Malcolm X Park. I thought he was an interesting brother.

Kwasi was straight from the ghetto. I never knew him to smoke, drink or use drugs, so when he told me he used to use drugs, I was initially shocked, but then I took it all in stride. It was part of that bad boy mold that I so admired. But Kwasi always seemed so singularly focused on the movement that the thought of a romantic relationship with him never even entered my mind.

He frequented General Hassan's Black Man's Development Center on Kennedy Street, located walking distance from my family's house. He was, unquestionably, a leader. While there he conceptualized a new organization, The Center for Black Unity. This was 1972-73, during my senior year in high school. He was the president of his new organization. Other members included Brother Akili who later renamed himself Brother Imani, and then went into the army and became a Muslim. There was Brother Kamau, who later became a Transcendental Meditation (TM) master, and there was me. The Center for Black Unity was Kwasi's brainchild and whatever Kwasi said, we did. My pet nickname for him was The Dictator.

The first Kwanzaa I ever celebrated in 1972, I also organized with Brother Kwasi. The Dictator was set on the Center for Black Unity hosting a Kwanzaa celebration on all seven nights. I thought one night was sufficient and we should enjoy ourselves at other celebrations around the community on the remaining evenings. I lost this battle and was relegated to baking carrot cakes every night at the community Kwanzaa programs we hosted at the Center for Black Unity.

After I went off to college, the Center for Black Unity kind of fizzled out. I didn't find out Kwasi had romantic feelings for me until my college days, after Jerry and I had also drifted apart. And boy, did Kwasi lay it on thick. He frequently brought me groceries from a store he was managing, and prepared scrumptious meals for me in my dormitory room. He truly had artistic qualities, hence his last name, which was Kiswahili for "artist." One day he presented me with a beautiful picture he drew. It illustrated a strong Black man draped in a dashiki, alongside a queenly woman adorned in an African headwrap with a baby nestled in her arms. The drawing was beautifully and artistically prophetic.

Chapter Three[20]
"Soul Rebel"

Chapter Three, Section 1
College Student, Revolutionary Poet

In 1973, I entered Howard University, my parents' alma mater. After my all-White, all-girl high school experience, I hungered for an all-Black co-ed environment. In my mind, there was never a question that I would attend Howard. Yes, the school had a reputation in the D.C. Black community for being "bougie," but what the hell, it was melanin-rich and I was craving chocolate. I always felt cheated because I missed out on the heyday of Howard University's activism by five years. In 1968, the school's rebellious spirit was punctuated by the four-day takeover of the Administration Building by over 2,000 students. When I arrived in 1973, things were back to normal, so to speak, but I maintained my revolutionary spirit and I remained ready!

Although I was a native Washingtonian, my parents agreed that I could live on campus in the dormitory. My first housing assignment was Truth Hall, part of the Harriet Tubman Quadrangle, the same dorm my mother was assigned when she attended Howard thirty years earlier. The Quad housed several women's dormitories named after four inspiring Black women leaders – Sojourner Truth, Prudence Crandall, Phyllis Wheatley, and Julia S. Caldwell-Frazier. In my first year, my roommate was Margo Smith, a serious student with a pleasant personality, intent on going to medical school. She is now a celebrated physician. My second year at Howard I met Adjoa Deborah Jackson. We vibed immediately and roomed together in Crandall Hall. Today, she is an amazing artist.

My Tubman Quadrangle dormitory buddies included Gerri Allen, then an aspiring pianist who later became a jazz musician, and close friends Ayanna Barbara Murphy and Macharia Louise Cook. We all spent many evenings in the dorm's social room just hanging out, rapping about community and world events. At times Gerri sat at the piano strumming out jazzy tunes; other times composing music to my love poems. Ayanna and I wrote poetry together and Macharia and I together worked with the Black Women's United Front. I spent my last two years at Howard living off campus at the University's Meridian Hill dorm, across the street from Malcolm X Park.

I idolized my English teacher, Esther Vassar. She appeared to me to be socially conscious and wore her hair natural when she was not sporting an African headwrap. She was pregnant during my first year at Howard and looked simply radiant. I reveled in writing papers for her class, one of my favorite being "Black Love is Black

Wealth: Nikki Giovanni and her Works." Professor Vassar loved it as well, commenting in the margins, "Excellent! I am happy I taught you English 02 and 03!"

At Howard, fellow student Leroy Davis and I were founding members of the school's new Chancellor Williams Historical Society (CWHS). I was working toward a double major in history and education. Williams' classic, *The Destruction of Black Civilization*, had recently been published and was right up my alley. It expertly and boldly detailed the history of the White assault of the African continent. "The white man is our bitter enemy," Dr. Williams penned. "This is not the ranting and raving of wild-eye militancy," he resumed, "but the calm and unmistakable verdict of several thousand years of documented history."

On the evening of March 18, 1976, we met with this audacious historian. Dr. Williams emphasized the expanding role of historical societies in Black universities. He stressed that "we must think and plan," and counseled that the Chancellor Williams Historical Society should underscore the importance of history as fundamental to all disciplines, whether medicine, law, science, etc. He suggested that the Society include as members all those interested in history, regardless of their department, as well as alumni. He concluded, cautioning that as long as we rely on White historians to write Black history for us, we should keep quiet about what they produce. "They write from the Caucasian viewpoint, and we are naïve indeed if we expect them to do otherwise," he lectured.

I was proud to serve as President of the new CWHS. One highlight of our society was bringing the author and anthropologist Ivan Van Sertima to Howard. He had recently published his seminal work detailing the African presence in North America, *They Came Before Columbus*. It was stimulating and invigorating to be in the presence of such genius. Undeniably, these and many other events were part and parcel of the greatness of Historically Black Colleges and Universities, HBCUs.

In college, just as in high school, I rarely let an opportunity slip to compare and contrast the Black struggle in the United States with struggles occurring internationally. In one of my college papers, "The Political Economy of the Black Ghetto," titled after a book of the same name by William Tabb, I argued, "A colonial relationship presently exists between the Black ghetto and the larger society, having many similarities with the same oppressive dependence that exists between many underdeveloped countries and industrial nations." My paper's conclusion was that the "Black ghetto was also a colony whose situation closely paralleled the political and economic relationships existing between many Third World nations and the industrially advanced countries."

For another class, I analyzed Frantz Fanon's book *The Wretched of the Earth* – a literary masterpiece detailing the effects of colonialism and decolonization on a society. Although Fanon speaks specifically about the conflict between the French and Algerians in Africa, I argued that his scrutiny was generally applicable to any struggle for liberation and, in particular, to the liberation struggle of Blacks in America. In my opinion, his analysis of the process of dehumanization of the oppressed should be required study in any serious consideration of American history.

Fanon died from cancer in 1961 at only 36 years of age. However his systematic analysis of the psychological and sociological effects of war on society, and the national consciousness and culture arising from the process of decolonization, is still studied and taught by revolutionaries worldwide. Little did I know that decades later I would share platforms with his daughter, Mireille Fanon Mendes-France, a Member of the United Nations Working Group of Experts on People of African Descent, jointly advancing the case for reparations.

I took the course, Blacks in Antiquity, taught by long-standing Howard University Professor, Dr. Frank Snowden. Interestingly, my father took the same class at Howard over 25 years earlier. Snowden's course was ground-breaking during my dad's time in the early 50s, appealing during my college years, but would probably be considered, no pun intended, antiquated today. Hippocrates is often referred to as the Father of Medicine. However, my father and I had many discussions about that title belonging more appropriately to Imhotep of ancient Egypt who lived 2,000 years before.

I learned as a teenager from personal study that Hippocrates and most Greeks were little more than hypocrites and plagiarizers because they knew that the inhabitants of ancient Africa were skilled and wiser than they themselves were. It was our dexterous fingers that performed intricate eye operations in the medical school of the University of Sankore in the city of Timbuktu in Songhay. The Western world still has not figured out our secret of preserving bodies through the process of mixing and combining herbs and substances to mummify. But the Blacks in Antiquity course was merely the tip of a colossal iceberg. Since then historical giants such as Dr. Yosef ben Jochannan, Dr. John Henrik Clarke, Ashra Kwesi, Anthony Browder, Runoko Rashidi, Maulana Ron Karenga and more, have upped the ante with their own expert analyses of our African past.

A professor who taught an Afro-American history class, Dr. Denys Van Cook, took a group of us students to St. Helena Island, one of the Sea Islands in Beaufort County, SC, to work with the Gullah people on issues of Black land loss in the South. We conducted research at the Penn Center, once a school that educated formerly enslaved West Africans and now is a center that preserves the culture, history and environment of the people of Gullah, also known as Geechee. Fittingly, in the 1960s, Dr. Martin Luther King, Jr. and other civil rights advocates chose Penn as a place to hold campaign strategy meetings.

On my trip, it really hit me how imbalanced my life was. I could spout the latest political theory or cultural diatribe, but I didn't know the latest dance. It became rather embarrassing when we went out to a club one night while in Beaufort. While others were having fun doing the hustle, the robot, and the funky chicken, I stood by the wall self-conscious, feeling awkward and uncomfortable, not wanting my classmates to think I had no rhythm and danced like White people.

Although I missed the heyday of Howard activism (or so I thought), it was still a Black mecca and cultural haven. I loved Black books, Black art and Black plays. I hobnobbed with notable fellow students skilled in the written and spoken word – such as the decades-long Howard University literary icon E. Ethelbert Miller, writer Peter Harris, playwright Ajamu Crawford, poet Gerard Brown, Howard Hilltop editor Hodari Ali, and student body president Hisani Mweusi.

I soaked up plays at Howard's Ira Aldridge Theatre, staged by the legendary D.C. Black Repertory Theatre, founded by Robert Hooks, and directed by Tony Gittens. This was long before "diversity" became a buzzword and morphed beautiful Blackness into broad, watered-down multi-culturalism.

At the D.C. Black Repertory Theatre I loved the musical, "Changes," by Motojicho. The play also featured as vocal director Bernice Reagon, who would later found my favorite a'capella group, Sweet Honey in the Rock. There was also Lyn Dyson who, in that play, was listed as stage hand, but would later become executive director of The Black Repertory Theatre's successor, D.C. Rep Inc. as well as head of the Multi-Media Training Institute. I was enthralled with the productions of "Sister Elena Got the Gift," by Joann Bruno; "Day of Absence," by Douglas Turner Ward; and "Owen's Song," a tribute to Howard legend Owen Dodson. Artist Ron Anderson prepared the set design and sculpture associated with this production. He would later become known as Brother Akili, and I would work with him in the community. My love for Black plays is just as strong now as it was then.

I joined a writer's organization, the Black Literary Artists of Creative Kingdoms (B.L.A.C.K.), founded by master storyteller, Lorenzo Lord Callender. I signed up for a writing class taught by poet-educator Haki Madhubuti (formerly known as don l. lee), who was a writer-in-residence at Howard and someone I knew from the independent Black schools movement. Brother Haki was also the publisher of *Third World Press*, and founder of Chicago's New Concept School.

A fellow student was Denise Rolark, who had been my classmate at Rabaut Jr. High.

Years into the future she would become publisher of the long-standing D.C. newspaper founded by her father, Calvin Rolark – *The Washington Informer*. Denise and I focused on our respective passions in Madhubuti's class. Denise presented a thoroughly researched project on the history of the Black press, while I focused on the Independent Black School movement.

The Black Arts Movement was strong, and Howard's Institute for the Arts and Humanities hosted several National Conferences of Afro-American Writers during my time at the University. I eagerly attended them all. Many of the Institute's staff I would encounter in other phases of my life; including research associate James Early, who much later became instrumental in creating the Smithsonian's National Museum of African American History and Culture; and the Institute's secretary, Virginia Blandford, whose children I would later teach at Watoto School. Veteran photographer Roy Lewis was ever-present, documenting not only the Institute's conferences but also just about every important socially conscious event in the Washington, D.C. community for decades.

These National Writers' Conferences featured luminaries I admired, such as actors and playwrights Ossie Davis, Lonne Elder III, Bill Gunn, Clay Goss and Alice Childress; poets Maya Angelou, Haki Madhubuti, Askia Muhammad, Kalamu ya Salaam, Mari Evans and Ishmael Reed; and authors Sam Yette, Sharon Bell Mathis, Lucille Clifton, June Jordan, John Steptoe, Quincy Troupe, John Henrik Clarke, Piri Thomas, Eugene Perkins, Paule Marshall, and many more. I was influenced by them all and was more than greatly enriched being in their midst.

But I was most influenced by John Oliver Killens, chair of the Institute and a prolific writer. His book for teens, *The Cotillion*, had earlier enthralled me. His novel, *Great Gittin' Up Morning*, provided much of the historical background I later used for my saga about Denmark Vesey in *Shining Legacy*, the children's book I would later write. John Killens was, without question, a literary icon, visionary, and my mentor.

In a keynote address during one of the Conferences, Killens emphasized, "The awesome task facing Black writers is to undo the million of little white lies America had told the world about Black Americans." He maintained that Blacks themselves have been the prime believers of these myths. Killens gave considerable discussion to topics such as the treatment of Black female characters and the impact in literature of the Black cultural revolution of the 60s, stressing the details with colorful, raunchy illustrations. I enthusiastically joined the John Oliver Killens Literary Guild.

I will never forget the time I traveled with some friends from D.C. to his home in New York for a workshop. Entering his humble castle was an experience within itself. Adorning seemingly every crevice of his home were plaques containing words of wisdom from our African forbearers. My love for African proverbs was fertilized during that trip and I remember feverishly scribbling down as many of these literary gems as I could capture, later using them to embellish the walls of my own home.

At Howard I continued the creative writing I loved during high school. My militancy, far from being muted, blossomed on pages into passionate tirades against oppression in society. Between 1973 and 1977 I wrote many poems, performed my work in the spoken word of the day, and was a ravenous reader of books that nourished my inquisitive mind and fed my hungry soul. I wrote about my disdain for pork:

Swine ... Hog
Hotdogs, ham, bacon, baloney, "shitlings," spareribs, pig feet
Triconosis ... Hypertension
Also a name for cops (pigs)
They both kill if
u
mess with them!

***

I wrote how I felt about the 1969 murder of Black Panther leader Fred Hampton:

Fred
i never met u
But i
Have known u
i cried
When i heard what they did
The lies ...The fabricated charges
But
the spirit
of the people
was not
quenched
The people brought
the shit
out into the open
NEVER WILL THE PEOPLE FORGET
The MURDER of FRED HAMPTON

***

I wrote about Angela Davis:

Angela, u are
Black Female Revolutionary Communist
They
Are seeking to eliminate u and your
Knowledge ...
They will not succeed
We are a Black Trojan horse
Inside the walls of Babylon
A horse 50 million strong
The year is 8AM (After Malcolm)
And
The Empire still stands
We will have a people's victory
we will win, without a doubt
"Alright gentlemen --- we're taking over now" – Jon Jackson.

***

I wrote about my brothers who survived the Nam:

Tough tight together
Dap-slapping Blacks
Courage in one hand ... weapon in the other
My comrades ... guerrilla ... friend
Embrace the Cong ... Eliminate the Swine
The wretched ... the scorned ... the truth
Any necessary means for freedom
Drink Deeply my Blacks
From the Source of the Revolution
Which is within us all. So be it.

***

And a poem about the Underground:

Who will be the soldiers
Who will take the load
Who will protect Black POWS
Who've escaped on the Underground Railroad?

Who will be on the frontlines?
Who will watch our backs?
Who will protect the POW's?
Who'll take up the slack?

Who will design the disguises?
Who will open their doors?
Who will protect the brothers and sisters?
Who are escaped prisoners of war?

Who will sing the songs?
Who will write the poems?
Who will speak the speeches?
Who will sound the horns?

Black secretaries, chemists, pilots, and electricians
Black lawyers, teachers and computer technicians

Who is you
Who is me
Who is us
Who is we

Who will struggle TOGETHER
So we all can be free

***

I wrote a poem in 1980 dedicated to Zimbabwe's independence, entitled, "Not in a Thousand Years, He Said"

Come on Southern Africa,
Hurl those spears
Aim the rifles
Set the mines
Protect the villages
Teach the children
Train the warriors

From the north to the south; from the east to the west
The struggle continued
From the war elephants of Hannibal

To the battle cries of Shaka
From the strength of Yaa Asantewaa
To the victories of Queen Nzingha

FRELIMO knew
MPLA knew
SWAPO knew
ZANU knew
ZAPO knew
PAC knew
ANC knew knew knew and knows

That the Struggle Continues and soon all of Southern Africa
Will celebrate a juicy victory
Juicy with the red pulp of white colonialist blood
Juicy with the sweet taste of liberation
Juicy with the necessary task of re-construction
Of re-building, of re-volution

PAMBERI CHIMURENGA! Forward with the Revolution
PAMBERI CHIMURENGA!
Revolutionary leaders thrown in prison for using that slogan
Revolutionary ZANU said, "No one cracks through our wall of forests
Nor through our fortress of wills joined as one"

Ian Smith had the audacity to say:
"Black rule would not come to Zimbabwe in a thousand years."
The Spear says, "Unless the three years that passed were light years, it
has been proven in Zimbabwe that we could care less what has-beens like
Ian Smith believe."

"Not in a thousand years," he said
Yet, Victory has come to Zimbabwe!
Tens of thousands tasting victory
Tens of thousands Black rule

But, let us not yet drink too deeply
From the calabash of celebration
Let us not drink too deeply
From the gourd of festivities
Lest we forget Patrice Lumumba and what happened to the victory in The
Congo

Lest we forget the Mau Mau and what happened to the victory in Kenya
Les we forget Toussaint L'Ouverture and what happened to the victory in
Haiti

For, in the calabash of celebration
flows the seeds of the bitter fruit of neo-colonialism
The seeds of the bitter fruit of puppet regimes
The seeds of the bitter fruit of destruction

Unless the calabash of celebration is tempered with the vigilance of wise
minds, ready bodies, and elimination of traitors
The sweet juicy victory could turn sour and dry

"Not in a thousand years," he said
Yes, Victory has come to Zimbabwe
Tens of thousands tasting victory
Tens of thousands Black rule
Tens of Thousands
SHONA, KHO KHOI, ZULU, XHOSA, SAN, MATABELE
Tens of thousands ... to VICTORY
STAY UP ZIMBABWE!

***

It is really scary just how relevant this poem is today with the crisis in Zimbabwe, the destabilization in Haiti, and more.

One of my favorite poems, however, was originally written in 1975.[21] It was the epic poem I titled "Re-Birth," with beautiful, long-winded verses that traversed the historical continuum, searching for my soul mate from the magnificence of the African past through the horrors of, and resistance to, the enslavement era, down through today.

I proudly recited this at a Howard event one evening and was unceremoniously shot down by one of my Marxist-Leninist friends. I wasn't prepared for the criticism. In the poem I called Black men "Kings" and they called me "Queen." I admit that I fantasized a lot, but how could one not? We had been so deprived of knowledge of Black history and culture that any accomplishment of our ancestors once brought into our awareness deserved to be celebrated. This knowledge made me feel good about myself, and I elevated it in my writings.

My Marxist friends, however, didn't see it that way and disdained my tales of kings and queens and royalty. They likened it to feudal times, hierarchal class structures and capitalism. Apart from our ideological differences, there were other contradictions as well. Generally speaking, my Marxist-Leninist friends wore plain clothes, whereas I adorned African garb. Most smoked cigarettes, which I absolutely abhorred. Despite our differences, I loved the intellectualism, the exchange of opposing ideologies, and the in-depth analyses. I just wanted my own flavor for it.

In analyzing American and world history, I was searching for a worldview that was African-centered. I wrote a play entitled *Bullshitting on the Way to the Revolution*. I predicated it on what I saw as contradictions within the Movement. During the 70s, it appeared that most of the conscious people on Howard's campus and the conscious Black community were splintered into essentially two camps – the Black Nationalists and the Marxists. I felt I straddled the fence because I embraced elements of both. I loved the culture of nationalism that included the Independent Black School movement, celebration of Kwanzaa, and African attire; but, I also related to the principles of socialism.

For the play I used observations from my work with organizations on Howard's campus such as the Youth Organization for Black Unity (YOBU),[22] the African Liberation Support Committee (ALSC),[23] the February First Movement (FFM)[24] and the All African People's Revolutionary Party (AAPRP).[25]

As part of the February First Movement, I participated in study groups probing answers to questions such as why was it necessary for Black student organizations to join together to build an anti-imperialist student movement? What is the fundamental task that progressive students need to be addressing today? Are all members of an ethnic or racial grouping equally oppressed? What is the role of education in the capitalist system? What are some manifestations of imperialist control of education at Howard University? And, why is it necessary to connect the struggle against national oppression with the struggle against imperialism?

With the African Liberation Support Committee there were more questions, discussions, and debates. What does 'Black workers take the lead mean?' What should be the correct policy in developing relationships, alliances, and coalitions with Whites and other oppressed nationalities? Is there a single working class within the U.S. or are there two distinct working classes – Whites and oppressed nationalities? What is the nature of the contradiction between the Black bourgeoisie and what should be the proletarian policy toward them? Is there any validity for a Black United Front in the U.S.? What is male chauvinism; how has it manifested itself in the African Liberation Support Committee, and how can we eradicate it? What is a colony? Do Blacks in the U.S. represent an internal colony? What is an anti-imperialist and anti-racist stance?

In addition to spearheading the first several African Liberation Day celebrations, the African Liberation Support Committee also supported community struggles in Washington, D.C., including the growing tenant movement against slum landlords, real estate agencies and banks, supporting struggles for stronger controls on rent increases, and stopping wholesale evictions. Besides attending meetings and study sessions, I was part of the ALSC information distribution committee, handing out material about African Liberation Day at bus stops, to community groups, and at high school functions.

All the groups I interacted with on campus and the questions raised above influenced my militancy and were the perfect fodder for my creative piece. My play centered on the contradictions within each of the following categories – what I called the bump-boogie get-high crowd, the Nationalists, and the Marxists. I used one of the African Liberation Day (ALD)[26] celebrations initiated by the All African People's Revolutionary Party as the backdrop for the scene from my play. ALD's zenith was during the 70s and 80s and, during those days, I missed none of these commemorative celebrations.

The last part of the play features an excerpt from a fictional me telling it like it is:

(The setting is Malcolm X Park).

Narrator:
… About one month later at a large gathering in Malcolm X Park, brothers and sisters from all over Washington, D.C. got together. There was something there for everyone. A band for the bump/boogie crowd. Speakers for those with a little more than partying on their minds. African drummers and dancers for cultural entertainment. Vendors pushing jewelry, pipes and paper. Food stands filled with carrot cakes, apple juice and other foods. *Muhammad Speaks, The African World, The Daily Worker, Unity and Struggle, Drum,* and hundreds of other papers and leaflets circulated and covered the ground.

MC: (Getting on stage after African dancers have finished)

"OK beautiful Black people we're going to slow the pace down a bit and listen to what this sister has to say. What's your name?"

"Sista Nkechi."

"What? Ok Sista. Folk, 'Na Key Chee' says she has something to share with all of us. Come on people. Give up some love."

Everyone claps, most hesitantly. Sista Nkechi rises to the platform.

"Sistas and Brothers, before I begin let us all reach out and touch somebody Black cause I want y'all to FEEL the vibrations of Black Unity present today in this park."

Joe and Reggie and their crowd give up dap and power signs. Kamili and Malaika hug some brothers close to them. Pat shakes somebody's hand, and Scooby grabs one of the African dancers in a tight embrace.

Sista Nkechi:
"This poem I would like to share with you is called 'Bullshittin on the Way to the Revolution,' and brothers and sisters, if the shoe happens to fit, don't wear it but try another size! Here we go!"

"Brotherme, the revolution is MORE than a nickel bag of smoke
You can't get over on the beast with herb
You can't sniff him out with coke, or jab him with SCAG
You are no longer the oppressed, but are becoming the oppressor
Because you are just BULLSHITTIN ON THE WAY
TO THE REVOLUTION.

You brothers are not blind. Can't you see what drugs are doing to your already meager earnings, or shall I say muggings?
A lot of u spout bout spilling blood
The revolution is more than white blood being spilt
Yeah we all know it will be spilt or we will be kilt but must we waste all our creative
energies on destruction????
We are just BULLSHITIN ON THE WAY TO THE REVOLUTION

We need creative minds to build and design
For our new nation to shine
We need creative minds to build and design
For our new nation to shine

I repeat my brothers
The revolution is more than a nickel bag of smoke
You cannot GET OVER on the beast with herb
You can't sniff him out with coke, or jab him with scag

It is all too easy for the oppressed to become the oppressor
We don't need stagnated brains to destruct and destroy and fill our people

with unnecessary pain

We need creative minds to build and design for our new Black nation to shine.

Sisterme, the revolution is more than workers' unite. Stop trying so hard to fit Marx's theory to Black people's plight. The solution may not lie in Black and White. We must first get our own to unite.

Now you comrades who follow Marx
Yeah that's cool by me
Just as long as you never forget where you came from
Yes, your African family tree.

You can spout words and theories all day long trying to convince the masses that yours is the correct scientific way, but unless you have some thing concrete to establish in place of all this madness, to hell with you the masses will say.

You speak loosely of a dictatorship of the proletariat after power has been seized
But don't realize that we must begin now to create independent Black institutions
for the further education of our offspring; food coops – all the necessary things so the transition to the new society will come more easily.

Those of you who follow Marx, yeah that's cool by me
But as long as you oppose natural childbirth and foods
And accept abortions and birth control clinics
Together you and me will never be.

And you sisters over there with the African geles wrapped around your hair.
Beware of possessing apprehensive, closed minds.
Remember, the liberation struggle exists on many fronts and
Black people – there are many different kinds

An African proverb goes, 'Not to know is bad, not to wish to know is worse'
If you are apprehensive of Marxism, study it, learn it, and understand it
Only arguing off the top of your head about a white boy's ideology is not good enough for we all know that Marx only stole and plagiarized the seed of the ideology he taught from the ancient system of communalism,

which existed on the continent of Africa before
the white man could even talk.

As for today's Great Debate, it ain't nuthin' but dirt
Cuz when two elephants fight, it is the grass that gets hurt.
The grass symbolizes the masses of Black people who are caught in the
middle of the two elephants or ideologies debating
in the Black community

Let's all stop thinking that ours is the only solution. The struggle exists
on many fronts. WE ARE ONLY BULLSHITTING ON THE WAY TO
THE REVOLUTION.
So Sistas all I have left to say dealing with the ideas the Black
Nationalists and Marxists have to say, is be careful in this
great debate war, So the grass will be hurt no more.

And brothers u over there with eyes so wide. Wishing under the
sista's dress your hand can slide, explaining you are dealing
with the revolution by collecting a harem of Black females
Because of the so-called shortage of Black males and you call that
the solution??! Brothers,
Y'ALL ARE JUST BULLSHITTING ON THE WAY
TO THE REVOLUTION.

The best way to deal with the shortage of Black males is not by having
a harem of females, but rather struggling and striving to free Black males
from the prisons and jails.
NOW THAT'S REVOLUTIONARY.
Making babies is fine. But raising and molding them into men and
women is on time. Instead of concentrating on how many sisters
you can hold, why not deal
With the reason of shortage and be bold.

So you brothers over there with eyes so wide
Wishing under the sista's dress your hand can slide
You need to go someplace and hide
Cuz you ain't nuthin but jive."

***

I penned many creative pieces and loved performing, often accompanied with the
rhythms of D.C.'s master drummer, Baba Ngoma, and with a group formed by

Brother Randi Payton, called The Pyramid Poets. Besides my own lines, I often spouted the lyrics of Nikki Giovanni, the Last Poets, Gil Scott Heron, Oscar Brown Jr. – all great precursors to today's spoken word artists.

Although I loved performing my spoken word, I always had a major problem with extemporaneous speech. A brief encounter with a fellow Howard student is illustrative.

While walking across the campus one Saturday morning with my signature gele headwrap, long dangle earrings and hip-hugger bell-bottom tight jeans, I noticed a poster on a tree informing passersby that Guyanese revolutionary Walter Rodney will speak on his book, *How Europe Underdeveloped Africa*, that evening.

A student who happened to be a brother from the Continent, was also reading the poster. I turned to him, smiled widely, and expressed my desire to hear Rodney speak because I felt he wrote a dynamic book on the subject. My African acquaintance laughed and mocked, "You believe that?!" referring to the title of Rodney's publication.

"Of course. I definitely believe that Europe underdeveloped Africa," I indignantly replied. "Don't you?!"

The brother proceeded to explain to me how Africa would not be as advanced as it is now without the expertise and intervention of the European. His analysis was that Europe developed, rather than underdeveloped, Africa.

At that point in the conversation I attempted to call upon all the knowledge I had gathered over the past years concerning the controversial subject. I tried to conjure up concepts from the extensive reading I had done – from Fanon to Rodney and from Mao to Malcolm. Unfortunately, all my thoughts were jumbled up in my mind and, try as I did, I could not assemble them coherently into oral communication at the time.

Frustratingly unable to organize my facts on the spur of the moment, I decided to let one older and wiser than I defend the opposite point of view, and strongly suggested he go to the meeting and debate the subject with Walter Rodney himself. Thus, the essence of the rest of our conversation was spent with the brother praising Europeans for barging in on a society which I feel was advancing along its own course of development, disrupting it, and in its place instituting the values and machinery of the most corrupt and inhumane people on earth.

My inability at times to express my thoughts verbally is an articulation problem I have always had. This weakness affected my self-confidence for years. When the words I wished to speak fail to materialize, I would get nervous, sweat and have digestive system issues. Despite this deficiency, I always try to understand the opinion of people from their point of view. This is one reason I didn't explode when the brother ranted that Africa would not be where she is now if it had not been for the White man.

I peeped into what I felt to be his field of experience and could empathize with his point of view. This brother was a student from Nigeria with probably a British elementary and secondary school education. This foundation is undoubtedly what indoctrinated into him the feeling that Black people could not accomplish anything successfully without the guidance of the European – feelings no different from the Euro-American indoctrination we receive in this country.

Nevertheless, I'm thinking to myself, How am I gonna be a lawyer if I can't express my thoughts extemporaneously? This failure and lack of confidence would gnaw at me for a long time and thank goodness, even though I still prefer having my notes by my side, I no longer get gas when I'm nervous!

Chapter Three, Section 2
Jesus Was Black and Had Two Wives?

Although Howard was melanin-rich, I spent more time in Chocolate City, a popular term of endearment for D.C., rather than being enmeshed in the sometimes cloistered air of campus life. I frequented events at Independent Black Schools such as Ujamaa Shule and Bookstore/African Shop at 9th and V Streets, N.W.; NationHouse Watoto School on Park Road, N.W.; Nia Shule on R Street, N.W.; and Roots Activity Learning Center on North Capitol Street, N.E.

Yet there was no institution during my college years that moved and grooved me more than the incredible Temple of the Black Messiah, located at 14th and V Streets, N.W. "Now who was this Black Messiah; wasn't Jesus White?" I would be asked by curious minds in different ways at different times. Still others more aware would inquire, "Don't you mean the Shrine of the Black Madonna?" The answer to both oft-asked questions was, "No."

Although both The Temple of the Black Messiah based in Washington, D.C., and the Shrine of the Black Madonna[27] based in Detroit were both part of the Black Christian Nationalist Movement, they were separate religious institutions headed up by different ministers.

The minister of the Temple of the Black Messiah was Rev. Ishakamusa Barashango, a fiery light-skinned brother sporting a wild-looking, naturally curly Afro hairstyle.

He was affectionately known throughout the community as Brother Shaka. At the time, the Temple of the Black Messiah in Washington, D.C. was located in the middle of the ghetto. Today, that area is a completely gentrified neighborhood. This was before the D.C. Reeves Municipal Center was erected around the corner, before the revitalization of the U Street Corridor, and before the landmark Busboys and Poets restaurant opened across the street.

The Temple was originally a humble, nondescript storefront that had been majestically transformed into a powder-blue and gold, gorgeous, grassroots temple, complete with a dome-like frame. Brother Shaka, a printer by trade, had his print shop, IVth Dynasty Press, strategically situated above the Temple. In addition to being a minister and prolific orator, he was also a skilled craftsman, responsible for professionalizing publications and flyers circulated by the D.C. Black Nationalist community before computer technology.

Brother Shaka was truly a trailblazer. He wrote and published his own groundbreaking books, *God, the Bible and the Black Man's Destiny*; *African People and European Holidays: A Mental Genocide I and II*; and *Black Woman – The Original Guardian Angel*. He also published my very first book, *New Afrikan Children of the Sun*, a coloring book co-authored with long-time friend Brother Imamu Kuumba. But

nothing filled me up like Reverend Ishakamusa's sermons, which expertly infused Black history with religion and culture. I listened intently to his lectures; everything made so much sense to my youthful, inquisitive mind.

One example was a sermon he delivered in which Jesus, whom he called in a folksy manner, 'Jerusalem Slim,' had been married with two wives. "Jesus had to have been married," Brother Shaka preached. "There was much circumstantial evidence," he continued. "Jewish culture would have demanded it."

His facts and figures seemed to add up to me. "Early Israelites barred unmarried men from the priesthood," he taught. "Jesus ben Joseph, commonly referred to as Jesus Christ," Shaka taught, "would have been powerless if he had no wife." It was part of the atmosphere and culture under which he lived. "The Hebrew Torah states," Brother Shaka fired on, "If a man is not married by the age of 20, let him rot!"

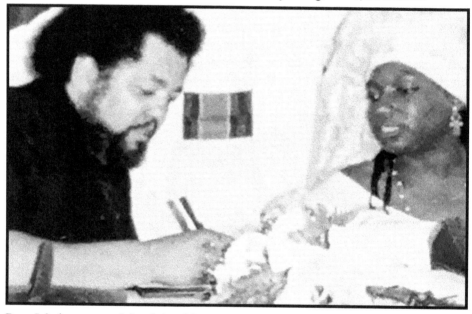

Rev. Ishakmusa explained that history tells us that women did things to Jesus no unmarried woman would have done, such as anointing his body with oil. In the Bible verse John 12:3, Mary of Bethany is administering ointment of spikenard to Jesus. "Spikenard," Brother Shaka expounded, "was a special oil only used to anoint Kings or high priests of Israel. And it was customary for Kings to be anointed by their wives." The fiery Reverend continued persuasively. "In order for Jesus to have been proclaimed King of Israel, he would have to have had a wife to give him an heir. And in his case, he likely had co-wives – Mary Magdalene and Mary of Bethany." And yes, Brother Shaka had a sermon about Barabbas, whom he suggested could have been Jesus's son, but I have no surviving notes or remembrance from that Sunday lesson to share.

Brother Shaka preached about the "historical Jesus who was Black as midnight and dedicated to the cause of independence," and compared him to what he described as the mythological Jesus, "a co-opted, bleached out version of the original, with blond hair and blue eyes."

He taught that Jesus was a Black Nationalist freedom fighter who fought for the liberation of his people and was lynched on a cross, according to the Roman form of punishment used to eliminate freedom fighters of that day. He articulated that the phrase, "the kingdom of heaven is at hand," translated into the mantra, "It's Nation Time!"

Brother Shaka often took jabs at current day customs, critical that Blacks didn't have the proper historical understanding. "Wearing a cross around your neck is like wearing a noose or electric chair, or gas chamber around your neck," he analogized.

From Brother Shaka I learned that the ancient world commemorated the date of December 25th as the birth date of Horus in Egypt, long before Jesus was born. Horus or Heru, one of the many manifestations of the sun, was the halo (sun disc) son of Isis and Osiris (also known as Auset and Ausar), born some 4,000 or more years ago – at least 2,000 years before the New Testament's Christ.

Brother Shaka told us that in those days, December 25th was also observed as the birthday of Tammuz, the Babylonian god of love and the nativity of Mithra, a sun deity also depicted with a brilliant halo of light around his head. Brother Shaka explained, "The concept of a savior dying and coming back to life again was not unknown to the ancient world, nor did it originate with the coming of European Christianity."

I was never much into traditional Christian religious practices, although I always considered myself a very spiritual individual. The Temple of the Black Messiah somehow answered many questions I was seeking about religion and seemed to crystalize everything for me. And to top it off, Baba Ngoma, D.C.'s original master drummer and resident instrumentalist at the Temple, hypnotized me with his rhythms.

The songs we sang to the beat of his drums, and the sermons preached by Brother Shaka, were exciting new experiences for me. The Methodist church in which I grew up did not specialize in old Negro spirituals and I was largely unfamiliar with most of them. I was likewise unfamiliar with many of the Civil Rights freedom songs, as I had not really come of age during that era. So as we sang the songs in the Temple, I did not realize that many of them were makeovers from old Christian and Negro spirituals infused with the Civil Rights freedom songs from the 60s.

At the Temple I belted out with the others, "I woke up this morning with my mind, stayed on freedom. Woke up this morning with my mind, stayed on freedom, Hallelu, Hallelu, Hallelujah. I'm gonna walk about and talk about and fight for, my precious freedom…". It would be years before it dawned on me that the song came from the spiritual, *Woke Up This Morning with my Mind, Stayed on Jesus.*

We also chanted Yoruba praise songs, singing tributes to the pantheon of Orisa[28] who are here to help us: Orunmila, Eshu, Yemoja, Osun, Ogun, Shango, Oya and more. It was exhilarating and electrifying as Baba Ngoma put so much energy and spirit into the drumming and the songs he taught and led. It was a fitting prelude to the impassioned and enlightening messages delivered each Sunday at 3 p.m. by Rev. Ishakamusa.

Kwanzaa at the Temple of the Black Messiah was always a highlight during the 1970s. We were packed like sardines into the little one room that housed the Temple. Seemingly hundreds of Black and Brown faces congregated, seated on the benches and the red-carpeted floor, December 26th through 31st for the candlelighting service, before spiriting off to various city-wide celebrations. Baba Ngoma captivated us with his drums. We sang Kwanzaa songs, culminating in seven "harambee's," meaning let's all pull together, where our fists were raised and lowered with each incantation.

Three decades later on the evening of January 17, 2004, I found myself in a van with D.C. cultural activists Baba El Zulu, Baba Ngoma, Baba Imamu, Baba Rasafik, and Sister Alemitu. We were on our way back to D.C. from Philadelphia, after attending the celebration of life of this great man, Brother Dr. Reverend Ishakamusa Barashango. Four days earlier he began his transition to become an ancestor, after succumbing to a heart attack at age 66.

Brother Shaka left such a huge imprint on my life. He also left his mark on Washington, D.C., which he affectionately renamed "Banneker City," just as he had renamed Philadelphia "Richard Allen City" and Baltimore "Harriet Tubman City." In fact, upon information and belief, it was he who renamed Meridian Hill Park "Malcolm X Park." His apartment was located adjacent to it, when he lived in D.C. For decades Black people and others in D.C. have almost universally referred to this location as Malcolm X Park.

Often calling me his spiritual daughter, I felt a unique obligation to make the service. Walking out in the middle of a board meeting of the National Coalition of Blacks for Reparations in America (N'COBRA), I joined the van and sojourned to Richard Allen City. Rev. Shaka's daughter, Daima, who I had worked closely with in the Republic of New Afrika, Khalid Abdur-Rasheed, her former husband, and their many children were all there in force. The children were now grown, but I could still discern who they were even with the passage of time since I saw them as babies. Their drumming brought the roof down, awakening ancestral spirits eager to join in the reverie.

Mama Masani, the mother of Brother Shaka's younger set of children, had oiled and prepared his body. His current wife, Lydia,[29] was the sister of political prisoner Mumia Abu Jamal. Present also at the service were Dr. Yosef Ben Jochannan and Brother Ashra Kwesi. Brother Shaka was put into the ground in grand style. Amidst the drumming, chanting and possessions, much liquid spirit was poured upon the plain pine coffin. The display of love and admiration captivated one of the cemetery ground caretakers, a brother. "I've never seen anything like this!" he repeated over and over, clearly awestruck.

Today, it appears that Brother Shaka's legacy is not more than a faint memory. His presence pre-dated the internet, and live video of his early sermons are scarce. Audio of some of his later speeches are online, but footage of his vibrant delivery are all but absent. In listening to some of his messages, it is today clear that he, like many Black Nationalists and organizations of that day, spouted views that progressives may now consider backward. Back then, however, few eyebrows were raised. And to me, any politically incorrect imperfections he may have had were far outweighed by the electrifying influence he had on my inquisitive mind.

Ominously, the oft-quoted goal from the FBI's COINTELPRO[30] documents, "to stop the rise of a messiah who could unify and electrify the militant black nationalist community," could have drawn part of its inspiration from Rev. Ishakamusa's Temple of the Black Messiah.

Chapter Three, Section 3
Putting Spice in Life Is Not Always Nice

I met Sister Halima at the Temple of the Black Messiah. Halima and Brother Atiba, her roly-poly, ever-present chauffeur, protector and all around good guy, were my hangout buddies. As years passed into decades, I often wonder whatever became of Halima as she was another one of my female idols who sported a large African headwrap covering her huge Afro.

Sister Halima lived in Southwest D.C., in the projects on Delaware Avenue. She was the youngest, most vivacious grandmother I ever knew. She couldn't have been much older than 30, which was uncommon for a grandmother during the mid-70s, although it is rather commonplace today.

It was through Halima that some of my friends from Howard University and I got involved with the Black Women's United Front. We met and drove down to Virginia to Lorton Reformatory, the prison for people with convictions from Washington, D.C. We visited the brothers and presented uplifting, consciousness-raising programs that included drumming, African dancing, poetry and discussions. Sometimes we visited brothers in the visiting room. The first time I came to the visiting room, I couldn't believe my eyes. Some women visiting their men wore long dresses or skirts. Naively I thought the attire was due to modesty, but in actuality these dresses were used to shield prohibited sexual activities from the nearby guards. Women sat on the laps of their sex-starved men, spread their dresses wide and got busy. These visits were affectionately called "Mother's Day."

"Sista, you needs to put some spice in your life," Sister Halima lovingly teased me.

That statement nudged me to step outside of my comfort zone. I tried to put some spice in my life and experienced a contradiction that impacts me to this very day.

There was a brother from New Jersey who my father would classify as a bad boy – that is, if my father had even known this brother existed. I decided to put some "spice in my life" and traveled to Jersey to spend the weekend with this brother who was then my boyfriend. The details are hazy now, but he was living with some other brothers. There was some beautiful artwork and posters on the walls of their communal house. I naively took my camera and snapped some pictures of the revolutionary art on the wall. I didn't give it a second thought, but you would have thought I had committed a cardinal sin.

"What?!! They think I'm an agent?!" I shrieked to my friend that evening after he told me his housemates had a meeting about me.

"Well, Sista," my beau responded. "You know I trust you, but the other brothers, they don't know you. After all, you live in D.C., and that's where the FBI headquarters is."

"Oh my God, how ridiculously absurd can one get?!" I yelled. "Take the damn camera. I'm outta here!" Actually, I was just naïve and, of course, the furthest thing from an FBI agent. I quickly left the city on the next train out, but didn't realize I was pregnant. Well, I had put some spice in my life all right! Talk about a major contradiction. Here I was, a senior in college and preacher of natural things, who shunned abortion as genocide against Black people. However, my personal situation had me seriously contemplating what it meant to have the right to choose. It's hard to believe today, but the ink on *Roe v. Wade*[31] had barely dried three years earlier.

To this day, I don't know if I made the right decision. Sometimes it can be very hard to practice what you preach. Many Black people, classified or seen as liberal, and even those who work every day on progressive issues, have what could be considered as conservative values. Many times the politically correct position is taken publicly, and although we may even believe it, behind closed doors or in our everyday private lives, we may take a different tack. Thus was the dilemma with my pregnancy, which shook me to the core of my being.

Even my experience at the abortion clinic gave me great pause. On the day of my initial interview, I sheepishly entered the facility. The receptionist was a White woman who, I swear, looked like she came straight from the devil's lair. It wasn't just that her physical features were witch-like (which they were to me), but her personality and attitude sent shivers up my spine. Now, decades later, I don't remember exactly what she said, but I've often wondered if that was some message from the metaphysical world that I, Nkechi, had no business in such a place, and to get the hell on out of there.

But I stayed. I later called to complain about her and was told that the receptionist had been fired. That gave me a little solace, but I still wonder if that was a spiritual test that I failed.Years later I began attending classes and events at the Ausar Auset Society.[32] They had an Auset ritual at a beach for women who had had abortions. They said it was to wash away the guilt of the experience. Interestingly enough, the bus was packed. No one asked any questions. No one had to testify. It was a sisterly ritual of forgiveness that was also an exhilarating experience. We entered the soothing waters and sang, chanted and danced to the female deities, Auset and Het Heru. I can't say that it absolved me of all my guilt, but it was comforting to know that I was not alone in my sorrow.

Again, it is amazing how much we as women keep inside. I didn't even tell my best friend that I had an abortion. I didn't confide in my political comrades. I did not tell my family. I often wonder if and how my life would have changed had I given birth at that time. Would I have gone to law school? Would I have traveled around the world? Would I have experienced difficulty the following decade when I was anxiously trying to get pregnant? I don't know the answers to these difficult questions. I only know that as conscious Black women, our lives are more complicated than one would ever imagine.

Chapter Three, Section 4
The Garvey Movement Was Personal to Me

The assistant minister of the Temple of the Black Messiah was Rev. Alton Akinsegun. We called him Brother Akin. He and Brother Imamu Kuumba were the primary people I recall always talking about the Honorable Marcus Garvey. I had heard of Garvey, but there wasn't much information out about this incredible Black leader during this time. I think Garvey resonated so much with me because of my Uncle Ambrose. So I studied Garvey's movement, wrote papers in college on his movement, and was always amazed at what I discovered.

Of all the movements that began in the 20th century that preceded my generation, it was the Garvey movement that was the most personal to me because of the link to my Uncle, who was the first son of island-immigrant parents born in New York.

My Uncle Ambrose, born in 1910, was not a radical or a revolutionary. He was a skilled artisan and a carpenter, like his father. To thousands of his father's Harlem-based contemporaries, the Garvey movement was part of the course of affairs. It was commonplace to see politicians, preachers and others honing their oratorical skills propped up on street-corner soapboxes, and Garvey was no different. My Uncle, no doubt, as a youth stopped to listen to Garvey's inspirational speeches on the way to his father's carpentry shop where he was an apprentice.

Marcus Garvey created the Universal Negro Improvement Association (UNIA), under the motto, *"One God, One Aim, One Destiny."* The UNIA had a communications arm in the form of a weekly newspaper, *The Negro World*, which quickly became a leading and important vehicle for the promotion of the philosophy and opinions of Garvey. This publication had a regular circulation of at least 50,000, and up to 500,000 at its peak, and a national and international readership several times that number. Although I never saw a copy, my Uncle regularly read the publication in his day. Indeed, this spurred his love for the written word, making him a frequent visitor to Harlem's Schomburg Library throughout his life.

The UNIA had an economic arm and Garvey was in the forefront promoting the importance of economic independence. Garvey often said, "A race that is solely dependent upon another for its economic existence sooner or later dies." He coined the expression, 'Buy Black.' As the result of Garvey's teachings to patronize Black businesses, people flocked to my Uncle's carpentry business, including notables such as the Harlem Renaissance poet Langston Hughes.

One of the businesses Garvey established was the Negro Factories Corporation in 1919, which had a market capitalization of one million dollars. Offering stock to Blacks at $5 a share, the company planned to provide loans and executive or technical assistance to Blacks who needed help in establishing their own small businesses. The corporation helped to develop a chain of cooperative grocery stores, a restaurant, a steam laundry, a tailor and dressmaking shop, a millinery store and a publishing house. The UNIA initiated the Black Star Steamship Line whose purpose, Garvey declared, was "to serve as a commercial and spiritual tie among Blacks wherever its ships traveled." And yes, Uncle Ambrose had shares in the Black Star Line but, regrettably, no memorabilia of the time came to my attention and, presumably, none was preserved by our family.

The UNIA also had a political arm and Garvey's vision was not confined domestically. In 1920, he called for the first international convention of the UNIA, with delegates representing all parts of the world. There were several thousand delegates from every one of the then 48 states, and more than a score of countries spanning three continents. I don't know whether my Uncle attended this historic convention but if he did, he would have been in the company of others in attendance such as Viet Nam's Ho Chi Minh; Ghana's Kwame Nkrumah; India's Mahatmas Ghandi; Malcolm X's father the Rev. Earl Little; and Elijah Poole, who later became the Honorable Elijah Muhammad. In later years all of these luminaries would draw upon the teachings of Garvey from that convention, fashioning struggles for victory around the world.

The UNIA had a cultural arm and Garvey developed the concept of the red, black and green, which became incorporated into flags throughout the African world. He advocated for the sale and production of Black dolls, rather than support the sale of White superiority created by White advertisers of the day. Garvey also organized grandiose parades, the most famous one being in Harlem in 1920. Among those marching in these huge parades were units of African Legionnaires, the military arm of the organization, prepared for self-defense. I'm sure my Uncle Ambrose was there, not as a Legionnaire, but simply accompanying his father as one of thousands of ordinary young Black men and women who yearned for a better life.

Another uniformed regiment of the UNIA at the Harlem parades was the Black Cross Nurses. Their existence indicated the readiness of the UNIA to come to the aid of stricken people all over the world. Although outsiders may have ridiculed the elaborate procedures of Garvey's organization, none should overlook its importance in restoring the all but shattered Black self-confidence.

One may then ask what caused the downfall of Garvey's movement? The answer would be the same thing that plagued the movements before Garvey and since Garvey – tactics of disruption, destabilization, and destruction.

Almost simultaneous with the birth of the UNIA was the beginning of the Federal Bureau of Investigation. Garvey was one of the first targets of its director, J. Edgar Hoover, whose devious methods later morphed into the FBI's COINTELPRO campaign to disrupt and destroy Black nationalist and other movements. We are still recovering from that disastrous and highly successful covert operation, which has been resurrected in current days by the FBI under the label, Black Identity Extremist.

Although the original Garvey movement began to disintegrate, many people held fast to its ideals and gave birth to new formations. The man who became Elijah Muhammad was at that 1920 Convention. The discipline and order the UNIA created was clearly a foundation for the discipline and order that is the hallmark of the Nation of Islam as founded by Elijah Muhammad. From Elijah Muhammad sprang Malcolm X, whose father and mother (Earl and Louisa Little) were both Garveyites.

Malcolm X sprouted other movements, among them the Black Panther Party for Self-Defense, the Provisional Government of the Republic of New Afrika,[33] the New Afrikan Independence Movement, the Independent Black School Movement, and the Sankofa Movement for ReAfrikanization, to name a few. And the influence of Queen Mother Audley Moore, another Garveyite, in keeping the issue of reparations alive is a story yet to be told.

Chapter Four
"A Change is Gonna Come"[34]

Section 1
You Mean We're Not Really U.S. Citizens?

One of the most pivotal lectures I heard while a student at Howard University came not from a professor or PhD, but from a speaker in a room on the first floor of Frederick Douglass Hall. The speaker was tall, dark-skinned and sported a bald head. It was probably sometime around the end of 1973 or early 1974. He was talking history, my 'thang,' and my ears were on fire. He ran down the specifics of the 13th and 14th amendments to the U.S. Constitution. "The 13th amendment freed you, but the 14th amendment could not have made you a citizen. You had to have been asked if you wanted to be a citizen. And we were never asked."

My eyes were wide with amazement.

Wow, I never looked at it that way before, I mused to myself incredulously. You mean we're not legally citizens of the United States?

Just as Brother Malcolm X ruminated when he was sentenced, and concluded that Whites were "devils," I too thought over the 300-year existence of Blacks on this American soil. The brutal lynchings. The blatant disrespect. The need to be better just to have a chance at equal upward mobility.

I found the anonymous brother's argument compelling. His rationale affected me greatly, although who he was will remain one of the lingering mysteries of my life. Several months later I saw a flyer announcing an organizing meeting for something called the Republic of New Afrika (RNA) and its National Black Elections. The meeting was to be held at D.C.'s All Souls Unitarian Church. When I got to the meeting and heard what I heard, I had an "aha" moment as I remembered the anonymous brother's speech from Howard's Douglass Hall that had so intrigued me. We were not citizens; we had never been asked and, as such, we were entitled to the international right to self-determination. I knew this was the movement I had been seeking. But little did I know it would become the movement that would occupy the elephant's share of my time and energy for the next fifteen years.

The Republic of New Afrika was founded at a convention of Black Nationalists in Detroit, MI, in 1968. At that convention the nation was anointed with its name, the Republic of New Afrika. A provisional or temporary "pre-independence" government was established to carry on the political life of the government. Five states in the deep South – Louisiana, Mississippi, Alabama, Georgia and South Carolina – were identified as the subjugated national territory of the nation. A constitution called the Code of Umoja was written, as was a Declaration of Independence from

the United States under a mandate to "Free the Land."

Needless to say, as a young college student with aspirations of one day becoming a lawyer, I was fascinated with the concept of an independent Black nation with formal laws and a constitution, all buttressed by international law. And added to my attraction was the fine, dark-skinned, dashiki-clad brother with the big Afro and nicely trimmed goatee who was leading the meeting. His name was Tyehimba Peyton. It was no question that Brother Tyehimba melted many a sister's heart and most likely inspired scores to join "The Struggle." Except me, of course. I was already in "The Struggle." And anyway, I had a boyfriend. It was Jerry at the time.

But Tyehimba sure was fine. We developed a connection that transcended time and movements. Our friendship probably survived over the years because we respected each other's relationships and our brother-sister, I-got-your-back relationship deepened. Whenever I had a problem, when I called 'Tye,' he would come. It didn't matter whether it was to keep some miscellaneous guy from messing over me, to participating in my weddings, or to helping me out with ideas for a speech.

Tyehimba became my first mentor in the RNA movement. And it didn't take long to enmesh myself into this cause for Black Liberation. It seemed to be the answer to my calling. The movement was nationalistic. It was scientific. It was cultural. I could be a "new" Afrikan. I didn't have to be straddled with lappas that I could never seem to tie correctly around my waist; my signature jeans more than sufficed.

These were exciting times with new and old acquaintances in "The Struggle." In addition to Brother Tyehimba there was Brother Imani Mahdi, who I had previously worked with at Kwasi's Center for Black Unity. Brother Imani, who now wore all black, was quiet, intense, and mysterious. There was Brother Patrice Toure, formerly Wesley Stevens, and at the time the husband of Sister Nkenge, who I remembered from my previous Panther paper-selling days. There was Brother Imamu Kuumba, who I would see every Sunday at the Temple of the Black Messiah and became a lifelong friend. There were Brothers Fati, Sami, and Changa, and Sisters Njeri, Tuere, Sala, Louise, and Johnetta.

And there was one of my most staunch political mentors, Brother Kwame Afoh, a father figure whose birth name of Edell Lydia I vaguely recalled from my teenage Black Land Movement days several years earlier. Kwame had been with the RNA for a while, and his analysis of the issues and movement was always sharp, perceptive and precise. Amidst his distinctive fast-talking, and hard to decipher Texas vernacular, he imparted much knowledge, which I enthusiastically absorbed.

Thus, I was distressed when soon after I joined the RNA movement, Brother Kwame was considering leaving. He had three young daughters and was seeking more depth to the spiritual side of his life, wishing to delve deeper into African traditional religion. He became a part of the African Cultural and Religious Society, under the tutelage of Nana Kwabena Brown, who would subsequently also become pivotal in my life. Brother Kwame would later come back to working with the Republic of New Afrika, even serving as President.

We were all the early stalwart members of the D.C. RNA cadre. We were revolutionaries, but were also regular human beings. I will never forget the day when Brother Kwame actually carried a small television with him to our Sunday meetings so as not to miss the football game.

Our cadre would meet, alternating in Southeast at Tyehimba's apartment on Ely Place, or on 15th Street across from Malcolm X Park at Patrice and Nkenge's apartment. Sometimes we would meet at my parent's home, because during the summer I did not live on campus.

Tyehimba's fond memory is of the brothers sitting up after one of our characteristically long meetings, drinking my father's homemade wine. Interestingly, my father never put my RNA comrades in the "bad boy" category. They were all, sisters included, affectionately referred to by him as "the Black Brothers" and were, in his lingo, all part of what he called, "the Black Brother Movement." It's no question that my father liked them. My comrades were clean and respectful. We were about building a Black Nation, under the precepts of the New Afrikan Creed, the beginning sentence being, "I believe in the spirituality, humanity and genius of Black people, and in our new pursuit of these values."

Tyehimba was my guide. From watching him, I learned how to run a meeting blind; put on a program with one hand tied behind my back and get up on a platform and speak (always provided I had my notes with me, of course). But my naivety back then astounds me, and we still laugh over it.

Tyehimba claims that the day after I got my driver's license, he had me behind the wheel of a car assisting with driving the long ride from D.C. to Mississippi. I know I had my license before then, but I will never forget being frantic on the highway because I couldn't see the road behind me at night, not realizing that it was the headlights from cars behind you that illuminated the road where there were no streetlights.

And I remember the time when Louise and I were driving together in a rented vehicle from D.C. to an RNA meeting in Detroit. Neither she nor I could figure out how to turn the high beams on. It amazes me today how we in "The Struggle" did so much driving across the country in those days, to meetings and conferences, whereas now, we just hop on a plane. Of course economics had a lot to do with it, and we had practically no money in those days and, of course, no virtual meetings or conference calling options.

I was the incessant political worker bee. But after a while I noticed that, by and large, the wives or girlfriends of the brothers I worked with were not involved in "The Struggle;" not required or even encouraged to attend the endless and often non-productive meetings; and not up on the stage like me pontificating before crowds. They were at home. Raising children. Having a life. I'm thinking. What's wrong with this picture? Why am I sacrificing not going out to parties or to the movies or otherwise just having fun, to sit up all night with mostly married or betrothed menfolk discussing and debating politics, history, or culture? But I pushed these thoughts to the back of my mind and just continued to bury myself in the work.

At that first RNA organizing meeting at All Souls Church, Brother Tyehimba fervently appealed, "Help us elect a Black government!" And so, over the years, I did. "Help us work with the National Black Elections!" And so, over the years, I did. "Help us Free the RNA-11!" And so, over the years, I did. "Help Free All Political Prisoners!" And so, over the years, I did. "Help to work for reparations for Black people!" And so, over the years, I did just that.

Brother Tyehimba was the catalyst of my work with the Republic of New Afrika, but several years later he announced he would soon move to California. I was devastated. Brother Kwame had already exited, although he would later be back, and now Tyehimba would be gone as well. Despite his confidence in me, I didn't know what I would be able to do to continue organizing with this new-found movement without his guidance. So I made sure to learn the stories and the politics so I would be able to recite the party line on demand. One of the major issues was the case of the Republic of New Afrika Eleven (RNA-11).

I could not believe it. I learned that in the wee hours of the morning of August 18, 1971, a force of approximately 40 heavily armed and bullet-proof vested Jackson, MS policemen and FBI agents, complete with Jackson's infamous "Thompson tank," secretly surrounded the official residence of Republic of New Afrika president, Imari Abubakari Obadele. Brother Imari, as many affectionately called him, had been elected as the second President of the Black Nation in North America, the Republic of New Afrika.

Inside Brother President Imari's official residence were seven persons – including 15-year-old Karim Njabafudi, Brother Offogga and his pregnant wife Njeri, Brother Chuma, and three visitors – RNA Vice President Hekima Ana and his wife Tamu (who had recently returned from the University of Ghana), and Brother Addis Ababa. Brother Imari and three others were spending the night at the new RNA office several blocks away. Unbeknownst to the occupants, a smaller force of police and FBI agents also surrounded that building.

At the residence following a pre-determined plan, the police and FBI agents, sup-

posedly seeking a fugitive who was not even there, gave the sleeping occupants a mere 75 seconds to come out of the building. The miniature army then opened fire into the bedroom windows with lethal rockets carrying gas charges. The occupants defended themselves. During the attack two policemen, along with an FBI agent, were wounded.

At the RNA office Brother Imari, oblivious to what had just occurred at his residence blocks away, walked out, challenging the policemen and agents as they moved in. They refrained from gunning him down in plain view of neighboring Blacks. All four at the office were arrested, as were those who defended themselves at the attack on the house. The seven men and women at the residence were beaten and paraded half-naked through Jackson streets in chains. After the police lieutenant later died of his wounds, all eleven were originally charged with murder, assault and "waging war against the state of Mississippi." Nine were also indicted by the U.S. for conspiracy to assault federal officers and for having assaulted them.

This case hit close to home and the attack was personal. Almost immediately it occurred to me that Tamu, a college student, could have easily been me. Karim was only 15 years old, and Tawwaub Nkrumah was the son of the acclaimed poet Margaret Walker, who I admired for her writings, especially her classic poem, "For My People." These were some of the defendants who were part of the RNA-11 case.

I was so enthused with this movement that was so very new to me, I decided to write a letter to the President of the New Afrikan nation in North America while he was in prison.

> *Dear President Imari. I am sorry that you are imprisoned. I work with the Provisional Government in Washington, D.C., under the leadership of Brother Tyehimba. I hope to go to law school one day. Please let me know if there is anything I can ever do to help you. Free the Land! Sister Nkechi.*

I didn't know it then, but I quickly learned that you don't write Brother Imari and ask what you can do to help without being fully committed. I received a ten-foot long list detailing step by step, point by point what was needed. I found myself doing things I had never done before – contacting lawyers, calling the FBI and Justice Departments, writing letters all over the country to influential Black professionals. I was glad I was an unknown name. I was a mere college student, and a sometime poet. I was definitely not a diplomat used to talking to Amnesty International or telephoning the United Church of Christ and other huge groups requesting large sums of money.

One of the specific responses from Brother Imari, to my innocent offer of assistance, was that I chair the National Committee to Free the RNA-11. I didn't realize it at the time, but his willingness to put me in such a responsible position demonstrated the desperateness of the times and the depths to which the movement had sunk. It was hard to believe that I, a new convert to this movement, would lead such a monumental effort.

But many years later, I understood. The nascent Black independence movement had become destabilized. It was a low point in the movement, and we will never know how much of it may or may not have been stoked by nefarious government sources. The seeds of this dispute had been brewing a long time, but I knew none of this when I wrote my innocent letter to help.

Brother Imari directed me to solicit members to join the National Committee to Free the RNA-11. It would become quite an illustrious Committee. Under his direction I sent letters to Congresspersons Charles Diggs, John Conyers and Ronald Dellums; Ministers Rev. David Eaton, Rev. Ishakamusa Barashango, and Rev. Louis Farrakhan; and Professors Dr. James Turner, Attorney Derrick Bell, and Dr. Ronald Walters. Also included on my list of people to contact were esteemed poets such as Haki Madhubuti, Kalamu ya Salaam, and Sonia Sanchez. Community leaders such as Baba El Senzengakulu Zulu of Ujamaa School and Bookstore and Julian Richardson of Marcus Books were also invited to participate. When I made the follow-up calls, everyone responded immediately, "Yes, I will lend my name. Anything for Brother Imari."

Even our Committee's letterhead reflected "The Struggle," thanks to the skillful work of the gifted preacher by day, printer by night Rev. Ishakamusa. It featured the infamous image of the brothers and sisters of the RNA-11 being paraded down a Mississippi street half-dressed, barefoot and in chains. The dehumanizing spectacle was reminiscent of captured runaway slaves being unceremoniously marched to the town square for execution.

When it was later revealed that the FBI had arranged for highly prejudicial stories against the RNA to appear in the press and had also forged inflammatory letters to spouses, friends, cadres and supporters of the Republic of New Afrika, I was outraged. I read evidence from the FBI's own files that they even tried to inspire violence between the Mafia's La Cosa Nostra and Black numbers runners in Detroit who were thought to be supporting the Black nationalist movement. This was infuriating. The nerve.

I examined shocking text between the copious blocks of blacked out pages unmasking FBI tactics to promote violence between RNA personnel and the Black Panther Party. I inspected letters on fake RNA letterhead addressed to the Black Panther

Party over Brother President Imari Obadele's forged signature. One letter insinuated that the Republic of New Afrika was "a better group" to join. What type of reaction would be generated to the Black Panther recipient of such a letter? FBI agents were incentivized to be creative in devising new and innovative ways to disrupt and destroy the Black movement in general and the Republic of New Afrika in particular. I wonder what type of incentive the agent who thought of the forged signature ploy received?

As I scrutinized page after page of notorious FBI documents revealing scurrilous lies to defame the reputation of Brother Imari and other Black freedom fighters, I knew I could not rest until he and the other defendants of the RNA-11 were free.

In addition to our early D.C. unit, I worked very closely with others as the 1970s were coming to a close and the next decade was beginning to try to free the RNA-11 and carry out the mandates of the Republic of New Afrika. These included the Temple of the Black Messiah's Rev. Ishakamusa, and Baba El Zulu, a former SNCC organizer who now headed up Ujamaa Shule, the first independent Black school in Washington, D.C. Brother Thomas Stanley and Brother Bomani Sekou were two great additions to the D.C. unit.

Brother Bomani had recently become my boyfriend and was a member of The People, an organization that had adopted the precepts of the Republic of New Afrika and conducted study sessions on its concepts. Our D.C. cadre worked closely with the Philadelphia RNA unit, the leaders of which were Rev. Ishakamusa's daughter, Sister Daima, along with her husband, Brother Khalid, and their comrades – Brother Kamau Amin, Sister Samira, and others. The Chicago unit was under the leadership of Brother Khaleed London, and we were all adamant about freeing Brother Imari and the RNA-11 from unjust incarceration, and continuing to build the movement for land and sovereignty.

Later, Sister Fulani, daughter of RNA's unfaltering Minister of Defense Baba Alajo Adegbalola, along with her new husband, Bilal Sunni Ali, who once played the saxophone with Gil Scott Heron's Midnight Band, came to live in D.C. They sought to whip some discipline into our Black Cultural Nationalist RNA unit. Although I greatly admired Sister Fulani who, despite being perpetually pregnant, was a serious drillmaster, I must say I was intimidated by her. In D.C. we weren't used to filling out lengthy security forms or training in Malcolm X Park at daybreak. But I was honored that she entrusted her two oldest children to my care who became part of a Saturday School I had earlier founded in 1973.

***

The Temple of the Black Messiah was the long-standing venue for my Saturday School, which started out as a Black Studies class I conducted for children through the organization, True Brothers and Sisters, at the S.E. home of its leader, Brother Colonel Hanif Martin. In September of 1975, I moved the Saturday School to the Shaw PAC building, then housed at 913 P Street, NW. My mentor Sister Anuli Street and her friend Sister Nnoshi, coordinators of NTU Productions, brought added value to the school. I recalled that a workshop they conducted was the first time I had ever experienced a guided meditation, and I fell in love with the practice.

My Saturday School curriculum included history, nutrition, drama, poetry, health education and self-defense, as well as field trips. I originally named the Saturday School, Kuumba Weusi.[35] After I became a part of the Republic of New Afrika, the Saturday School moved to the building of the Temple of the Black Messiah, and I changed its name to the Imari Obadele New Afrikan Shule.

Stalwarts of the Saturday School included Sister Anuli's children Akim, Makini and Kamau; Patrice and Nkenge's children Frelimo and Kianga; Bilal and Fulani's children Aiyisha and T'Chaka (whose blood father is Brother Ahmed Obafemi); and several of the youth living in the neighborhood of 15th and V Streets, N.W. My Saturday School instruction was tight, complete with lesson plans, pledges, songs, poems, games and even home assignments. We served cookies, juice and snacks.

Assisting me with the school on Saturdays was my best friend Tami, Brother Kwasi, Sister Johnetta, Brother Imamu, Baba Oraefo and others. We took the children on field trips to the playground, and they viewed the new exhibit on King Tutankhamen at the Smithsonian. We even took them on a trip to Chicago to participate in the Council for Independent Black Institutions' Annual Science Fair. The parents entrusted their children to my care, and I did not let them down. However, over time, the participation of the neighborhood children began to trail off, despite the fact that they always seemed to enjoy the activities.

I will never forget the day I found out the FBI had visited parents of children in the neighborhood, warning them not to send their children to my school because we would poison them. The gall of this tentacle of the U.S. government. The Saturday School was free, and we were all volunteers trying to bring more value to the lives of our youth. To have been subjected to such treachery was reprehensible. Brother Imari was still in prison. Although we knew that he and the Provisional Government of the Republic of New Afrika were targets of FBI surveillance and illegal tactics, at the time we had no definitive proof of dirty tricks as the government continually denied any wrongdoings.

After the 1977 release of the FBI's first ten pages of COINTELPRO documents on Obadele and the Republic of New Afrika, I had a deeper understanding of the lengths to which the government would go to disrupt and destroy Black nationalist groups and leaders and to, in their own words, "stop the long-range growth of militant black nationalist organizations, especially among the youth." And the attempted destabilization of my Saturday School was a personal, prime example.

Chapter Four, Section 2
Who Were These Henry Brothers?

Unquestionably, Imari Abubakari Obadele had a monumental impact on me, and naturally I dug into his history. I found out he was not just Brother Imari; he was from the influential Henry family of Philadelphia and they were phenomenal. Indeed, I found that one could not really talk about nation-building and the principles, practices and philosophy of the Republic of New Afrika without talking about not just Brother Imari, but the Henry brothers as a whole.

Dr. Imari Abubakari Obadele was born Richard Bullock Henry, the ninth of twelve children born in 1930 to Walter and Vera Henry of Philadelphia. I dare say he was the single most important person responsible for the philosophy, principles and practices of what would become the Provisional Government of the Republic of New Afrika and the New Afrikan Independence Movement.

It frustrates me that we seldom hear anyone talking about or writing about Imari Obadele.[36] Similarly, we all know the name of Angela Davis, but why are most people in this country ignorant about Assata Shakur? How is it that the world knows about former D.C. Mayor Marion Barry, but not former Jackson, Mississippi Mayor Chokwe Lumumba?

Organizations and movements do not materialize within a vacuum: they are shaped and molded by the triumphs and travails of real people. I remember Brother Imari telling me once that when he was growing up during the 1940s, he was reading and studying about the great author J.A. Rogers at his kitchen table. How many of you have even heard of J.A. Rogers' *100 Amazing Facts About the Negro, Africa's Gift to America*, or *The World's Great Men of Color?* And these are just only a few of Rogers' masterpieces.

Brother Imari often said that immersing himself in Black history was an integral part of his upbringing. He would casually speak of one of his brothers, Walter. It would be years before I found out that Dr. Walter Lester Henry was head of the medical department at Howard University Hospital and its chief endocrinologist.

But the relationship between Brother Imari and his older brother, Milton, was most profound. Milton, later to be known as Brother Gaidi, had been a veteran of World War II's elite all-Black Tuskegee Airmen, and one of the leading Black military officers who fought against discrimination and segregation in the military.

He and Brother Imari formed a civil rights group in the early 60s that once even featured W.E.B. DuBois as a speaker. The brothers Gaidi and Imari worked together to form the Group on Advanced Leadership (GOAL), a civil and economic rights group in Detroit. GOAL successfully used consumer boycotts to effect economic justice in the city. Brother Imari became president of GOAL, and because of his leadership, boycotts were successfully used to improve the situation of Black employees. GOAL also encouraged chain stores doing business in Detroit to carry products manufactured by Blacks. Brother Imari once told me that the racist head of a large bank in Detroit was quickly persuaded to hire Black people after he sat down and had a brief conversation with him.

His brother, Gaidi Milton Henry, was an articulate attorney and is credited with possessing one of the sharpest legal minds in the country. A little-known fact to most people is that Gaidi was also a personal confidante of Malcolm X. Through GOAL, Gaidi and Imari brought Malcolm X to Detroit, where Mal-  colm delivered his auspicious speech, *"Message to the Grassroots."* At the speech's end Malcolm said, "Milton Henry and the brothers who are here in Detroit are very progressive young men and I would advise all of you to get with them in any way that you can to try and create some kind of united effort toward common goals, common objectives."

Malcolm was so impressed by Gaidi and Imari that he often said, "If the Henry brothers ever need me, all they have to do is call and I'll hop on a train and be there."

It was Gaidi who accompanied Brother Malcolm to Cairo to attend the second Organization of African Unity conference in the summer of 1964. It was Gaidi who recorded the first of three major Detroit speeches by Malcolm X, all of which were released posthumously as long-playing records: *Message to the Grassroots*, *The Ballot or the Bullet*, and *The Last Message*, delivered at a Black Image Awards ceremony organized by him on February 14, 1965.

If that date rings a bell, it's because Malcolm X's home was firebombed early that same morning. However, Brother Malcolm was so committed to supporting his friend Gaidi that he refused to cancel the speaking engagement, despite suffering from smoke inhalation. Titled *The Last Message*, it was Malcolm X's last public address. Tragically, he was assassinated a week later and Gaidi served as a pallbearer at the great leader's funeral.

Malcolm's *Message to the Grassroots* speech had a huge impact on Brother Imari. He once told me that the "light bulb" in his mind was set on fire in 1966 in a park in Detroit. "I was listening to Yoruba Temple leader Baba Oseijeman Adefunmi talk about how the Harlem People's Congress was formed. He spoke of how he was crowned king. Now that was self-determination," Brother Imari counseled. "You see Sister Nkechi," he wisely continued, "Self-determination means you make it plain that you don't wait for someone else or someone else's law to tell you to be independent. Self-determination, my sister, means you claim it for yourself."

Shortly after this self-determination revelation, Brother Imari formed The Malcolm X Society, a new organization designed to carry on and accelerate the teachings of Malcolm X. Although recorded information about the Malcolm X Society is scant, one document reveals both its boldness as well as the Society's commitment to community uplift and development. During the Detroit rebellion in 1967 on its second day, a telegram was sent to the Detroit Mayor and other city officials, titled, "Regarding the insurrection in Detroit, speaking for Malcolm X Society."[37] The telegram stipulated:

> We will ask for cessation of all hostilities by insurrectionists by seven PM today provided the following eight points are accepted.
> 1. Withdraw all troops
> 2. Release all prisoners
> 3. Give amnesty to all insurrectionists
> 4. Set up district police commissioners
> 5. Agree to urban renewal veto by residents
> 6. Divide city council and school board by districts

7. Provide funds and community owned businesses
8. Institute compensatory and compulsory equal employment enforcement.

'Who are these Negroes who claim they can stop a riot,' I'm sure officials from local police and the FBI fumed. But, of course, they knew. They had been surveilling the activities of the Henry brothers for years, and this new Malcolm X Society formulation no doubt raised speculation in some law enforcement minds about whether the Detroit and other uprisings were spontaneous or, in some fashion, strategically and militarily coordinated. Regardless, the Society was not taken up on its offer and, as such, hostilities did not cease by 7pm.

Coordinated Black military retaliation, however, could have been the manifestation of a "second-strike capability" that Brother Imari was theorizing in his writings—the importance of a secret underground army as a force to make the U.S. stop attacking Black people. Whether the Malcolm X Society was cognizant of such a force and/or had any power or influence over its undertakings, we will never know. But it is safe to assume that, if so, authorities would have felt that the authors of the audacious telegram should not 'have that much power.'[38]

A week before Malcolm's assassination, he and Brother Imari talked at length in his Detroit hotel room, discussing programmatic directions a new movement could take. Although Brother Imari felt Malcolm's death left the movement without a clear path, he realized that Malcolm's teachings had already set out all that should be done. Thus, in October 1966 while on an international flight, Brother Imari penned a manuscript about how to achieve land and power. The Malcolm X Society later revised and published it under the title, *War in America: The Malcolm X Doctrine*.

As a major result of this powerful booklet, the Malcolm X Society organized a Black Government Conference for March 30-31, 1968 in Detroit, MI. The Society utilized three themes from *War in America* to guide the conference: independent land, internationalization, and self-defense. Brother Imari was chosen by the Malcolm X Society to write the final documents to submit to the conference attendees, including proposed procedures, laws, programs, and a declaration of independence from the United States.

The New Afrikan Declaration of Independence excited me. Just as I had earlier memorized the preamble to the U.S. Constitution, I likewise gleefully memorized the RNA Declaration, which begins:

We the Black People in America, in consequence of arriving at a knowledge of ourselves as a people with dignity, long deprived of that knowledge; as a consequence of revolting with every decimal of our collective and individual beings against the oppression that for three hundred years has destroyed and broken and warped the bodies and minds and spirits of our people in America.

I loved this stuff! It moved and grooved me. And I would recite it with fervor and expression, practicing in front of the mirror:

In consequence of our raging desire to be free of this oppression, to destroy this oppression wherever it assaults mankind in the world, and in consequence of our inextinguishable determination to go a different way...

"Inextinguishable determination." Those words spoke volumes to me, and I would especially accentuate the word, "inextinguishable." I continued:

... to build a new and better world, do hereby declare ourselves forever free and independent of the jurisdiction of the United States of America and the obligations which that country's unilateral decision to make our ancestors and ourselves paper-citizens placed on us.

The Declaration went on to assert our claim to reparations and the recognition that our revolution "is against our oppression" as well as the oppression of all those in the world and is a revolution "for a better life" and a "surer harmony with the forces of life in the universe." Each and every word in the Declaration resonated with me, and I would get goosebumps reciting it.

Chapter Four, Section 3
A Black Nation in the South?

Over 500 Black nationalists attended the March 31, 1968 Black Government Conference in Detroit. They adopted this Declaration of Independence for the Black nation in North America and named the nation, the Republic of New Afrika. The Conference approved the basic laws drafted by Brother Imari, and identified five states of the deep South consisting of Louisiana, Mississippi, Alabama, Georgia and South Carolina as its national territory.

The conference organizers explained that all Blacks, descendants of Africans enslaved in the U.S., are citizens of the Republic of New Afrika by birth. This automatic citizenship resulted from being kidnapped from Africa and molded by a common history of oppression into a New Afrikan nation in the world, geographically separated from the continent of Africa, but a new branch of the African family tree on the western side of the Atlantic ocean.

The attendees were told that despite the repression of language, religion and history, the essence of African cultures from different regions of Africa survived, fused into a new culture – a new nation, birthed by experiences in America. Blacks may choose to give up their New Afrikan citizenship, may choose dual RNA/USA citizenship, or may opt for exclusive RNA or USA citizenship. This right of choice is key, it was excitedly explained, and the crux of the right to self-determination.

At no time, however, was a national plebiscite or people's vote held to inform Black people of these options under international law. Therefore, an informed and collective determination could not be made about our political future. Instead, the organizers taught, U.S. citizenship was a unilateral decision thrust upon citizens of the Black nation and, as such, was not legally binding on those who may choose otherwise. What is needed, the organizers surmised, was "land and power, a separate, free, progressive, rich, powerful Black nation, in our time, and on this continent."[39]

This political analysis was markedly distinct and abundantly more ambitious than the predominate nebulous calls for a vague Black nation, and represented the next logical phase to the evolution of Malcolm's thought – identification of a specific land base, buttressed by international law, and protected through self-defense.

Robert Williams, author of *Negroes with Guns*, was praised amongst Black nationalists for promoting armed self-defense in Monroe, North Carolina in 1961. At this 1968 founding conference of the Black Nation, Williams was named as first President, despite the fact that he was in exile in China. Gaidi Obadele was named first Vice President. According to Brother Imari, Sister Betty Shabazz, the wife of Malcolm X, whispered into his ear that she wanted to be a Vice President, and was enthusiastically appointed Second Vice President. Imari Obadele was designated as Minister of Information. Herman Ferguson, an Assistant Principal in New York's Ocean Hill-Brownsville school system,[40] was named Minister of Education. Longstanding reparationist, icon-activist Queen Mother Audley Moore, who had earlier been part of the Garvey Movement, was designated Minister of Health and Welfare. H. Rap Brown was named Minister of Defense; Raymond Willis was Minister of Finance; and Joan Franklin was named Minister of Justice. Amiri Baraka, Maulana Karenga, and Oseijeman Adefunmi were selected as co-ministers of Culture.

The year was 1968, and it appeared that just about everyone in the Black Power, Black cultural or Black political circle wanted to be a part of this dynamic new movement. Queen Mother Moore was the first signer of the Black Nation's Declaration of Independence. To be the first signatory was of great consequence, and rumor has it that she tripped Detroit's Poppa Wells so she could beat him to the punch. General X. Rashid Ali asserts that he was the 99th signer. Unfortunately, I have yet to uncover the original or any copies of this historic document, and none to date have come to my attention from disclosures of FBI files.

Some of the early signers and participants were involved in name only; others never served, and some stayed active until their death. Whatever their level of involvement, the clear message being delivered was that this was the birth of a new era

and a new movement of nationalism, which came to be known as the New Afrikan Independence Movement.

Brother Imari and others flew to Tanzania to meet with Robert Williams, where he was then situated, prophetically, at Dar Es Salaam's New Africa Hotel. Williams accepted the Republic of New Afrika presidency from exile. Brother Attorney Vice President Gaidi Obadele was instrumental in negotiating terms of his return to the United States from exile. However, after travelling from Africa to England, Williams was blocked from proceeding to the United States. Brother Imari described the support built by the new RNA Provisional Government as "militant and substantial."

As Minister of Information he issued a fiery statement that the RNA was insulted and would declare war on Great Britain as the result of the President of the Republic of New Afrika being held incommunicado by Great Britain. A letter was sent to the British chancery detailing the way the war would be waged: the RNA would stop and detain British citizens traveling through the Republic of New Afrika's national territory.[41] RNA citizens would boycott all British products and demonstrate in front of embassies and other locations.

Attorney and RNA Vice President Gaidi traveled to London and met with officials, arguing that they had no legal grounds to keep Williams. I am not sure whether it was Imari Obadele's militant stance, Gaidi Obadele's expert legal maneuvering or some other unknown reason, but Robert Williams was finally allowed to fly back to the United States unimpeded. Black Legionnaires, the military wing of the new Black nation named by Queen Mother Moore in honor of the Garvey Movement's defense arm, assembled at the Detroit airport to meet him.

Brother Imari later recounted to me that although RNA citizens eagerly awaited hearing from Robert Williams, their newly appointed President, they were dis-

appointed when he refused to speak, citing possible harm to his impending court case. An emergency meeting was held in Brooklyn at the home of Sonny Carson,[42] to question him and request his resignation. Williams declined to attend the meeting. Brother Imari told me that this was "the first instance when RNA citizens began losing faith in their new government." It would be nearly a decade before revelations of calculated U.S. governmental sabotage and destabilization against the Republic of New Afrika and its founders would come to light. Whether the Williams' debacle was a part of such sabotage, I cannot say, but the full extent of government disruption against the Black movement has yet to be revealed.

Chapter Four, Section 4
Attack on Aretha Franklin's Daddy's Church

I have always been fascinated with peoples' personal accounts of the first anniversary celebration of the Republic of New Afrika. I was in junior high school at the time and, although aware of the Black Panther Party, was completely oblivious of the founding of the RNA. The anniversary was held on March 31, 1969, in Detroit at the famous church pastored by Aretha Franklin's father, the great Rev. C.L. Franklin.

Brother Ike Ridley, from D.C., was there. He later told me he observed over 200 people in attendance and said that, by the end of the day, many were still milling around the full glass-doored lobby preparing to leave. He described sisters in beautiful flowing African garb, dashiki-wearing brothers "getting their rap on," children running around, and vendors hawking their wares. Some were saying their goodbyes, arranging transportation, or finding out where the after-party would be. General Rashid was there, relating to me the trauma he still feels just speaking about the incident. Faya Rose Sanders, then in law school, and her good friend later to be husband and Alabama State Senator, Hank Sanders, were also there. All were traumatized by what happened.

Brother Imari told me that President Gaidi[43] left the celebration of the RNA's first anniversary early, flanked by four guards, two with rifles. Outside, other Black Legionnaires[44] with rifles lined the side of the church building. I have to keep reminding myself that back then, it was legal to carry loaded rifles in Detroit streets. Also outside was an unarmed Legionnaire, Brother Chaka Clarence Fuller. Brother Imari later characterized him to me as a "man marked for destiny." The popular account of what happened next is as follows.

Police cars pulled up and officers rudely shouted, "Hey, nigger, put down that gun." Other police took aim to shoot. A police officer was shot. However, no one inside the church was aware of the commotion erupting outside. Brother Imari's 13-year-old son, Imari II, walked outside, spotted the armed police phalanx advancing towards the church and immediately dove back through the church doors into the crowd milling about the lobby, shouting, "Everyone get down, now!"

What happened next "was incredulous," Brother Ike Ridley fumed. "We were chased back inside the church," he blurted, "by a hail of bullets fired indiscriminately upon innocent children, women and men. I heard a woman scream. I presume she had been struck by gunfire." Lamenting, Brother Imari recalled that "the huge glass windows of the church caved in, showering the brothers and sisters inside with shards and slivers of glass."

Faya Rose Sanders, now a noted civil rights attorney and founder of the Bridge Crossing Jubilee in Selma recalled, "The police rushed inside the church with their guns blasting. We all plunged to the floor when the shooting started," she described. "Whenever anyone tried to get up, they were shot down. It was not until after the Black cops came in did they stop shooting."

General Rashid divulged to me that General Chui, the head of the Black Legionnaires, quickly ordered the RNA security force personnel to lie on top of the women and children and "try to save as many as they could." General Rashid reminisced that he was personally guarding Queen Mother Moore and Sister Iyaluua, the wife of RNA Minister of Education Herman Ferguson, and made sure they got to the church basement to relative safety. Inside the church neither he nor anyone else knew what had happened outside. He said he did not know that "a cop had got wasted." He described Legionnaires within the church, clutching children and holding them down so they would not be shot. "The best we could do was hold people down," he raged.

The scene was "utter pandemonium," Brother Imari thundered, despite his normally calm manner of speaking. "The intense barrage of bullets forced people to the back of the church." He described brothers and sisters scrambling in terror under the sanctuary's church pews. "But the only safe escape," he explained, "was back towards the front of the church, through a door that led to the basement." However, the shooting got closer and bullets could be heard striking the sanctuary. Taking control of the situation, Brother Imari said he ordered calmly but sternly, "Turn the lights out. This is Imari. Follow my voice. Come this way."

He described people one after another crawling forward, some on their elbows and knees, others on their bellies, through the pews to the glass-shattered front of the church. Upon reaching the front bench, they quickly darted across the exposed aisle to where Brother Imari was, and scurried down the stairway into the basement. Brother Imari later scoffed, "Far from killing us, the New Bethel Baptist Church incident made the RNA an instant international reality."

Miraculously, the 800 rounds fired into Aretha Franklin's father's church by Detroit police killed no one, although several people were seriously wounded.

Interestingly, Brother Imari asserted that one reason no massacre occurred was because of what he described as the "presence of a handful of stony-faced Black officers," similar to what was later described to me by Faya Rose Sanders as "an appeasing force." Brother Imari articulated that the Black officers' demeanor made clear that first, "they did not appreciate a Black church being shot up," and second, "that they would, without extreme additional provocation, turn their guns on their white fellow cops."

Unbelievably, all of the nearly 200 people who had been inside the church were arrested and, because the jail was not large enough to hold them, they were all herded into the basement parking lot of the police station. Women, children and men were forced to stand for nearly 90 minutes with their hands stretched tortuously over their heads.

Rose and Hank described to me a particularly horrendous scene that forever left an indelible mark on them.

"There was a Black woman with a baby," Rose exclaimed breathlessly. "A cop bellowed to her, 'Put your hands up on that wall or we will shoot you.'"

The woman vehemently repeated over and over, continuing to hold her baby, "I'm not gonna do it. I'm not gonna put my baby down!"

Hank, feeling immobilized in the face of possible death, blurted out in fear without thinking, "Put that baby down or we'll all get killed!"

He later lamented that he had never felt more embarrassed or guilty in all his life. "I blamed the strong Black woman, instead of the racist cop," he moaned. "This was the most powerful lesson I have ever learned."

"If it were not for Judge George Crockett, Rev. Franklin and others getting out of their beds to come to the police station," Rose said, "we would have been there all night." Crockett, who later became a Congressman, demanded to the police at the station, "If you have no evidence you must release them." He was successful in first getting all the women and children released, and then the men.

Rose noted that she was one of the last women to be released. "They took everything," she grumbled disgustingly. "Our purses, driver's licenses, money, and we never got anything back." She continued, "They later came to Harvard to question me. I was just a mere 20-year old and they threatened to contact my parents. I was so scared but my mother had already seen a girl in a gold leather coat she knew was mine on the news, so she already knew I had been in Detroit."

Brother Imari would later acknowledge, "Rev. Franklin said he knew we hadn't shot up his church. He knew that the police did it totally and without provocation." He continued his reflection. "The pastor stood in defense of us, even after they put severe pressure on him by attempting to ruin a music benefit he had planned by denying him insurance and trying to plant marijuana in his suitcase."

Days later, the police issued warrants for the arrest of three New Afrikans: Rafael Viera, Brother Chaka Fuller and Alfred 2-X Hibbitt. They were charged with assault to commit murder. But the trumped-up charges didn't stick, and they were each acquitted by a Detroit all-Black jury. Tragically, however, Brother Imari said that some months later Brother Chaka was found in an alley, mysteriously murdered, with his wallet still on his person. His wife revealed that he had been harassed almost daily by the police since the New Bethel attack. Although his murder was never solved, there was never a doubt in Brother Imari's mind that his death was the result of law enforcement revenge.[45]

Chapter Four, Section 5
Free the Land, the RNA-11 and COINTELPRO

A year later, in 1970, Imari Obadele, Chokwe Lumumba[46] and others in the New Afrikan Independence Movement moved the center of the struggle to the South. The following year, in March 1971, a Black farmer entered into an agreement with the RNA for the purchase of land in Hinds County, Mississippi. A Land Celebration Day to consecrate the land as "El Malik," the capitol of the new Black nation was publicized. A member of the Klan, however, appeared on TV that night saying, "The RNA has no business here and they will not have no capital in this state. We will run them out."

The KKK passed out leaflets that taunted, "They'll be no meeting here Sunday niggers."

I listened with awe to Brothers Kwame Afoh and Imari Obadele tell me the story of the 40-to-50 car caravan of Black nationalists on the highway headed to the Land Celebration. They described a highly charged and dangerous scene with the Klan throwing rocks and bricks on one side of the highway, and the FBI and other vigilantes brandishing weapons on the other. Despite the threatening presence of the authorities and vigilantes, there was no outright attack, perhaps, Brother Imari would say, because of the "visible show of Blacks prepared to defend themselves."

The slogan, "FREE THE LAND" rang out everywhere, and it became popularized as the movement's official welcoming greeting.

However, the New Bethel attack and the El Malik Land
Celebration were not the first
nor the last times the RNA
would defend itself against
police violence. I was always
awestruck whenever there
was reference to the pre-dawn
attack on the RNA residence
in Jackson, MS, in the wee
hours of the morning of Au-

gust 18, 1971 that would have ended in the assassination and murders of RNA officials and citizens, had they not been superbly prepared for self-defense.

African priests connected with the Republic of New Afrika had conducted readings
and counseled the RNA against going to the South. Although Brother Imari, a Christian, appreciated traditional West African spirituality, I once overhead him remark
that, with all due respect, he "didn't need shells and bones" to confirm that they
would face violence in Mississippi. The issue, he said, was not whether they would
be confronted by violence, but "whether they would be prepared for defense." And,
as demonstrated on more than one occasion, they were.

For example, if the brothers and sisters who had been attacked by the U.S. government's pre-dawn raid at the RNA's official residence in Mississippi, just blocks

from Jackson State University, had not been prepared for self-defense, they likely
would have been slaughtered.

"Jump!" commanded 15-year-old Karim Njabafudi to the sleeping occupants inside
the RNA house as he went from room to room alerting them with the pre-arranged

warning of a possible attack. Karim was the guard on front porch duty whose vigilance that early morning in spotting the oncoming mass of police force enabled the now woke people to immediately spring into position – some at windows; others descending into a partially completed bunker that was to lead to an empty lot across the street.

The RNA had learned well from police attacks on Black Panther Party members across the country; one of the most tragic being the December 4, 1969 murders of Fred Hampton and Mark Clark while sleep in bed. And, closer to home, Black folk in Mississippi were still numb from the May 14, 1970 killing of two students after police indiscriminately opened fire on Jackson State University.

As such, RNA citizens were tenacious in preparing themselves for defense, so as not to fall victim to police attacks and to be prepared for any eventuality. The tunneling of a bunker underneath the Lewis Street residence was part of that preparation and, in tandem with other preparations, was part of the self-defense formula that ensured their survival during the course of the unprovoked August 18, 1971 pre-dawn attack.

However, if it weren't for Rosa Parks, Brother Imari acknowledged, the RNA-11 may possibly have been murdered in the Hinds County jail, particularly after the police lieutenant died of his wounds. Word had gotten to Congressman John Conyers that one of his Detroit constituents, Imari Obadele, was imprisoned in Jackson. Mrs. Parks, who worked for Representative Conyers in his Detroit office, called down to the Mississippi jail, inquiring about his welfare. Brother Imari always believed that as a result of this high-level attention, he and the other jailed RNA citizens did not meet an untimely demise.

They did, however, as described by RNA-11 defendant and then Vice President Hekima Ana, carry on political education classes behind bars in the jail – the men confined on one side of the jail and the women on the other, with the lessons being taught loud enough to be heard by all.

Among the 37 pre-trial motions filed by the brilliant legal team of RNA defense lawyers (Attorneys William Miller, John Brittain, Ray Willis, Fred Banks, Milton Henry, Lew Meyers and law student Chokwe Lumumba), it was the historic Article III brief that most intrigued me. Brother Imari, who by this time had been elected President of the Republic of New Afrika, had extended coverage of this Constitutional

Article, that dealt with the concept of Sovereign Immunity, to include U.S. jurisdiction over Afrikan-descended people in North America. The motion argued that the RNA, not unlike the indigenous nations in North America, was a nation separate from, though held captive by, the U.S. As such, RNA attorneys argued that U.S. lower courts had no jurisdiction over officials of the RNA government in general, and particularly its president.

This was the epitome of New Afrikan Political Science and the legal motions and briefs passionately laid out the history of the Black nation in North America. The legal documents described the rights of New Afrikan people under international law and stated that as the president or sovereign of the nation, President Obadele could not be tried or imprisoned in a U.S. court. Brother Imari audaciously demanded that U.S. courts recognize his political status of immunity, which was in accord with the Universal Declaration of Human Rights, the United Nations Charter, Article III of the U.S. Constitution, and the 13th Amendment. Brother Imari then concluded that if the courts refused to recognize his status, then the U.S. government must comply with the provisions of the Geneva Convention as they relate to prisoners of war. Not surprisingly, these motions were overruled, denied and avoided by various judges.

It's hard to now believe that all this history – the 1968 founding of the Republic of New Afrika, the 1969 New Bethel attack, the 1970 El Malik land celebration, and the 1971 RNA-11 attack – all transpired a mere three to five years before I walked into that organizing meeting at All Souls Church and responded to Brother Tyehimba's appeal to work with the Republic of New Afrika.

Years later, after we both were decades older, Brother Tyehimba and I mused over our early days with the RNA. We reflected on our seriousness at the rally we organized in front of the Supreme Court the night before Brother Imari was to report back to prison after the failure of his appeals, and the gravity of the discussions we debated about whether the President of the Black Government should go back to prison or go into exile. We commiserated on the sheer craziness of the times that landed some in prison, left others strung out on drugs, and many who lost their very lives – these realities of the struggle for liberation were mind-boggling to us both.

But what was most disturbing to me was the COINTELPRO[47] – whether the FBI could use secret, illegal methods against the Black movement, and whether criminal courts could help them to hide this. I distinctly remember March 30, 1977, as if it were yesterday. It was on that date that then-director of the FBI, Clarence Kelley, addressed Imari Obadele through correspondence.

Dear Mr. Obadele:

Reference is made to my letter dated December 1, 1976, in which you were informed that no indication had been located that you were ever a target of Counterintelligence (COINTELPRO) action. This is to advise that since my referenced letter, 10 pages of COINTELPRO information concerning you have been located. These pages are enclosed at no cost for duplication. We regret the delays encountered in this matter. Your patience and cooperation have been appreciated.

Sincerely yours,

Clarence M. Kelley, Director

Whoa! Kelley's 1977 letter was nice and polite. But the problem was that it was written six years too late, to be exact. It was written six years after eleven Black people in Jackson, Mississippi, went to prison on trumped-up charges. It was written after these brothers and sisters had exhausted their appellate means, and right after the U.S. Supreme Court had declined to review the case.

Consistently during the trials, RNA-11 attorneys had argued and insisted that there was some type of governmental wrongdoing and misconduct in the RNA case, and that the FBI/police attack on the RNA residence was part of a conspiracy to assassinate Imari Obadele and destroy the movement. Under oath during the trials, the FBI insisted and assured the judge that this was not so, and that the defense allegations of governmental wrongdoing were frivolous.

Now, after six years of denial and lies, the FBI finally admitted to conducting a counter-intelligence program against Imari Obadele and the Republic of New Afrika, aimed at destroying the movement. Since 1977, despite the mere 10 pages Kelley said they had finally discovered, the RNA has received thousands of pages of COINTELPRO documents detailing attempts to disrupt, destroy and neutralize the movement. Documents released show a frightful series of dirty tricks, forgeries, damaging anonymous letters and many other violations of human rights by the FBI against Imari Obadele and the Republic of New Afrika.

The Republic of New Afrika was part of the FBI's COINTELPRO directed against the Black Liberation Movement, which they smeared as "Black nationalist hate groups." But let's not get it twisted: it was J. Edgar Hoover and his FBI who hated

Black nationalists and clearly had a vendetta to destroy them. There was a COIN-TELPRO against just about every movement out there, and COINTELPRO spared no cause aimed at resistance.

In the FBI's own words, "the purpose of this new Counterintelligence endeavor [i.e. – against the Black Movement] is to expose, disrupt, misdirect, discredit and otherwise neutralize the activities of black nationalist organizations and groupings and their leadership, spokesmen, membership and supporters."

Never meant to be read or disseminated to the public at large, these millions of pages of documents reveal a coordinated, national program of war against the movement.

An FBI memorandum expanding the program described five goals for COINTELPRO:

1. "To prevent the coalition of militant black nationalist groups." The FBI even appropriated the African proverb, "In Unity there is Strength," asserting it to be "a truism that is no less valid for allits triteness."

Hoover went on to say that an "effective coalition of black nationalist groups might be the first step toward a real Mau Mau in America." At that time the Mau Mau in East Africa were strong as a liberation struggle, and the FBI Director fearfully opined that Black groups unifying could be "the beginnings of a true black revolution."

2. "To prevent the rise of a messiah who could unify and electrify the militant black nationalist movement."

Despite deleted names, the text of the memorandum was unmistakable. "Malcolm X could have been such a messiah, he's the martyr of the movement today. Martin Luther King, Stokely Carmichael and Elijah Muhammad all aspire to this position. Elijah Muhammad is less of a threat because of his age. King could be a very real contender for this position, should he abandon his supposed obedience to white liberal doctrines, nonviolence, and embrace Black nationalism. Carmichael has the necessary charisma to be a real threat in this way."

3. "To prevent violence on the part of black nationalist groups."

In reality, documents reveal that it was actually the FBI who was fomenting the violence they were supposed to be trying to prevent.

4. "Prevent militant black nationalist groups and leaders from gaining

respectability."

The FBI was very analytical, strategic and specific in this regard. The agents were instructed as follows: "You must discredit these groups and individuals to first – the responsible Negro community." The training continued to ensure that Black groups are also discredited to all segments of the White community – "both the responsible white community and to the liberals who have vestiges of sympathy for militant black nationalist groups simply because they are Negroes." The written tirade continued – "Third, these groups are to be discredited in the eyes of the Negro radicals–the followers of the movement." A final goal of this information arm of the U.S. government continued the rant:

5. "To prevent the long-range growth of militant black nationalist organizations, especially amongst the youth." The FBI instructed that "specific" tactics to prevent these groups from converting young people must be developed."

According to the Congressional Committee that investigated the activities of the FBI in the 70s, its Counterintelligence neutralization campaign, code-named COINTELPRO, was determined to be an illegal and unconstitutional abuse of power by the FBI. It wasn't me, Nkechi, voicing this. It was the conclusion of the Senate Select Committee on Intelligence, chaired by Senator Frank Church in the 70s, that characterized the COINTELPRO as "illegal and unconstitutional."

The Congressional Committee report stated that COINTELPRO is the FBI acronym for a series of covert programs directed against domestic groups. Many of these techniques would be intolerable in a democratic society, even if all the targets had been engaged in violent activity. But COINTELPRO, the Senate stated, went far beyond that. "The Bureau conducted a sophisticated vigilante operation aimed squarely at preventing the exercise of First Amendment rights of speech and association, allegedly to protect the national security and deter violence."

So how do we know about all this? The existence of COINTELPRO was discovered in March 1971 as the result of a break-in into the FBI's local office in Media, PA, where secret files were removed and released to the news media. Indignation deepened as Freedom of Information requests and lawsuits abounded, intensified by the public confessions of former agents. There was so much public outrage about governmental wrongdoing that the Senate conducted an investigation which resulted in the production of a comprehensive series of reports. These reports revealed seemingly unending revelations detailing FBI abuses under COINTELPRO.

Millions of pages of documents, despite being heavily censored with lines and even whole pages blacked out, reveal the harrowing nature of the FBI's neutralization campaign. It was the FBI that used the term "neutralization" – a military term used during times of war. They were talking about war against people who were simply trying to exercise their rights and stand up for justice.

And it was a war, waged against groups such as the Southern Christian Leadership Council, the Revolutionary Action Movement, Deacons for Defense, the Black Panther Party, the Student Nonviolent Coordinating Committee, Students for a Democratic Society, the Nation of Islam, the Weather Underground, the Republic of New Afrika, the National Lawyers Guild, the Young Lords, the American Indian Movement, the Socialist Workers Party, the Committee in Support of the People of El Salvador, American Friends Service Committee, and countless other civil liberties, civil rights, religious, peace, labor and social action groups. By the late 60s, the Black Panther Party had become one of the Bureau's primary targets and dubbed "public enemy number one" by President Nixon.

The FBI established networks of agents, spies and provocateurs who infiltrated countless organizations and the Bureau coordinated with other law enforcement agencies at every level of government. Organizations and individuals were subjected to illegal wiretaps, physical surveillance, anonymous or forged letters, burglaries, tampering of bank records, psychological warfare, bogus propaganda publications, evictions, grand jury subpoenas and false arrests. Participants in these organizations were sometimes framed for crimes they did not commit, and in other cases activists were targeted for assassination.

The FBI agents were always encouraged to be "imaginative" in their attempts to disrupt organizations. For example, they planted news articles:

> ...the Bureau approved a Jackson division counterintelligence suggestion regarding [deletion] the publishing of an article about the Republic of New Afrika (RNA), showing the RNA in an unfavorable light and enumerating examples of the RNA's violent nature... He published extensive front page articles showing the RNA in an unfavorable light on 7/30/70, 7/31/70, and 8/4/70. This newspaper has the widest distribution of any paper in Mississippi.

The FBI then analyzed the "tangible results:"

> As a result of the articles which appeared in the 'Jackson Daily News'... showing the RNA in an unfavorable light the RNA conference in Jackson ...was disrupted...and the RNA received considerable bad publicity in Jackson and throughout Mississippi and the conference was generally a

failure as a result.

Other egregious actions by the FBI against the Republic of New Afrika are detailed in excerpts from the following memorandum:

Detroit is authorized to send the letter…concerning the financial status of the Republic of New Afrika (RNA) to RNA officials in other states. Take the usual precautions to ensure this letter cannot be traced…Further, Detroit is authorized to mail the second letter…to prospective members of the Black Panther Party (BPP) in Detroit and certain BPP officials… This letter is addressed "Dear Brother and Sister;" and notes that the letter invites the recipient to consider membership in RNA instead and is on RNA stationary and signed by the RNA Minister of Information…

The first letter regarding the financial status of the RNA was previously mailed to local RNA members as a counter-intelligence measure. It caused considerable disruption in RNA ranks in Detroit. Detroit now recommends, and we concur, a second letter that is designed to create tension between the RNA and the BPP…by making it appear the RNA is attempting to defect potential BPP members and officials. RNA stationary was previously made available and this counterintelligence action will not jeopardize our sources.

We now know that during the 1960s and 70s, activists received a steady flow of anonymous letters and phone calls, ostensibly thought to be from their comrades but which were actually from the FBI. The letters were either unsigned, used bogus names, or as in the case of Brother Imari Obadele, had either forged signatures or signatures from unknown people in phony or actual organizations.

The FBI concocted highly prejudicial stories in the press, forged letters to spouses, friends, cadres and supporters. They utilized tactics to try to inspire violence between La Cosa Nostra and Black numbers runners in Detroit who were thought to be supporting the Black nationalist movement. The FBI sought to provoke the Jewish Defense League into acts of violence against the RNA and interviewed White people in Mississippi sympathetic to the Ku Klux Klan to gauge their willingness to join in any Klan action against the RNA.

The FBI falsified and spread malicious rumors to defame the reputations of President Imari and others. All of these COINTELPRO actions and physical attacks comprised vicious acts of violence against the RNA and those organizing to create an independent nation in the deep South a reality.

As a result of the rampant abridgments of human rights in the case, Amnesty International designated Imari Obadele as a prisoner of conscience, a political prisoner. This was a major recognition, and we used the designation to help boost support for the case of the RNA-11.

Imari Abubakari Obadele was the chief architect and visionary of the philosophy, principles and practices of the New Afrikan Independence Movement, which was led, initially, by the Republic of New Afrika. Many people, including and especially Chokwe Lumumba and Assata Shakur, not only adopted the philosophy, but used their own experiences to expand and conceptualize it.

I attended a rally on November 5, 1979, in front of the United Nations when a statement was read from Assata Shakur who had escaped from prison a mere three days earlier. She declared unequivocally, "Malcolm X had his dream and his dream was land and nationhood, and his dream has become my dream." And at age 24, this was my dream as well.

That rally was where I first met Yuri Kochiyama, a Japanese-American activist who was present at the Audubon Ballroom that fateful day of February 21, 1965, when Brother Malcolm X was assassinated. It was she who administered mouth-to-mouth resuscitation to Brother Malcolm. I felt so honored that Yuri was impressed with the poem about COINTELPRO I had earlier authored and delivered quite forcefully at the rally.

An excerpt:

Cointel's got Blacks in Hell
They open up our mail
Tap our phones and kick our bones
And railroad us to jails

Angela Davis, Rev. Ben Chavis
Brother Imari and Assata Too
Ruchell Magee all want to be free
From You Know Who

FBI went so low
They invented COINTELPRO

To stop the rising fire
Of a Black Messiah who could unify and electrify the masses to revolutionize
Co is for counter, which means to use against
Intel is for, intelligence
Pro is for program, they thought it was the perfect solution
CounterIntelligence Program, to crush the revolution ...

***

Many organizations and individuals did not survive the FBI neutralization program. Some were destroyed, some seriously weakened and many others were destabilized. Countless people were unjustly imprisoned, others were driven underground, and some were outright murdered. The only two FBI officials ever convicted for COIN-TELPRO abuses, Mark Felt[48] and Edward Miller, were pardoned by Ronald Reagan before they even began to serve their sentences.

The Church Committee hearings of the 1970s need to be re-opened. We need hearings today on these unsolved issues from over 40 years ago. Although the Congressional Committee chaired by Senator Church rightfully condemned the FBI's COINTELPRO as illegal and unconstitutional, it failed to establish remedies for those who were victims of COINTELPRO actions. There remain scores of political prisoners still languishing in prison or in exile from that era. Where is their justice?

Chapter Four, Section 6
Love Me Some New Afrikan Political Science

Just as I drank from the spiritual cup of knowledge held by Rev. Ishakamusa Barashango, I also studied at the political feet of Imari Obadele. I heard Brother Imari speak so often for so many years that I sometimes don't know where his words ended and where mine began. My political philosophy fused with his, and I often mimicked, quoted or paraphrased his words, tone and inflection. I learned the history, politics and New Afrikan political science from Brother Imari in his own words, and from his own strong, uncompromising voice.

I learned from him that freedom, independence, and self-determination, all aspects of Black nationalism, have been objectives sought by Black people ever since we were kidnapped and forced to come to this country. He would often teach about the great and mighty Black nations built by our ancestors, some of the better-known being Carthage, known in ancient times as Khart Haddas; Egypt, known as Kemet; and Ethiopia known as Kush, in the East. Brother Imari would talk about how our ancestors built Monomotapa and Angola in the south of the African continent; Ghana, Mali, Songhay in the west of the continent; and on and on and on. He would always conclude with the declaration that "we were quite used to Black nation-building."

And time after time, on these bitter Western shores, Brother Imari would reflect, Black people gave their lives for what was dearest to any oppressed human being: freedom, self-determination and land. "Just what was it that possessed us?" he often mused. "It was none other than the spirit of Black nationalism, the spirit of freedom, the spirit of independence," he would teach.

"It was that same spirit which propelled brothers and sisters like Denmark Vesey, Jean-Jacques Dessalines, Gabriel Prosser, Nat Turner, Fannie Lou Hamer, Queen Mother Moore, Paul Robeson, Sekou Odinga and Assata Shakur to be freedom fighters on the frontlines," he emphasized.

Just listening to my mentor Brother Imari over the years made me eternally grateful for the sacrifices of so many of our people throughout the centuries who possessed the spirit of nation-building, independence, and the spirit of carrying on the tradition of resistance.

Ever since our ancestors were snatched from our homeland of Africa, there have always been people who fought back and fashioned resistance movements to regain freedom and independence. Brother Imari taught that it was military forces nurtured in the hills of Santo Domingo that brought independence to Haiti. One-hundred seventy-five years before that, we revolted and established the legendary Palmares Republic, which lasted over 100 years, located in what is now Alagoas, Brazil, bordering Bahia. Even today, there are more people of African descent in that region than there are in the U.S. This maroon state stood as the greatest challenge to European rule in so-called Latin America.

The Quilombos of Palmares had hundreds of homes, churches, and shops. Its fields were irrigated African-style with streams. It was a structured society that had courts to carry out justice for its thousands of citizens. It was an elected republic of free, united people, living communally and in prosperity. Unlike the colonizer's sole emphasis on sugar cane for export, in Palmares, maize, beans, potatoes and vegetables were also planted. Ownership of land was collective, a tradition Blacks brought from Africa.

Periodically, the people of Palmares ventured from the hills to rescue others who were enslaved, obtain arms, powder, and tools and also to mete out justice to overseers. Despite military expedition after expedition, the Republic of Palmares remained independent and was not destroyed by the Portuguese until nearly a hundred years later.

After a 42-day siege, many of the warriors flung themselves over a cliff rather than surrender to the Portuguese. The ruler, Ganga Zumbi, was captured and beheaded by the enemy. In a case of sheer terrorism, his head was barbarically displayed, "to kill the legend of his immortality," according to the 'civilized' Europeans. For generations, the Republic of Palmares had united many people under an African form of government and culture, and had successfully defended itself from invaders. After each victory, they returned to planting and harvesting abundant crops, and continuing the quest for sovereignty.

It was clear to me that Brother Imari idolized the Palmares model of an independent government and military system, despite it having occurred during the eras of enslavement and colonialism. He emphasized that in the U.S., free communities set up by escaped Africans in Florida, Georgia, and elsewhere in territory claimed by the United States, were also continuously sought out for destruction.

He stated, "every time we ran away, it didn't matter whether we went away quietly in the night like Harriet Tubman. It didn't matter if we organized elaborate insurrections like Denmark Vesey. It didn't matter if we fled to Pennsylvania or New York – they always came after us, with their armed forces, paddy rollers, militia, and dogs."

"Why didn't it matter?" Brother Imari would stridently quiz.

"Because the White folk had decided they were going to live here!" he thundered in response to his own query. "Wasn't gonna be no 100 years of Palmares liberation."

The Europeans vowed that they would not just let us walk off into the woods and swamps and develop our own communities. They refused to go back to France or England or Spain because it got too hot. This was not going to be their vacation spot. They came, and they planned to stay. Free labor was integral to their plan. So they chased us and pursued us, tracked us down and beat us, and castrated and lynched us. They sought to quell all forms of resistance and Black nation-building.

"Sister Nkechi," Brother Imari would stress, always pronouncing my name as 'N-Ket-Chi, similar to how it is pronounced in Nigeria. "You must internalize the history of Black resistance to enslavement. Study the case of *U.S. v. Libellants and*

Claimants of the Schooner Amistad," he advised, "where international law was applied in a U.S. court and served as a springboard to release kidnapped Africans from enslavement."

"You should know about Peter Poyas, Gullah Jack and Denmark Vesey who, in 1822 masterminded a scientifically elaborate plan to seize the state of South Carolina. That's part of the RNA national territory today, my Sister. It took discipline and organization to mobilize over 9,000 enslaved people, and we must have discipline and organization today," he counseled.

"How many countless Gullah Jacks were out there that did not make the history books?" Brother Imari would ponder. "We must never forget about Nat Turner in 1831 seeking control over Virginia. We must know about David Walker who called for mass rebellion in his fiery pamphlet, *Appeal to the Coloured Citizens of the World.* What are the countless names we do not have?" he wondered out loud. "What are the deeds we do not know?" he pondered as his voice trailed off to a whisper.

It was always Brother Imari's position that to the African people who were forced to come to this land, Black Nationalism was not viewed lightly. It was the dream of many. Self-determination was what most Blacks wanted.

"Well," Brother Imari often queried facetiously in his speeches, "Why not just join this new White nation that was coming up on these shores?"

"We did not come here voluntarily," was his answer. "We came as the result of war. And without question all of the available evidence bore a crystal clear message for the enslaved African on this land, that White folk did not intend for Black people to be citizens of the White nation they were founding."

"The country's first politicians all owned slaves – Thomas Jefferson, George Washington, Patrick Henry. We forget far too easily. We must remember the origins of the Black nation in North America," Brother Imari taught. "We are the descendants of Africans illegally kidnapped and transported to the U.S., with the explicit complicity of the U.S. government and every arm of the U.S. lawmaking and law enforcing machinery. This included U.S. federal law, state law, high court decisions, lower court decisions. Our enslavement in the 13 colonies and the U.S. was a matter of war – war conducted against Africa under the authority of the U.S. Constitution."

"Let us start with Article One, Section Nine," Brother Imari would preach. "This Article expressly guaranteed and sanctioned the continued importation of kidnapped African prisoners of war to every state that might desire enslaved people until the year 1808. We need to remember that the U.S. upheld in its Constitution in Article One, Section Two, Clause Three the further dehumanization of the African prisoner of war by relegating their status to that of 3/5 of a White man. This clause was not an admission that the enslaved possessed a percentage of humanity, but simply to allow slave states to profit even further from our presence through increased representation in Congress."

"It was war conducted against the African nation in America under the authority of yet another constitutional provision – Article Four, Section Two, Clause Three, known as the fugitive slave provision. This Clause mandated that no African, even if he or she had reached a free state, was safe. And it was the duty, the legal obligation, and the constitutional responsibility, of every White person to track down runaway people and deliver them up to the government."

I finally understood why Harriet Tubman could not just stop at Pennsylvania or New York. The "free" states were no longer safe. She had to continue bringing escaped people all the way outside of the country – to Canada.

The 13th amendment to the U.S. Constitution was passed in 1865, recognizing the freedom of all Blacks. Notice I do not say the 13th amendment "freed" enslaved Africans. I learned well at the feet of Brother Imari. As human beings, we were already free. That status, however, was not recognized by the United States. Moreover, and quite tellingly, it is important to note that the Amendment passed in 1865 is quite succinct. It states that neither slavery nor involuntary servitude shall exist in the United States.

Although the next clause exempts people from freedom "who have been punished for a crime," the 13th amendment contains no statement of citizenship, Brother Imari often stressed. In fact, the Dred Scott case, *Scott v. Sanford*, had been decided scarcely eight years prior. A Supreme Court Justice ruled in that case that Blacks in America "had no rights which a white man was bound to respect," and that neither Dred Scott nor any other Black person could be a citizen of the U.S. in the manner in which that word is used in the Constitution.

Brother Imari stressed that Justice Taney's ruling strongly implied that any law which attempted to make Black people citizens of America at any time, would be unconstitutional, simply because it was against the intentions of the White founding fathers who wrote the Constitution. You see, we must be clear, I was counseled by Brother Imari, "that when they wrote, 'We the People,' they meant, we the white people."

Brother Imari taught me that because the formerly enslaved were now a free people, the Black nation was possessed of rights, irrespective of action taken or inaction by the United States. The newly freed persons began to ask questions. How do we wish to govern ourselves? Should we leave or stay here? What did this right to self-determination entail?

Brother Imari analyzed that this right to self-determination would extend to the right to return home to Africa, since we had been in America as the result of a vicious kidnapping, unmatched in human history. He taught that the right to self-determination would extend to the right to general emigration, as our families had been cruelly fragmented and spread across the diaspora. The right to self-determination would also extend to the right to seek admission as citizens to the American community and strive to make a multi-racial democracy real.

He concluded forcefully, "and the right to self-determination would extend to the right to establish an independent separate territory of our own." This was justifiable because we had been illegally denied the rights and privileges afforded those in the American community. The Black Nation had legally been constructed outside of the American community, and as a consequence, we found ourselves in great numbers, enforced illiteracy, and severed homeland ties on soil claimed by the U.S.

When I first heard this analysis, it made me think about the original Native inhabitants of this country. Again, the brilliant Brother Imari, from the RNA Kush District also known as Jackson, Mississippi, laid it out and answered that question in my mind in 1975 with his penned response, "Let No Man Question Us."

> We apply to ourselves – and believe it also logical, humane, and legally correct, for the world to apply to us – the same standards that permit the Cubans, who are descendants of Indians, Africans, and Spaniards, to claim the land they claim; Jamaicans to claim the land they claim, and Haitians, Trinidadians, Guyanese and Mexicans to claim the land they each claim. All of us and each of us are migrant peoples who came into possession of the land as the majority and traditional populations in the wake of a campaign of genocide waged by Europeans – English, French, Dutch, and Spanish – against the original and rightful possessors: the Amerindians. We, the New Afrikans, gladly acknowledge the fundamental rights of the Indian in the land. But, if no one questions the claims of the Cubans or the Jamaicans or the Mexicans, let no man question ours.

Brother Imari explained that for almost three years after the 13th amendment, the newly freed people were deciding their destiny. In 1868, however, the U.S. government essentially insisted that we had no right to self-determination. It attempted to nullify our nationalistic options by unilaterally declaring us citizens of their nation. The audacity, I thought. How could you take a "free" person and tell him he's got to become a part of your family? You didn't ask him if he wanted to join your family. It didn't matter if she wanted to start her own family. If the African were free, and there has been no debate as to the authenticity of the 13th amendment other than the outrageous prison slavery clause, no one, not even the ex-slaveholder, could define a future status for the freed people and impose a status upon them. I learned from Brother Imari that this right belonged to the formerly enslaved, and it was the African's alone. It was the fruit of the right to self-determination.

Brother Imari and the Republic of New Afrika taught me that international law prohibits Portugal from going to Angola and telling the Angolan people that they are Portuguese citizens. That same law prohibits France from making the Algerian people French citizens. Yet that is exactly what we have accepted from the U.S. government, without debate. They said the 14th amendment made us citizens, and we accepted that message, lock, stock and barrel – despite our rights under international law, and despite the repressive actions of the U.S. government and its White citizenry.

Brother Imari stressed, "It is not too strong to say that all this was and is, war," though not being declared with the usual solemnities. Despite this war by the stronger nation against the weaker, "Black nationalism," he declared, "survived and persisted to the present day."

"The problem," Brother Imari often stated, "is that White nationalism and fraud has left many otherwise fine African minds among us functionally unable to think of independence and land as a viable option for nationhood." He continued. "Some of us, however, feel that freedom cannot be amorphous and misty. It must be, as Brother Malcolm once stated, for land and sovereignty." Brother Imari further taught me that unless the struggle is for land and independence, "it is a domestic matter between citizens of a nation who are treated right and those who are treated wrong, and it is to be settled as a domestic matter between them." Unfortunately, we have suffered the tragic results of the lack of such a settlement process for over 100 years.

The wise sage continued. "For years our people talked about, asked, or begged for land…anywhere. That's what Edwin McCabe said in the 1880s. He wanted Oklahoma and said, 'Black folk, let's go and make this a Black state where we can take our families and live in peace.'"

"Pap Singleton and Henry Adams took over 40,000 Black people and went up into

Kansas. During Reconstruction, the twin demands of Black people everywhere were what? Land and education. And after that, our brothers and sisters insisted, 'Give us land...anywhere. You name it.'"

"It was on the back of the *Muhammad Speaks* newspaper year after year after year. 'Give us land. Anywhere.' Malcolm X preached it. He staunchly believed that land was the basis of freedom and independence. The Black Panther Party paper demanded, 'give us land, bread, housing, clothing, education, justice and peace.'"

And so the founders of the Provisional Government of the Republic of New Afrika followed in 1968 and defiantly proclaimed, "Yes, we are entitled to land and independence." With chilling conviction they declared, "Since you won't name it, we will. We envision a Black nation that spans the states of Mississippi, Louisiana, Alabama, Georgia, and South Carolina. Furthermore, we're gonna write a declaration of independence for the nation and create a government and an army!"

And that's when all hell broke loose.

"You see," Brother Imari explained, "They didn't care if we flew the red, black and green flag and sang freedom songs. They didn't care if we marched and demonstrated. They really didn't care if we called them honkies and pigs and devils. As long as we didn't talk about creating the answer to Marcus Garvey's probing questions during the 1920s. 'Where is the Black man's government? Where is his king and kingdom, his President, his army, his navy, his men of big affairs?'"

"There was no problem as long as we didn't talk about creating a government to lead the Black nation," my mentor explained. "No problem as long as we didn't talk about an army to defend our government. No problem as long as we didn't talk about reparations to restore some of the African cultural identity that they systematically sought to destroy."

Brother Imari continued, "They didn't care if we went back to Africa, as long as we did not mind jumping into the ocean and swimming there, naked. There was no problem as long as we didn't attempt to internationalize our struggle."

This was some sho-nuff New Afrikan political science for the New Afrikan Independence Movement. I could and I did, rock it!

Brother Imari stressed that we were always a nation, but the formation of the Republic of New Afrika was the first time we sought to create a state structure since the U.S. put down our attempts at self-government during the Civil War. Most people thought that the idea of a state structure was ludicrous because for a long time Black nationalists had only talked about nationhood. "However, a nation and a state," Brother Imari clarified, "are almost the same thing except for two major differences." First and foremost, he taught, "A nation evolves historically." He added, "Queen Mother Moore didn't make us a nation, and neither did the Honorable Elijah Muhammad, or Brother Malcolm X."

He continued teaching:

> We know we came from Africa, but from which nation in Africa? Were our ancestors from the Kingdom of the Congo, or were they from Ashanti, Dahomey, Angola, Mozambique, or Ghana? We didn't just come from one particular nation in Africa, but from many different nations. Once we got here, the Europeans made sure that we were separated in order to subjugate us. We were forced to intermingle, so we forgot the languages unique to our particular region. We were forced to speak English in order to communicate with our captors, as well as with each other. The use of the drum as a major form of communication was denied us. Our captors raped our women and they declared that all the children of those sexual assaults were Black.

"As some of our ancestors ran away and sought to escape enslavement, they were aided and abetted by Native peoples who knew the lay of the land. Further racial intermingling took place and many Blacks can trace their ancestry to a Cherokee grandfather or a Seminole grandmother. So for over 200 years," Brother Imari continued expounding, "we developed as a people and as a nation. A New Afrikan nation. We originated in Africa, but now we have formed a new branch of the Afrikan family, with genes fused from several races, on this side of the Atlantic Ocean."

Brother Imari's teachings were nonstop, and I gobbled them all up eagerly as he continued uninterrupted. "We didn't start this Black nation, Sister Nkechi, and we're all in it because of our common history and culture. It's not a club and you can't put me out of it because I shoot dope or snort cocaine or because I set up the Mayor. I'm born into it. You can't push me out because I follow the god of Shango. You can't keep me out because I'm short. You couldn't keep me out if I were tall. Because I'm born into it."

"But what about a state, Brother Imari," I quizzically probed. "You said there was a difference. What is it?"

"First," he responded, "A nation can exist even where there's not a state. A nation can exist without a government. A nation has all those other things – it's got people with a common culture. It's got land and if they don't occupy that particular land or don't control it, then you've got a liberation struggle on your hands. You've got to get control of it."

"So the elements include people and land," I slowly parroted. "And you may not have a government or you could have a government but it may be a subjugated government, like the Navajo," I excitedly babbled. "Let's see," I continued, grasping the concept. "The Navajo occupy some land but their government is a subjugated government authorized by U.S. colonial law. Regardless, it's still a government."

"That's correct, Sister Nkechi," the revolutionary mastermind marveled. "And the second most important difference," he illustrated, "between a nation and a state is that a nation evolves historically. So let's say me, you, Dick Gregory, Queen Mother Moore, and all of us in this room decide to get together. We might decide to take over some uninhabited island and draft a constitution. Then we declare that this is our law, and this is how we're going to govern ourselves. We might even include some Latinos and some of those radical White folk. Well, what we have created is a state, but we're not a nation. Due to the fact that we can't just 'make' a nation. It has to evolve, historically."

I cannot put into words the profound impact the teachings of President Imari Abu-bakari Obadele and the doctrines of New Afrikan Political Science have had on me. These teachings, although preceding my law school years, greatly informed my legal studies. I was blessed to later enter law school with a politico/legal consciousness unparalleled to that of my law school classmate peers. I had already been introduced to criminal law, civil procedure, international law and the practice of law in the public interest before ever setting foot in a law school classroom. It can never be overstated the influence of Obadele's wisdom upon me, and it is my hope that one day he and his philosophies will be elevated to their rightful place in the annals of history.

I would be remiss, however, if I left you with the impression that this was a perfect man. Far from it. I would soon find out that my revolutionary nationalist mentor, whom I respected and admired immensely, was not as forthcoming as he should have been about problems in the Movement.

Chapter Four, Section 7
Manipulators and Liquidationists?

There were two major constitutional crises that afflicted the Republic of New

Afrika's Provisional Government (PG), neither of which I was aware of when I joined. They involved what direction the PG would take, and Brother Imari was at the center of both.

The first calamity was a major disagreement and falling out between the two blood brothers, Imari and Gaidi, in 1969 precipitated by the state violence of the New Bethel attack on the first anniversary of the founding the RNA. Brother Gaidi favored a political organizing approach in the North as the safest and most viable way to achieve their aims. Brother Imari advocated moving the center of the struggle to the South, beginning the necessary building of "New Communities."

There was, however, an overarching legal issue – the terms of the officers elected in the 1968 RNA founding Convention had expired, and a constitution had yet to be adopted to establish guidelines for succession. As a temporary solution, Gaidi advocated holding open elections of new officers in Convention; Brother Imari, however, favored a popularly based approach with regionally based elections.

A special tribunal organized for the issue ruled that an election in convention could only occur if 40% of the electorate was represented. Gaidi disagreed with the decision and he, along with others including Queen Mother Moore, resigned, thereby handing Imari, by default, control over the direction of the government. Elections were held with Brother Imari chosen as President. A new PG-RNA cabinet was installed with Hekima Ana as Midwest Region Vice President, Dara Abubakari as Southern Region Vice President, and Alajo Adegbalola as Eastern Region Vice President. And, as desired by Brother Imari, the center of the struggle was re-located from the North to the deep South.

I knew nothing of this 1st Constitutional Crisis when I first entered All Souls Church in 1974, after seeing the advertisement for a planning meeting for the RNA's first National Black Elections. Incredibly, it would be several years working with the RNA before I even heard anything about that conflict, despite the fact that a very similar 2nd Crisis involving the RNA Constitution was already looming when I arrived on the scene.

Barely a year after the RNA's move to Jackson, MS, as accounted earlier, eleven RNA workers including its now President, Brother Imari, were arrested and imprisoned on bogus murder and conspiracy charges, as well as "waging war against the state of Mississippi," a scurrilous charge later dropped. But the fact that the RNA President was incarcerated lay at the root of the 2nd Constitutional Crisis that threatened the nascent Provisional Government.

Did the RNA's Constitution, the Code of Umoja, equate incarceration with incapacitation and, if not, could the president of the Black Nation carry out his duties behind enemy walls? That was the technical basis for the Crisis. Underlying it, however, was continued buzz and heated debate as to whether the establishment of the Provisional Government itself was premature; this time led by Brother Chokwe Lumumba.

It was during this time that I became a "conscious citizen"[49] of the Republic of New Afrika and mailed my innocent letter to the imprisoned President Imari if there was anything I could do to help him. I knew nothing of Gaidi, or Chokwe, Dara, or Alajo. I had never heard of Queen Mother Moore. After receiving his long list of directives, all I knew was that the President of the Black Nation needed help from me, and our committed group in D.C. sought to provide that. Before long, however, the seeds of the ideological conflict percolated and grew.

Our Brother President's seeming vehemence towards leaders such as Brother Chokwe and others who had differences of opinion surprised me. Brother Imari labeled them "liquidationists," because, in his words, they were trying to "launch a coup to destroy the popularly elected government."

Brother Imari, on the other hand, was characterized by Brother Chokwe and other critics as "manipulative" and "dictatorial," and probably other adjectives I was not privy to. This was an unfortunate low point in the Movement.

And, he was in prison. Although the Code of Umoja addressed the issue of incapacity, it was silent as to whether imprisonment constituted incapacity.[50] Regardless of the advisability of one running a government behind bars, President Imari definitely was not incapacitated in terms of work product, communicating instructions, and being knowledgeable about news and events. There were, however, very legitimate and practical concerns about the lack of confidentiality in a prison setting.

 I recall hearing Brother Chokwe Lumumba speak at a gathering around the late 1970s. I was captivated by his fiery presentation. "We aren't talking about a mere question of police brutality," he admonished. "We're not talking about a question of civil rights," he stressed. "We're talking about a question of war. You may not be at war, but you're certainly in war!" he argued.

Lumumba movingly addressed other issues as well, including Africa, Native peoples, land and the underground. He opined, "Yes, we need obviously a strong and unified Africa. But most of all, we need some land and some independence. We need a plan to get the land. When the Native American tells you they have a problem, then there's time for dialogue. Seminoles, Choctaw, Cherokee – there flows much blood between us," he emphasized.

"You see, when we struggle for land," Brother Chokwe declared, "it intensifies the Native American's struggle for land, and the Chicanos. You cannot separate the blood of our ancestors from that land. We can best help Africa in a revolutionary struggle if we have a revolutionary struggle. There're different ways of talking to the world," he explained. "You can talk from a platform, or you can talk like the BLA.[51] It has a different voice."

He charged on. "We need a plebiscite and we need a military campaign because even if we don't fight, we die. And people need to know the difference between a crook and a freedom fighter because if we leave it to CBS, we'll never know!"

I happened to be sitting near the back of the audience, next to Brother Atiim. I leaned over to him, remarking softly, "Wow, Chokwe's presentation was simply excellent. I didn't disagree with anything he said!"

Atiim whispered back, "I didn't either."

"So what the hell is the problem?" I exasperatingly fumed, alluding to the split between Brothers Imari and Chokwe.

"That is the question!" Atiim replied.

Me: "So what's the answer?"

Him: "The solution is us – some of the younger element within our divided family will have to forge our desired unity; we have to become more active and outspoken, given the reality that we really don't disagree."

I never forgot Atiim's words and, from then on, while still remaining loyal to Brother Imari, I sought to forge my own relationships and seek unity whenever and wherever I could.

There were now two Provisional Governments operating, each claiming to be legitimate, sanctioned by the Code of Umoja. Brother Imari was the President of one wing of the split, and Dara Abubakari, a former Vice President and close associate of Queen Mother Moore, was President of the other side.

A three-judge tribunal was subsequently convened to resolve the constitutional issue. The Code of Umoja was interpreted to equate imprisonment with incapacity. No one is perfect. Even geniuses have flaws. This is when it really became clear to me that one way or another Brother Imari was going to have his way. He resurrected the long defunct Malcolm X Society, renamed it the Malcolm X Party, and used it as the vehicle to hold the constitutionally mandated 1978 and 1980 National Black Elections. Rev. Ishakamusa Barashango was appointed Chairman, Baba El Senzengakulu Zulu was Secretary, and I was always the "mover and shaker" to make things happen and get things done.

The National Black Elections for the officers of the Black Nation was conducted by the Central Committee of the Malcolm X Party in 1978 and Imari Abubakari Obadele was elected President by nearly 1,000 votes through the direct popular elections process as provided for in the Code of Umoja. In all honesty, there were questions in my mind as to the wisdom of our street corner elections where people were ignorant as to officers and judges they were electing and their qualifications for the office. But I admired Brother Imari immensely and respected his position.

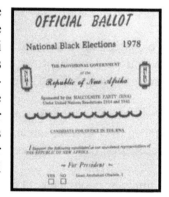

So, who was the real government? The answer depended on who you asked and whom they were aligned with. This is the reason why today's internet searches on officers of the RNA are sometimes either vague or inconsistent. It's not so much a matter of intentional revisionist history, but more so an accurate accounting based on which faction of the government one held allegiance to.

At one point, I was chairperson of the People's Center Council while at the same time another person professed to hold that position. And the same was true with other PG officials. There was drama galore that could have succumbed to COINTELPRO machinations, but composure was kept and we all engaged in operational unity.

After much discussion, debate and endless meetings over the course of several years, a reconciliation government was established in 1984, reuniting leaders of the struggle for independence and land in North America into a single, Provisional Government. The unity government operated with a co-presidency in the persons of Brother Imari Obadele and Sister Dara Abubakari.

"We need unity," urged co-President Dara Abubakari, who resided in New Orleans, LA. "We need principled unity first, between Black individuals and organizations inside the Nationalist Movement, and also with Black people who have never heard of or thought about us having our own independent nation. This is the only way we're going to get our freedom!" she declared.

Co-President Imari Obadele agreed and pronounced, "This is an historic occasion. It is rare that Black groups who go through times of internal and external upheaval can come together in unity and still forge ahead! We are the first to do this and there are major plans in progress for the future."

I would later write in *The New Afrikan* newsletter, "This momentous agreement marked not only a triumph for the New Afrikan Independence Movement, but a decisive defeat for the U.S. government which had tried for 15 years to destroy the Independence Movement."

The dispute had pinpointed the issue of elections and whether the concept of a government to lead the life of the Black Nation was premature. Ironically, however, and still an amazing story to be told, four decades later Brother Chokwe Lumumba himself would use the same route of popular elections to first win a City Council seat and then, later, become mayor of a city within one of the five states of the subjugated national territory of the Republic of New Afrika.[52]

It would be dishonest to imply that everything was perfect after the establishment of the Unity Government. As expressed by African anti-colonialist leader, Amilcar Cabral, "Tell no lies, claim no easy victories." And the Unity Government surely was no easy victory for either side. Emotions were still somewhat tepid, but there was a mutual feeling that we would take the high ground, agree to disagree, and move forward.

Brother Chokwe and others put their energy into forming the New Afrikan People's Organization as an additional vehicle in the New Afrikan Independence Movement to mobilize the grassroots. The Provisional Government under the presidency of Brother Imari was solidified and elections every three years continued to be held.

Through it all, Assata Shakur was liberated,[53] the Brinks trial[54] began, the MOVE compound was bombed,[55] an Independent Black Foreign Policy[56] was developed, and the National Coalition of Blacks for Reparations in America (N'COBRA)[57] was birthed. But perhaps most indicative of principled unity in the early days after the split occurred in the wake of the arrest of Sister Fulani Sunni Ali. Fulani, who worked closely with Brother Chokwe, had been elected RNA Minister of Health and was living in New Orleans at the time. Ostensibly as the result of a witness claiming to have seen her cleaning out a safe house in New York the day a Brinks armored truck was commandeered, she, along with her father, another sister and 11 children also in the house, were arrested.

Sister Fulani was vociferous. "I am not a terrorist. Instead it is I who has been terrorized by the FBI. Two hundred FBI agents, local police armed with automatic weapons, tanks and air force helicopters, harassed and tried to intimidate not only myself but my children as well."

She raged on. "They wanted to terrorize me, break my spirit, unnerve me... But I am innocent. From the beginning I knew I had an airtight alibi."

And she did. Concrete evidence forced the U.S. Attorney to withdraw the complaint against her.

I was pleased when Brother Imari agreed to provide testimony in support of Sister Fulani, on the distinction between the Provisional Government of the Republic of New Afrika as an 'overground' government, and the Black Liberation Army as part of the underground. He testified to the fact that Fulani, as Minister of Health, was part of the government, functioning overground.[58]

Chapter Four, Section 8
Carry on the Tradition of Resistance

I was in my early 20's when I started writing to political prisoner/prisoner of war Sundiata Acoli in prison; but it was during law school in my late 20's that I first visited him at Marion Penitentiary. That was nearly four decades ago. As of 2019, he has yet to be released. Sundiata is the co-defendant of Assata Shakur, and his name deserves to be lifted up and celebrated whenever her name is. Sundiata is incredible and a steadfast, unfaltering human being. He is a gifted writer, penning a comprehensive summary and historical analysis of the New Afrikan prison struggle of the 70s and 80s. His book, *Sun Views*, should be required reading in college classes.

So what keeps him behind bars? Pure vindictiveness. One of the many letters I have written in support of his parole, follows:

January 29, 2010
Chairwoman Volette C. Ross
New Jersey State Parole Board

Re: Letter in Support of 2010 Parole for
Sundiata Acoli (NJ#54859/Fed#39794-066)

Dear Chairwoman Ross:

Mr. Sundiata Acoli, NJ #54859/Fed#39794-066) has been imprisoned since 1973. He turned 73 years old in January. Incarceration for thirty-six years is long enough. Mr. Acoli becomes eligible for parole, again, this February, after having twice receiving two-digit parole setbacks. His request for parole must be granted this time.

Although there are numerous reasons why Mr. Acoli should be released, I will emphasize three. First, he is an elder. At 73 years old, he has served enough time. There is no danger to the community should he be released. Studies show that the recidivism rate for elderly prisoners is minimal and the chances that they will commit a violent crime upon release are extremely low. Moreover, the older prisoners become, the more costly it is to the state or federal government to support the intensive medical care of an increasingly geriatric population.

Second, Mr. Acoli has an impeccable institutional record with no violations or write-ups in decades. He is an extremely talented artist, writer, and educator. He has worked with high school and college classes across the country, providing information and insight, as well as providing support to other prisoners who seek to further their education. Mr. Acoli himself has a very impressive educational and work background. During the 1960s he worked at NASA in Texas as a computer programmer. He once told me that he used to help former astronaut Neil Armstrong with his mathematics homework. Mr. Acoli left his promising career at NASA to travel to the South to help register Black people to vote during the Civil Rights era. During his activism with organizations he contributed to community, educational, health, and legal programs.

Third, Mr. Acoli is a father and a grandfather. His greatest desire is for the opportunity to watch his grandchildren grow up.

Please do not deny him the opportunity this time. I personally met Mr. Acoli in the early 80's when he was incarcerated at Marion Penitentiary. I met a kind, considerate, and caring individual. I met a man who had been part of a turblent era, an era fraught with issues, many of which remain unresolved today. Several decades have passed since that time. I have a fulfilling career, am married, am raising a daughter, and am caring for my elderly mother. Mr.

Acoli likewise has a loving family. Justice is not served by the continued denial to him, after over a quarter of a century, of the opportunity to spend his remaining years with family. Compassion dictates that Sundiata Acoli's request for parole be granted.

Sincerely, Nkechi Taifa, Esq.

***

Are there political prisoners in the United States? Some say the answer depends on whom you ask, and how you define the term. The official position of the United States government has been that there are no political prisoners in U.S. prisons. However, former U.S. Ambassador to the United Nations, Andrew Young, at one point stated that there were hundreds, perhaps thousands, of political prisoners in the

United States. Not surprisingly, he was almost immediately removed from office.

"Freedom Now," the National Campaign for Amnesty and Human Rights for Political Prisoners, lists 132 political prisoners. The book, *Can't Jail the Spirit*, lists 67 political prisoners. During the 1980s I helped to form a group, the New African Network for Political Prisoners and Prisoners of War (NANPPOW). We in this group, spearheaded by Dr. Nubia Kai, Attorney Jacque Reardon and Brother Imani Mahdi, created a definition of a political prisoner in the context of Black people in the U.S.

From our vantage point, we described a political prisoner as "one who is imprisoned, either awaiting trial, serving a sentence, or in any other status, who is incarcerated by reason of ideas, beliefs, associations, and/or actions that are contrary to the domestic and/or foreign laws and policies of the U.S. in pursuit of these goals and that contribute to the repression, impoverishment and suffering of oppressed people."

Our political prisoner definition included those initially imprisoned for "social crimes," who have become politicized and transformed themselves inside of prison to the cause of social justice, such as George Jackson,[59] the author of the acclaimed books, *Soledad Brother* and *Blood in My Eye*.

We continued our description of what a political prisoner is. "They have protested and or resisted while incarcerated. As a result, like George, they have received extended prison terms, been denied release and/or were targeted for repression." We acknowledged that there are also prisoners who engage in right wing political activity and actions. "However, since the right wing is fighting to establish and maintain the system of White supremacy, we do not consider them to be political prisoners, at least not our political prisoners."

NAN-PPOW stressed that Prisoners of War (POWs) are a form of political prisoner. These people are members of oppressed nations who have been captured and imprisoned by forces of another nation in the course of warfare, declared or undeclared. POWs usually take the position, consistent with international law, that U.S. courts have no jurisdiction over them, and therefore they may and often do refuse to participate in legal proceedings, including their own trials.

There is a great deal of documented international law to support this position, including the Geneva Convention Protocols One and Two, and Resolutions 1514 and 3303 of the UN General Assembly, which state that colonialism is a crime against humanity and those captured fighting against it are prisoners of war.

Indeed, over the past several decades scores of New Afrikan prisoners have applied to U.S. District Courts for recognition as prisoners of war and enforcement of that status – which includes the right to exchange to another country and the right not to be held in penitentiaries. These applications have been blatantly opposed, despite arguments that the U.S. is a party to the Geneva Convention. Article V of the Convention requires governments to accord POW status to prisoners who have requested it until a competent tribunal determines whether the applicant meets the criteria.

It is critical to recognize that identification of a person as a political prisoner, or prisoner of war, doesn't necessarily imply agreement with the acts, tactics, associations or specific ideology of the person. It does imply a commitment to the struggle for their human rights and recognition of their commitment to the struggle for justice for oppressed people.

One of my countless speaking engagements over the years occurred in 1990 before a group called the Student Committee Against Racism (SCAR). I spoke to the integrated gathering about what appeared to be the imminent release of Nelson Mandela, who had been illegally imprisoned by the South African government since 1962. I shared with the audience that Mandela's imprisonment was not isolated – that he was part of a resistance movement and his arrest, conviction and confinement could not be divorced from that movement.

"I cannot overemphasize," I told the group, "that there are freedom fighters – political prisoners and prisoners of war – who have been languishing in U.S. prisons for more than twenty years."[60] I acknowledged that everyone in the room knew the name of Nelson Mandela, and the majority of them could recite a sentence or two, at the very least, about who he is.

Then I asked the group, "Raise your hand if you have ever heard of Sundiata Acoli, or Herman Bell, Anthony Jalil Bottom, Albert Nuh Washington, Leonard Peltier, Abdul Majid, Bashir Hameed, Sekou Odinga, Eddie Conway, Assata Shakur, Richard Dhoruba Moore, Geronimo Pratt, Mumia Abdul Jamal, Filiberto Ojeda Rios, Mutulu Shakur, Kuwasi Balagoon, Safiya Bukhari, Henry Sha Sha Brown, Masai Ehehosi, or Imari Obadele?" Few hands went up.

I then demanded. "How dare we teach Patrick Henry or George Washington or even Nelson Mandela, and completely obliterate Sundiata Acoli and Geronimo Pratt and Sekou Odinga from the annals of history? Freedom fighters in this country," I continued, "political prisoners and prisoners of war, need to be supported. Their names need to be remembered. The deeds they were convicted of need to be analyzed, not in the context of the Hollywood media hype which glorifies the state, as exemplified in *Badge of the Assassin*[61] or *The Big Dance*.[62] Instead, their deeds must be examined through the lens of our evolving strategies for liberation."

My legal mentor and brother in the New Afrikan Independence Movement, Attorney Chokwe Lumumba, often stressed that one of the reasons it is sometimes difficult to organize around the issue of political prisoners in the U.S. is because they are largely convicted of acts of resistance. "It didn't matter whether they actually committed violent acts, or whether they were framed," he taught. "Acts of resistance in the context of a liberation struggle or independence movement was something many Blacks shied away from."

"But is it wrong to resist?" I often questioned.

Assata Shakur answered that question in her writings.

She reminded us that "It was none other than the spirit of resistance, the spirit of struggle, the spirit of freedom, the spirit of independence that propelled brothers and sisters like Denmark Vesey and Dessalines and Gabriel and Fannie Lou and Nat Turner to be on the frontlines."

"They embodied the spirit of independence and were determined," Assata stressed, "to carry on the tradition of resistance."

I told the Student Committee Against Racism that the endless names of freedom fighters that began to resist and respond to the war the White nation had been waging against the Black nation on this soil should be common household parlance. I stressed that we must honor, respect and teach about them and their resistance to oppression.

Sundiata Acoli once said that the media rarely say where freedom fighters come from or why they appear. Assata Shakur has stated that the resistance movement calling itself the Black Liberation Army (BLA), rose during the 70s and continued the response to the war that had been waged against African people since the time of the slave trade.

"The idea of a BLA," she said, "emerged from conditions in Black communities. Conditions of poverty, indecent housing, massive unemployment, poor medical care, and inferior education. The idea came about because Black people are not free or equal in this country."

It came about because Black people were being lynched and killed and disrespected every day by the colonialist power structure. Because Black women in Chattanooga, TN, were being shot at; because Black men's hearts in Buffalo, NY, were being cut out; because cross burnings never ceased and police attacks grew more beastly; and Black people complained and demanded that something be done about all this madness.

"So we are told that the Black Liberation Army emerged from the ranks of the Black Panther Party and started doing something about it. Thus, the BLA became a part of that resistance movement," Assata concluded.

Using Sister Assata's theme, I continued my speech before the Student Committee Against Racism. "It is important to understand that the resistance movements of today are part of the same resistance movement that Sister Yaa Asantewaa raised against the British; the same resistance movement that Queen Nzingha raised in Angola; and the same resistance movement that Toussaint and Dessalines waged against the English, French and Spanish in what would become Haiti."

I emphasized, "Our movement is part of the same resistance movement the maroons waged against the slaveholders; the same resistance movement that built the Palmares Republic; the same resistance movement Vesey and Prosser attempted to organize; and the movement Nat Turner struggled for. It was the movement David Walker wrote about; the movement Sojourner Truth spoke about; and the movement Harriet Tubman lived."

"We unequivocally admire and respect the resistance movements of yesterday," I persisted. But just as we applaud and demonstrate in support, and provide material aid to resistance movements of today around the world struggling for independence, we also need to respect and support resistance movements in the U.S. today," I stressed. "So what does that mean?" I challenged my listeners. "It means that when people who are part of resistance movements are captured, tried, and imprisoned, they must be supported. Their names must be remembered. They must not be forgotten."

Among the names I heralded was that of Mutulu Shakur.

Ahh, Brother Mutulu, I reflected. Genius of acupuncture, godfather to Tupac, and convicted of masterminding revolutionary acts. I remembered the teachings I learned from Brother President Imari Obadele and his persistence on the use of international law. One in particular was use of the international Geneva Conventions and their Protocols, as a defense to the incarceration of Black prisoners of war in the United States, along with various other international law instruments emphasizing the rights of colonial peoples to self-determination.

Unbeknownst to me until internet revelations after the turn of the 21st century, I discovered that legal memoranda I wrote years ago at Brother Chokwe's behest for the trial defense of Mutulu Shakur was part of the official record in *U.S. v. Buck.*[63] Mutulu had been charged with being the architect of the November 2, 1979 liberation of Assata Shakur from prison, as well as the October 20, 1981 Brinks expropriation.

To my surprise, there my name was, big and bold, in the court record, Nkechi Taifa-Caldwell, along with my long-ago title, "Minister of Justice of the Republic of New Afrika."

Okay, I'm thinking. And I thought back to how I believed I was being what I humorously termed "incognegro" while a new lawyer. But I was proud that my name was included as amicus curiae, right next to that of Chokwe Lumumba, Chairman of the New Afrikan People's Organization, and Lennox Hinds, Permanent Representative to the United Nations for the International Association of Democratic Lawyers.

In an unprecedented fashion the judge, Charles Haight, ordered the prosecution to respond to our allegations that the acts in the indictment were political acts; that Mutulu Shakur was a prisoner of war, subject to the dictates of the Geneva Convention; and that as such, the indictment must be dismissed under international law. And, also unprecedented, the prosecution submitted our papers to the U.S. Department of State who recruited a team of five attorneys from the Departments of State, the Army and Defense, who prepared a 36-page memorandum opposing our claims.

My revolutionary legal arguments were not only inspired by the theoretical writings of President Imari Obadele, but also by the real life words of Sister Safiya Bukhari, who was arrested in 1975. I beamed when I heard how she bravely stood up in a U.S. courtroom along with her co-defendant Masai Ehehosi and challenged adamantly, "You cannot try me in your courts of law. I am a prisoner of war and a citizen of the Republic of New Afrika."

Safiya and Masai boldly maintained that the State of Virginia had no jurisdiction over them because they were "descendants of persons kidnapped from Afrika for purposes of slavery, not allowed to return to Afrika after slavery." They demanded their release from custody from Virginia because they were "prisoners of war," captured while in active status as soldiers in the Black Liberation Army in the U.S., and as such, should be released to the authorities of their nation, the Republic of New Afrika, released to another friendly country, or held under circumstances provided for prisoners of war by customary usages of international law and the appropriate conventions to which the U.S. is a party.

Brother Imari regularly wrote "President to President" letters to highlight concerns impacting the Black Nation in North America. In a letter to President Gerald Ford, dated May 14, 1975, and enumerated later when testifying in support of Sister Fulani, President Imari advised:

> I wish to remind you, Mr. Ford, that the RNA Provisional Government neither directs nor controls the Black Liberation Army, nor did we found it. Indeed until recent events, including the arrest and subsequent statements of Sister Safiya, we could not be certain that such an Army even existed. Today, We still do not direct or control it or encourage the Army in offensive military operations. But it is quite clear that the BLA does exist. An armed struggle for the liberation of the Black Nation and its land is going on in North America. And when members of the BLA who are citizens of the Republic of New Afrika – as all Blacks born in America are – call upon their Government to represent them, we are obliged to respond.

Similarly, in his letter to President Jimmy Carter,[64] dated July 16, 1978, President Imari admonished:

> In United States prisons are such persons as Sister Safiya Bukhari and Brother Masai in state prison in Virginia; James Haskins at Terre Haute, Herman Bell at Atlanta, and others, all members of the Black Liberation Army and citizens, like all blacks, of the black nation, the Republic of New Afrika, who have declared in U.S. Courts that they are prisoners-of-war, having been taken in acts of belligerency against the United States, which is waging a war of genocide against the black nation. Despite the fact that the United States is a signatory to the Geneva Convention of 1949, not one of these persons, not one Indian or black in American jails, has been extended the protections of the Treaty. (These protections include, among other things, the right to be free from slave-labor, the right not to be kept in penitentiaries, and the right to be exchanged.) This stubborn refusal of

the United States government to extend coverage of the Treaty to New Afrikans and Indians is a clear violation of the Geneva Convention's Article Five, which reads, in part:

'Should any doubt arise as to whether persons, having committed a belligerent act and having fallen into the hands of the enemy, belong to any of the categories enumerated in Article 4 such persons shall enjoy the protection of the present Convention until such time as their status has been determined by a competent tribunal'.

Years later after her release from prison, and as a staunch supporter of the New Afrikan Independence Movement, Safiya Bukhari came to speak at Howard University Law School, invited at my suggestion by members of the Black Law Students Association. They also invited Gloria Rolando to talk about her new film about Assata Shakur, *Eyes of the Rainbow*.

Safiya, who had come from the ranks of the Black Panther Party, told my law students who were thirsty for knowledge, that "the media didn't talk about the free breakfast programs. They didn't talk about waking up at 5 a.m. to feed hungry children. They didn't talk about the Panthers' work with sickle cell anemia. All they talked about were gun-toting cop killers."

The students shuddered as Safiya described how Black Panther Ruben Scott was tortured with cattle prods to his testicles. "Not in Viet-Nam," Safiya emphasized, "but in Louisiana." She spoke of Herman Bell, the victim of fingerprint forgery, and Black Panther member Joan Bird who was dangled by her feet by police out a third-floor window, to get her to give up information. And she described how Mark Holder, age 16, was tortured into giving information.

Safiya Bukhari became a Vice President of the Republic of New Afrika after her release from incarceration. She also became one of the masterminds, along with Brother Herman Ferguson and other staunch freedom fighters, behind the historic Jericho March to Free Political Prisoners and Prisoners of War. Inspired by a call made by political prisoner Jalil Muntaquim, Safiya described Jericho as "a movement with a defined goal of getting recognition that political prisoners exist inside the prisons of the United States, despite the government's denial."

Although I was not one of the major mobilizers behind the March 27, 1998 Jericho march and rally, I delivered an impassioned speech, along with Brothers Imari Oba-dele, Chokwe Lumumba and many other revolutionaries on the stage at Lafayette Park, overlooking the White House, demanding the release of our freedom fighters.

Safiya joined the ancestral realm in 2003. Fortunately, her papers were compiled by Laura Whitehorn in a book published posthumously, *The War Before: The True Life Story of Being a Black Panther, Keeping the Faith in Prison*, and *Fighting for Those Left Behind*. I am honored I had the opportunity to meet and work with my Warrior Sister Safiya Bukhari before her transition. And likewise, I am privileged to have had time to bond with Geronimo JiJaga Pratt after his release from 27 years of unjust imprisonment. His was a case I taught to my law students and consistently lifted up in my speeches. And I did so in my presentation before the Student Com-mittee Against Racism, as an illustration of the category of political prisoner who had been framed on non-political charges.

Geronimo was convicted of the murder of a woman on a Santa Monica tennis court in 1972 and sentenced to life imprisonment. He always maintained that the FBI, as part of COINTELPRO, framed him because of his leadership in the Black Panther Party. He was, in fact, a target of COINTELPRO, and the FBI identified him as a "Key Black Extremist." But at the time of his trial, neither he nor his defense coun-sel were aware of this. What's more, the chief prosecution witness was an FBI in-formant, though he denied being one during the trial. The FBI also planted three informants on Geronimo's defense team.

Amnesty International investigated Geronimo's case and issued a report about him in 1988. "Amnesty International is concerned in case irregular conduct by the pros-ecuting attorneys may have jeopardized his right to a fair trial in violation of inter nationally agreed standards for the protection of human rights," the report stated.

Geronimo's main line of defense was that it was im-possible for him to have committed the murder, given that at the time of the woman's death, he was 350 miles away, in Oakland, attending a Black Panther Party (BPP) leadership meeting. FBI surveillance logs from the Bureau's bugging of Party head-quarters, he alluded, would prove his point. At the trial, however, the FBI lied under oath, denying that any such bugging had occurred.

Years later, when it was proven that the government had indeed bugged the BPP facilities, his attorneys once again demanded the relevant logs. This time, the FBI claimed to have lost the crucial material. Appallingly, during a 1988 parole hearing, an Assistant District Attorney went before the Parole Board to explain why Geronimo should not be released. She stated, "because he is still a revolutionary man."

For over 27 years and 16 denials of parole, Geronimo steadfastly maintained his innocence. Judge Everett J. Dickey, a Reagan-appointed judge in conservative Orange Country, listened to the facts told by his attorneys Stuart Hanlon and Johnnie Cochran, and the rest is sweet history.[65]

Shortly after Geronimo's 1997 release, Attorneys Gilda Sherrod Ali, Adjoa Aiyetoro and myself from the D.C. Chapter of the National Conference of Black Lawyers organized, in less than a week, a massive hero's welcome home, held in the spacious backyard of my home. Geronimo sauntered across the lush grass, wearing a black, white and gold "Emerge"[66] tee shirt, flanked by New Afrikan People's Organization Brother Watani Tyehimba, and Tavis Smiley of the Tavis Smiley Show, with whom "G" had just completed a taping.

The backyard was bursting with Black nationalists, community activists, cultural artists, academics, and law students. My mother and father were there, as was my three-year-old daughter, oblivious to the significance of the occasion, but delighting in repeatedly sliding down the bright orange and pink jungle gym slide adjacent to where Geronimo would address his well wishers. The former political prisoner's brother, Timothy Pratt, a good friend of mine who had worked tirelessly for his freedom, was also there.

The turn-out in such a short timeframe revealed how much Geronimo was loved

and respected. Those in attendance were a virtual who's who of the D.C. activist, cultural and academic communities. Gazing over the crowd that had gathered, I saw Al Malik-Farrakhan, founder of Cease Fire Don't Smoke the Brothers and Sisters, maneuvering the grass in his wheelchair. The Umoja Party's mover and shaker, Matsimela Mark Thompson, was there. Brother Kokayi Patterson of the African Wholistic Health Institute; Senghor Baye with the UNIA; Donald Temple and Everett Bellamy with the Charles Hamilton Houston Preparatory Law Institute; students from the Howard University School of Law; and Paul Coates with Black Classic Press were there to bear witness. Also represented were leaders of the National Coalition of Blacks for Reparations in America; Mothers on the Move Spiritually; and the African Freedom Fund Treasury.

The D.C. Coalition to Free Mumia Abu-Jamal, as well as the New Afrikan Network in Defense of Political Prisoners and Prisoners of War, were represented at this momentous occasion. Organizers with the Provisional Government of the Republic of New Afrika, the New Afrikan People's Organization, and the All African People's Revolutionary Party were present.

Mamas Nia Kuumba and Marilyn Killingham, along with Baba Oraefo Karamoko and Kalonji and Kupenda Olusegun brought their blessings. The schools of Nation-House Watoto, Ujamaa, Roots and Kamit Institute were there. Sankofa Bookstore along with representatives from the radio stations WOL-AM and WPFW-FM showed up to show their support.

Nana Kwabena Brown from the Temple of Nyame delivered a rousing libation on Geronimo's behalf, acknowledging to those gathered that "the ancestors walk with him and give him strength."

The Ujamaa School dancers and drummers paid their respects to the newly freed brother with their energetic beats and rhythmic body movements. Geronimo was spellbound, and I overheard him chuckle wistfully that he wished he "could share all the beautiful dancing and drumming with the brothers in the hole."

Speaking over the occasional drone of aircraft hovering above, Adjoa introduced Geronimo, noting "this brother showed me a revolutionary spirit – he would express more concern about others than himself. Geronimo is an example of a person who stood on principle and did not compromise."

It was, indeed, a hero's welcome, but Geronimo insisted, humbled by all the attention, "I'm not a movie star; I'm a revolutionary!" To thunderous applause, he continued, "I'm from the underground. I always said I was a prisoner of war because we are in a war and we must stand on these principles. We have a right to be free.

We have a duty to be free."

He spoke of his upbringing in Louisiana; that his elders sprang from the
Deacons for Defense and the UNIA.
"There were things we could not talk
about in the 60s because of our own
security," he intimated. "We dedicated

our lives, not for no monetary gain, but for the movement. Ruchell Magee is still
in there," he charged. "Sundiata, Sekou, Mutulu – we gonna get the rest of the soldiers out; get them out of those dungeons because very soon they will be coming
after y'all," he ominously warned.

"If they would have just one comprehensive investigation[67] into COINTELPRO,
everyone will be able to walk out of prison," he blurted, "and Assata would be able
to come home." Geronimo spoke of White revolutionaries Marilyn Buck and Susan
Rosenberg, emphasizing that White people needed to follow examples set by anti-
slavery abolitionists such as Levi Coffin. He uplifted the work of Brother Imari
Obadele, proclaiming, "that man taught so many people in prison more about international law than anyone."

"It's not about the personalities," he added, likely alluding to the split in The Movement. "It's about the principles." He continued with ideals from the New Afrikan
Independence Movement and the importance of the plebiscite and offices in the
Government. "What kept me going, is the belief that Adjoa can be our Prime Minister; Nkechi can be our Prime Minister," he marveled.

Brother Lasana Mack delivered a rousing poem, "Too Righteous, Too Strong," and
the heavenly jazz singer Sunny Sumpter, with her ensemble, blessed the gathering
with song.

Gilda Sherrod Ali concluded the celebration, reminding the rapt crowd, "Our people
are at war with the police in the U.S. We are at war on crack cocaine in the U.S. We
have a lot of work to do."

I hosted a welcome home celebration years
earlier in 1990 for Dhoruba Bin Wahad
shortly after his release from imprisonment, and years later in 2016 for Sekou
Odinga after his release. Neither celebration, however, was as elaborate as this one
in Geronimo's honor.

Geronimo is sorely missed as he is no longer with us, having transitioned on June 3, 2011, at the age of 63. Thankfully, his legacy will live forever, not only in the U.S., but in Tanzania as well. With part of the proceeds of a state settlement from his 27-year unjust incarceration, Geronimo financed a well that now provides water for an entire village in Arusha[68] at the foot of Mount Kilimanjaro.

Many revolutionaries, however, are leaving this earthly plane without transmitting their rebellious footprint for the benefit of future generations. Brother Imari Obadele[69] for example, in my humble opinion, lived before his time. He had the aura of a distinguished statesman, a resolute leader, the chief executive of an independent New Afrika, if there ever could be one. His 1984 memoir, *Free the Land*, is all but forgotten. Never having received wide distribution, the manuscript was seized and held hostage in the files of the FBI for decades. Many of the tidbits  he shared with me can be found within those pages, and I am happy to be able to share them with you, on these pages, as well.

Brother Chokwe Lumumba is gone prematurely, another great leader who should be triumphantly heralded in the annals of history. Not only was he a brilliant attorney, a Vice President of the Republic of New Afrika and helped to found both the New Afrikan People's Organization and the Malcolm X Grassroots Movement, but quite incredibly he became the mayor of Jackson, MS, a city designated as part of the deep South five states of the Republic of New Afrika. Although Brother Chokwe authored no memoir, his son, Attorney Chokwe Antar Lumumba, continues in his legacy as mayor of Jackson, MS.

Although there are always legitimate explanations accompanying the deaths of some of our freedom fighting leaders, I have always considered the premature demise of freedom fighters in the Black Power Movement to be mysterious, and ruminate whether some type of conspiracy accompanied their passings – Chokwe Lumumba,[70] Geronimo Pratt,[71]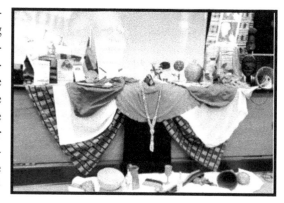

Kwame Ture,[72] Ishakamusa Barashango,[73] and Kwame Afoh,[74] to name a few. Perhaps, if there had been more visible security measures surrounding them, then the possibility of sabotage could be ruled out in my mind.

I often scoff at being subjected to Nation of Islam (NOI) security; one instance in particular comes to mind, prior to being cleared to enter one of their events featuring Minister Louis Farrakhan. A treasured miniature backscratcher I always carry in my purse due to a chronic itchy back was discarded during the mandatory search as it was considered "a weapon that could do harm to the Minister [Farrakhan]."

I coolly acquiesced, thinking, *Little does this sister know that I once had dinner with her great leader at Imari Obadele's mama's house in Philly, during a time shortly after the death of the Honorable Elijah Muhammad when the NOI abandoned him with no security.*

I'd like to have been able to tell her, as she rifled through my purse, *And yes my sister, during our dinner conversation, we were strategizing the future of the Black Nation. I can assure you no harm will come to him as the result of my benign backscratcher.* In reality, I don't recall what Brother Imari, Minister Farrakhan and I talked about at that dinner table. But I do remember in detail the scrumptious, home-cooked meal Mrs. Henry prepared for her son and his friends – fried chicken, macaroni and cheese, collard greens, candied yams, and cornbread. I honestly don't think we talked about anything consequential. It was just an idyllic day in Philadelphia where two prominent leaders, along with lil ole myself, just kicked back, relaxed, and enjoyed a lovingly prepared meal.

I could never explain all of that to the young NOI sister who unilaterally rejected my coveted backscratcher. I could not explain to her that her leader graciously accepted my appeal to him on behalf of President Imari many many years earlier to join the National Committee to Free the RNA-11. I could not tell her that it was the

RNA that provided security at public events for the Minister when the Nation deserted him, and that Minister Farrakhan has forever been grateful for that assistance.

What I can say to her though, is 'thank you.' Although I was pissed and inconvenienced and still think she was wrong in not allowing me to enter the hall with my backscratcher, I thank her because she was simply doing her job as a security officer, which dictates that no one should be above scrutiny.

And what I can say is that the Nation of Islam's security methods have kept probably one of the most uncompromising and controversial leaders of our time safe, despite incessant threats, denouncements, political intrigues and negative media sensationalism.

Although once quite astute in the realm of security consciousness, many movements of today with historical roots have become lax with safety and defense and many new movements have no systematic plan for security. Perhaps we all need to take a lesson from the NOI's page, as well as pages from the RNA's early history, and reprioritize the protection, safety, and security of our leaders.

Chapter Five
"Get Up, Stand Up for Your Rights"[75]

Section 1
Who'll Pay Reparations on My Soul?[76]

I was influenced by the Black Power Movement very early in my life and today, one of its fundamental tenets, reparations, is part of mainstream conversation. The spark for me occurred during a lull one afternoon while a high school student selling Black Panther Party newspapers on the streets of downtown Washington, D.C., in 1971. I sat down on the curb and turned the pages to the Party's 10-point program, "What We Want; What We Believe." The graphic assertion of Point Number 3 always particularly grabbed me:

We Want an End to the Robbery by the Capitalist of our Black Community – We believe that this racist government has robbed us and now we are demanding the overdue debt of forty acres and two mules…promised 100 years ago as restitution for slave labor and mass murder of Black people. We will accept the payment in currency which will be distributed to our many communities. The Germans are now aiding the Jews in Israel for the genocide of the Jewish people. The Germans murdered six million Jews. The American racist has taken part in the slaughter of over fifty million Black people. Therefore, we feel this is a modest demand that we make.

The absence of justice continually flustered me because, even at that young age, I knew that Black people had been kidnapped and brought to this country to labor for free as slaves, stripped of our language, religion and culture, raped and tortured, and then subjected to a Jim Crow era of lynchings, police brutality, inferior education, substandard housing, and mediocre health care. I did not know then about the massacres in Rosewood, FL; Tulsa, OK; or Wilmington, NC. I did not know about the merciless experimentations on defenseless Black women, devoid of anesthesia, that led to modern gynecology; and, I did not know about the enormous profits made by corporations, insurance companies, the banking and investment industries, and academic institutions from slavery.

On a psychic level, however, I could feel in my bones the enslavement era's inhumane cruelty to Black children, its destruction of kindred ties, economic exploitation and cultural deprivation, and there was an incessant gnawing in my soul for amends and redress. I was passionate about injustice, felt the idea of reparations to be reasonable and fair, and vowed to talk about the concept whenever and wherever I could. My analysis, however, had not crystallized and matured beyond a monetary check.

However, to just verbalize the word "reparations" was a starting point to its validity. And so talk about it I did, despite my views being often rejected, ridiculed, or otherwise summarily dismissed. Standing on the street corner that afternoon, little did I realize that over forty years later I would be in the company of leading academics, economists, historians, attorneys, psychiatrists, politicians and more, domestically and internationally, promoting the right to, and the need for, reparations.

But that day would be far into the future. Despite my advocacy and that of many others during my high school, college, and law school years and beyond, the issue of reparations for descendants of Africans enslaved in the United States was not fashionable, but fringe, and definitely not part of the mainstream popular discourse. One would often be branded as a militant or a revolutionary (both of which, admittedly, I was), or just plain crazy (which I was not). In today's dubious governmental surveillance parlance, I would have been labeled a "Black Identity Extremist."[77]

It is critical to understand, however, that the demand for reparations in the U.S. for unpaid labor during the enslavement era and post-slavery discrimination is not novel or new. The claim did not drop from the sky with Ta-Nehisi Coates' brilliant treatise, "The Case for Black Reparations," in *The Atlantic*, or from Randall Robinson's impassioned book, *The Debt: What America Owes to Blacks*, both of which galvanized the issue in different decades and thrust it into national conversation.

Although there have been hills and valleys in national attention to the issue, there has been no substantial period of time when the call for redress was not passionately voiced. The first formal record of a petition for reparations in the United States was pursued and won by a formerly enslaved woman, Belinda Royall. Professor Ray Winbush's book, *Belinda's Petition*, describes a petition she presented to the Massachusetts General Assembly in 1783, requesting a pension from the proceeds of her enslaver's estate (an estate partly the product of her own uncompensated labor). Belinda's petition was successful, yielding a pension of fifteen pounds and twelve shillings.

Former U.S. Civil Rights Commissioner Mary Frances Berry illuminated the case of Callie House in her book, *My Face is Black is True*. Callie, along with Reverend Isaiah Dickerson, headed the first mass reparations movement in the United States, founded in 1898. The National Ex-Slave Mutual Relief Bounty and Pension Association had six hundred thousand dues-paying members who sought to obtain compensation for slavery from federal agencies.

During the 1920s, Marcus Garvey and the Universal Negro Improvement Association galvanized hundreds of thousands of Black people seeking repatriation with reparation, proclaiming, "Hand back to us our own civilisation. Hand back to us that which you have robbed and exploited of us … for the last 500 years."

During the 1950s and 60s, New York's Queen Mother Audley Moore was perhaps the best known advocate for reparations. As president of the Universal Association of Ethiopian Women, she presented a petition against genocide and for self-determination, land and reparations to the United Nations in both 1957 and 1959 and was active in every major reparations movement until her death in 1996.

In his 1963 book, *Why We Can't Wait*, Dr. Martin Luther King proposed a Bill of Rights for the Disadvantaged, which emphasized redress for both the historical victimization and exploitation of Blacks as well as their present-day degradation. "The ancient common law has always provided a remedy for the appropriation of labor on one human being by another. This law should be made to apply for the American Negroes," he wrote.

After the Black Panther Party's "payback for slavery" stance in 1966, the Republic of New Afrika proclaimed in its 1968 Declaration of Independence, "We claim no rights from the United States of America other than those rights belonging to human beings anywhere in the world, and these include the right to damages, reparations, due us for the grievous injuries sustained by ourselves and our ancestors by reason of United States' lawlessness."

In April 1969, the *Black Manifesto* was adopted at a National Black Economic Development Conference. The Manifesto, presented by civil rights activist James Forman, included a demand that White churches and synagogues pay $500,000,000 in reparations to Blacks in the U.S. The amount was based on a calculation of $15 for each of the estimated 20 to 30,000,000 African Americans residing in the U.S. He touted it as only the beginning of the amount owed. The following month, Forman interrupted Sunday service at the Riverside Church in New York to announce the reparations demand from the *Black Manifesto*. Notably, several religious institutions responded with financial donations.

In 1972, the National Black Political Assembly Convention meeting in Gary, Indiana adopted the Republic of New Afrika's Anti-Depression Program, an act authorizing the payment of a sum of money in reparations for slavery, and a negotiating commission between the United States and the Provisional Government of the Republic of New Afrika to determine type, dates, and other details of paying reparations.

Consistently, the Nation of Islam's publications, *Muhammad Speaks*, and later, *The Final Call*, have demanded that the United States exempt Black people "from all taxation as long as we are deprived of equal justice."

It was the end of the 20th century that brought broad, national attention to the call for reparations for people of African descent in the United States with the founding of the National Coalition of Blacks for Reparations in America (N'COBRA). The spark for its founding emanated from a 1987 conference on Race and the Constitution spearheaded by the National Conference of Black Lawyers (NCBL) and held at Harvard University. Reparations had always been part of the Nationalist and Pan-Africanist agenda, but now there was interest from the National Conference of Black Lawyers, fueled by receptiveness from a key NCBL leader, Adjoa Aiyetoro.

She invited me, Imari Obadele and Chokwe Lumumba to join economist Richard America on the panel at Harvard to discuss whether the U.S. Constitution should be amended with a reparations demand. The three of us, long-standing champions in the New Afrikan Independence Movement, jointly concluded that there was no need to amend the U.S. Constitution because the basis for the Black Nation's claim for reparations already existed within it. Our presentations from the conference were later compiled in a small but power-packed book, *Reparations Yes: The Legal and Political Reasons Why New Afrikans – Black People in the United States – Should be Paid Now for the Enslavement of Our Ancestors and for War Against Us After Slavery.*[78]

Eight Dollars (U.S.A.)

REPARATIONS
YES!

The Legal And Political Reasons
Why New Afrikans – Black People In
The United States – Should Be Paid
Now For The Enslavement Of Our
Ancestors And For War Against Us
After Slavery

THIRD EDITION

Contains
THE U.S. ACT GIVING REPARATIONS TO THE JAPANESE
And
THE CONYERS REPARATIONS STUDY BILL
NOW IN CONGRESS
And
A DRAFT REPARATIONS BILL

ARTICLES BY
CHOKWE LUMUMBA,
IMARI ABUBAKARI OBADELE &
NKECHI TAIFA

Our articles in the book were replete with historical precedents for reparations, New Afrikan Political Science, and analyses of international law with revolutionary fervor promoting the right to self-determination peppered throughout. Our contributions highlighted the RNA's 1972 Anti-Depression Program submitted to and approved by the National Black Political Assembly Convention meeting in Gary, IN, and its acceptance by the Mississippi Loyalist Delegation to the Democratic National Convention that same year.[79]

We examined the specifics of the Second Act of this Anti-Depression Program, which called for the authorization of the payment of a sum of money ($300,000,000) at the time, in reparations for slavery and unjust war against the New Afrikan nation. We also examined an act authorizing negotiations between a commission of the U.S. and a commission of the RNA to determine kind, dates and other details of paying reparations. We discussed the significance of "government to government" reparations as the negotiated settlement that follows conclusion of war.

The issue of reparations for Brothers Imari and Chokwe, as well as for myself, was nothing new, special or separate from what we had been engaged in for years. Although normal to us, our positions were likely viewed by Movement outsiders as militant and extreme. As a lawyer and an activist, I recognized this conundrum and, as such, have always credited Brother Imari for taking the high ground in sublimating his independence politics to issue the call for reparations-loving people to convene in Washington to discuss, among other agenda items around foreign policy, how to move the issue of reparations for Black people in the U.S. forward.

Out of that historic September 26, 1987 gathering, the National Coalition of Blacks for Reparations in America (N'COBRA) was born, bringing together diverse groups under one umbrella. Black Nationalist politics clearly dominated the room. The Provisional Government of the Republic of New Afrika and its Foreign Affairs Task Force were there in numbers, as were members of the New Afrikan People's Organization chaired by Chokwe Lumumba. Kalonji Olusegun, the meeting's facilitator, was a PG-RNA official and New Afrikan judge. Dorothy Lewis worked closely with the Provisional Government through her organization, the Black Reparations Commission. Others present included Adjoa Aiyetoro from the National Conference of Black Lawyers, the African People's Socialist Party's African National Reparations Organization, and others.[80]

The Movement had essentially crowned Queen Mother Moore as the undisputed Mother of the modern-day Reparations Movement in the U.S. Although the genius and role of Brother Imari Obadele is largely absent from the popular annals of reparations lore, I have always felt that he should be universally acknowledged as the Movement's Father.[81]

Since the creation of NCOBRA, the demand for reparations in the United States substantially leaped forward, generating what I've dubbed, the modern day Reparations Movement. It was the perfect storm. The Black Power Movement was open and receptive to a broad-based approach to further the issue of reparations. The Black legal community sanctioned the largely Black Nationalist effort. And we were all invigorated by the recent passage of the Civil Liberties Act of 1988, which granted reparations to Japanese-Americans for their unjust internment during World War II. And so it was in the throes of this fertile environment that N'COBRA picked up the long-standing mantle of justice, reinvigorated the demand for reparations for African Americans, and broadened the concept through massive public education, accompanied by legislative and litigation-based initiatives.

Also encouraged by the Civil Liberties Act and in response to the dogged persistence of a Detroit constituent known as "Reparations Ray" Jenkins, Congressman John Conyers expressed interest in introducing a reparations bill in Congress. N'COBRA worked closely with his staffers, and in 1989, legislation was introduced.

The bill would "establish a commission to examine the institution of slavery and subsequent racial and economic discrimination against African Americans and the impact of these forces on Black people today." This commission would be charged with making recommendations to Congress on appropriate remedies. The bill was later numbered H.R. 40, in remembrance of the unfulfilled 19th century campaign promise to give freed Blacks 40 acres and a mule. In essence, Representative Conyers' Commission to Study Reparation Proposals for African Americans Act provided the cover and vehicle to have a public policy discussion on the issue of reparations in the Congress of the United States.

The bill was modeled on the 1988 Civil Liberties Redress Act, which began in 1980 as a study commission. The final bill authorized the payment of $20,000 to each Japanese-American detention camp survivor, a trust fund to be used to educate Americans about the suffering of the Japanese-Americans, a formal apology from the U.S. government, and a pardon for all those convicted of resisting detention camp internment.

It is a sad commentary that the U.S. government has not taken formal responsibility for its role in the enslavement or post-slavery apartheid segregation of millions of Blacks. It has never attempted reparations to Black people for the extortion of their labor for many generations, deprivation of their freedom and human rights, and terrorism against them throughout the centuries. The U.S. Senate and House of Representatives did pass symbolic resolutions apologizing for slavery and segregation. However, the 2009 bill passed by the Senate contained a disclaimer that those seeking reparations or cash compensation could not use the apology to support a legal claim against the U.S.

Since the introduction of H.R. 40, N'COBRA members and organizers helped to influence several state legislatures and scores of city councils across the country to pass reparation-themed legislation or resolutions endorsing H.R. 40. In 1990, the Louisiana House of Representatives passed a resolution in support of reparations. In 1991, legislation was introduced into the Massachusetts Senate providing for the payment of reparations for slavery, the slave trade and individual discrimination against the people of African descent born or residing in the Commonwealth of Massachusetts. In 1994, the Florida Legislature paid $150,000 to each of the eleven survivors of the 1923 Rosewood Race Massacre and created a scholarship fund for students of color.

In 2001, the California State Assembly passed a resolution in support of reparations. After a four-year investigation, the Tulsa Race Riot Reconciliation Act was enacted in 2001. Oklahoma legislators settled on a scholarship fund and memorial to commemorate the June 1921 massacre that left as many as 300 Black people dead and

40 square blocks of exclusively Black businesses, homes, and schools obliterated. That same year a bill was introduced in the New York State Assembly to create a Commission to Quantify the Debt Owed to African Americans.

And while bills are pending within several other state legislatures, the reparations movement isn't just targeting state houses. City councils in the states of Arkansas, California, Georgia, Illinois, Maryland, Michigan, Mississippi, Missouri, New Jersey, Ohio, Pennsylvania, Texas, Vermont, Virginia, and the District of Columbia have all passed resolutions in support of H.R. 40.

More recently, Alderman Robin Rue Simmons of the Evanston, IL City Council successfully spearheaded the passage of a $10 million reparations initiative to address racially exclusionary policies which contributed to the lack of opportunity and underdevelopment of Black families and neighborhoods which perpetuated and exacerbated the racial wealth gap in Evanston. An historic marker and possible blueprint for other jurisdictions, this reparations initiative will be funded from city tax revenue received from the sale of recreational marijuana.

Reparations advocates such as my colleague Deadria Farmer-Paellmann have also challenged corporations who benefited from the profits made from the trafficking in human beings during the enslavement era. Countless companies and industries benefited and were greatly enriched from the profits made as a result of chattel slavery.

There are companies that sold life insurance policies on the lives of enslaved persons, such as Aetna, New York Life, and AIG. Financial gains were accrued by the predecessor banks of financial giants such as J.P. Morgan Chase and Bank of America. Others with documented ties to slavery included railroads like Norfolk Southern, CSX, Union Pacific and Canadian National, as well as Newspaper publishers that assisted in the capture of runaway persons such as Knight Ridder, Tribune, E.W. Scripps, and Gannett.

The financial backers of many of the country's top universities were wealthy slave owners, and it has been disclosed that the reason Georgetown University stands today is because the Jesuits who ran the college used profits from the sale of Black people to save it from foreclosure.

Survivors of torture by Chicago police received an unprecedented compensatory package based on a reparations ordinance passed by the Chicago City Council in 2015. Numerous civil and human rights organizations, religious groups, professional organizations, civic groups, sororities, fraternities, and labor unions, have also officially endorsed the call for reparations, along with other organizations who had been working for decades on the issue. These include Queen Mother Dorothy

Lewis's Black Reparations Commission, the African People's Socialist Party's African National Reparations Organization, the National Black United Front, the December 12th Movement, and the Black Radical Congress, to name a few. In 2016, the Movement for Black Lives Policy Table released its platform, which prominently featured the issue of reparations.

The role that governments, corporations, industries, religious institutions, educational institutions, private estates and other entities played in supporting the institution of slavery and its vestiges are roles that can no longer be ignored, dismissed outright, or swept under the rug. The time is now ripe that their involvement be recognized, examined, discussed and addressed.

Although a lifetime member of N'COBRA, I am also part of the inaugural cohort of Commissioners on the National African American Reparations Commission (NAARC), convened in 2016 by Dr. Ron Daniels, President of the Institute of the Black World 21st Century. The Commission's preamble asserts that "no amount of material resources or monetary compensation can ever be sufficient restitution for the spiritual, mental, cultural and physical damages inflicted on Africans by centuries of the MAAFA, the holocaust of enslavement and the institution of chattel slavery."

Recognizing these as "crimes against humanity" as acknowledged by the 2001 *Durban Declaration and Programme of Action* of the World Conference Against Racism in South Africa, the preamble goes on to assert that "the devastating damages of enslavement and systems of apartheid and defacto segregation spanned generations to negatively affect the collective well-being of Africans in America to this very moment." NAARC has advanced a comprehensive, yet preliminary, reparations program to guide reparatory justice demands by people of African descent in the United States.

Although my primary focus has been on obtaining reparations for the descendants of Africans enslaved and/or subjected to Jim Crow laws in the U.S., it is important to recognize that our quest is also part of the international movement for reparations. As such, I have worked closely with supporters of reparations throughout the world, recognizing that the success of the movement for reparations for diasporic Africans anywhere, advances the movement for reparations by Africans and African descendants everywhere.

I am thrilled that my quest to have reparations seen as a legitimate concept for Black people, begun during the 1970s, is today becoming a reality. The issue has become more precise, less rhetorical, and has entered the mainstream. And while cash payments remain an important and necessary component of any claim for damages, it is crystal clear today that a reparations settlement can be fashioned in as many ways as necessary to equitably address the countless manifestations of injury sustained from chattel slavery and its continuing vestiges.

Some forms of redress may include land, economic development or scholarships. Other amends may embrace community development, repatriation resources, or truthful textbooks. Still, other areas of reparative justice may encompass the erection of monuments and museums, pardons for impacted prisoners from the COINTELPRO era, and repairing the harms from the so-called "War on Drugs."

Nearly half a century after I was first exposed to the issue of reparations, I'm optimistic. It's hard not to be when H.R. 40 was updated after 30 years to include not just a study, but also the development of reparation proposals. It's also hard not to be optimistic when a Senate companion bill to H.R. 40 was introduced in the 116th Congress, and even more astonishing when some Democratic candidates for the 2020 presidential race assert that they will sign the legislation if elected president.

Despite a resurfacing of White supremacy in the U.S., I can see the light at the end of the tunnel. I am appreciative that leaders in the New Afrikan Independence Movement had the humility to tone down their analysis and distinct ideological positions in favor of facilitating broader acceptance of the concept of reparations and allowing new voices to come to the fore.

I am buoyed by the reemergence of the spirits of Belinda and Callie House, and the resilience of "Reparations Ray" Jenkins who kept the fire alive in Congressman Conyers to introduce H.R. 40 year after year.

And my hat goes off to the Mother of the modern-day Reparations Movement, Queen Mother Moore, and its Father, Imari Abubakari Obadele, both of whom symbolize the influence of the Black Power movement in contemporary society.

Chapter Five, Section 2
Educate, Agitate, Organize

Although I always wanted to be a lawyer, I had no legal mentors to guide me in my early life. Other than the urgings from my father, there was no one to advise me to go to law school and get it over with. After graduating from Howard undergrad in 1977, I must say that by then I was tired of school. Although there were no "gap years" in those days where colleges allowed you to defer enrollment for a year, that is essentially what I took rather than going straight to law school. I decided to teach at an Independent Black School, NationHouse Watoto Shule.

The first interview of my career after graduating from college was both informal and unconventional, yet the most satisfying that I have ever experienced. It was a lazy, sunny spring day, with just a slight breeze. Baba Akili Ron Anderson interviewed me outside on the front steps of the NationHouse family's 13th Street home. This communal abode was conveniently located a walking distance from Watoto Shule, a picturesque red brick house-turned school building, located at the time near Park Road and Water Street, N.W.

I was still clad in my characteristic tight blue jeans, bodysuit blouse and towering gele with hoop earrings. Much to the chagrin of the institution's founders, I never really got the feel of the "lappa" – African fabric wrapped around the waist the way Ghanaian women wore them. But I was ready to teach and was thankfully hired.

The Independent Black Schools were a national movement, under the governance of the Council of Independent Black Institutions (CIBI), at that time under the leadership of Brother Kofi Lamotey. From Uhuru Sasa Shule at "The East" in New York, to New Concept Development Institute in Chicago; to the African People's Action School in Trenton; to Ahidiana in New Orleans, these and many more "liberated zones" for the education of Black youth were dotted across the country. In D.C. alone, in addition to Watoto School, there was also Ujamaa Shule, founded by former SNCC activist Baba El Senzengakulu Zulu; Roots Activity Learning Center headed up by Dr. Bernida Thompson; and Nia Shule. And my very own Imari Obadele New Afrikan Saturday School was part of that movement as well.

For several years, CIBI conducted Teacher Training Institutes (TTI) to support the development of African-centered schools by providing curriculum content and teaching methodologies to their educators. I had already decided to attend the third annual TTI session that summer of 1977 in Detroit, Michigan. I registered for it upon graduation from Howard University, even before my front-step interview.

TTI was a phenomenal experience, spearheaded by Imani Humphrey of the Alexander Crummell Center and Aisha Shule in Detroit. I met many people that summer of 1977, including Brother Malik Yakini, who went on to found his own independent Black school, Nsoroma Institute, and years later became the architect of the Detroit Community Food Security Network. I met Carol Blakes, a prolific teacher I would later work alongside with at Watoto School. We all came to TTI united by one purpose: to prepare, empower and inspire Black youth with positive education.

That fall I taught the Zulu class at Watoto School. The class was roughly the equivalent to first grade. Some of the other instructors at Watoto during my tenure, along with Mama Carol, included Mamas Nana, Cecelie, Sherifu, Afia, and Baba Mamadi. Baba Agyei Akoto was the headmaster and the glue that held everything and everyone together. Mama Kamili was the cook who prepared wholesome, vegetarian meals during my early days teaching at the school.

The four and five-year-old students in my class eagerly learned to read. I developed many of my own teaching materials and creative methods by which to impart information. I remember some of the names of my early students – Bavu Blakes, Sekou Crawford, Yao Tyus, Haziq Ali, Shaka Densu, Osei Akoto, Malik Keene, Damani Goode, Ama Tyus and more. These were students who grew up to be doctors, musicians, rocket scientists, educators, African dancers, architects and more.

It was at Watoto that I wrote my children's book, *Shining Legacy: Story Poems and Tales for the Young, So Black Heroes Forever will be Sung*, and later, *The Adventures of Kojo and Ama*. It was at Watoto that I participated in Nation Studies. And it was at Nation Studies that I met Brother Bomani, a nice-looking, soft-spoken brother.

Some time after we met I invited him to a holiday dinner at my parent's home. While waiting for the meal to be served he retrieved a newspaper from the coffee table, and proceeded to peruse the headlines. Intently reading the news, my new suitor had not noticed my father scrutinizing him from the kitchen. Eventually looking up and seeing him staring, Bomani inquired respectfully, "Mr. Caldwell, is everything alright?"

"Well, son," Daddy slowly, but emphatically replied. "I must say I'm impressed. I don't think I've ever seen any of the black brothers my daughter brings around here ever reading anything!" Although peeved that he was comparing my new boyfriend to others, Daddy was basically right. Like the title of today's anthology by Gloria Edim, *Well Read Black Girl*, Brother Bomani was most definitely a "well read Black man." I loved that about him, as well as everything else. Yup, I was smitten in love for the next four years, and everyone knew it.

His name was not Bomani when I met him but, before long, he graciously accepted the African name, Bomani Sekou. Although he did not fit my traditional "bad boy" mold, we made a great team, not just romantically, but politically as well. Not only was he well-read, but his library of consciousness-raising books rivaled mine. The organization he was a part of, The People's Organization, consistently produced a newsletter and other literature promoting the importance of the resistance movement, political prisoners, and the Republic of New Afrika. Unfortunately, however, because he never wanted to "tie the knot," we drifted apart, but remain great friends down to this day.

***

Nation Studies was one of the many brainchildren of the founders of NationHouse Positive Action Center, which housed NationHouse Watoto School. Baba Agyei Akoto and his physician wife, Mama Akua Akoto, were the stalwarts and architects behind the genius of NationHouse; along with artist Akili Ron Anderson and jazz and classical singer Kehembe Eichelberger. For decades NationHouse opened its Park Road, N.W. doors to the cultural, revolutionary, nationalist and Pan-Africanist D.C. community. It, along with the D.C. Independent Black Schools of Ujamaa and Roots, provided much-needed, free and low-cost venues for countless programs and events that I would both frequent and host over the years.

Nation Studies, the interactive lecture/discussion series at NationHouse Watoto School, held its lectures way up on the third floor of the house-turned-school, and

later, on the 3rd floor of the newly acquired building down the street. The community was blessed to have two presenters on a regular basis, the phenomenal scholar activists Dr. Ronald Walters and Dr. Acklyn Lynch. These political masterminds came to lecture whenever they were called. They educated me about Pan Africanism, global politics, and community affairs. Their political analyses were sharp and insightful. They were academic geniuses and cultural giants.

Baba Hannibal Afrik, founder of Shule Ya Watoto in Chicago, was another key influencer from my time with NationHouse. I was honored to later work closely with him in both the Republic of New Afrika and N'COBRA. He often travelled to the Washington, D.C. area to conduct his signature Survival Skills trainings on land in Virginia, which the Black Nationalist community designated as "liberated."

Out of many conversations I have had with Baba Hannibal, I never forgot the dialogue with him during Survival Skills training one particular afternoon. At one point our survival group had to carefully balance ourselves, separately one by one, across a narrow bridge consisting of a lone, willowy tree log precariously positioned across a rocky creek. Needless to say, I was totally out of my comfort zone.

While still on steady ground, I leaned over to Baba Hannibal, 20 years my senior, and confided to him that I was scared to cross. He studied my frightened eyes and confessed, "Sister Nkechi, I'm afraid as well, but I don't allow fear to conquer me. Do as I do. Concentrate and stay focused on your goal, for that is how you become victorious." Although inwardly trembling, I did as he said, and crossed without falling. I never forgot his advice, and although concentration and focus has at times been hard to live up to, Baba Hannibal increasingly became significant in my life, both as a reparationist and a nation-builder.

***

My first apartment after graduating from Howard was a tiny, one-room efficiency on 8th Street, N.W, near Georgia Avenue. I used a bamboo screen to separate the kitchen from the rest of the room. One wall was adorned with the black and white poster of Malcolm X peering out the window with a rifle in his grasp. There was also an orange and black "Boycott Gulf" poster featuring an Angolan sister with a baby on her back and a rifle on her arm. On the other wall was my favorite – a pink and black poster portraying members of the RNA-11 being paraded down a Jackson, MS street, half-clothed and in chains. The outline of the five states of the Republic of New Afrika's national territory loomed in the background. It was in this tiny beautiful room in August of 1981 that New Afrikan Arms Training, or NAT, was born.

The acronym "NAT" was also chosen in remembrance of our freedom-fighting ancestor, Nat Turner. Several of us had seen the need for an organization that would gather and research correct information about firearms and disseminate this information to the Black community. NAT was the creation of security expert Ike, pronounced EE-kay, Ridley. The nuclei of the organization were myself and my boyfriend Bomani Sekou, along with Mba Mbulu, Yao Brewer, and Kyana Mtima.

I was a founding member and secretary for NAT, Inc., and a registered member of the National Rifle Association. NAT taught basic firearm safety classes, firearm purchase and counseling, advanced instructor training and more. We published a training manual, introducing the various chapters with inspirational quotes, such as:

He that hath a Purse, let him take it, and likewise his scrip (money); and he that hath no sword, let him sell his garment, and buy one.
(Jesus Christ, Luke 22:36)

No obstacle is able to stop men carrying arms for liberty.
(Toussaint L'Ouverture)

Any attempt at disarmament when half the world oppresses the other half is but a farce. (Marcus Garvey)

We will be non-violent with people just so long as they are non-violent with us. But if someone raises a hand to harm us, he will take back a stub. (Malcolm X)

As NAT instructors, we cautioned against romanticized, unrealistic views of how casually firearms are used and the consequences of such use, recognizing that many of these acquired views came from the media.

Although I learned how to shoot and clean a weapon, the most important skill I learned as part of NAT, Inc., was the proper attitude to have regarding firearms. I learned to treat every firearm as if it were loaded. I learned to always keep a firearm pointed in a safe direction. I learned that a gun is not a toy. I learned that children should not be taught that guns are toys, and guns should never be given as such. NAT taught that a firearm is a dangerous tool and when in control of one we cannot allow TV images or power fantasies to influence our behavior.

We regularly traveled to Virginia to a range we constructed. While practicing at the range I learned that it didn't necessarily matter if my shots failed to hit the bull's eye. "You develop accuracy when your shots stay in a tight group," Ike instructed, so I practiced and excelled in getting my shots in as tight a group as possible.

Historically, traditional civil rights organizations spouted the principle of non-violence. However, I can assure you that for survival, they relied on "covert armed protection." Years later, Georgia State Professor Akinyele Umoja expertly explored the issue of armed self-defense in his book with the beautifully audacious title, *We Will Shoot Back*. He documented oral histories of Mississippians meeting violence with armed resistance, particularly after the unprovoked 1964 murders of civil rights workers Chaney, Schwerner and Goodman, dispelling the myth that the civil rights movement was always about "turning the other cheek."

My work with NAT, Inc., was decades ago. Today, I have mixed feelings when it comes to the issue of guns. On the one hand, it is axiomatic that self-defense is imperative. On the other hand, there is rampant Black-on-Black crime in our communities. There are also lots of unstable people experiencing Post-Traumatic Stress Disorder (PTSD), Post-Traumatic Slavery Disorder (PTSD) and, in the words of radio host Roach Brown, Post Incarceration Slave Syndrome (PISS), amongst other types of emotional illnesses. Nevertheless, on balance, history has made clear the importance of preparation and the necessity of self-defense. Thus, it is imperative that we all be prepared for self-defense for our survival, while at the same time educating people not to use these skills against those in our own communities.

There is a song with a refrain I used to love to recite, *"How we gonna make the Black Nation rise, Agitate, Educate and Organize."*[82] I was the epitome of these three maxims and the embodiment of Black Power by being part of the building of a Black Nation. I was educating children and writing Black children's books, while at the same time fertilizing my own mind. The lectures I absorbed at NationHouse, as well as Ujamaa Shule, which held similar discussions every Friday night, complemented the historical/spiritual teachings I drank up from the Temple of the Black Messiah on Sundays. I spear-headed Kwanzaa events every year, studied survival skills and engaged in firearms training.

My community cultural/political education and organizing fused with my revolutionary nationalist underpinnings, and both helped inform the next phase of my life. I was stepping outside of my insulated, Black Power community into a larger constellation of activists and advocates, and a new chapter in the continuation of my quest for justice.

Chapter Five, Section 3
Go On and Get That Darn Law Degree

After three years of teaching at Watoto School, I realized if I was as serious about being a lawyer as I claimed I wanted to be all my life, I needed to do what Daddy had always chided me to do – to "go on and get that darn law degree." I took the Law School Admission Test without any prep course. Naïve ole me didn't even know there were prep courses. My first choice was Howard Law School, but I was about to start working during the day at the Washington Office on Africa and Howard did not offer an evening program. My second choice was Antioch Law School, but it likewise did not offer evening classes. I ended up applying to George Washington University National Law Center. It was the only law school I applied to.

Incredibly, I was accepted. Either the ancestors were looking after me or I was the beneficiary of Affirmative Action–in fact, it was both. The April 11, 1980 letter read:

> Dear Ms. Anita Caldwell. The Special Committee on Student Life and Recruitment would like to congratulate you on your acceptance. The National Law Center, in cooperation with the Special Committee, is actively seeking minority students to attend the law school...Your registration at the law school would enhance the continued diversity of the student body.

My plan was to work full time during the day, attend law school in the evening, and continue with "The Struggle" during any remaining moments. I was still a rebel against oppression worldwide, a militant and a self-proclaimed revolutionary.

I wrote the following words on the back of my September 30, 1980 law school class notes:

> I saw *Jaws* in the movies, but no one tells the story of the 100 million Afrikans caught in the jaws of the thousands of sharks who followed the trail of the slave ships on the Middle Passage. I saw *Holocaust* on TV, but no one tells the story of the 100,000,000 Afrikans slaughtered on the voyage across the Atlantic during the Middle Passage. I saw *Raiders of the Lost Ark*, but no one tells the story of the greedy filthy swine who raided and plundered Mother Afrika during the European scramble. I refused to see *Superman* because I knew it would not portray the true supermen and women – Black giant heroes – who relentlessly fought against European domination, from Hannibal to Shaka Zulu; from Nzingha to Yaa Asantewaa; from Harriet to Fannie Lou; and from Garvey to Malcolm, just to name a few.

Needless to say I did not receive a good grade in that class. It was hard paying attention in class when my mind was full of activism and revolutionary fervor. Working full time during the day and attending law school at night was far from ideal, especially when there were only five melanin-enriched people in the entire George Washington University National Law Center evening division when I began. Out of the five of us, only Wilbert Nixon graduated on time; one student became pregnant and withdrew from school; another dropped out; and one left to become the head of a prestigious union. As for me, I graduated a semester late because I found out I was short two credits and had to stay an additional semester to make them up.

Although I attended evening classes at GW, the curriculum, professors and assignments were identical to those of the students who attended day classes. I tried to be active in the Black American Law Students Association (BALSA); the "American" in the title was dropped several years after my law school experience. Always seeking to insure I injected aspects of "The Struggle" into my life, I succeeded in getting an informative article published in the GW BALSA Bridges newsletter on the issue of political prisoners in the United States.

Overall, my law school experience was relatively uneventful. I divided my time between working full time at the Washington Office on Africa, studying for my law school classes, and organizing in support of the Republic of New Afrika and the New Afrikan Independence Movement. I often wondered how much I would have digested had I not been working full time in a critical organization engaged in history-making issues. I wonder how much more of law school I would have retained had I been able to give full attention to my studies?

Moreover, it was difficult for evening students to engage in clinics; even more so as the clinical experience was extremely limited in those days, even for day students. There were no Critical Race Theory courses in those days, no Feminist Legal Studies courses, no seminars based on the television series, "The Wire." My law school experience was, for the most part, conventional boring doctrine.

Despite the curricular limitations of the day, one of the courses I liked most was Crime Lab, and I was fascinated by the section on fingerprint forgery. I sent my final paper on that topic to imprisoned former Black Panther Party member Herman Bell as the issue of a fingerprint was central in his case, which had COINTELPRO all over it. I don't know if it was ever helpful to him, or if he ever even received it, but I do know it would be over 35 years later before he would finally be released on parole in 2018.

Shortly after graduating from law school, the International Convention on the Prevention and Punishment of the Crime of Genocide was ratified by the U.S. Senate and signed by President Reagan. I was now thrilled to add the issue of genocide to my arsenal of advocacy. During this time, I was assisting Brother Imari Obadele in advocating for the release or transfer of New Afrikan prisoners of war, pursuant to the Third Geneva Convention and its protocols. I had no law school classes addressing contemporary international law issues; however I spent a lot of time outside of law school scrutinizing international law doctrine.

While I did not have the benefit of participating in clinics or sexy law school classes, I completed law school successfully. I received my degree, albeit a semester late, and finally my credentials as a bona fide attorney. I finally passed the bar exam after two unsuccessful attempts; the second time missing the mark by only a couple of points.

COINTELPRO was full of unscrupulous deeds, corrupt actions and "dirty tricks." Based on my work with the Republic of New Afrika, I had good reason to believe I was under surveillance. The FBI had visited and questioned me. I was convinced there was a conspiracy to keep me from being a credentialed lawyer. But the third time I took the bar exam was the charm, and it became less of an obsession to investigate whether my test scores were being illegally manipulated as the result of my revolutionary activism. I proudly joined the tiny ranks of Black lawyers in the United States.

According to the National Bar Association, in 1984 there were only 20,000 Black lawyers out of 650,000 lawyers nationwide, and, upon graduation, I guess I made the number 20,001. Although desiring to be a lawyer ever since seeing that poster of Huey Newton up on the wall of my 8th grade Black Studies class, I am so very glad my father pushed me to pursue my dream. I heeded his sage advice and went on and got "that darn law degree!"

Chapter Five, Section 4
Sex, Lies and Videotape

I was a Black power advocate. I was poised to be a Black movement lawyer. But I was also a human being. Throughout my life I made good decisions, and bad. I was happy, and sad. I had the challenges and personal frailties that define what it is to be human.

I once caused a decent relationship to go down the drain because of pride and a lack of trust. Although nowadays the recording of near nude and naked gyrating and twerking bodies in music videos, on snap chat and in other forms of social media is widespread, people were more discrete in the not so distant past. But once the video camera came on the scene, it was not uncommon for consenting couples to make home videos. And so it was with me and a former boyfriend.

One evening, pursuant to a pre-arranged plan, he carefully positioned the video camera on the dresser opposite the bed, and we made love. The video in my opinion, although spicy, was nevertheless (no pun intended) tasteful; yet portrayed me in poses I would not want splashed across a big screen. Becoming increasingly embarrassed and panicky over the next several days, fearing he had shown or might show the tape to his friends or that it might somehow fall into the wrong hands, I was obsessed to get it and destroy it.

So what did I do? I shamefully admit I did what any woman on a mission to preserve her self-respect would have done. I tore up his house looking for that daggone VHS tape. No, not really, but I searched everywhere. In closets, in drawers, under the bed. No tape. Then I ventured to the attic, and, lo-and-behold, there it was. What an absolute relief. My reputation would remain intact. I was saved. Hallelujah!

And then, I saw them. In seconds I went from relief and immense elation, to anguish and gloom. They were love letters – current love letters – stuck up in the attic, from some other woman. I couldn't believe it. The videotape was now a distant second fiddle. He had been lying and was cheating on me, and I was hurt. How could he?! I had thought we were close. When I confronted him about the woman, he was furious.

"You violated my privacy," he angrily charged.

"You cheated on me," I hotly countered.

I couldn't believe his nerve! He justified his infidelity because I violated his privacy. I thought that was some twisted logic. He became the victim. I was the intruder. I was the bad guy. I was the guilty one. And all I was trying to do was get that tape back.

"How can I ever trust you again?" he raged.

My boyfriend (by now ex-boyfriend) said he felt violated. In retrospect, he was correct. I violated his trust, his home and his privacy, to protect my own vulnerability and vanity, and stumbled across something that was not my business. He has never forgiven me for that transgression. But the chilling part about it all is that I don't really know whether there is another copy of that infamous tape lurking around somewhere. With my snooping around to find the tape and stumbling across love letters, I sacrificed what had been a good and fulfilling relationship, as well as a warm friendship. It reminds me of an African proverb – "one who digs too deep for a worm may come up with a snake."

Thinking back upon the incident today, some 30 years later, I grin. Although I was so very cautious back then about not wanting anyone to see an aesthetically graphic, yet lascivious view of me, now that I am in my 60s, maybe it would be nice to look back at an old tape of a younger and much thinner me!

Chapter Five, Section 5
Free Southern Africa!

My full-time day job while attending law school in the evening was working under the tutelage of Dr. Jean Sindab, a badass, brilliant unsung Black woman. I fell in love with her the moment I laid eyes on her. Jean sported natural hair and a strong, fierce confidence that bolstered my own. I was proud to call her my boss.

She was the Executive Director of the Washington Office on Africa (WOA), a church- and union-sponsored organization that advocated for a progressive U.S. policy towards Southern Africa. My interview was with Jean and her associate, Ken Zinn. Jean and I hit it off royally. Ken, her young White colleague, was cool, too. I was still wearing my iconic, sky-high African head wraps daily, accompanied now with long skirts as opposed to tight jeans. I don't know exactly what they thought of me, but I got the job. My first position at WOA was as Office Manager; the role of Network Organizer came next. It was a perfect fit.

During the interview, Jean hesitated when I told her I would be attending law school in the evening. However, I assured her my studies would never get in the way of my work. She later agreed that I kept that promise. When it came to "The Struggle," however, that was a different matter. To this day I have no clue how I was able to juggle a full-time, demanding job, the rigors of law school, and being a full-time Sista in "The Struggle."

Jean Sindab was the quintessential organizer, a powerhouse of energy, and she was smart and savvy. Those were the days when Southern Africa was under apartheid rule and liberation movements such as the African National Congress, Pan Africanist Congress, Southwest African People's Organization, Zimbabwe African Nationalist Congress, and the Black Consciousness Movement, among others, were struggling against White colonial domination. Jean Sindab was the African American head of the Washington arm of the American Committee on Africa. WOA's mission was to be a faith-based lobby in Congress.

The Washington Office on Africa challenged South Africa's efforts to gain support for its racist apartheid system in the United States. It also exposed U.S. complicity with White minority regimes in Southern Africa. We were only a three-person office at the time (Jean, Ken and myself), but we provided much-needed informational resources to educate, motivate and agitate for an end to U.S. support for the unjust racist regime. Our vehicle was an educational publication, *Washington Notes on Africa*, which kept the community informed about U.S. policy towards Southern Africa.

This publication was chock full of information and played a pivotal role in the struggle for the liberation of Southern Africa. During my 1980-1983 tenure, we produced several resource packets. They included *Stop the Apartheid Bomb*, detailing U.S.-South Africa nuclear collaboration; *Free Namibia*, a special resource on Namibia and U.S. policy; and *Campaign Against Investment in South Africa*, which provided background materials for state and local divestment campaigns.

I fondly remember writing the following words for a speech Jean delivered to an enthusiastic audience gathered to celebrate WOA's 10th anniversary:

> When the Washington Office on Africa opened in 1972, Richard Nixon was President and U.S. policy towards Southern Africa was based on Henry Kissinger's analysis that Whites were in Southern Africa 'to stay.' Not only have we survived Nixon, we have continued to carry out our mandate through three subsequent Administrations – struggling for an end to U.S. support for racist minority rule in Southern Africa.

Attended by over 500 people, we held the gala affair on November 6, 1982, at the Capital Hilton Hotel in Washington, D.C. I was the principal coordinator, galvanizing the attendance of diplomats, Congressional aides, African scholars, church groups and grassroots organizers. The honorary sponsors included Senators Paul Tsongas and Edward Kennedy, as well as Congressmen George Crockett and Stephen Solarz.

I organized a stellar reception as part of the program featuring the a'cappella singing sensation, Sweet Honey in the Rock, the Cosan African Dance Ensemble (headed up by my friend, Karen Daniels) and South African poet Fatima Dike. The evening's speakers included the Ambassador of Botswana, Theo-Ben Gurirab (a frequent visitor to our office and the SWAPO Observer to the United Nations), and Ted Lockwood, former director of the Washington Office on Africa.

During my time at WOA, South Africa's 4.5 million Whites ruthlessly controlled the political, social and economic lives of the country's 26 million Blacks. Although Whites represented only 16% of the population, they controlled 87% of the country's land. They denied Blacks access to employment and education opportunities, as well as all political rights. Those who opposed this system were jailed, and often tortured or even executed.

Years later I conversed with my esteemed elder Leonard Dunston, who reminisced conundrums faced by African Americans during apartheid South Africa. Although

I was aware of the regime's schizophrenically racist policies wherein Black partici-pants in sport, trade or diplomatic matters were granted the status of "Honorary White" to allow them to circumvent apartheid rules, it had not dawned on me the impact of similar exceptions with visiting African Americans.

Baba Lenny told me the story of Cenie "Jomo" Williams, the first national president of the or-ganization they were both members of – the Na-tional Association of Black Social Workers (NABSW). In 1972, a group of Black social workers in South Africa had invited Williams to the country to help organize a NABSW chapter there. As a national Black figure, they had ar-ranged for him to stay at a hotel in Johannesburg. However, the only way in which U.S. Blacks dur-ing the apartheid era could stay in White hotels while in the country was to be afforded the status of "Honorary White."

Cenie Williams, Baba Lenny disclosed, contemptuous of the apartheid govern-ment's racist policies, chose to stay in the Black township of Soweto in solidarity with the oppressed people, rather than be listed as an "Honorary White." That spoke volumes to me, and I never forgot his principled stance.

The U.S. government under the leadership of Ronald Reagan was increasingly sup-portive of South Africa's White minority regime. The Reagan Administration's cozy policy, known as "constructive engagement," renewed the alliance between the U.S. and South Africa by increasing political, military, and economic support to the apartheid government. At WOA, we asserted that Reagan's policy bolstered U.S. corporate investment by allowing access to strategic minerals. The policy under-mined human rights and self-determination. Rather than constructive engagement, we branded the U.S. actions as "destructive engagement."

For example, Reagan asked Congress to repeal the Clark Amendment, an important law that prohibited covert U.S. military intervention in Angola. Such aid was being used to undermine the liberation struggle in Angola. He vetoed a resolution in the UN Security Council to impose sanctions on South Africa because of the racist re-gime's refusal to compromise on reaching a Namibia settlement. Reagan allowed several nuclear sales to South Africa and approved the export of 2,500 electric shock batons to South Africa. He lifted the ban on sales of "non-military" items to South Africa, including the military and police, and allowed the sales of computers, air-planes and helicopters to the military and police.

President Reagan entertained South African Foreign Minister Pik Botha in the White House. The apartheid leader became the first foreign minister from Africa to be invited to and visit the Reagan White House. His Administration attempted to deport exiled South African poet and anti-apartheid activist Dennis Brutus, who once celled next to Nelson Mandela on Robben Prison Island, from the U.S. The Reagan Administration introduced an obstacle to Namibian independence by insisting on an agreement of withdrawal of Cuban troops from Angola as precondition to settlement. And the Administration rejected international efforts to censure South Africa for continued illegal occupation of Namibia.

The Washington Office on Africa's position was that Reagan's election to the White House signaled a new, closer alliance between the U.S. and South Africa. This alliance successfully deflected the efforts of the international community to achieve Namibian independence. Authored by the U.S. Assistant Secretary of State for African Affairs, Chester Crocker, the policy of "constructive engagement" viewed Southern Africa through the lens of the Cold War. WOA contended that this meant a "new partnership with the staunch anti-communist South African regime in joining efforts to stop perceived Soviet expansionism, undermine the achievements of the Angolan, Mozambican and Zimbabwean revolutions and hold the line against the liberation movements of Namibia and South Africa, SWAPO and the African National Congress."

One of WOA's major campaigns was "Stop the Apartheid Bomb," designed to halt U.S./South African nuclear collaboration. Rep. Charles Rangel introduced legislation to ban all nuclear exports to South Africa and end the training of South Africans at U.S. government nuclear facilities. On December 19, 1982, four bombs exploded at South Africa's Koberg nuclear power reactor, which had been a direct beneficiary of the Reagan Administration's "constructive engagement" policy. The African National Congress took credit for the explosions. It was said they were set off in retaliation for Pretoria's brutal attack on land-locked Lesotho, in which 42 people were killed ten days earlier. The sabotage delayed the nuclear power reactor for several months.

Little did I know that this bombing in South Africa occurred during the same time period of politically-motivated bombings against political and military institutional targets in the United States, or that later that decade as a lawyer, I would defend the revolutionary bombing suspects in federal court. Armed expropriations against financial entities in the U.S. were also occurring during this period. Reportedly, the expropriated funds were to help resource liberation movements in Southern Africa, one of many stories from the Black underground in the U.S. yet, and possibly never, to be told.

Perhaps most pivotal, today's activists could use the massive divestment and cultural boycott campaigns during the 1980s against corporations and entertainers profiting from doing business with South Africa as a model. The divestment campaign, in which stockholders intentionally sold their assets from corporations doing business in South Africa to influence social change, sparked unprecedented city and state initiatives around the country. These initiatives helped to create a political climate for national legislation curtailing investment in South Africa.

Proudly, the D.C. divestment bill was the most comprehensive municipal bill to be introduced in the nation. It barred deposits of city funds in banks that had lent to the South African government or to corporations and banks active there. It also required the District's pension funds and housing finance agencies to sell their holdings in any bank or corporation with financial links to South Africa. The proceeds were to be re-invested in acceptable firms.

During my tenure at WOA, both the divestment and the cultural boycott against South Africa picked up steam. The apartheid regime had drastically intensified its efforts to woo U.S. entertainers and athletes to perform in South Africa, hoping to strengthen apartheid and give it international legitimacy. Pretoria spared no expense, offering as much as $2 million to artists to come and perform. Those who succumbed to the huge sums of money justified their visits to South Africa by arguing the false dichotomy of separation between culture and politics.

All the while, South Africa shrewdly combined politics and culture as an additional weapon in its propaganda arsenal. The widespread cultural boycott offered an excellent opportunity to raise the visibility of the apartheid issue. Large grassroots constituencies mobilized for political work. Jean Sindab often stated, "We must tell these entertainers who dance to Pretoria's tune that if they perform in South Africa, they will pay a higher price than the huge sums of money they receive from that racist regime."

What I feel took the issue over the top were the efforts of the newly formed advocacy group, TransAfrica. Under the leadership of Randall Robinson, the group launched a national campaign and formed the coalition, Artists and Athletes Against Apartheid. They designed the campaign to inform the U.S. entertainment industry about the UN-sanctioned ban on tours of South Africa.

Besides WOA and TransAfrica, there was also the Southern Africa Support Project (SASP), under the leadership of D.C. veteran advocates Sylvia Hill, Sandra Hill, Adwoa Dunn and Cecelie Counts, along with the Lawyers' Committee for Civil Rights. The circle was now complete and a "Free South Africa" movement burgeoned. WOA lobbied Congress on behalf of mainstream churches and unions.

TransAfrica became the voice of the Black community on the hill. SASP coordinated the grassroots and direct action on the ground. Gay McDougall mobilized lawyers. A mere peon in this escalating movement, I gobbled up all the tactics and strategies to use later at various points throughout my career.

These were the days long before the personal computer. I remember when WOA first purchased an IBM Seletric III typewriter. It was a master invention, with unheard of self-correcting tape. Jackie Wilson, our top-notch secretary who, when hired, brought the WOA team to four full-time staff, fell in love with this new invention. She also fell in love with one of the SWAPO representatives who frequented the office. When independence came to Namibia, he became an Ambassador and Jackie became part of the government of a free Namibia as the ambassador's wife. To this day I stand in awe of her many accomplishments in Namibia. And, I stand in awe of students who once interned at WOA during my tenure, who today are change-makers, such as Lisa Crooms, long-term professor and Associate Dean of Academic Affairs at Howard University School of Law; and Sherrilyn Ifill, voting rights genius and Executive Director of the NAACP Legal Defense and Educational Fund.

Dr. Jean Sindab, ten years my senior, died prematurely in 1996 at age 51, after a year-long battle against cancer. Among her many accomplishments after leaving WOA was heading up the World Council of Churches Programme to Combat Racism. Driven to right injustices, Jean directed a program for the National Council of Churches on issues of environmental justice, hunger and sexism. She also worked tirelessly against the stigma of casteism confronting the Dalits, an underclass in India. She addressed however she could the needs of indigenous people worldwide. Dr. Nellie Jean Pitts Sindab was my idol and anchor for years. An absolutely unforgettable woman.

I am grateful for the opportunity Jean gave me to work and learn alongside her at such a pivotal moment in world history – the dawning of a free Southern Africa. Although neither she nor hardly anyone else in either the anti-apartheid movement or my law school career knew of my pursuits with the New Afrikan Independence Movement, it was exhilarating engaging in activities with not only the liberation movements in Southern Africa, but a key one at home as well.

***

1996 was an emotional year for me. Not only did Jean pass that January, but in April, two other close colleagues and friends made their transitions as well – Haywood Burns and Shanara Gilbert. They were traveling in South Africa at the time, attending a conference in Cape Town on democracy and international law, when the car they were riding in was tragically struck.

Shanara was truly a trailblazer, particularly on the issue of the death penalty and lobbying to achieve passage of the Racial Justice Act, which sought to address the issue of race in the application of the federal death penalty. The last time I recalled her physical presence was during the October 1995 National Conference of Black Lawyers board meeting in Washington, D.C.

Even upon his death at the young age of 55, Haywood was already a legend in law. He was a founding member of the National Conference of Black Lawyers, had successfully represented Angela Davis on trumped up kidnapping and murder charges; had coordinated the legal defense of the Attica prison rebellion case; was the second dean of the City University of New York Law School; and, ardently opposed the Nixon proposed Supreme Court nominations of Clement Haynesworth, G. Harrold Carswell, and the H.W. Bush Administration's Supreme Court nomination of Clarence Thomas.

I feel blessed that I could always call upon Haywood, and he would always respond. He was often a professional reference for me for employment positions. He always positively responded to my requests to speak on programs.

He was a big brother and mentor in my career development. And he even once referred me to his wife, Jennifer Dohrn, a midwife, for consultation on the birth of my daughter. The last time I was in his company was two months before his death in D.C., at a meeting with key staffers from the Congressional Black Caucus (CBC) seeking a civil rights investigation for Mumia Abu-Jamal, and requesting CBC hearings on the impact of the FBI's once-secret COINTELPRO program.

The day of the fateful accident in South Africa, I was reviewing a document for a speech I was to deliver the next day. It was ironically jointly prepared by Haywood and Shanara on behalf of Brother Attorney Chokwe Lumumba, who had disciplinary charges pending against him for allegedly expressing a personal opinion out of court that a particular judicial decision was 'racist.' The Letter and Memorandum to the Disciplinary Committee from Haywood and Shanara brilliantly demonstrated the racism inherent in the U.S. administration of justice. The document concluded:

Institutional or societal denial of the existence of racism will not eradicate it; only courageous, honest acknowledgment and conscious efforts will do so. The law itself has great potential for eradicating racism in society, provided that the human beings behind the law have the requisite sensitivity to weave social reality into the logic of the law. Practitioners of the law, who are in a position to see the debilitating effects of race-based decision-making, even if unconscious in the operation of the legal system, have an obligation to identify it and to use all legal means, including those means protected by the First Amendment, to challenge and defeat it. In doing so, they embody the most noble of values and of character as professionals and citizens.

In reflecting on Jean, Haywood, and Shanara, I lift up a statement that was quoted frequently in the Black Panther Party newspaper that went something like this, "Whenever death may surprise us, let it be welcome. Provided that this, our battle cry, reach some receptive ear. That other voices may come forward to pick up the struggle where we left off, with new cries of battle and victory."

Jean, Shanara, and Haywood, your passing will not be in vain. I vowed to myself that I would carry on "The Struggle" and continue standing up for rights. I hope throughout the years I have done justice to that pledge.

I left the Washington Office on Africa in 1984 upon my graduation from law school. Jean was still working there at the time; and I never had the pleasure to work with her successors, Damu Smith and Imani Countess, who continued in her footsteps through the triumph of a free South Africa. WOA's Board of Directors honored me upon my graduation with an all-expense paid trip to anyplace in Africa I chose. Gleefully, I picked Senegal.

Friends who visited the country had always recommended it as a first trip to Africa and as "an unforgettable return home." Senegal, they said, had the ambience of traditional African culture and dress, and an extraordinary historic experience that included the bone-chilling slave castle at Goree Island. The only drawback for those colonized with the English tongue was that French is the official language of the country.

Rev. Jesse Jackson was running for the U.S. Presidency during my first trip to the Motherland. It was an exciting time. People in Senegal loved Jesse. Someone had given me a slew of Jesse Jackson post cards before my trip, and they were my number one bartering chip. Armed with my cache of iconic Jesse postcards, coupled with a supply of New York-themed tee shirts, a stock of school supplies and nail polish galore, I cleaned up in the marketplace!

I was greeted by cries of "My Sista" everywhere I went. Most of the Senegalese I encountered thought I was from the islands. They knew I was not likely from the African continent based on how I styled my gele headwrap. Some erroneously surmised I was from Jamaica. I did not speak French, and disappointedly, my knowledge of the Senegalese Wolof language was limited to "Nga def" (hello). But despite it all, I loved the trip and had a fabulous time.

Years later I took my mother and father to Senegal, for their first (and only) trip to Africa. The three of us stood silently in the arch of the "Door of No Return"[83] at Goree Island, solemnly gazing upon the oceanic waters of the Atlantic. It was at that very moment, in that very sacred place, and squeezed between my loving parents, that an animating ancestral wind traversed my being, and revealed in no uncertain terms, that I must connect the dots of generations, and continue their collective quest for justice.

Chapter Five, Section 6
Plastic Cuffs and Momentary Deprivations of Liberty

My legal career began with a bang. I was arrested in 1984 as soon as I graduated from law school. I had joined others demonstrating outside of the South African Embassy on Massachusetts Avenue in D.C. We were protesting to urge the release of Nelson Mandela from unjust imprisonment and the ending of racist apartheid. Our arrests were totally staged, orchestrated, and negotiated with plastic cuffs and the probability of dismissed charges. Nevertheless, a nervous shiver coursed through my body as I was handcuffed and unceremoniously marched to the waiting police van for delivery to the precinct. After processing, I was fingerprinted and led to a large room where I waited for what seemed like an eternity before they finally called my name for release.

The protest and arrests were facilitated by legal observers with the National Conference of Black Lawyers and the National Lawyers Guild, two organizations I would come to love for their steadfast commitment to movement lawyering. At different intervals, the names of Jesse Jackson and Dick Gregory were called out to be released. I don't remember who else joined me at the police precinct, but there was quite a mass of protestors.

While waiting for my name to be called amidst the remaining crowd of similarly detained protestors, I mused about Steve Biko, leader of the Black Consciousness Movement in South Africa. I recalled that he was tortured and subsequently murdered while in police custody. Knowledge of the torture of Chicago police station detainees by Officer John Burge had not yet been uncovered; however, the 1973 torture of former Black Panther Party member Ruben Scott and others in a New Orleans police station had been revealed. At the time, I was oblivious to both outrages. It would be several decades before the U.S. Army and CIA-orchestrated tortures against detainees at Abu Ghraib in Iraq would occur. Nevertheless, after my release from voluntary detention for peacefully demonstrating in front of the South African Embassy, I resumed my everyday activities.

Since then, I have been arrested on two other occasions: Once outside the Congressional Longworth House of Representatives Building to support statehood for the District of Columbia, and once outside of the White House to support democracy in Haiti. Each time, the arrests were en masse and staged. The organizers negotiated with the police and prosecuting authorities before the demonstrations. They made sure that plastic cuffs would be used and all charges would be dropped. After each dismissal, I gave not a second thought about the arrest and went on with my life. I had experienced a mere inconvenience of perhaps several hours until processing was completed.

Let me be perfectly clear: these staged arrests and momentary deprivations of physical liberty were a far cry from the terror, dogs, fire hoses and nooses of the past. I humbly realized that I could engage in these struggles because my predecessors were on the frontline battlefields of justice, whether from the Civil Rights or Black Liberation Movements. They sacrificed, struggled and paid the price for a new generation to pick up the baton and fight against new manifestations of injustice.

But there was a fourth occasion when I was detained, but not voluntarily. Little did my daughter know that when she was five months in utero, I was listed as an enemy of the state. I had flown to Grenada in December 1993 to participate in the wedding of my good friend Kianga, whose family was from the island nation. I was excited to go, not only because it was the venue for my friend's wedding, but also because Grenada had been the home of the legendary Maurice Bishop, who 10 years earlier as its revolutionary Prime Minister, had been assassinated just prior to a U.S. invasion of the country.

Returning to the U.S. at the conclusion of the wedding festivities, I was unceremoniously stopped and herded into a secure room at the Puerto Rican airport.

"Why am I being detained," I demanded. "What is the problem?! I'm an officer of the court."

"We know who you are," one security officer stiffly replied. "You've been to Libya, haven't you?" he stridently insisted.

The accusation totally threw me for a loop. I'd been to many places, but unfortunately Libya had never been one of them.

"Nope, that wasn't me," I countered. "I've never been to Libya."

"You have," the other officer brazenly piped in. "Your name is on the list."

"List, what list?" I demanded. "Where is it? Let me see it!" I angrily persisted.

Ignoring me and disregarding my entreaties, his eyes remained transfixed on the computer as he scrolled through the screen's pages.

Here I am, noticeably pregnant, imprisoned in some back room with two White airport security guards, pre-TSA. Who knows what list they claim I was on. Who knows what associations they connected me with. Now of course I knew several comrades who had traveled there, several times. That, however, was a question not asked and information not necessary for me to proffer.

Libya was a revolutionary government. It was well known that Muammar Gaddafi, like Kwame Nkrumah before him, had impressive plans to create a unified Africa, empowered with a new African economic system. And, most importantly, he wanted to financially assist the work of Black people in the U.S. Although I did not accompany comrades in those trips to Libya, upon information and belief, some successfully used Republic of New Afrika passports issued by the RNA Ministry of Justice to gain entry into the North African nation.

Yes, I probably was on some list the U.S. deemed nefarious, but if the authorities had actually done their homework, they would have known I was never amongst any of the groups that traveled to the country. However, even if I were, don't tell me I can't travel to the continent my ancestors were stolen from, particularly as it was your ancestors that stole my people. The audacity. Don't brand me an enemy of your state, when you have desecrated mine. The nerve.

Having no grounds whatsoever to detain me, I was eventually released after about an hour to resume my travel home.

But again, this and my other momentary deprivations of liberty pale compared to what would become much of my legal career's work – unmasking the horrifically lengthy periods of incarceration meted out by U.S. courts that disproportionately impact so many Black brothers and sisters. This life's work would become a major calling for me, pushing the envelope to illuminate the severity of the problems we face, and questioning whether such outrageous deprivations of liberty amount to justice or solely, just-us.

Chapter Five, Section 7
Cutting My Legal Teeth in Prison

My first job after graduating from law school in 1984 was as a staff attorney for the National Prison Project of the American Civil Liberties Union Foundation. But my dream had been to work as a public defender. I eagerly applied to the Public Defender Service (PDS) for the District of Columbia, which had a reputation for being one of the best public defender offices in the country. I was very idealistic and naïve, unaware of the undue emphasis placed on the prestige of the school attended, grades, and other indications of status and success.

When I was not hired, I was crushed! How could they not hire me? Sure, I had not attended an Ivy League school, but George Washington University Law School definitely wasn't the lowest school on the totem pole. However, I knew my law school grades were far from stellar. While I graduated magna cum laude from undergrad, I always felt that I got out of law school, Thanky you Lawdy!

To this day I am convinced PDS made a mistake in not hiring me. I was so disappointed, and I was not used to failure and defeat. Hadn't just about everything in my life gone the way I wanted it to? Didn't I get into the only law school I applied to? Didn't I receive a grant from the D.C. Commission on the Arts and Humanities for my storypoems? In retrospect, I wonder why I stayed upset for years that I was not hired by PDS. What difference would it have made, I ruminate? What would I have learned from PDS that I did not later learn after going into private practice as a court-appointed lawyer?

Let me not kid myself. Had the Public Defender Service hired me, I would have been taught how to litigate as opposed to making a spectacle of myself stumbling through the process alone by trial and error. As a court-appointed lawyer during the late 80s, I had no access to investigators. I had no mentors in criminal law. I had taken part in no mock trials. I had no practice sessions before trials.

If I had access to any of these preparatory essentials, I might not have been so nervous during my very first jury trial that I forgot to deliver my opening statement. I might not have been flustered trying to figure out how to get a document introduced into evidence after finding that a policeman had lied.

The esteemed and prestigious Criminal Practice Institute at D.C.'s Public Defender Service, open to lawyers at-large, had not yet been established. If the young lawyer I was then had access to its support, I would have been better prepared to manage the inherent stress of knowing that an individual's future – their very life – might be determined by my advocacy, or lack thereof.

At the same, if I had gotten my dream job at the Public Defender Service, I likely would not be where I am today. When you pull away one thread of your history, it is difficult to say how many other threads would have unraveled, or what kind of life you'd be left with. If I had gotten the PDS job, I likely would not have applied to the National Prison Project. I would not have gotten to know Adjoa Aiyetoro, a union that led to the mainstreaming of the reparations movement. I may have never come to the attention of Mort Halperin, who hired me first at the ACLU Legislative Office and later, provided me with an incredible opportunity at the Open Society Foundations.

Had I not worked at the ACLU, I may never have been inspired to engage in advocacy on the crack/powder disparity issue, which was a catalyst for the changes to that egregious law nearly two decades later. If the Open Society had not hired me, I might never have led the Justice Roundtable Coalition, whose working groups helped to change the landscape of federal criminal justice reform. Who knows what could have been. I remain grateful for what was, which has led me to where I am in this very moment.

As it turns out Al Bronstein, director of the National Prison Project of the ACLU Foundation[84] was the one who took the chance and hired me as a staff attorney right out of law school. Thirty years later I was asked to make formal remarks at his memorial service. I proudly stated:

> Al was not just an effective lawyer. He was a phenomenal lawyer. A brilliant lawyer. A courageous lawyer. An inspirational lawyer. He was the quintessential lawyer's lawyer. But most important for me, he was a lawyer who practiced what he preached and was always on the cutting edge of social change. I vowed that is what I wanted my legal career to be, on the cutting edge, and most definitely I wanted to engage in the practice of law in the public interest for social change, like Al.

Being at the National Prison Project was not like being at a traditional law firm. Instead of making $224,600 my first year, my starting salary in 1984 was $24,600. But I would never have traded the experience I gained from being on the front-lines of prisoner rights' advocacy. I was escorting expert witnesses through prison facilities. I was interviewing prisoner clients. I was researching, writing and filing briefs.

I was actually litigating. Largely because of Al, there was never a feeling of what I could not accomplish in the field of law. He deepened in me the qualities of perseverance, creativity, ingenuity and the determination to never give up.

I have fond memories of my days at the National Prison Project and of colleagues such as Attorney Elizabeth Alexander who was lead counsel on my primary case in Michigan; Steve Ney, who went on to head a Maryland disability organization; Mary McClymont, who later led a foundation; Ed Koren, whom I considered the prisoner rights historian; Dan Manville, a formerly incarcerated person who later went to law school; Urvashi Vaid, an Indian American lawyer who would become one of the most ardent LGBTQ advocates in the country; Jan Elvin who later married Al and became a noted author; Lynthia Gibson, who has remained a close colleague of mine through most of my professional jobs over the decades; and, of course, Adjoa.

Adjoa Aiyetoro was a dynamic, bodacious, outspoken, Black female attorney at the National Prison Project. My earliest recollection of her is that she was in a horrible accident. She was making tea, and her nightgown caught fire. Adjoa was seriously burned over much of her body. However, her indomitable spirit undoubtedly led to her not only surviving, but thriving. During those early  years of our working together, Adjoa was confined to a compression bodysuit so that the skin grafting could take effect. Her face was unscarred, but her hands were disfigured. One thing about Adjoa was that once you got to know her, you discovered that her personality was so strong and frank that you never even noticed the burns.

Adjoa was, to me, a masterpiece. She became my mentor in the practice of law, and I was her mentor in Black Nationalism and reparations. She introduced me to the legal activist world of the National Conference of Black Lawyers (NCBL). Through her I became acquainted with its great leaders such as Haywood Burns, Lennox Hinds, Charles Roach, and Margaret Burnham. I introduced Adjoa to the revolutionary world of Black Nationalism, reparations, and political prisoners. I think her openness to my politics put her at odds with some NCBL masterminds, who probably leaned more towards Marxism than Black Nationalism. Adjoa, however, uniquely straddled both worlds and was the one I consider instrumental in helping to bridge ideological gaps in the movement.

I admired her legal acumen, and her proclivity and openness to the issue of reparations for enslavement and post-slavery discrimination. During that time one of the foremost experts espousing reparations was Brother Imari Obadele of the Republic of New Afrika. It was Adjoa who helped to engineer the Harvard NCBL conference, which brought Brother Imari, Chokwe Lumumba, and myself to Cambridge to advance the dialogue about reparations. This gathering catalyzed the birth of the National Coalition of Blacks for Reparations in America (N'COBRA).

I cut my legal teeth at the National Prison Project. We litigated large-scale class action prisoner lawsuits against state governments. This was long before the passage of the 1996 Prison Litigation Reform Act, which cut out the receipt of attorney fees in such cases. My primary case was a 'conditions of confinement' lawsuit against the Michigan Department of Corrections. It required me to travel often throughout Michigan, from Jackson State Prison in Jackson to Ionia, which housed mental health prisoners, to all the way upstate at Marquette prison. I was learning on the job, and my seemingly insatiable passion for social justice lawyering was being fueled.

On October 28, 2015, four days after Al passed, I received the following Facebook message from a long-ago client in the Michigan case:

> Nkechi, the last time I saw you, you were with Elizabeth and Adjoa before Judge Enslen in Kalamazoo. I was one of the named plaintiffs who attended the hearings. I won parole and was released last year. I am attending the ICAN conference next month in D.C. I see you are a keynote speaker. Will be awesome to see you after so long. Regards, T.J. Spytma.

"Amazing, T.J. I remember your name, but that was oh so long ago. I was just out of law school. Your memory is so good. I'm impressed. That was my first case," I replied.

"How could I forget?" he fired back. "You three kicked butt. The AAGs [Assistant Attorney Generals] didn't know what hit them. I was impressed then and remain so today."

The National Prison Project brought experts through the institutions, inspecting prison conditions of confinement for their constitutionality, ensuring access to the courts through the adequacy of the law library, and investigating claims of racial discrimination. We toured the institutions' kitchen facilities, dormitories and individual cellblocks. Walking through the prisons, I was never scared of its residents. I was actually more apprehensive of the guards. The prisoners knew we were there to help. "Hey Sista," the brothers shouted, just like they did on the streets of Harlem when I was a teen. "Shorty, come on over here!" they jested. My background was political prisoners. I was comfortable interacting with the brothers. I loved it. I felt at home.

I developed friendships among the prisoners, including one special brother, Damu Abantu, who was part of the Melanic Brotherhood. Now, over 30 years later, I wonder where he is today. Is he gainfully employed, with a house, wife and family? Is he incarcerated on possibly another charge? What collateral consequences of his conviction has he been saddled with? Is he still with the Brotherhood movement, which sustained him so well while he was at Jackson State Prison? I have unanswered questions about many of the brothers I met years ago. Overtime, I found myself inundated with prisoner mail. Little by little, much to the chagrin of those behind bars seeking legal advice, companionship, or just a lifeline to the outside world, I eventually disengaged from mostly all institutional correspondence.

While at the National Prison Project, I also investigated the Maryland Department of Corrections AIDS Unit. It was horrific. Food trays were pushed through dirty slots. The living quarters were dilapidated. One word sums up the experience – abysmal.

One brother, Marshall Eddie Conway, was incarcerated within the Maryland Department of Corrections. This was 20 years before his release in 2014 after 44 years of unjust imprisonment. Eddie was the former Minister of Defense of the Baltimore Chapter of the Black Panther Party. Although the drumbeat for his release was kept up by Black Classic Press's Paul Coates over the decades, Eddie would likely still be imprisoned today had it not been for revelations of erroneous jury instructions in pre-1981 Maryland cases.

These revelations led to the unprecedented release of nearly 200 aging people serving life sentences, including Eddie. He now very successfully serves as an Executive Producer of The Real News Network (TRNN), host of the TRNN show "Rattling the Bars," and author of *Marshall Law: The Life & Times of a Baltimore Black Panther*, and *The Greatest Threat: The Black Panther Party and COINTELPRO*. But for the chance ruling that resulted in his release, he would likely still be behind bars; his talents and contributions to society, unrealized.

Chapter Five, Section 8
The "Ketchup in My Face" Case

I left civil litigation with the National Prison Project in 1987 to hang out my own shingle. I wasn't getting any younger and really wanted to try my hand at criminal defense. Just three years out of law school, I now had more experience than most of my counterparts slaving in corporate law firms. I was not pushing paper; I was escorting experts through prisons. I was not getting coffee for bosses; I was deposing clients. I was defending depositions. I was examining witnesses. I was writing briefs. I was not at a thankless job. I was making a difference. Sure, I wasn't raking in the big bucks, but I was surviving financially, and emotionally speaking, thriving.

My first case in private practice was a PWID (possession with intent to distribute) drugs, which would be the charge in most of my court-appointed cases, as the infamous War on Drugs was about to kick in high steam. My client was dying. He had full-blown AIDS, and this was during the time when there was not a lot of information about the disease. He looked weak, sick and horrible. He smelled too.

I took a deep breath and timidly approached him in his Howard University Hospital bed to have him sign some papers. I remember not wanting to touch the pen after he signed, which was such stupidity on my part. But like many people at the time, I was ill-informed about the ways in which HIV was transmitted. Nevertheless, I advocated zealously on his behalf and got the case dismissed.

Although most of my D.C. Superior Court cases were PWID, others included regular, run-of-the-mill, adult criminal defense and juvenile cases, including solicitation, theft, robbery and simple assault, as well as work in landlord/tenant court. I also handled child abuse and neglect cases.

My first jury trial was an excellent example of a prosecutorial waste of time, a squander of taxpayer dollars, and outright ridiculousness. The case would decide the fate of an 18-year-old Haitian youth charged with throwing ketchup in the face of a White girl in a carryout in D.C.'s upscale Georgetown neighborhood. Although the charge was a misdemeanor, it was a very serious situation for my client because of his non-citizen immigrant status. Hell, I'll admit, I was nervous!

I was worried because of the collateral consequences of a criminal conviction, if that were the outcome. This teen's future was in my hands, and I had not had the benefit of a criminal clinic in law school. I had never picked a jury before, and here I was, with this maze of a chart in my hands. The only thing I remember was trying to get as many Black men on that jury as I could. The only one I can recall getting through jury selection was a middle-aged, African American gentleman with horn-rimmed glasses who was a professor at a local university.

I had crafted a carefully prepared opening statement that I wrote down and practiced delivering from memory in advance of the trial. I felt confident that the statement I would give followed the rules I learned from reading about trial techniques. I would make sure I provided a preview of what the evidence in the case would show. I would say, "Before I talk about what we believe the evidence will show, I want to make one fact perfectly clear to each of you. P.L. did push ketchup in the face of the plaintiff, A.H., on April 26, 1987, in the carryout in Georgetown. That fact, however, is not the issue in this case." I would then pause for dramatic effect. "The issue in this case, ladies and gentlemen, is whether or not P.L. was defending himself when the incident occurred, and whether his defense was reasonable."

Next, I would espouse the regular mantra of any good defense counsel. I would state emphatically, "We as the defense do not have to prove anything. Rather, it is the prosecution that has to prove, beyond a reasonable doubt, that P.L. was not justified in defending himself." I would then state unequivocally, "We believe that the evidence will show that he was in fact justified in reacting as he did and thus is guilty of no crime."

I had the main points of my opening statement memorized and I would deliver it with poise and passion:

> Now I am sure that many of you are curious as to what really did happen in the carryout early that morning. You will hear P.L. answer that question. You will hear him tell you he and some friends entered the carryout, that his friends got fries and found stools, and that he went to get ketchup and then searched the crowded carryout for a stool to take to join his friends. He will tell you that he saw an empty stool by the front window, and that he proceeded to move it over to where his friends were sitting.

> He will testify that a young woman – the complaining witness A.H. – was seated on the stool next to the one he was taking, and that he asked her could he have the seat. P.L. will tell you her response was, 'Don't you see someone sitting there?' P.L. will tell you that no one was sitting on the stool, and he told her he wanted to take it and sit down because there were no other stools. P.L. will tell you that the woman followed him as he dragged the stool, shouting obscenities and racial slurs at him. He will tell you that he paused, holding on to the stool in one hand and the ketchup in the other, and told her that he does not like anyone talking about his mother.

> He will tell you that the woman then tried to knee him in the groin, striking the inside of his thigh instead. P.L. will describe to you the painful apprehension that shot through his body as the thought of being kneed in his private parts became real. He will tell you that his first reaction was to get this girl away from him, which he immediately did by pushing her with his hand – the same hand that was holding the napkin with ketchup on it.

> Mr. P.L. will tell you that A.H. never got the opportunity to try and knee him in the groin again because she slipped on the dirty wet floor and fell.

> D.W. will also testify. D.W. will tell you he saw much of the incident. He

will tell you that A.H. was ranting and raving, loud and wild. He will testify that he saw A.H. knee P.L. in his groin area, and that P.L. immediately reacted by pushing her away from him.

We hope that you listen carefully to all the evidence that will be presented, and render a verdict in favor of my client, the defendant, P.L.

I had read in my trial practice manual that the defense has the option of giving her opening statement right after the prosecution, or waiting until the defense case-in-chief and rendering it at that time. I thought that made sense, as there would be no interruption in the minds of the jury once we started our defense. Thus, after the prosecutor delivered the government's opening statement, I self-assuredly announced that the defense would give its opening statement at the beginning of our case-in-chief – the statement I had so carefully prepared and practiced reciting.

The prosecution then called its only witness, the complainant, A.H., to the stand. A.H. gave an elaborate and exaggerated rendition of her version of events – that she was assaulted by my client, and thrown to the ground not once, but two times and sustained injuries.

My cross-examination sought to establish that 1. she was with other people; 2. that she had been drinking; and 3. that she was disrespectful to my client. Portions went as follows:

> Me: "You say you were out dancing that night, into the wee hours of the morning, is that correct?"
>
> A.H.:   "Yes, I was."
>
> Me: "And you were out with some friends of yours?"
>
> A.H.:   "Yes, I was."
>
> Me: "And you and your friends had some drinks that night, didn't you?"
>
> A.H.:   "One or two."
>
> Me: "Do you remember cursing at P.L.?"
>
> A.H.:   "No, I don't."

This was a poor choice of words. Of course the answer would be she doesn't re-

member. I should have phrased it, "You cursed at P.L., didn't you?"

Me: "Do you remember talking about his mother in a derogatory fashion?"

Another inappropriately worded question.

A.H.:   "That I did not do."

Me: "You do remember saying, 'your mama,' though, don't you? Is that your testimony?"

A.H.:   "That's all I said."

OK, I thought, I could go with that admission. I knew she had no eyewitnesses, otherwise they would have been called to the stand before the prosecution rested its case. I knew she had made inconsistent statements. I had a police officer who would testify to that. So, now it was my turn to stop this absurd prosecution and set young P.L. free. After re-cross examination, the prosecution rested its case.

I was ready to roll. I called my first witness, P.L., to the stand. That was a colossal mistake! I was so daggone nervous after picking the jury and hearing the complaining witness exaggerate and lie, that I had forgotten to deliver my carefully prepared Opening Statement. I froze. "Damn it," I muttered to myself and asked to approach the bench.

"Excuse me your honor," I humbly pleaded. "I inadvertently neglected to deliver my opening statement to the jury. I seek permission to deliver it at this time."

"Ms. Taifa," the judge responded sternly. "You have already called your first witness. Your case has begun."

"But your honor…" I tried to appeal to his compassion.

He turned toward opposing counsel. "Government, what is your position?"

At that point I knew I was sunk, and that it would be futile to expect mercy. I was correct.

"Judge," the government's attorney loudly chimed in. "She has already started her case. It would not be right at this point to allow her to go back."

And so I was forced to proceed, and things continued to spiral downhill. I elicited favorable testimony from my client, P.L., about the dirty and wet condition of the carryout, about how loud and brazen A.H. was, and that she appeared drunk. P.L. also described how it felt to be almost kneed in his groin.

But I couldn't figure out how to counter A.H.'s testimony of the assault. I had the police report, which contained no record of the victim being thrown to the ground multiple times, sustaining injuries. However, the police officer who had promised to show up in court to testify was nowhere to be found. Embarrassingly, I had failed to subpoena him. So I found myself frantically requesting to approach the bench once again to request a brief recess. The judge shook his head and sighed, but granted the request.

I flew into the courthouse hallway searching for someone, anyone who could tell me how to introduce a daggone document into evidence when the witness was not available. A veteran African American attorney came to my rescue, and I returned to the courtroom armed with the method. I had the PD 251 police report, which did not corroborate her statement of being thrown to the ground by my client twice, and had no mention of any injuries that A.H. now claimed she sustained. I was able to get police report entered into evidence, as an exception to the hearsay rule.

After having P.L.'s friend D.W. testify, I used all the elements I had studied in my trial practice manual, including laying out my theory of the case, using rhetorical questions, volunteering weaknesses, and pointing out the weaknesses of the other side. I wielded it all into a closing argument, and forcefully and persuasively presented it to the jury.

As you know, this incident took place in a little carryout in Georgetown. You heard testimony that the carryout was crowded on April 26, 1987, and that the floor was dirty and wet in places. You remember P.L. telling you how he went to get ketchup to share the fries his friends had purchased. P.L. however never got a chance to share those fries. He never got a chance to sit down with his friends, and at the close of the incident that night, he never even got a chance to tell his side of the story. And that, ladies and gentlemen, is what he finally had the opportunity to do today – to tell his side of the story. To tell what really happened.

"And what did P.L. tell us?" I continued.

He told us that as he was taking the stool, A.H. got up in his face, called him derogatory names, racial slurs and talked about his mother. He told us he smelled liquor on her breath and that she was acting like she was drunk.

P.L. testified that he told her he doesn't like people talking about his mother. Those words, however, were the end of the verbal bickering between the two, because A.H.'s response was to attempt to knee P.L. in his groin. Luckily for P.L., she missed, and hit the inside of his thigh. Now, what would an ordinary prudent man under those identical circumstances do? What would you do if you just got hit in that sensitive area and felt you were about to be hit again?"

I asked that last question, looking directly at the bespectacled African American gentleman in the jury box. The Professor watched me intently as I continued with feigned confidence.

First of all, it is undisputed that P.L. pushed ketchup in the face of A.H. But he pushed ketchup in her face to get her away from him. It is his testimony that she fell because she slipped on the dirty, wet floor.

But let's go back to A.H. for a moment. Between April 29 and today, July 16, three different stories have emerged as to whether or not my client, P.L., knocked her down. First, there is the version in defendant's exhibit #1, the PD Form 251, which contains no mention of P.L. knocking the complainant to the floor. Then there is Form 163, which states that he did knock her to the floor. And there is A.H.'s July 3 signed statement that he knocked her down, she got up, and he knocked her down again. And then her testimony today.

It really doesn't matter which of A.H.'s tales are true, if any of them are, and which are false, because P.L. actually believed and had reasonable grounds to believe that it was necessary to use force to protect himself from imminent bodily harm and, as a result, he was justified in using the reasonable amount of force that he did.

I made eye contact with the jurors and stated with certainty:

There was no mention in any of the police reports that A.H. was injured, bruised or swollen in any shape, form or fashion. Nor is there any account in any of the police reports that A.H. was knocked to the floor twice. Yet she claims she was.

I shook my head in disbelief.

But the most incredible thing was A.H.'s testimony on the witness stand today. If, as the prosecution has been claiming all along, the incident happened the way the plaintiff said it did, then why isn't there any corroboration? Wouldn't you expect that of all the people who were inside the carryout that night that they could find one person, just one, who could back up her testimony? Even her own friends didn't see anything. One would think if there really was all of that being knocked down once and getting knocked down again for 15 long minutes, it would have left an impression on somebody to come forward and talk about it.

In my final attempt to convince the jurors, I wagged my index finger, narrowed my eyes, and stated with conviction:

This case is not an open and shut case. It is a case that makes you hesitate. It makes you pause. His Honor will tell you that the government has to prove its case beyond a reasonable doubt. Now what does that mean? It means that if you have one reason, just one, to believe my client P.L. acted in self-defense, you must find him not guilty.

But you don't just have one reason in this case. You have several. Reason #1- A.H. was drunk, and shouted obscenities and racial slurs at P.L. Reason #2 - In a fit of rage, because she did not want him taking the empty chair, A.H. tried to knee P.L. in the groin, striking the inside of his thigh instead. Reason #3 - A painful apprehension shot through P.L.'s body as the thought of being kneed in his private parts became real. Reason #4 - His first reaction was to get this girl away from him, which he immediately did by pushing her with his hand – the same hand that was holding the napkin with ketchup on it.

I concluded with what I hoped the jurors would also feel was evident: "And that ladies and gentlemen, is self-defense!"

While the jury deliberated, I was nervous and panicky. The negative consequences of convictions were in the embryonic stages of public discussion, and a conviction, albeit misdemeanor, could serve as a basis for deportation should P.L. find himself in court again.

Well, in the end, I didn't win the case. But I was just as ecstatic as if I had. The jury could not come to a unanimous verdict; in other words, the jury was hung. I have no idea who or how many hung the jury, but I will nevertheless say "Thank you middle-aged African American gentleman with the horn-rimmed glasses!"

If the prosecution decided to go back and retry the "ketchup in my face case," I swear I would have retired my law license. Bringing that first trial was stupid. A second one would have been preposterous. The prosecution didn't seek to retry, so P.L. went free. He was a very personable and charming young Black man and I hope he never again got caught up in the system.

Chapter Five, Section 9
The "Capitol Bombing" Resistance Conspiracy Case

On November 7, 1983, at approximately 11 pm, a bomb exploded in the United States Capitol in Washington, D.C. The Senate had adjourned around 7 pm that evening, followed by a crowded reception held near the Senate Chamber. The reception ended around 9 pm. Two hours later, a deafening blast went off in a public corridor directly in front of the Senate Republican Cloak Room. It blew off the door to the Office of Senator Robert Byrd from West Virginia, who at one time was a member of and recruiter for the Ku Klux Klan. The bomb shattered glass windows and blew a hole through a wall partition, showering glass and debris into the Republican cloakroom. It also destroyed mirrors, chandeliers, tile flooring, artwork and furniture in the surrounding corridors and offices.

Just minutes before the explosion, a caller to a Capitol switchboard operator warned of the existence of the bomb. The caller said the bombing was "in support of the struggle against American military aggression in Grenada and Lebanon." The following day, National Public Radio received what was called a communiqué from an organization calling itself the Armed Resistance Unit, which took credit for the action and described the bombing as "retaliation against imperialist aggression." *The Washington Post* received a tape-recorded message, which stated, "We purposely aimed our attack at the institutions of imperialist rule rather than at individual members of the ruling class and government. We did not choose to kill any of them at this time. But their lives are not sacred."

An investigation ensued. It would be five years before a federal indictment was unsealed, and suspects named and charged. The May 11, 1988 indictment claimed that in addition to the U.S. Capitol, there were also bombing targets in New York, and other areas of Washington, D.C. The New York targets were the Federal Building on Staten Island on January 28, 1983, the Israeli Aircraft Industries Building on April 5, 1984, the South African Consulate on September 26, 1984, and the offices of the Patrolmen's Benevolent Association on February 23, 1985. The indictment charged that the Armed Resistance Unit was also the same group responsible for bombings at the National War College at Fort McNair on April 26, 1983, the Washington Navy Yard Computer Center on August 18, 1983, and the Washington Navy Yard Officers' Club on April 20, 1984.

The 23-page indictment charged the defendants with conspiring together and with unnamed others "to influence, change and protest policies and practices of the United States government concerning various international and domestic matters through the use of violent and illegal means."

Several days after the 1988 indictment was unsealed, I found myself in a federal courtroom as part of the legal defense team of what was initially pegged by the media as the "Capitol Bombing Case," but later retitled the "Resistance Conspiracy Case" by The Movement. Incredibly, I was representing the lead defendant, Laura Whitehorn, the result of her strong desire for a Black attorney.

Strategically, the government unsealed the indictment the same day that one of the defendants, Marilyn Buck, was convicted in the Southern District of New York, found guilty of assisting with the liberation of Assata Shakur from prison, among other charges. Shakur was a former Black Panther and member of the Black Liberation Army. She escaped from prison in 1979, four years after being convicted in the death of a New Jersey state trooper. Marilyn became a suspect in Assata's escape as soon as the FBI believed that White people might have been involved.

Also among the indicted in the Resistance Conspiracy Case were other White supporters of Black Liberation, including Susan Rosenberg and Tim Blunk, each already serving 58-year sentences on explosives and weapons charges. Linda Evans was serving a 35-year prison sentence on false identification and harboring charges. Alan Berkman, a medical doctor, was serving a 10-year sentence on weapons charges, after being indicted for treating a gunshot wound incurred by a fugitive in a politically motivated armored truck expropriation. But the bombshell, no pun intended, was that my client, Laura Whitehorn, was the only one of the defendants facing trial for the Capitol bombing who was not currently serving time for any crime, although she was being detained in a pending case in Baltimore.

The defendants were all middle-to-upper class White people who shunned their bourgeois class identity to work clandestinely in support of and under the leadership of movements for liberation. There was always a distinct difference between those who worked "above-ground" in the movement and those who worked "underground." I was always an "above-ground" Sista. Whether in the community or the courtroom, I maintained visibility – passing out flyers, talking on the radio or making speeches. While I may romanticize what it would have meant to trudge through thick brush in the night with Harriet Tubman 125 years earlier, secreting escaped slaves from safe house to safe house, the reality of the modern day underground I'm sure, is far from romantic.

I can only imagine the persistence, patience and discipline people must have had to hold down ordinary jobs as clerks and salespeople to fit into society, pretending to be the very people they are fighting against, while at the same time manufacturing fake identifications, donning disguises and conducting reconnaissance. I'm sorry, Harriet. I definitely could never conduct reconnaissance. I have always been horrible with details and it's difficult for me to even read a simple map. Honestly, I'm not sure I would have been able to do it. So, how could I not salute, support, or represent those who did?

The bold, successful liberation of Assata Shakur on a modern-day Underground Railroad touched my soul as one of the most daring revolutionary actions imaginable. And the fact that some defendants in the Resistance Conspiracy Case were either convicted, indicted or non-indicted as "co-conspirators" along with Black revolutionaries in her emancipation from prison gave me added inspiration to passionately advocate on their behalf. This was the epitome of being a "People's Lawyer" or "Movement Lawyer," and my advocacy in the case was most definitely client-centered.

Today, activists with the Black Lives Matter Movement often chant a quote from Sister Assata, which has caught on like wildfire amongst progressive youth. "It is our duty to fight for our freedom. It is our duty to win. We must love each other and support each other. We have nothing to lose but our chains." As I got to know my clients, I saw that they believed in, loved, and lived, that duty.

It was clear early on that the Resistance Conspiracy Case would not be the ordinary run-of-the-mill criminal case. It was going to be a political trial. A multi-defendant case, my main co-counsel included the politically conscious attorney Mary O'Melveny; the social justice law firm of Bernabei and Katz; New York activist attorney Danny Meyers; D.C. Public Defender Service attorney Shawn Moore; and death penalty expert attorneys Russell Canan and Robert Morin (both of whom would later become judges). And then there was lil' ole me, the newest lawyer and only Black woman on the legal team.

Although unspoken, I felt my clients presumed I would stand up to the non-activist lawyers in the case and tow the revolutionary line. Now I was really in a quandary. My client, Laura, her co-defendants, and the movement at large were all unaware that, despite my years-long activism and dedication to "The Struggle," now that I was a lawyer I was really trying to "get on the plantation" as opposed to getting thrown off. I think my inner strife showed early on, and I had a nagging feeling that my revolutionary comrades were disappointed in my lack of aggression.

Is this the Nkechi Taifa of New Afrikan Independence Movement fame that we had heard so much about? Where is her fire? Where is her spirit? I cringed as I felt the sting of their unspoken words. I was feeling positively schizophrenic. I didn't want to alienate the judge, or the legal defense team. I also didn't want to be typecast as a militant. Yet here I was, once again, on my familiar side of the fence, with the proverbial clenched fist raised high and a microphone to my mouth.

Speaking at a rally of mostly White Resistance Conspiracy Case allies staged by the Washington Area Committee for Political Prisoners, I quoted the words of U.S. Attorney Jay B. Stephens from a *Newsday* article that ran the day after my client was indicted.

"Let this be a warning," the U.S. Attorney had stated, "to those who seek to influence the policies of the U.S. government through violence and terrorism. We will seek unrelentingly to bring them to justice."

I disdainfully countered that warning as I looked into the sea of mostly White activist faces at the rally. "How many of you remember the bombing of those four little Black girls who were blasted to smithereens in a church in Birmingham, Alabama in 1963? I don't remember a similar vow on the part of the U.S. government to 'seek unrelentingly' to bring those perpetrators to justice."

I also cited the bombing of the children of MOVE members in Philadelphia in 1985, and the bombing of civilians in Libya in 1986, as similar instances where there were no vows to "seek unrelentingly" to bring anyone to justice.

"What the government actually meant," I argued forcefully, "is that these defendants would never see the light of day outside of prison." In fact, I pointed out, "four of the defendants are already serving lengthy sentences ranging from 12 to 58 years each for convictions related to some of the underlying charges of the indictment."

I reminded the audience that the Resistance Conspiracy Case also highlighted the repressive features of the Bail Reform Act of 1984. "My client, Laura Whitehorn," I continued, "has been held without bail longer than any person in the United States since Puerto Rican independentista Filiberto Ojeda Rios." As I examined the room of multi-racial supporters, wondering who might be on the FBI's payroll, I expounded, "The U.S. government has unlawfully used the 1984 Bail Reform Act to create pretrial detention conditions which are, in fact, punitive and politically motivated."

I straightforwardly concluded, "The international and domestic matters our clients are accused of trying to change include the Contra War against Nicaragua; the invasion of Grenada; U.S. support for South Africa in violation of U.N. sanctions; the colonization of Puerto Rico; and racist attacks by the police against the African American community and other Third World people in cities across the United States."

The consummate Black revolutionary Ahmed Obafemi approached the podium next and stated with conviction: "Whether you support armed struggle or not; whether you support revolutionary violence or not; whether you support liberation movements or not; you must support those who are struggling against the state if you claim solidarity with the progressive movements."

"Our charges are criminal, but our case is political," the defendants declared in a taped statement that was aired at the rally. "We use the slogan, 'Resistance is not a Crime.' The government says that we are committed to violence. This is not true. We are committed to social change and political struggle."

In their own words, our clients described the policies and practices they were indicted for:

- The U.S. practice of slaughtering thousands of Nicaraguan civilians through the proxy contra army;
- The U.S. invasion of Grenada, the first Black socialist non-aligned nation in this hemisphere;
- The U.S. policy of establishing brutal dictatorships in El Salvador, Guatemala, Honduras, and Chile that murder their own people to make their countries safe for U.S. investment;
- 90 years of U.S. colonization of Puerto Rico;
- The U.S. policy of aiding and abetting the racist governments of Israel and South Africa;
- The centuries-old practice of racial genocide and oppression of Black, Puerto Rican, Mexican, Asian and Native American peoples here, and of promoting racism and racist violence; and,
- The U.S. government's denial that Prisoners of War and political prisoners are held in U.S. jails, targeted for isolation and destruction.

Their statement continued, "Do we want to change these policies and practices? Wholeheartedly. They violate every tenet of international law and human decency."

To contest their portrayal by the government as terrorists, the co-defendants stressed:

Each of us charged in this indictment has committed our life to fighting for social justice here and to extending solidarity to national liberation movements around the world. Each one of us has been involved in supporting the just struggle of the Vietnamese people, in fighting against the Ku Klux Klan and racist violence, in supporting the struggle for Black liberation/ New African independence and for Puerto Rican independence. We have participated in and supported the movement for women's liberation and sought an end to gay and lesbian oppression. We have been anti-imperialist activists and organizers for many years. Fighting against poverty and oppression, and inspired by a vision of collective and personal liberation, people from South Africa to Palestine to Central America to the ghettos of the U.S. are struggling to change the conditions of their lives. With them we say, 'No Justice, No Peace.'

Our legal defense team successfully advocated for confidential legal meetings with our clients in a special group room at the D.C. Jail where they were detained awaiting trial. We spent many long nights in that room. I brought in my Republic of New Afrika comrades, Brothers Kwame Afoh and Thomas Stanley, to assist me as paralegals. In between legal strategy discussions about preventative detention, the security wall and how we would present the evidence, we also engaged in heated discussions on the topic of lesbianism. My clients branded my Black Nationalist paralegals and I as "narrow nationalists" and "homophobic."

We vigorously argued, "Is it homophobic to believe in the preservation of the Black family?" To this day I still would not describe our views as homophobic. We did not feel we were phobic in any way, or fearful of homosexuality. It was just that in the late eighties, the LGBTQ movement had not really hit the cultural Black Nationalist community. The term "homophobic" was probably not the correct term for us. "Homoignorant" of the issues and concerns may have been the better nomenclature.

It was also at our D.C. Jail legal meetings that I first heard about mobilization around the case of former Philadelphia Black Panther member and journalist, Mumia Abu-Jamal, who had been sentenced to death in 1982 for the alleged murder of a White police officer. Our clients appeared more concerned with strategizing to achieve his freedom, and the freedom of other political prisoners, than focusing on their own case. But that was their nature. And in the true tradition of client-centered lawyering, we implemented a strong client-led strategy, which, however disconcerting to me, ended up benefitting everyone except my own client.

We submitted collective motions challenging the government's case based on unconstitutional delay, prosecutorial vindictiveness and vagueness. We filed a motion challenging the ominous courtroom security, a motion we affectionately dubbed

"Tear Down the Wall." Other motions included the most critical one – the issue of double jeopardy.

Because Laura was being held in preventive detention, I individually filed a motion for her release in the Washington, D.C. indictment. Most of our motions were denied in whole or in part. The preventive detention motion I filed for my client was successful, albeit totally academic. Although the judge, Harold H. Greene,[85] ruled favorably on my petition and released Laura in the current Capitol Bombing case, she would be going nowhere. There was a detainer on her for earlier charges in Baltimore, MD, that she would be required to face at the conclusion of the Washington, D.C. case.

To enter the District of Columbia federal courthouse, visitors are required to pass through a screening magnetometer, similar to one you would see for airport security. However, an additional magnetometer was placed in front of the courtroom where our proceedings were being held. On top of that, a camera was directed to the well of the court where the defendants, counsel, judge, court staff and jury sit, and another was trained on the courtroom's spectator section. This was intimidating and appalling. Our motion argued that our clients were being expressly singled out to jurors and others as dangerous.

Judge Greene agreed that the cameras should not be used for intelligence purposes. "A court is a public place where justice is dispensed, and it is a place anyone should be able to attend without fear that his attendance will be recorded and used to link him to criminals or others of interest to police or intelligence agencies. Safety from such practices is one of the characteristics distinguishing a free society from a totalitarian one," Judge Greene ruled, allowing the continuation of the cameras for monitoring purposes, but directing that no tape recordings be made.

Our fight to "Tear Down the Wall," the plexiglass partition dividing the area where the public sits from the well of the court, was fruitless. Judge Greene found our reasoning absurd. Although we argued that The Wall deprived our clients of their constitutional presumption of innocence, the judge did not buy it and proceedings continued in the divided courtroom.

The double jeopardy motion was based on the prior cases of Susan, Tim and Alan. Triumphantly, Judge Greene agreed with our motion that the government would use the same evidence they used to convict the three in previous trials, again in this case. This was a flagrant violation of the double jeopardy clause. Although his ruling was overturned after a lengthy appeal, the charges against the three in the double jeopardy motion were dropped as part of a later plea agreement.

The plea affirmed that Laura, Linda and Marilyn would agree to plead guilty to conspiracy and destruction of government property, in exchange for charges being dropped against Susan, Tim and Alan. Laura also agreed to plead guilty to possession of false identification documents in her pending Baltimore case. As part of the agreement, Linda would receive an additional five-year sentence on top of the 35 years she was currently serving. Marilyn was already serving 17 years on previous convictions, and was later sentenced to 50 years in the New York Brinks/Assata Shakur liberation case.

My client, the resolute Laura Whitehorn, the only defendant not already serving any time, would receive a whopping 20-year sentence, inclusive of the pending Baltimore charge. As a revolutionary, I felt victorious. Although Laura received a lengthy sentence, the greater good was that three revolutionaries would eventually go free, including Alan, who had recently been diagnosed with cancer. However, as a lawyer, I felt like a fool. Despite my client's willing acceptance of the deal, 20 years was hard for me to stomach.

On December 6, 1990, while standing erect at counsel table wearing a green suit jacket trimmed in black, enhanced with a straight black knee-length skirt, I turned around and gazed at the multiracial courtroom packed with supporters who had come to witness the sentencing. The crowd jeered and booed the prosecutors and judge and cheered when our clients entered the courtroom. Laura walked in with her clenched-fist raised, as high as it could while handcuffed. Inside the secure courtroom we were still subjected to the ten-foot high bullet proof glass wall. Sharpshooting snipers and armed guards encircled the building's exterior. Judge Greene admonished my client, stating, "You have committed acts of violence which are not excused by good purposes or political purposes." He continued somberly, "The effects of these kinds of violence are just as devastating to the victims and to society at large as if they were motivated by greed."

When the judge finished, I stroked my favorite little red, black and green Africa-shaped earrings which adorned my neatly trimmed Afro, took a deep breath, rose to my feet at the counsel table, and delivered a powerful statement on behalf of Laura, summarizing the case as a "vindictive prosecution" that ended with a "vindictive sentence."

After going through the evidence and summoning the spirits of pertinent historical figures such as Rosa Parks, whose defiant act against the state I cited occurred four days and 35 years earlier, I concluded that the 20-year sanction against Laura Whitehorn "shows that the sentence a person receives depends on whether their politics fall on the right or left side of the political spectrum." I pointed out that it was Judge Greene himself who, several months earlier, sentenced former Reagan National Security Advisor John Poindexter to a mere six months in prison for his role in the Iran-Contra scandal.[86]

Laura was sentenced in 1990. Within the next two decades, all the defendants who went to court as part of the Resistance Conspiracy Case had been released. During that time the media and mainstream society all but forgot about the policies and practices our clients struggled against. Nelson Mandela walked out of prison and became the President of a free South Africa. Barack Obama was elected the first Black president in the United States. Yet, Puerto Rico remained colonized. Racial oppression of Black and other people of color in the U.S. still flourished, and domestic acts of violence by right-wing extremists boomed.

The sentences of both Susan Rosenberg and Linda Evans were commuted by President Clinton in 2001, on the last day of his term. Tim Blunk was paroled after serving 12 years of his original 58-year sentence. Marilyn Buck was paroled after serving 33 of her 80-year sentence and died a month after her release from uterine cancer. Alan Berkman, released in 1992, served eight of his original 10-year sentence. He died from cancer in 2009. Laura Whitehorn was released on parole after serving 14 of her 20-year sentence.

All the co-defendants were engaged in impressive and impactful social activist endeavors while incarcerated. They became poets, authors, quilters, tutors, and HIV/AIDS activists – all the while continuing to support work for other political prisoners. Their work within the prison system made a huge positive impact on other prisoners.

I have met many formerly incarcerated women today who served time with the women of the Resistance Conspiracy Case. These formerly incarcerated women all state that they respected my former clients for their efforts to help others. They said they bonded with them, learned from them, and taught them as well.

There were other lasting impacts of the Resistance Conspiracy Case. The 1983 bombing was the dawning of intensified security proceedings in federal buildings throughout Washington, D.C. In an effort to prevent future attacks, metal detectors were installed at entrances to the Capitol, Senate and House of Representatives. A portion of Pennsylvania Avenue in front of the White House was closed to traffic, and a security-laden walkway was established in its place.

While I am thrilled that my Resistance Conspiracy Case clients, all of whom are White, are no longer incarcerated, it continuously gnaws at me that scores of Black revolutionaries still languish behind bars and have not received the same preferential parole or clemency treatment as their White compatriots.

I am still aggravated that, years later, despite being a lawyer with a 6th amendment obligation to zealously represent my clients within the bounds of the law, I was nevertheless forced to don the humiliating red security badge and required to be personally escorted while on White House grounds. I still ask myself what led to the infamous red badge? It was likely not just my representation of the lead defendant in the Capitol Bombing case, nor the legal memoranda I submitted that Brother Chokwe used as a basis for the Prisoner of War status legal papers in Mutulu Shakur's case. It was more likely the sum total of myriad people, associations, connections and events that have been an integral part of my righteous quest for justice for my people my entire life. Perhaps I can live with that as the rationale. But I'm still pissed about it, because it flagrantly violates the U.S. Constitution's First Amendment right to free speech and association.

Chapter Five, Section 10
The "David v. Goliath" ABC Case

While waiting in the courtroom to be called for one of my criminal cases, I observed the tail end of a case that intrigued me. The African American comedian-turned-social-justice-activist Dick Gregory, was on trial for one of his many acts of civil disobedience. I don't remember the exact charge, but he was being represented by the legendary attorney Mark Lane of John F. Kennedy and Martin Luther King, Jr. conspiracy theories fame.

Mark catapulted to national acclaim during the mid-1960s, challenging the "magic bullet" theory of President John F. Kennedy's 1963 assassination of a lone gunman with one bullet that ploughed through Kennedy's body, struck a Texas Governor riding in the car's front seat, and emerged intact. He stridently contended that Lee Harvey Oswald could not have acted alone in killing the President, a theory later supported in part by the House Select Committee on Assassinations in 1979.

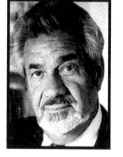

Mark published the results of his government conspiracy theory in his 1966 blockbuster expose, *Rush to Judgment*, which was followed by *Plausible Denial*, a 1991 book arguing that the CIA was involved in Kennedy's murder. His books contributed to movies such as *JFK* and *Executive Action*. He teamed up with Dick Gregory to advance conspiracy theories about the assassination of Dr. Martin Luther King and co-authored with Gregory, *Code Name Zorro*, which alleged that the FBI may have been involved in the King assassination.

Lane had previously successfully represented American Indian Movement leaders convicted of murder and conspiracy after an uprising and a 71-day standoff at Wounded Knee, South Dakota. He narrowly escaped with his life from the jungles of Guyana, South America, the day California Representative Paul Ryan and members of his delegation were killed just prior to the deaths of 900 children, women and men followers of People's Temple cult leader, Jim Jones who ordered they drink cyanide-infused Kool-Aid. I knew most of this when I saw him in the courtroom that day.

I studied the flamboyant, controversial lawyer intently. He was a tanned White man with a shock of black and white peppered hair. His posture exuded poise and self-confidence, and his demeanor commanded respect and afforded him unequivocal control of the courtroom. I must say that I was impressed, which is rare for me. He was an early champion of many civil rights issues, and was one of the first Freedom Riders to go to the South in the early 60s, enduring many arrests. During a break in the court proceedings, I followed the living legend into the hall.

"Excuse me, Attorney Lane," I boldly began. "My name is Nkechi Taifa. I've always admired your work. Although I'm a new lawyer in private practice, here's my business card. If you ever need any assistance, please don't hesitate to give me a call."

I have no memory of what his exact response was. I had the impression that he politely brushed me off as an immature nuisance. Needless to say, I was stunned when I received a phone call from him about a week later. He wanted to know if I was interested in assisting him with an ongoing case that had started in 1986. I nearly fainted. Composing myself, we set an appointment to meet at his home office, located directly across from the side of the U.S. Supreme Court building.

Lane's home was an elegant, majestic house that he and his wife Trish were in the process of renovating. The case itself was fascinating. Two African American graphic artists employed by ABC News, Michele Shepherd and LaRue Graves, had sued the media conglomerate on charges of sexual harassment and racial discrimination. I couldn't believe that I was actually going to be co-counsel with Mark Lane on the lawsuit.

The case against the American Broadcasting Corporation (ABC) was a classic case of David versus Goliath. Solo practitioners Mark Lane and myself being David, battling the giant Goliath in the form of three major blue chip law firms armed with their powerful credentials and endless resources.

The complaint alleged that our clients were discriminated against, disparately treated, and singled out because of race. It also alleged that they experienced retaliation for meeting with other ABC minority employees to discuss company grievances. Amidst constant denials, it was revealed in court that ABC sent an informant to the meeting to spy on the proceedings. Mr. Graves was fired shortly after the meeting and the pleas and grievances of Ms. Shepherd, who worked the "graveyard shift" at the television station, went unheeded.

Our clients had been discriminated against, but we could not prove it. We were at a stalemate. Then, on the eve of trial, the unimaginable happened. LaRue was at a summer concert at D.C.'s Carter Barron outdoor amphitheater when he just happened to bump into the secretary of the vice president of ABC News, an African American woman. They engaged in casual chit-chat, and just before going back to enjoying the concert, she asked whatever happened to his legal case. He sighed and told her the case was at an impasse because he could not prove he and Michele were retaliated against. He mentioned the grievance meeting of minority employees, and the fact that he and Michele were at the meeting, but that when the minutes of the meeting were provided during discovery, their names were not there. The secretary was quite surprised.

"LaRue, that's really weird," she said. "I know Michele Shepherd was at that meeting because I remember typing her name on the list of attendees."

"Whoa, well, what about my name?" LaRue asked excitedly.

"Honestly, I don't recall, but I know about Michele because I did not know she was a member of the minority. I recall going to the file to look her up after typing her name. Because she worked at night, we never had the opportunity to interact."

This was just the ammunition Mark needed. I watched a legal mastermind at work.

"They lied, and I knew it!" he blurted loudly when he received the news. "They manipulated the evidence by deleting their names," he fumed to me. "This is absolutely colossal. We've got to demand sanctions! Nkechi, find out everything you can on default judgments," he ordered.

I complied. In addition to conducting detailed research, I borrowed a brief on the issue of default judgments from one of my law colleagues, Debbie Katz. Debbie had been instrumental in helping our legal team on the pending Capitol Bombing case, which was on an extended hiatus as the result of a lengthy interlocutory appeal. Her brief was excellent and greatly assisted our legal strategy. Mark and I demanded sanctions and immediately sought an unprecedented default judgment, not only against the media mogul, but its lawyers as well. We then called for an emergency hearing into our allegations of false representations and fraud.

U.S. District Court Judge Royce Lamberth was incensed at the thought of impropriety and immediately granted our motion, which resulted in an extensive four-day evidentiary hearing that same week. The secretary could not have been a more sincere witness. She was soft-spoken, professional and credible, with a demeanor that exuded honesty. On the credibility scale of 1 to 10, her score was off the charts, past 10. We had to subpoena her because she did not want to testify against her boss. She did not want to testify, period. I know she wished she had never gone to the Carter Barron concert that weekend. She turned out to be the epitome of the perfect witness.

In the evidentiary hearing, it was revealed that ABC not only engaged in fraudulent concealment, but produced during the discovery period a doctored and altered document. They then sought, by foul means, to unfairly secure a dispositive decision from the court based on their ruse.

The judge mulled over the blatant evidence from the hearing for nearly three years. Clearly dismayed with the actions of the corporate defendant and its lawyers, he penned a 34-page ruling. He wrote that the "defendants and their counsel have taken substantial and inappropriate actions to prevent the emergence of the facts." Perturbed by what he characterized from the evidentiary hearing as the "I Don't Remember Syndrome," "the use of artful language to deceive plaintiffs and the court," and "outright untruths," the judge mandated that the most severe sanctions for abuse of the judicial process must be imposed on ABC. He struck the defendants' Answers, thereby throwing out the corporation's case. Ruling that the imposition of a lesser sanction would only reward the defendant for its misconduct in the litigation, the court found that "policy considerations of deterrence for recalcitrant behavior was necessary."

We won! Judge Lamberth granted our motion for a default judgment on all our claims against the television network.

On April 16, 1992, the *Washington Post* ran the article, "Artists Win Race Discrimination Suit Against ABC." The article quoted a New York University legal ethics expert calling the judge's ruling "quite remarkable," noting that there probably are fewer than five such judgments in federal courts a year. The expert concluded that it was even more remarkable because of the involvement of a high caliber law firm, "the bluest of the blue chips," he observed. "Judges tend to be tolerant of lawyer misconduct," he noted.

Judge Lamberth observed that ABC and its lawyers failed to produce the internal memo prepared by the informant it sent to the meeting, despite it being forwarded to four senior network officials. He was incensed that ABC "could provide no explanation whatsoever as to how four separate documents containing original date stamps could have disappeared."

Calling our evidence of misconduct "impressive," Lambert concluded that ABC "submitted witnesses who did not recall circumstances which they should have recalled, and witnesses who remembered nothing on cross-examination but who were willing to adopt the prearranged line of the defendants." In revealing his disgust in the actions of the defendants and their counsel, the judge's opinion berated ABC and their lawyers for "conflicting testimony," "evasiveness," "equivocations," "false assertions," "signing of false statements," "harassment of witnesses" and "retaliation."

Whew! Asked by a reporter for my view of the court's decision, I responded with conviction:

> As a result of the fraud practiced against our clients and the court by ABC, we were denied crucial and central evidence that supported our clients' claims. Sanctions in the form of a default judgment were essential because the destruction and alteration of a critical document in this case denied us the right to a fair and impartial trial. For nearly seven years we relied on the false representations of ABC and their lawyers.

I continued, trying to contain my excitement.

> On literally the eve of trial we stumbled upon information which caused their elaborately constructed story to crumble. ABC's actions in surreptitiously directing a management informant to spy on the minority employee's grievance meeting backfired.

I ended the interview thoughtfully:

> Indeed, the Court's ruling should serve as a lesson to this and other defendants that they have nothing to gain but everything to lose by lying. I applaud the plaintiffs, Ms. Shepherd and Mr. Graves, for taking a courageous stance against discrimination and despite the passage of many years, re-

fusing to give up the fight for justice.

In his 1994 memorandum opinion on our application for attorneys' fees and costs, U.S. District Court Judge Royce Lamberth praised our efforts: "The court extends its commendation to Mr. Lane and Ms. Taifa for obtaining exceptional results for their clients in this case against a powerful opponent. Counsel contributed to the development of the law of sanctions in this Circuit and served the court in the highest tradition of the bar."

Although my co-counsel Mark Lane revealed a strong, brash personality to the outside world, I often saw the softer side of him. He was well-known for his assassination conspiracy theories, but I think the case that touched him the most was a little known one reaching back 20 years, involving an African American man, James Richardson, who was convicted by an all-White Florida jury of killing his seven children. As the result of Mark's advocacy, a special prosecutor appointed to the case named Janet Reno, who would become a future United States Attorney during the Clinton Administration, agreed with Lane that Richardson had not received a fair trial and should be set free. Winning this case and having Richardson released to his custody brought tears to the eyes of Mark, who witnessed his client walk free.

Over the next several years, I co-counseled with Mark Lane on several other cases. He was a brilliant lawyer and an amazing strategist. His legal reputation was so strong that in one of our cases, the defendant law firm rapidly settled rather than be subjected to a trial with him at the helm. One of the things I learned from my experience with him was that a strong presence is paramount. I also learned to be unafraid to go up against the odds. "If you firmly believe in your case," he once schooled me, "You must pull out all stops to advance justice."

Unfortunately, I also learned first-hand that even lawyers I admire and respect have flaws. Despite all the work I did on the ABC case, after our victory it appeared as though my illustrious co-counsel was going to seek to diminish my role in the representation of our clients and thus, my compensation on the case. What I learned from him I deftly used against him. I stood up to my Goliath and vigorously challenged his trying to cheat me out of my earned share of court-ordered attorneys' fees. Fortunately, my efforts appealed to his better judgment without my having to initiate legal proceedings. After that, I think he had a newfound respect for me – recognizing the strong advocacy I learned from him. Touché!

And as for ABC, I am so glad that chapter passed, as 20 years later I relished racing home from wherever I was every Wednesday night to glue myself to my local ABC affiliate, Channel 7, to enjoy *Scandal* – producer Shonda Rhimes' new hit TV series starring a badass Black woman lawyer!

Chapter Six
"What's Going On?"[87]

Section 1
Give the Brother a Break?

After I saw the name of a youth in the *Washington Post* that I had quite successfully diverted from detention, now running guns up and down the East Coast, I decided I wanted to go into policy. Closing out my regular "run of the mill" cases and while the Resistance Conspiracy Case was on a lengthy interlocutory appeal, I worked as a policy counsel for the Women's Legal Defense Fund (WLDF).[88]

The decision to work with the WLDF was notable for me, particularly as I was never really into the women's liberation movement, which I had essentially written off as consisting primarily of hypocritical White women. Many of their histories included complicity and muteness during the enslavement and Jim Crow eras, and being the primary beneficiaries of the affirmative action that was originally designed to eradicate discrimination on the basis of race, creed, color or national origin. But, of course, there were White women who risked their own lives shielding runaways and freedom fighters from the atrocities of enslavement or imprisonment. So it was with mixed feelings that I even applied for the position.

There were two other phenomenal sisters at WLDF during the major time of my employ there, Claudia Withers and Judith Winston. Claudia, an expert in policy, government and programmatic development, would go on to serve as Chief Operating Officer to several nonprofits. Judith, amongst many other impressive accolades, would go on to serve as Executive Director of President Clinton's Initiative on Race. But at the Women's Legal Defense Fund, they were two veteran Black women attorneys I looked up to as a young lawyer trying to find my place in the profession.

Years later, while seated together during the intermission of a civil rights conference, Claudia evoked an awkward memory from our WLDF days that brought raucous laughter to us both. As Black women working in a primary White organization, of course we were supposed to be the experts on any and everything race-related. Rev. Jesse Jackson, a two-time Democratic presidential candidate, had recently popularized a movement toward use of the term "African-American" to describe Black people, and there were many discussions about it in the Black community.

During a staff meeting one morning we – the Black women lawyers – were asked by the organization's executive director what we personally preferred being called. Judith's response at the time was "Black." Claudia announced her preference as "African-American." And, characteristic of my Black Power cultivation, I emphatically stated my preference as "African *in* America."

My most memorable experience working at the Women's Legal Defense Fund, however, was the time we spent opposing the Bush Administration's nomination of Judge Clarence Thomas to the U.S. Supreme Court. I helped to produce WLDF's report, *Endangered Liberties: What Judge Clarence Thomas' Record Portends for Women*, an in-depth review of the nominee's record. The report stated that the Thomas nomination was critical because "the margin by which cases are decided has become increasingly important. Without diversity on the Court, the Rehnquist majority will be even more emboldened to produce aggressively conservative opinions."

My work at WLDF on this nomination fit in perfectly with my work with the National Conference of Black Lawyers (NCBL), which had also taken a position in opposition to the nomination of Clarence Thomas. NCBL concluded, based on the concepts Thomas had embraced in his legal writings, speeches and to a lesser extent, his record on the Court of Appeals, that he would "champion the rights of the privileged and powerful rather than the rights of the oppressed and dispossessed." Our position opposing the nomination conflicted with the prevailing view in the Black community that, as a Black man, we should "Give the brother a break."

We, however, felt that the Thomas nomination served two purposes for the Bush administration: first, as a Black candidate, the nomination "continued the façade Bush projected that he supported civil rights;" second, the conservative politics of Thomas "continued Bush's effort to stack the judiciary against the interests of people of color, the poor and women."

His nomination represented another one of those moments of chagrin for African Americans. While the nomination of a person of African descent to the country's highest court is important, it is also critical to have a candidate who has demonstrated a clear commitment to equal justice and fundamental rights. Judge Thomas had shown no such commitment. His history of protecting the rights of the politically, economically and socially oppressed was dismal and fell far short of the legendary record of Thurgood Marshall, whom he would succeed if appointed.

On August 21, 1991, NCBL, in conjunction with the Howard University School of Law class of 1993, hosted a community education forum, "Rights at Stake: The Nomination of Judge Clarence Thomas to the U.S. Supreme Court," which was held at the Howard University Law School's Moot Court Room. C-SPAN was seeking to cover the Black community's response to the Thomas nomination, and I was thrilled that they decided to cover the event.

I secured the panelists, which included Dr. Ronald Walters, Chair
of the Political Science Department at Howard University, and
my colleague, Claudia Withers, Director of the Employment Rights
Project for Women of Color at the
Women's Legal Defense Fund. I was pleased to also secure Wade Henderson, Director of the Washington Bureau of the NAACP who had recently persuaded his organization to oppose the nomination; and Haywood Burns, Dean of the City
University of New York Law School and Chairman Emeritus of the National Conference of Black Lawyers. Tyrone McCall, President of Howard University's School
of Law Class of 1993, gave an enthusiastic welcome. I served as the event's moderator.

I provided what I deemed a thorough, in-depth introduction; however, it may have
been a bit much for the middle-of-the-road, White-led WLDF that I now worked
for. While WLDF was not a co-sponsor, I, as WLDF policy counsel, was clearly a
mover and shaker of the Black-led public event. In my overview I started out by
quoting the great Black historian, Carter G. Woodson, stating forcefully, "If you control a man's thinking, you don't have to worry about his actions." I questioned,
"What better candidate for the Bush administration to nominate than one whose actions you don't have to worry about." I then asserted that "Thomas' record reflected
anti-Affirmative Action, anti-civil rights and anti-reproductive rights views." So far,
so good.

I next cited anti-lynching crusader, Ida B. Wells-Barnett, and Emmett Till, victim of
a vicious lynching, as examples of those on whose shoulders we all stand. Then I
became a bit more edgy. "Clarence Thomas was able to live in his upper middle
class neighborhood in Virginia, although years ago it would have been impossible,
or illegal for him to live in such neighborhoods, solely because of the color of his
skin," I said. I took it a step further. "He was only able to live there because of the
civil rights movement and drum majors for justice such as Dr. Martin Luther King, Jr."

I noted that when Thomas was a young man, it would have been illegal for him to
marry his current wife, a White woman, not only in his native state of Georgia but
also in his current residence in Virginia. At this point, some White folk in the audience squirmed in their seats, but I was greeted by what seemed like thunderous
applause. Thomas's supporters in the audience appeared uneasy, but I continued like
a dog with a bone.

I stated emphatically that his ability to marry outside his race was preceded by heinous murders, lynchings, and beatings historically endured by Black men. "Clarence Thomas is standing on the shoulders of a lot of Black men and women who have kicked open doors that he has been able to walk through, although he now wants to negate these struggles." I opined, "If he were a White man, I doubt there would be many supporters in the Black community."

Addressing the Black people in the audience and attempting to make eye contact with an elderly African American gentleman in the back, I cautioned, "Historically, the upholding of race without an equal commitment to principle by Blacks not working in the interests of Black people has led to our downfall."

I pointed out the case of Peter Poyas, who warned enslavement era insurrectionist Denmark Vesey, "Beware of those eating scraps from Massa's table; those wearing Massa's old clothes." I used the example of COINTELPRO and the Black man who provided the map marking the spot where young Black Panther leader Fred Hampton slept.

I continued to reference instances of "Black people not working in the interests of Black people." Among them were the Black men who shot Malcolm X, and the Black prisoners who, on orders of White guards, viciously beat Fannie Lou Hamer for trying to register to vote. In conclusion, I asserted that Clarence Thomas was not working in the interests of Black people and would work to undermine the very laws he himself benefited from. And today, in observing his now decades-long record on the bench of the highest court in the land, my assertion has unfortunately been correct.

Our forum at Howard Law was one of the first organized gatherings to oppose the nomination of Clarence Thomas to the U.S. Supreme Court. It occurred a little under two months before the sexual harassment allegations of Professor Anita Hill publicly surfaced in early October 1991. Hill accused the nominee, who was her supervisor at both the U.S. Department of Education and the Equal Employment Opportunity Center, of inappropriate conduct. An all-White, all-male Senate Judiciary Committee mercilessly grilled Hill, eliciting graphic testimony about penis size, pubic hair, and pornography. The hearing was out of control.

Witnesses who had earlier testified against his confirmation before the Senate during September, including my colleague Adjoa Aiyetoro representing the National Conference of Black Lawyers, and Haywood Burns, representing Supreme Court Watch, never had the opportunity to share on the record the sexual harassment allegations as part of their opposition to the nomination.

Although Harvard Professor Charles Ogletree admirably served as Anita Hill's attorney, preparing her for what would be a rambunctious Senate hearing, it was becoming obvious that it was a no-win situation and Thomas would be seated, regardless of the strength of the opposition or the seriousness of the allegations against him. The WLDF and other women's groups such as the National Women's Law Center were not standing alone in opposition to the Thomas nomination. The fact that civil rights organizations such as the NAACP under the leadership of Wade Henderson and the Leadership Conference on Civil Rights headed by Ralph Neas stood strongly on principle against "giving the brother a break," speaks volumes.

Chapter Six, Section 2
People's Tribunal Mumia Abu-Jamal

On December 6, 1997, I served as an attorney in an innovative, historic mock proceeding in Philadelphia entitled the People's International Tribunal Investigating the Case of Mumia Abu-Jamal. The all-day proceeding included a well-known and respected international panel of jurists, political leaders, labor and community activists, cultural figures and others concerned with social justice.

The powerful indictment, crafted for the mock proceeding, charged various Pennsylvania officials – including the Governor, several Pennsylvania Supreme Court Justices, the State Attorney General, the Pennsylvania Department of Corrections, the Mayor, the Fraternal Order of Police, various Pennsylvania District Attorneys, the FBI, the Department of Justice, and the trial judge – with conspiracy to silence Mr. Abu-Jamal using false charges, a fraudulent trial, brutal imprisonment, and imposing the death penalty in an attempt to silence him forever.

As the lead prosecutor in the Tribunal, I was honored to craft and present the Opening Statement, which included these words:

> May it please the Tribunal, counsel and members of this honorable jury. My name is Nkechi Taifa and I represent the People, on behalf of Mumia Abu-Jamal and other Victims of Human Rights Violations Perpetrated by the Defendants. We are at the part of the proceeding called the Opening Statement, wherein I will provide this distinguished body with an overview of the evidence you will hear.

> There are a number of persons whose names will be frequently mentioned in this case, and I would like to tell you a little about one of them – the principal complainant and victim, Mumia Abu-Jamal, who is currently sitting

on death row as the result of the abuses inflicted upon him by the defendants. Mr. Jamal is a father, a grandfather and a husband. He was born into a poor family in Philadelphia.

It was in the 1970s, during the emergence of the Black Power Movement, that Mumia and hundreds of thousands of Black youth began to develop a broad, political consciousness that challenged the national norm of White supremacy. It is in this context that a 14-year-old Mumia attended and protested the Philadelphia appearance of then presidential candidate George Wallace. Mumia and several friends were each beaten savagely by hordes of White plain-clothed Philadelphia police officers and arrested for their protest.

It was at this time, at the tender age of 14, that Mumia was selected as a target of the FBI's COINTELPRO operation where, as a private individual exercising his rights of free speech, he was marked and filed as an agitator to be followed, reported on, and surveilled by the government.

In the fall of 1968, Mumia helped to found the Philadelphia chapter of the Black Panther Party for Self Defense, where the teenager was assigned the rank of Lieutenant of Information. COINTELPRO efforts against him were increased in order to disable, disrupt and destroy a promising young man. Trained by the Black Panther Party as a revolutionary journalist, Mumia left the Party in the 1970s.

He then published articles and broadcast critical radio shows challenging the Philadelphia Police Department and Mayor Frank Rizzo. He rejected Rizzo's version of the paramilitary 1978 siege of the MOVE organization's Powelton Village home with radical advocacy. His stance resulted in him being fired from news media jobs. Although once elected president of the Philadelphia Association of Black Journalists, Mr. Jamal found it necessary to also work as a cab driver at night to support his family.

The evidence in this tribunal will be presented in two phases. The first phase will scrutinize and place in historical context evidence of the climate of abuse, corruption and institutional racism that prevailed in Philadelphia and permeated its police department, courts, and correctional systems. The second phase will delineate the legal aspects of the case of *Mumia Abu-Jamal vs. The Commonwealth of Pennsylvania.*

Noted journalist Linn Washington and Ronald Hampton, Executive Director of the National Black Police Association, will present evidence during the contextual phase of the Tribunal of the Rizzo years between 1972-1980, when Frank Rizzo served as Philadelphia's Chief Executive. These years were punctuated by a flagrant pattern and practice of police brutality, culminating in scathing reports, legislative probes, and an unprecedented federal civil rights lawsuit initiated by the U.S. Department of Justice against Mayor Rizzo and other Philadelphia city officials.

Mumia was among a handful of reporters who consistently reported on instances of police brutality in Philadelphia. His reportage of clearly newsworthy abuses perpetuated by a governmental entity earned Mr. Jamal the antipathy of Rizzo Administration officials and ostracism from his peers in mainstream media who considered police brutality to be an isolated phenomenon impacting individuals who deliberately provoked police. You will hear from former Black Panther Rosemary Mealey, who will provide testimony about the Black Panther Party in Philadelphia and Mumia's role.

You will also hear testimony about the FBI's once-secret counterintelligence program against the Black Liberation Movement in general and the Philadelphia Black Panther Party in particular. You will hear expert testimony on the COINTELPRO from noted author Ward Churchill who will testify on Philadelphia police political surveillance and cooperation with the FBI in scrutinizing the Black Panther Party and Mr. Jamal. Geronimo Ji Jaga Pratt, recently released from 27 years of unjust imprisonment and a victim of COINTELPRO, will also testify.

You will also hear about the MOVE years, from Pam Africa of MOVE, an organization which over the years has been subjected to brutal beatings, false arrests, malicious prosecution, mass murder, arson, and bombing.

Attorney Soffiyah Elijah will present testimony on the conditions of Mumia's imprisonment and his civil case against the federal authorities. You will hear testimony about the racist and disproportionate application of the death penalty and its violation of international law norms from Tonya McClary of the NAACP Legal Defense Fund, and Terry Rumsey from the Pennsylvania Abolitionists United Against the Death Penalty. Lastly, you will hear through video from the complainant himself, Mumia Abu-Jamal. His is the voice they are trying to silence.

Distinguished jurists of this Tribunal, what happened the day this tragedy occurred? Picture yourself near the corner of 13th and Locust Avenue on December 9, 1981, in the early hours of the morning. The area is bustling with night activity. Your attention is drawn to the street where a Black man is being viciously beaten about the head and shoulders by a White police officer. The police officer is shot by someone. Another Black man approaches the scene and bends over the officer to help him, but is himself shot by the officer. You see the shooter run away.

No less than five witnesses who were at separate locations and did not know each other told the police that someone ran from the scene, with two of them claiming it was the shooter. Mr. Jamal was the person shot at the scene and found within minutes by the arriving police sitting on the curb in a pool of blood. He could not have run away. He almost died that night. As an injured Black man at the scene, however, Mr. Jamal was assumed to be the perpetrator and was beaten by arriving police officers, thrown in a paddy wagon and driven around in the expectation that he would die.

Essentially, key elements of the state's case against Mr. Jamal are as follows: first, the state alleges that it has eye-witnesses who saw Mumia commit the crime; second, they claim that Mumia confessed to the shooting.

Evidence presented during this Tribunal will refute each of these allegations. During the original trial, it was stated that Mr. Jamal bragged about the shooting of Officer Faulkner at the hospital. Today's evidence will reveal that no such statement was ever made by Mumia. You will hear evidence about the official written report by Officer Gary Wakshul, who was with Mumia continuously and clearly stated, 'the negro male made no statement.'

So where did this concoction about a confession come from? You will hear that several months after his victimization by the police, Mumia filed police brutality charges. It was only at this point, over two months later, that the police suddenly claimed that Officer Bell, Faulkner's partner and a hospital security guard who personally knew Faulkner, claimed Mumia had made the statements. However, you will have the opportunity to see and hear Dr. Anthony Colleta from the emergency room via videotape, who contradicts these statements.

You will also hear from Ms. Lydia Wallace, sister of Mr. Jamal, who will tell you that Mr. Jamal told her that he was innocent.

William Singletary, a respectable businessman, will testify that he saw another man shoot Officer Faulkner and flee the scene. Singletary will testify that he was harangued, threatened and detained at the police station for hours after other witnesses were allowed to go home. He will tell you how police repeatedly tore up his written statements until he changed his story and signed a false statement dictated by the police.

Dessie Hightower, an accounting student at the time, will testify as he did during the original trial that Office Faulkner was shot by a man who escaped down the street.

Perhaps one of the most compelling pieces of testimony you will hear will be from Ms. Veronica Jones who, via videotape and sworn affidavit, will tell you that she gave false testimony at Mumia's 1982 trial. She will tell you how she, as a 21-year-old mother of three who was in jail facing serious felony charges was coerced, intimidated, and threatened by police into lying. She will swear that her original statement to the police – that she had witnessed two men run from the scene in which Officer Faulkner was killed and Mr. Jamal seriously wounded – was correct.

You will also hear how when Ms. Jones finally came forward to tell the truth about police pressure and coercion, she was threatened with seven years in prison for perjury and she was immediately arrested on the witness stand on a bench warrant for missing a court date two years earlier. All this was an attempt to silence her.

You will hear testimony from a newer witness, Pamela Jenkins, who provides still more corroboration in the chain of evidence against the police. You will hear that she was working as a teenage prostitute in the early '80s and knew the government's star witness, another prostitute named Cynthia White, well. She will also testify that she knew a lot of Philadelphia police officers as well. In fact, she will tell you that one of those officers was her boyfriend at the time. Ms. White will swear that she was asked by him to testify against Mumia and to falsely identify Mumia as the shooter, in spite of the fact that she was not even at the scene.

You will hear that Mr. Jamal never had the assistance of a constitutionally effective advocate during his original trial, so the Commonwealth's case was never subjected to a meaningful challenge. The Court unjustifiably stripped Mr. Jamal of his right to self-representation and forcibly removed him from significant portions of the trial. You will hear that with expert assistance or even competent counsel, Mr. Jamal would have shown that physical evidence disappeared, and that the Commonwealth's scientific tests were suspiciously incomplete and incompetent. In actuality, the physical evidence did not support the Commonwealth's claims. However, he was denied adequate resources with which to defend himself.

Finally, you will hear of improprieties regarding the jury selection process, causing it to be racially stacked against Mr. Jamal, and egregious testimony regarding the Philadelphia District Attorney's practice of using racially biased peremptory challenges to systematically remove Blacks from juries.

You will hear how the government used irrelevant information about Jamal's teenage Black Panther membership to inflame the largely White jury. You will hear testimony that the trial judge Albert Sabo clearly harbored a bias against Mr. Jamal and that Judge Sabo has presided over more cases that ended in death verdicts than any judge in the United States.

Members of this esteemed Tribunal, at the close of all the evidence we are confident that you will find the defendants guilty of each and every count in the indictment, and enter an order calling for the implementation of each and every one of the proposed remedies, including the immediate release of Mumia Abu-Jamal from prison.

His release must be accompanied by full compensation for the violation of his human rights, an immediate moratorium on the death penalty, as well as a thorough, independent and impartial judicial investigation into the Philadelphia Police Department and its treatment of people of color.

Also instituted immediately must be a thorough, independent and impartial judicial investigation into the FBI's counterintelligence program; a thorough, independent and impartial judicial investigation into the actions of any official entity that had any role in relation to the 1985 MOVE headquarters bombing; the removal from office of all public officials responsible for the deprivation of Mumia Abu-Jamal's human rights; and a request to the United Nations to call for reports on the case of Mr. Jamal from U.N. Special Rapporteurs.

Thank you for your attention.[89]

Chapter Six, Section 3
A Frying Pan, Baking Soda, and Crack[90]

In 1986, crack cocaine was hyped across the country in headlines as an urban menace that would spawn a generation of crack babies and an epidemic of violence. The public knew very little about crack other than the belief, later found to be erroneous, that nationally acclaimed University of Maryland basketball star Len Bias died from a crack cocaine overdose.

The Congressional Record was inundated with sensationalized news articles about crack. While there was no rationally sound data or analysis to draw conclusions from, Congresspersons, both Democrats and Republicans alike, concluded that crack cocaine warranted especially severe penalties. Congress mandated that a mere five grams of crack cocaine – equivalent to the weight of a couple packs of sugar – would carry the same five-year sentence as 500 grams of powder cocaine. This 100-to-1 distinction between the two forms of the same drug was, in the words of my colleague and former Congressional staffer, Eric Sterling, "essentially plucked out of a hat."

In 1991 I was hired by Mort Halperin and joined the American Civil Liberties Union Washington Office, during a time when the federal legislature was drafting and debating the omnibus crime bills that ultimately led to the epidemic of mass incarceration. It was the 103rd Congress that ultimately embraced the largest expansion of the death penalty in modern times, the federal three strikes legislation, the anti-gang provisions, and the prosecution of 13-year-olds as adults.

Other than the issue of the death penalty, which was the responsibility of my ACLU colleague Diann Rust-Tierney, it was my charge at the ACLU to fight to eliminate, or at a minimum narrow, these provisions. In the midst of my advocacy against the omnibus crime bills, the U.S. Sentencing Commission, an independent agency whose duty it was to advise Congress on sentencing policy, issued a call for public comment on an array of issues. Included was the differential in sentencing between crack and powder cocaine offenses.

A colleague from the D.C. Federal Public Defender's Service suggested that I focus the ACLU's comment on the crack cocaine disparity, an issue I was ignorant about at the time. Again, this was the early 1990s, when public opinion on the disparity between crack and powder cocaine was undeveloped and research was sparse. Racism in cocaine sentencing had not yet been taken very seriously.

This was during a time when Democrats were trying to "out tough" the Republicans on criminal justice issues. It was a time when it appeared the only criminal justice issue the NAACP felt comfortable fighting against was racism in the application of the death penalty. There was no "kum-ba-yah"[91] across party lines on criminal justice reform, and even I, despite my civil rights and civil liberties background, initially approached this subject with skepticism.

Aware of the devastation crack had wreaked on communities of color, and also influenced by exaggerated media images, I assumed because young Black men were so often shown spread-eagled on the ground by police (or on the way to the morgue from crack cocaine abuse), that they were the primary abusers of and dealers in that substance. I could not have been more wrong.

My research, however, disclosed that Blacks were less involved in crack use than Whites. Statistics from the National Institute on Drug Abuse documented that the majority of crack users were Caucasian. Whoa! These statistics, which were inconsistent with the astronomical increase in arrests, prosecutions, convictions and imprisonment of young African Americans, intrigued me.

The disproportionate increase in Black incarceration directly resulted from strategic decisions made to send more police to communities of color, coupled with the legislation mandating harsher mandatory minimum sentences for crack than powder. My voice on the crack issue was quickly transformed into zealous advocacy.

The problem I faced was a dearth of balanced information on the issue at the time. The only material I could scrounge up was a comprehensive feature article in *USA Today* by reporter Dennis Cauchon. The article became my rock and the foundation for my attack.

The internet was infantile in those days. There were no law review articles on the issue – no analyses, no reports. So I studied the *USA Today* piece inside out. One person highlighted in the article was a mother, Barbara Piggee, whose son Roderick, a first-time offender, was serving a 17-year sentence for a crack conviction. Ms. Piggee admonished, "These kids are not the Mafia. They are poor, uneducated people trying to survive. You can't just throw away a whole race."

The photo in the article of the African American judge from Minnesota, Pamela Alexander, who had recently issued a ground-breaking state court decision, captivated me. Her decision equalized the penalties between crack and powder cocaine in her state.

However, the math in this issue kept kicking my butt. Despite loving the lure of street life and my sordid history dating "bad boyz," I knew nothing about drugs. Grams, kilograms, 100-to-1 quantity ratio. Damn, that's not what I thought I would be dealing with as a lawyer.

I was embarrassed to overhear Congressman Bobby Scott once remark to his counsel, Bobby Vassar, something to the effect that "Nkechi keeps saying this wrong. It's not the sentence that is 100 times more severe, but the drug amounts that dictate what the sentence will be." So I sat at Eric Sterling's feet and made him break it down to me until I could parrot the disparity and the math effectively.

I submitted the ACLU's public comment and testified before the U.S Sentencing

Commission on the crack and powder cocaine disparity in the spring of 1993. The main feature of the testimony was that the disparity in sentencing laws for possession and distribution of crack and powder cocaine resulted in an enormous and unjust increase in the Black prison population.

When I finished, Mrs. Barbara Piggee from the *USA Today* article approached me to say she loved my testimony. She expressed that she had flown to D.C. from California to testify on behalf of her only son, Rod. He had been sentenced to 17 years in prison for an offense involving a kilogram of crack.

Barbara was now a representative of a grassroots organization she founded with her son, Families Against Discriminatory Crack Laws. She pleaded that their organization desperately needed a voice in Washington to help expose the crack/powder cocaine inequity. Impressed with her passion and seriousness of purpose, I told her I would do what I could. Within months, armed with statistics, commitment and a sense of righteousness, I had found my niche at the ACLU, a calling that would follow me for the next 17 years, and beyond.

Shortly after that hearing in the spring of 1993, I issued a formal call to organizations to mobilize on this issue. The call prompted an immediate response from a coalition of groups coordinated by my colleague Gene Guerrero. The coalition was already meeting at the ACLU Washington National Office seeking to establish more rational responses to crime. As a veteran of coalition-building, however, I knew our advocacy would lack credibility if the support was limited to the usual Washington suspects. We needed to reach the constituencies most affected by the crack disparity, and the organizations that represented them.

During those early years I felt it was crucial to view the disparity not as a crime issue, but as a key civil rights issue. That formulation made it easier to forge alliances with organizations not traditionally focused on criminal justice issues. I mobilized a coalition of over 25 civil rights, religious, criminal justice and grassroots organizations to come together to oppose the disparity. We dedicated our newly formed National Committee Against the Discriminatory Crack Law to what we identified as twin priorities for action: public education and legislative advocacy.

Almost two months after the initial call, we convened a national symposium on the 100-to-1 ratio, entitled *Racial Bias in Cocaine Laws*, on August 26,1993. Laura Murphy, who had recently come to the helm of the ACLU Washington Legislative Office, immediately agreed that the ACLU would host the sympo-

sium. It was co-sponsored by our newly formed Committee, the Congressional Black Caucus Foundation, the Southern Christian Leadership Conference (SCLC), and the Criminal Justice Policy Foundation. At the time, I was serving as chair of the Criminal Law and Individual Rights Section of the D.C. Bar. The Section also became a proud sponsor. The symposium was convened at the Congressional Rayburn House Office building, and fortunately was covered by the still young C-SPAN station.

We featured three substantive plenaries: "The Experts Speak," "The Families Speak," and a Roundtable Discussion moderated by American University's Law School Professor, Angela J. Davis, a friend of mine since our Howard undergrad days, whose African name is Amani.The luncheon keynote speaker was Bill Moffitt, then Secretary of the National Association of Criminal Defense Lawyers, and a dynamic brother. We also gave a special recognition to Judge Pamela Alexander of Hennepin County, MN, for her recent seminal ruling on the crack disparity.

The Symposium also featured presentations by Rev. Jesse Jackson and Rev. Joseph Lowery, President of SCLC. That segment was moderated by my political savvy new boss, Laura Murphy, the first African American and female director of the ACLU Legislative Office, who would go on to serve in that capacity for the next 17 years.

My organizing was in high gear. This was the first time criminal justice professionals, civil rights advocates, defense attorneys, religious leaders and family members had been brought together in a national conference to discuss the disparity. The message from the symposium was clear – increased sentences for crack cocaine were not medically, scientifically or socially supportable. Furthermore, the long sentences were highly inequitable against African Americans and, I asserted, added up to a national drug policy tinged with racism.

It was too provocative at that time to even utter the word "racism" in professional Washington circles – so I couched the message in nebulous terms such as "tinged with racism." Remember, I was working for a majority-White organization. But it was not just liberal White groups I had to tiptoe around; during those early days it was even difficult to convince the NAACP to vocally advocate on the crack disparity issue.

I tried hard to convince my colleague Wade Henderson, then chair of the NAACP Washington Office, to be an official part of the event on the Hill. Wade knew it was right to be there, and I waved from the podium when I saw him standing at the door. But I surmised he felt too constrained by the NAACP such that when it came to criminal justice, he had been vocal primarily on issues of racism in the application of the death penalty.

This was before the term "racial profiling" had become widely used. It was years before Michelle Alexander popularized the analogy of the war on drugs as the "New Jim Crow," and long before it became fashionable to say that "Black Lives Matter." Nonetheless, our determined little committee worked long and hard to lay the foundation for future proponents of racial justice to stand and thrive.

We worked with television stations to compose features on the crack/powder disparity and provided assistance to journalists and talk show hosts across the country. We produced an educational manual, the *Cocaine Equitable Sentencing Briefer*, which was chock full of information.

Coalition members were frequently called upon to testify as expert witnesses as lower courts began to hold evidentiary hearings on the disparity issue. Coalition members in the American Bar Association were instrumental in getting the organization to adopt a resolution to eliminate unwarranted distinctions that produced racial disparity in sentencing. Of course this included the 100-to-1 weight ratio between powder and crack cocaine.

Our early organizing on the issue in the early 90s helped to plant seeds that elevated public consciousness. Our efforts made the public aware of the plight of thousands of people like Rod Piggee who were languishing in prison under this unequal law.

Besides public education, we knew we needed a legislative vehicle to rally around. We held briefings for members of Congress and strategically lobbied Rep. Charles Rangel (D-NY) to consider introducing corrective legislation. He was a veteran member of the Congressional Black Caucus, had been former Chair of the House Select Committee on Narcotics Abuse and Control, and was known for his tough stance on drugs. He was the perfect sponsor and agreed to spearhead the legislation, introducing the Crack-Cocaine Equitable Sentencing Act in October 1993.

The proposed Crime Prevention and Criminal Justice Reform Act of 1994, affectionately known as the "Congressional Black Caucus Alternative Crime Bill" sponsored by Rep. Craig Washington (D-TX), became another legislative vehicle.

Rep. William Hughes (D-NJ) introduced the language of the Rangel bill that would fix the crack/powder disparity as an amendment to the 1994 omnibus crime bill being considered by Congress at that time.

That's when the drama began to escalate. The mark up session in the House Judiciary Committee became heated when some Members viewed the attempt to equalize the penalties for crack and powder cocaine with hostility. The focus began to shift away from achieving equity to instead advocating the raising of penalties for powder cocaine. This, they argued, would fix the perceived disparity.

To eliminate the risk of his proposal being voted down and replaced by one that would needlessly raise the penalties for powder cocaine, Congressman Hughes withdrew his amendment and instead yielded to a provision directing the U.S. Sentencing Commission to study the issue and submit recommendations to Congress by the end of the year.

The outcome of the Committee debate was not surprising. This was a mid-term election year with politicians clamoring to be among the toughest on crime. This political climate signaled an automatic defeat for any rational proposal seeking to lower drug sentences. Congress unanimously passed the amendment not to equalize the sentences but instead to mandate a cocaine penalty study. It was an easy vote since the Sentencing Commission was already in the process of reviewing cocaine penalties.

The prisons exploded with celebrations. Watching the debate on C-SPAN, many serving crack sentences erroneously believed that they had won a unanimous victory but, alas, it was just a unanimous vote to study the issue.

That was a sober and crushing defeat. However, the Sentencing Commission completed its mandated study and on May 1, 1995, transmitted to Congress its report along with amendments to equalize the penalties for crack and powder cocaine possession and distribution to eliminate the disparity.

Again, all hell broke loose. The Sentencing Commission's report provoked a debate on the floor of the House of Representatives that smacked of mean-spirited paternalism. I watched the proceeding on C-SPAN and was appalled to see how differently legislators could view the same set of facts.

White members of Congress, by and large, professed to know more than their Black colleagues about an issue directly impacting the Black community. For example, in the Floor debate regarding the appropriateness of increased penalties for crack because of the devastation crack had wreaked on Black communities, Representative Bob Barr (R-GA) rose to the floor and advocated higher penalties for crack.

He attempted to validate his viewpoint by recounting his conversations with impoverished Black residents in housing projects showing their interest in stiff punishments. "They told me this when I was U.S. attorney; they tell me now as a Representative in the United States Congress, '(g)et those people off the streets and put them away for a long period of time.'"

I was pleased as I watched Representative Sheila Jackson-Lee (D-TX) counter:

It is interesting that…[Mr. Barr] can talk about how he has traveled the highways and byways of inner city Atlanta. But let me say to you that it is all in the asker to the question as to what the responder says. I asked the same question in neighborhoods that I grew up in, and I asked a group of African American ministers. 'How many of you enjoy your community using drugs?'…I got no takers. But then I asked the fairness question: 'How many of you understand that those who sell crack get 100 times more sentencing than those who sell cocaine?' Shock came across their faces because they really understand the needs of their members day after day. They are in the homes of crying mothers who say, 'He simply wanted to have a job.' They are in the homes of crying families who say, 'Where is the treatment facility for those who are addicted?' That is what the question becomes.

I chuckled as Representative Maxine Waters (D-CA) expressed "surprise at much of the rhetoric…of these so-called conversations that my friends on the other side of the aisle have been having in minority communities."

And Black members of Congress were not alone in countering the paternalism. Representative Miller (D-CA) effectively stated:

> I appreciate what the gentleman from Georgia…said, but when you go into white houses and white neighborhoods, they want white dealers put away, that sell it to white people. But they do not say put them away for a longer period of time than black people…the suggestion that somehow because black people believe in law enforcement and do not like people selling drugs in the streets that that means they are for the unequal treatment of people is crazy…

The Sentencing Commission reported that they researched and analyzed the issue of cocaine and federal sentencing policy "from every conceivable angle and for many, many, many months, making every effort to consider this critical matter in a thorough and professional manner." Nevertheless, Congress summarily rejected the Commission's recommendations and rebuffed the wisdom of the very body of experts it had established to advise on sentencing policy.

Ironically, the vote occurred on October 18, 1995, just two days after the historic

Million Man March, where an unprecedented number of Black men converged at the steps of the U.S. Capitol demanding justice and equality. Adding insult to injury, Congress demanded that the Sentencing Commission revise its recommendations so as to maintain sentences for crack cocaine trafficking that exceeded those for powder cocaine trafficking.

I was crushed. This was yet another grave defeat. I thought surely that the high-profile Million Man March would have made an impact on this effort, but I was wrong. Now, Bill Clinton was our only hope. Despite the actions of Congress, the President had the power to veto the Congressional action and allow the Commission's recommendations to become law.

Without skipping a beat, we got busy and redoubled our efforts. Coalition members lobbied, wrote letters, convened high-level strategy conference calls, and met with members of Congress. ACLU director Laura Murphy and I joined awkward meetings with Attorney General Janet Reno and her deputy Eric Holder, which yielded nothing but vague excuses. Others met with President Bill Clinton.

Ultimately, none of our appeals were successful, as President Clinton, despite his address during this period stressing the need to "root out racism" from the criminal justice system, signed the Congressional legislation gutting the Commission's effort to equalize the crack/powder cocaine sentencing.

We were appalled and castigated the President. The NAACP, which had been an integral member of the Coalition for some time, stated their frustration, "President Clinton missed a critical opportunity to bridge the nation's racial divide...we are profoundly disappointed that the President failed to follow his eloquent speech on racial healing with the equally enlightening action of a veto."

In a joint letter to President Clinton, a coalition of civil rights organizations, analogizing the situation to the 1993 beating of motorist Rodney King, as well as the crooked detective in the then-current O. J. Simpson case, stated:

> Nothing undermines the racial fairness of the criminal justice system more than these crack laws: Mark Fuhrman and the beaters of Rodney King operate outside the system, but the racism of the crack laws is an official, written, legislatively sanctioned part of the system. Rooting out the Mark Fuhrman's will take time: rooting out discriminatory crack sentencing is as easy as the stroke of a pen.

I was disgusted, disillusioned and dismayed with the political process and felt betrayed by this Democratic President. Even the savior, the U.S. Sentencing Commission, apparently acquiesced two years later to the unfavorable "tough on crime" political climate. In April 1997, the Commission modified its principled 1995 call for the complete elimination of the crack powder disparity. Instead, it recommended increasing from five grams, the amount of crack needed to trigger a five-year mandatory sentence, and lowering from 500 grams the amount of power needed to generate the same penalty.

In a concurring opinion, Commission Vice Chairman Michael Gelacak chided the modification, stating that "political compromise is a function better left to the Legislature." In July of the same year, the Administration proposed to reduce the 100-to-1 ratio to 10-to-1. Although this new ratio would be a step forward, it was an inadequate remedy nonetheless. The proposal went nowhere and the law mandating the 100-to-1 quantity ratio between crack and powder cocaine remained unchanged for the next 13 years.

In November 2004, the U.S. Sentencing Commission issued a report analyzing 15 years of sentencing since the U.S. Sentencing Guidelines went into effect in 1989. The report strongly stated, "Revising this one sentencing rule [the disparity between powder and crack cocaine] would do more to reduce the sentencing gap between Blacks and Whites than any other single policy change, and would dramatically improve the fairness of the federal sentencing system." The report noted that Congress had yet to address any of the Commission's recommendations since 1995, despite appeals for reform in three separate reports.

I left the ACLU in 1996 to direct the Equal Justice Program at Howard University School of Law, helping to train and inspire the next generation of legal professionals to challenge the unequal administration of justice. After my departure, our crack coalition dispersed, but I never gave up and stridently continued my personal advocacy on the disparity with whoever would listen – students, the media, even taxi drivers.

"The evidence has been scientific and persuasive," I continuously argued. "Crack cocaine and powder cocaine are pharmacologically identical and have similar effects, they differ only in their manner of ingestion. Both forms of the drug are dangerous, but one is not more dangerous than the other."

In responding to the constant references to fetal harm, I countered, "the term "crack baby" is now widely understood to be a misnomer, with research indicating that the negative effects of both prenatal crack and powder cocaine exposure are identical and no more severe than the impact of alcohol or tobacco on the fetus. In actuality, all pregnant women should be educated and discouraged against using any dangerous substances," I emphasized.

The issue of violence was always just beneath the surface. I stressed, "significantly less drug trafficking-related violence is associated with crack than was previously assumed, and any cases involving weapons are subject to either enhanced penalties or stiff mandatory minimum sentencing for use of a weapon in connection with a drug trafficking offense."

The most persuasive reason for erasing the disparity, I constantly argued, is that "only a mere frying pan and baking soda stand between powder and crack. Thus, to apply a stiffer penalty for crack that is sold directly as crack, as opposed to powder cocaine easily transformed into crack, is irrational."

It would be a decade before another serious challenge to the crack/powder disparity would manifest. And again, I would be at its helm.

Chapter Six, Section 4
The CIA/Contra Crack Connection

Dark Alliance, a series of articles published in August 1996 in the *San Jose Mercury News* provided startling revelations of the origin of the crack epidemic that plagued Black communities across the United States during the 1980s and 1990s. According to the investigative series – which included declassified reports, federal court testimony and records, undercover tapes, and hundreds of hours of interviews – thousands of kilos of cocaine were pumped into Black neighborhoods in Los Angeles during the 1980s, with the millions in profits used to finance a Latin American guerilla army organized by the CIA.

Although the scarce, high-priced cocaine was virtually non-existent in Black communities prior to this unique "fundraising strategy," its new availability, combined with "bargain-basement prices," quickly became the ammunition which set off the explosion in crack cocaine – the repercussions of which included devastated communities, violence and killings precipitated by gang warfare, and inordinately lengthy mandatory minimum sentences for countless low-level players.

Journalist Gary Webb, who conducted the paper's year-long investigation and authored the series, stated, "It is one of the most bizarre alliances in modern history, the union of a U.S.-backed army attempting to overthrow a revolutionary socialist government and 'Uzi-toting gangstas' of Compton and South Central Los Angeles."

"The army's financiers," Webb continued, "who met with CIA agents both before and during the time they were selling the drugs in L.A., delivered cut-rate cocaine to the gangs through a young South Central crack dealer named Ricky Donnell Ross." *"Freeway Rick,"* as he was later called, turned the cocaine powder into crack and "wholesaled it across the country, becoming L.A.'s biggest crack cocaine dealer in the mid-80s. Trial testimony of Ross on cocaine trafficking charges…reveal that the profits received from the cocaine was used to buy weapons and equipment for the FDN, one of several anti-communist groups in Nicaragua popularly known as the Contras, created in 1981 when the CIA consolidated exiles into a unified force, hoping to topple the new socialist government."

Oscar Danilo Blandon, Ross' supplier and a founder of the Contra army, had connections to the CIA and a "seemingly inexhaustible supply of high-grade cocaine." At one time he was described by prosecutors as "the biggest Nicaraguan cocaine dealer in the United States." Blandon later testified, "Whatever we were running in L.A., the profit was going for the Contra revolution."

However, despite having admitted to crimes which have sent others to prison for life, and despite a federal judge being earlier informed that Blandon "had sold so much cocaine in the U.S. his mandatory prison sentences were 'off the scale,'" he was released by the Justice Department after reportedly serving just over 28 months, and worked as a full-time informant on the payroll of the Drug Enforcement Agency.

Freeway Rick, in an exclusive interview with the *Final Call* newspaper from his jail cell, was outraged. "When I see how [the government] twist[s] the rules for him and they want to give me a life sentence, to me, it's sickening."

Although Ross states he can be viewed as either a "villain or a victim," he stressed, "I was manipulated. I was just like the prostitute…The U.S. government put it in our hands. They financed it. It was their planes that brought it over here…their guy, Oscar Danilo Blandon, he set up the market. They picked me. I didn't go to Nicaragua. This could go higher than the CIA."

Freedom of Information Act requests filed by the *San Jose Mercury News* with the CIA and the DEA were denied and, at the time of the series, requests filed with the FBI, State Department and INS yielded nothing. Representative Maxine Waters requested a full investigation by the DOJ and the CIA, as well as hearings to be conducted by the House Judiciary Committee.

Chapter Six, Section 5
Taxation Without Representation is Still Tyranny[92]

Other than the crack cocaine disparity theme, another fulfilling issue I advanced while legislative counsel for the American Civil Liberties Union was Statehood for the District of Columbia. At the time, it was a subject largely unknown outside of D.C. On April 2, 1992, the House District Committee passed a bill introduced by D.C.'s delegate to Congress, Eleanor Holmes Norton, a non-voting legislator and a respected veteran of the Civil Rights Movement. The bill, H.R. 51, provided for the admission of the state of New Columbia into the Union as the 51st state.

As a lifelong resident of Washington, D.C., I was ecstatic. The legislation was approved along an expected partisan line. The Committee voted out a similar bill in 1987, but that legislation never reached the House floor. This time was going to be different, and I was going to be right in the mix of it.

The New Columbia Statehood Act would terminate Congress' power to overturn, amend or repeal all legislation passed by the District of Columbia. It would also entitle me, along with over 600,000 other politically disenfranchised D.C. residents, to representation by two U.S. Senators, one or two Congresspersons, a governor, a lieutenant governor and an attorney general, among other state officials.

Many folk outside of D.C. don't realize that the lack of statehood for D.C. means political disenfranchisement. It means that every law duly passed by District legislators is subject to the whims and political winds of Congress. It means that every cent allocated by the District must pass Congressional scrutiny. It means that D.C. lacks legislative, economic and judicial autonomy. It means that District residents must bear all the burdens of citizenship, including paying taxes and perishing in wars, but are prohibited from having a voice that counts on matters of policy.

Lack of statehood for District citizens means we have no one in Congress who can fully protect our interests. It means that we are the only entity subject to United States jurisdiction that is taxed but has no voting representation in Congress. Puerto Rico, Guam, the Virgin Islands and American Samoa are all U.S. territories, yet pay no federal income taxes. D.C. residents, on the other hand, are not only taxed, but pay more in federal taxes than eight states and more per capita than 48 of the 50 states.

The District paid a whopping billion dollars in taxes to the federal treasury during the time I worked on this issue at the ACLU. Taxation without representation was tyranny 200 years ago, and it is tyranny today.

It all made perfect sense to me. No magic formula was needed to bring the District into line with not only the 50 states, but with democratic countries all over the world. All that had been required for the admission of other states into the Union was a simple majority vote by both Houses of Congress, and the President's signature.

There was no Constitutional impediment to granting statehood to residents of D.C. The Constitution requires that Congress exercise exclusive control over a federal seat of government that does not exceed 100 square miles. Representative Norton's bill allowed the federal seat of government to be preserved by maintaining the District of Columbia as the "National Capital Service Area." It would be comprised of key federal buildings, agencies and monuments, with the remaining territory admitted into the Union as the state of "New Columbia."

A Constitutional amendment was not a prerequisite, the consent of Maryland was not needed, and retrocession to Virginia was not a viable alternative. To me, these were all smokescreens advanced to deny fairness and fundamental rights to the Chocolate City, as many of us who grew up in D.C. affectionately called it. Indeed, the reality of a predominately Black city with a large underclass has historically been an implicit undercurrent mitigating against statehood.

Today, now that Washington, D.C. is more akin to Vanilla Bean City in its complexion, and is 'upper crust' as the result of gradually gentrified demographics, I am convinced that the quest for statehood for the District of Columbia will one day become a reality.

Nevertheless, during the early 1990s we were far from that day. On November 20th and 21st in 1993, I witnessed the House of Representatives debate the entrance of the state of New Columbia into the Union, as part of its deliberations on Representative Norton's H.R. 51. This was historic. It was the first time the full House of Representatives debated D.C. statehood.

A massive lobbying and civil disobedience campaign spurred activity on the Hill. There were weekly demonstrations in the streets in front of the Congressional Office buildings. Hundreds of people, including me, were strategically arrested, focusing the media's attention on statehood. Thousands of people were mobilized to make calls to their legislators, asking that they support H.R. 51.

The debate and subsequent vote were momentous, spreading energy, life and legitimacy to a part of the Civil Rights Movement that for decades had been swept under the rug. The vote was the result of a broad coalition of civil rights groups, D.C. residents, and leadership of the House of Representatives, strategizing together. This coalition was under the aegis of the Leadership Conference on Civil Rights (LCCR), during the time Ralph Neas was at the helm. As legislative counsel for the National ACLU Washington Office with this issue in my portfolio, I enthusiastically co-chaired the LCCR D.C. Statehood Committee.

I watched with pride as Congresswoman Norton rose to her feet and became the first to speak on the House Floor in support of statehood. Ironically, she would not be allowed to vote on her own bill, precisely the issue H.R. 51 hoped to remedy. In a moving speech to the rapt Congresspersons and all of us in the packed Gallery, she spoke for her constituents, including me, and all the other unrepresented people of the District of Columbia. She spoke of justice, of the Constitution, and stated that this historic vote "was a vote for the principle of self-government and representative democracy."

I was one of over 650 supporters packed into the House gallery for those two days, and I could not have been prouder.

The ensuing debate, however, was mean-spirited and Rep. Norton had warned that statehood opponents would use every argument, good or bad, warranted or not, against enfranchising District residents. One Congressional adversary declared that if D.C. residents did not like their status, they could leave. "There was no citizen chained to the pillars of the Capitol," he added.

Another argued that D.C. was "a liberal bastion of corruption and crime...[its police] illiterate and border-line retarded," and "it did not even deserve a City Council." Other opponents argued that D.C. statehood was unconstitutional (despite the Constitution explicitly granting federal representation to all citizens) and that D.C. was too small (despite having a population larger than three states). They also stated that D.C. was not a viable economic unit, although at that time D.C. residents paid the second highest federal taxes per capita in the nation.

Still, speaker after impassioned speaker rose to register their support of statehood. Representative Ron Dellums (D-CA) stated, "I have waited patiently for 23 years for this moment to come." Rep. Norman Mineta declared that "200 years ago, we fought a revolution over...taxation without representation. We fought against tyranny of laws passed by a legislative body in which we had no voice and no vote...Yet today, the Congress regularly subjects one group of Americans to those same indignities, simply because they make their homes in the Capital."

Representative Neil Abercrombie, from the last territory admitted as a state, belittled the traditional anti-statehood arguments used against Hawaii and now D.C., as well. He stated unequivocally, "Violence and racism was at the root of efforts to stop almost every bid for statehood from every state that has existed." Rep. Charles Rangel asked Congress "to get above our biases, our prejudice, and do what is right for America…that we are not willing to deny people who love this country, who have fought for this country, who die for this country, to play according to a different set of rules."

As he closed the debate, Majority Leader Dick Gephardt asked passionately, "What would it be like to be a father here in the District of Columbia and have my son or daughter go [to war], and have no vote on the floor of this House?" After he finished, for the second time that day – the first being at the conclusion of Rep. Norton's remarks – we all spontaneously rose and gave him a standing ovation. Incredibly, the applause was not just from the supporters. Uncharacteristic for the House floor, much of the cheering and clapping came from the Members of Congress themselves.

Being in that auspicious room for those two days felt like riding on a rollercoaster. Every time supporters of D.C. statehood rose, my adrenaline rose with them, and every time opponents spoke, it sank.

Although H.R. 51 failed by a margin of 153 to 277, the historic vote proved the naysayers wrong. Over one hundred and fifty Representatives agreed with our coalition and voted "yes."

At a press conference afterward, Eleanor Holmes Norton pointed out that Alaska's bid for statehood failed eight times before it became a state. She stated that surprisingly, the number of "yes" votes greatly exceeded her expectations. The entire Democratic leadership voted in support of statehood. President Clinton actively supported statehood. Two-thirds of the Democrats voted "yes," as well as the entire Congressional Black Caucus, and most of the Hispanic caucus. That was 1993.

Today, over 25 years later, the quest for statehood continues.[93]

Chapter Six, Section 6
The Spirit World is Very Real

I once had a boyfriend who was an organizer with the National Black United Front and did a lot of work with RAP, Inc., a local substance abuse prevention and treatment organization. I knew he used to be a drug addict, but again this 'good gurl' liked the 'bad boyz'. Besides, he gave me very flowery compliments and often told me how beautiful I was. It was because of this brother that I finally ditched my glasses and donned contact lenses.

But he started seeing another sister and wanted a polygamous relationship. That simply wasn't my cup of tea, so we parted as friends. Years later, I received a phone call that rocked my world.

"Nkechi, this is Nkenge."

"Hey sis, what's happening?" I asked.

"I'm calling you because you're my sister and I'm not sure if you know."

"Know what?"

"About your Brother friend from Rap."

"What about him?"

"Well, he's in the hospital."

"Oh my God, I didn't know. I haven't talked to him in years."

"I just think you need to know."

"Know what? How's he doing?"

"He's dying from AIDS. You might want to get checked out."

Well, it would be a colossal understatement to say that I was freaked out. My sister Roberta was about to have a baby, and ridiculously frightening thoughts churned through my mind. I wondered fearfully.

Will I be able to hold the new baby? Would he or she become infected with AIDS?

I saw my life evaporating before my eyes. I just knew I probably had AIDS too. I mean, how could I not? It's transmitted sexually, and we definitely had sex, albeit years earlier. Although I dreaded having to do so, I knew I had to get tested. It was an agonizing, excruciatingly unbearable waiting period. Thankfully, the result was negative, and I heaved a mighty sigh of relief!

I kept putting off going to the hospital to visit my old boyfriend. What was I going to say? I don't know why, but I did not want to face him. Did the sister he two-timed me with know that she should get checked? I fretted. I didn't know how to reach her. Hell, I didn't even remember her name. By the time I had mustered enough courage to finally go visit him, I found out he had passed. I asked myself contemptuously, What kind of friend was I? I was so ashamed of myself and felt bad that I didn't visit him before he died. The entire ordeal shook me up.

One night soon after he passed, even before the funeral, I woke up with a start in the middle of the night. To this day the image is seared in my mind. And I don't care what anyone thinks, it really happened.

There he was, in my bedroom. Sitting down, not in a chair, but cross-legged on the ceiling. Yes, that's what I said. On…the…ceiling. He was up there on that ceiling, plain as day. He didn't speak out loud, but I knew exactly what he was saying. It was like mental telepathy. He expressed to me that it was all right and to stop beating up on myself. He silently communicated that he understood and was not upset with me for not visiting.

Needless to say, I was scared shitless and screamed! And other than him and me, I was alone in the house. It was undeniably real, and I was terrified. I mean, we often call upon the ancestors to visit and give us guidance, but I had not called upon him. He just showed up. When I do call upon the ancestors, I am usually meditating or doing a libation with my incense, Florida water and bells.

There was none of that in this situation. I was in bed asleep and woke up to an experience that was so very real. I was petrified, but then I remembered that to my mind, the spirit world is very real and is all around us. I'm reminded of the lyrics of the song, "The Ancestors' Breath" by Sweet Honey in the Rock. The lyrics express my sentiments exactly:

> Those who have died have never, never left
> The dead are not under the earth
> They are in the rustling trees
> They are in the groaning woods
> They are in the crying grass
> They are in the moaning rocks
> The dead are not under the earth …[94]

Even today, I know the Brother's spirit, and the spirits of countless others from my D.C., Africentric community are still here. There are many who left lasting impressions upon me, and whose spirits I feel still surround me. In calling their names, they include: Baba Agyei Akoto, Baba Ngoma, Rev. Ishakamusa Barashango, Brother Kwame Afoh, Dr. Jean Sindab, Brother Damu Smith, President Imari Obadele, Maulana Douglas Jones, Mamadi Nyasuma, Rabia Rayford, Nana Seshibe, Baba Oraefo, Ike Ridley, Za'hraa Mahdi, Iya Omitosin, Karega Dukes, Ngina Milner, Amensa Whaley, Lasana Mack, Dr. Frances Cress Welsing, Baba Dick Gregory, Mama Noni, Brother Vernard Gray, Brother Bey, Hodari Ali and Brother Ah. Sadly, the list grows daily.

Chapter Six, Section 7
My Big Fat New Afrikan Wedding, and Divorce

While at the National Prison Project, I realized that I was ready to settle down and have children. It was the beginning of my professional legal career, and my community work emphasized the importance of family. The second principle of the Republic of New Afrika's New Afrikan Creed is "I believe in the family as a community and the community as a family and I will work to make this concept live."

The first principle of the Nguzo Saba, the value system of Kwanzaa, is Umoja, which means "unity." I was a founding member of the Ankobea Society, a family-based society focused on the preservation of generations. I had taught first grade and had written two books for young people.

So when am I going to meet someone that I can build a family with? I kept asking myself. Although not with conscious intention, I had fulfilled Dr. Frances Cress Welsing's two requisites for marriage – I was over the age of 30, and I was employed. Damn, I was more than ready.

I met a brother at a book reception. I'd seen his name before, but I had never made his acquaintance. He was a journalist who wrote for the *Washington Afro-American* newspaper and had written for the *Washington Informer* weekly newspaper as well. He also worked as a writer for an international union. He came from a long-standing, civic-oriented, well-respected family in Minnesota. He was well-spoken and had adopted an African name. After dating for about five months, he asked me to marry him.

I was so ready to settle down. I wasn't getting any younger and was getting tired of people always asking me, "Nkechi when you gonna get married?"

So I told him "Yes."

He later showed me a letter Assata Shakur once wrote to him in 1973 while she was in jail. "Really?!" I exclaimed. *Damn, I was impressed, but wondered, How in the world did she even know anything about this young dude in Minnesota?* Then he told me he had been to prison, which seemed to be the case with most of the brothers I had relationships with up to this time. He said it happened when he was a juvenile and when released, he moved to Washington, D.C., enrolled at American University and had not missed a beat.

I was not really alarmed when I found out he had been to prison, but I was surprised at the charge.

"You bombed a department store!?" I shrieked, incredulously. "At fifteen years old???" "No, I was *charged and convicted* of bombing a department store," he retorted quietly.

I really would not have even believed him, but he showed me old newspaper clippings with his "slave" name and the facts of the case. Again, damn. There was no internet back then, but there it was in black and white, or rather yellow and faded print. I read that the bombing happened in 1970, during a time of intense police/community unrest in St. Paul, MN. There was growing opposition to the Viet Nam War and there had been numerous bomb threats and evacuations in the Twin Cities.

A woman, who ironically happened to be a civil rights activist, was seriously injured in the bombing. My husband-to-be, then 15, was arrested after bomb-making instructions, Black Panther material and a pamphlet on urban guerrilla warfare were found in his house. He was tried as a juvenile, transferred to adult court, convicted and sentenced to 20 years in prison. He served three years at a juvenile reformatory before being released on parole.

We never really talked much about the incident after we discussed it that one time. In "The Struggle" there was always the creed of "need to know," and after the passage of 17 years since the incident, I really did not have a need to know. Of course, none of his history was common knowledge in Washington, D.C., and it was something he rarely wanted to elaborate on or discuss, so we didn't.

Being married to someone convicted of a bombing didn't faze me. I accepted it because the charges were related to "The Struggle" and he had a background as a revolutionary. It wasn't until much later that reality began to sink in. I learned that in addition to aggravated arson in detonating a stick of dynamite, the charge also included 1st degree attempted murder. But at the time, I considered his reputation more significant than mine as just an "armchair" revolutionary. So, characteristic of my allure with bad boys, I took it all in stride. I said to myself, He's a militant, revolutionary man. I thought I had hit the jackpot. It was not long before I realized that he was no prize.

The wedding, however, was colossal. You may have heard of the movie, "My Big Fat Greek Wedding." Well, my first marriage could have been dubbed "My Big Fat New Afrikan Wedding." To ensure that I was being inclusive to all parts of my spiritual and political selves, I requested four spiritual leaders, all personal friends, to officiate: Reverend Ishakamusa Barashango, founder of the Temple of the Black Messiah; Nana Kwabena Brown, Chief Priest of the Temple of Nyame; Ur Aua Hehi Metu Ra Enkhamit, Paramount King of the Ausar Auset Society; and Brother Imari Obadele, President of the Provisional Government of the Republic of New Afrika.

I wore an elegantly gorgeous, cream-colored lace two-piece African-inspired peplum gown. An elaborately wrapped golden lace gele crowned my head. My bridesmaids

included my two sisters, Paula and Roberta, along with my girlfriends Tami, Soffi-yah, Kianga and Donna. Even Brother Tyehimba joined us from California as one of the groomsmen. The ladies wore flowing blue lace gowns with matching lace head wraps, and the groomsmen wore blue and black African print dashikis.

We held the grand affair at the Howard University Rankin Chapel and the reception followed at the Howard University Blackburn Center. We savored the traditional "tasting of the elements" ceremony – an essential feature of an African-inspired wedding that includes flavors representing the different emotions couples experience in a marriage, ranging from bitter and sour to hot and sweet.

After our elaborate ceremony and vows, which included a recitation of the Republic of New Afrika's New Afrikan Creed, we jetted off to a storybook Egyptian honeymoon. Ahhh, it all seemed so celestial. My husband, however, had another side to him and it became clear to me that this was not a marriage made in heaven. The dissolution of our marriage, however, had nothing to do with his past. Our union was simply a disastrous fit. We had irreconcilable differences that led to the divorce of the decade.

Not more than a year and a half into the marriage, he reveled in disseminating slanderously, sham information about me. He spread these falsehoods not only throughout the community and to my family but also to political prisoners I had been writing to, and to God knows who else.

I was totally shocked that he was trying to damage my reputation, saying stupid stuff like "late last year my wife, Nkechi, the revolutionary attorney and political activist, decided she didn't want to be married any longer to a strong Black man following her employment with the white female-led women's legal defense fund, where she found white feminist ideology more to her liking than the Black nationalism she has professed for more than 20 years. At that point she abandoned the concept of Black family."

It was some sho-nuff COINTELPRO-type stuff. I couldn't believe it. He even produced a maliciously defamatory flyer under the title, "Black Community Beware: My Complaint Against Nkechi Taifa." Reading his lying diatribes made me hyperventilate with anger. He accused me of fornication and adultery and of being "an informant guilty of espionage on the Black Community."

He invented ludicrous lies claiming I disavowed community decision-making processes and that I asserted that "Black leaders have no standing on such matters because the white man's law takes precedence." His flyer concluded:

> Therefore, I challenge YOU, the Afrikan community at large to DEMAND THAT YOUR LEADERS thoroughly question Nkechi Taifa and hold her responsible for her actions to the point that she should be BANISHED from all our homes, gatherings, meetings and events should she be found guilty of her crimes against the nation...I insist that each of you question her at every opportunity. Do you want an immoral woman setting examples for our sons and daughters? I say NO, NO, NO, NEVER! BANISH HER FOREVER!

A community Council of Elders was summoned to intervene and mediate. My lawyer friend Soffiyah Elijah from New York happened to be in town the weekend of the hearing, staying at my home. Although I did not know her during the late 70s, she had clerked for Brother Chokwe Lumumba the entire time she was in law school, and shortly thereafter served as one of the special tribunal judges in the 2nd RNA Constitutional Crisis I was involved in that interpreted the RNA Code of Umoja as equating imprisonment with incapacitation. Shortly thereafter she ended up representing Marilyn Buck in the N.Y. Brinks expropriation and liberation of Assata Shakur case, and I later ended up on Marilyn's legal defense team in D.C. as the attorney for one of her co-defendants, Laura Whitehorn.

Soffiyah and I laugh hilariously when reminiscing about how we first bonded. We had separately arrived in Atlanta, GA to receive an award, along with Sister Fulani

Sunni Ali and others, honoring women in the New Afrikan Independence Movement. Renting a vehicle to travel to the event for what should have been no more than a 15-minute drive, we talked for hours, not necessarily because we were interested in each other's lives, which we were, but mostly because we were lost, essentially driving around in circles.

This was long before the internet, before cell phones, and before Map Quest and Google Maps. We only had at our disposal real paper maps, and revolutionary me never learned how to read one. Although not really funny, we joked at how could I possibly represent radical clients where discovery in the case was brimming with maps and charts, detailed notes of reconnaissance, disguises and false id's, and me as their lawyer could not even decipher directions on a simple map!

Besides being an attorney, Soffiyah is now also a part of the Ausar Auset Society. People often ask how she became involved with the Society. That story is tied up with my big fat divorce. She solemnly describes the circumstances that led to her first encounter with the Ausar Auset spiritual society:

I had come in town from New York to interview my client, Marilyn Buck, at the D.C. jail. I was staying at Nkechi's house, and she was a total wreck. I took one look at her and seriously considered flipping through the phone book for the nearest hospital.

I honestly thought she was on the verge of a nervous breakdown. She had made a call to a friend she knew who was part of a spiritual group. Nkechi pleaded for help and received a return phone call, stating that she had to get some work done. I'm thinking, 'Work? It's the weekend.' I couldn't have been more surprised when Nkechi urgently said, 'Soffiyah, I need to get some lettuce and a watermelon. Let's go!'

Now I don't know where she thought we were going to get this watermelon in the middle of the winter, but we got it – and the lettuce as well. We went to this large house where Nkechi talked with a distinguished but ordinary looking brother. He instructed her to go to someone's apartment that she knew.

When we arrived, I saw women and some children in a room. They taught us some type of song or chant. One woman had white chalk put on her face, and she was dancing around Nkechi. I was literally about to bolt when I noticed that whatever they were doing to my friend, was working. Her distraught demeanor was being transformed right before my eyes!

They instructed Nkechi to tear up the slanderous flyer her husband had written into tiny pieces. They then burned the pieces and placed them in a little pouch which was put around Nkechi's neck. They then instructed her to throw the lettuce and melon into the river. We drove to the 14th Street Bridge, recited some prayers and chants, and sacrificed the materials to the water. I was completely dumbfounded. Nkechi was transformed before my very eyes. She was now the perfect epitome of calm and serenity.

"That was my introduction to the Ausar Auset Society," Soffiyah marveled.

The community Council of Elders' hearing was later that day. I was a totally different person from my usual hectic self and quite changed from the hysterical person I was earlier that morning. I was confident, calm, poised and polished. My husband was the hysterical one, vehemently objecting to Soffiyah's presence, shrieking 'It's not fair, it's not fair! She's a lawyer!'

"Well, this is a hearing that you called," Soffiyah coolly retorted. "So it is not out of the question that Nkechi would have a lawyer."

There was nothing he could do but sulk back to his seat. Needless to say the community Council of Elders quickly ruled in my favor. He was required to issue an apology, and soon afterwards penned a public retraction declaring that all of his charges were untrue. I was actually surprised at how quickly the retraction came. No one ever told me what conversations on the street, if any, they or others may have had with him, but I suspect that, again, brothers who always have my back secretly came to my aid and defense and I never heard a peep from him again.

When that marriage chapter closed, I vowed that I would never jump into a relationship again with someone I really did not know. Little did I know at the time, but that vow would be short-lived. As for the Ausar Auset Society, I credit them with getting me pregnant several years later after I remarried.

Chapter Six, Section 8
Miracle Birth Baby

Several years after my calamitous first marriage, and after a couple of other boyfriends, I reconnected with a blast from my past, Brother Kwasi, who I first met while still in high school in 1971. I credit him with giving me the very first headache I ever had in my life when I was a teenager. I nicknamed him "the Dictator" because he was always trying to tell me what to do. However, Kwasi, whose last name means "artist," once drew a beautiful and prophetic picture depicting him with me in a park, holding a baby in my arms. Twenty-three years later, the image became a reality.

At the time we reconnected in the early 90s, Kwasi had recently emerged from maxing out of a 10-year sentence in Mississippi at the infamous Parchman Prison Farm. The conviction was for armed robbery. Kwasi, however, always asserted his arrest resulted from being targeted due to the community organizing he was doing in the state.

When he asked me to marry him when he returned to D.C., I thought, *Well, at least this is someone I know, not some stranger.* I said, "Yes!"

We planned a very small wedding to be held in a park. He became my second husband and, as he had artistically prophesied decades earlier, became the father of my only child. Despite all of our many differences, disagreements and the fact that we later divorced, I will always be thankful for the gift from God of our daughter.

Although I had spent most of the 80s trying not to get pregnant, I had been having a very difficult time conceiving and had had a couple of miscarriages. I had an outpatient scan called a hysterosalpingogram to find out what was wrong and was informed that there was some type of blockage in my fallopian tubes. When the doctor told me I would not be able to have children, I was devastated. I tearfully chalked it up to Divine punishment for having terminated a pregnancy years earlier.

During this period of my life, I was deeply involved with the Ausar Auset Society, a Pan African religious organization that provides spiritual education and a social vehicle to the African-descended community. I attended classes, took part in rituals, and received spiritual readings using either the Metu Neter oracle cards or the I-Ching, a Chinese method of divination.

Shekhem Hames Metin,[95] an herbalist priest in the Society, prescribed a regimen of herbs to strengthen my reproductive system. I was excited that Ausar Auset was having a fertility mudram (ritual dance)[96] in January 1993, called Waamba Wu. I attended the jam-packed ritual for conceiving and birth, which was especially good for healing the womb of traumas that were preventing women from getting pregnant.

I blended in with the other sisters there, all of whom were adorned in flowing fabrics of yellow, green and pink. Rabia Rayford was there. She was a beautiful, carefree

Sista who is now in the spirit world. Mama Eshe Bernal was there. Our spiritual connection continues to this day. Countless sisters were part of this wonderful Waamba Wu fertility mudram, all either seeking conception or assisting others in their quest.

We all chanted, sang and danced to Auset and Het Heru in the Kemetian tradition. These were the same feminine energies of YeMaya and Oshun in the Yoruba tradition, or Nana Esi of the Akans. The magical outcome was that a number of us, including Sisters Rabia, Eshe and myself, all got pregnant within months, and had babies around the same time. Mama Eshe, in particular, later revealed to me a dream she had while on a trip to Egypt that two little babies from the spirit world were coming to the earthly plane together: one was her daughter, and the other turned out to be mine.

I prayed for my daughter before I was pregnant, and I honestly believe she heard my prayers from the ancestral realm, and chose to be born through me (and, okay, through her father too). This may sound crazy but, believe me, there were many signs. While Kwasi's memories of events differ slightly from mine, we both agree that they were signs.

Kwasi and I had driven to New York to purchase some fabric from the African Marketplace to use for my wedding dress when the first sign appeared. We were coming off the Roosevelt Freeway into Harlem. While stopped at a red light at a wide intersection, I saw what appeared to be a very old Black woman. She seemed feeble and ambled slowly across the street, kind of dragging one leg behind the other. She slowly made progress across the street, stopping whenever a car presented itself.

She was dressed like a beggar woman, looked like a beggar woman and acted like a beggar woman. I suddenly felt an overwhelming desire, a need, a must, to give her as much money as I could. I had never had that feeling before. As she approached our car, I handed her around $10, more than I would normally have given to someone on the street. I was obsessed and after the light changed and the car started moving again, I cried out urgently, "Kwasi, please turn around! I wanna go back to her. I really, really want to give that woman more money!"

He looked dubious, but dutifully turned the corner and returned to the spot where we had last seen the woman. I swear it could not have taken us longer than a couple of minutes to round the corner, but she was nowhere to be seen. She had been walking ever so slowly, with that one leg dragging behind her but, lo-and-behold, she was now magically nowhere to be seen. It was like she had…Poof!…vanished into thin air. I couldn't believe it and was also quite disappointed to have missed the opportunity to bestow more money upon her.

We were short on cash, as I had given the mysterious beggar lady practically all the money I had. While still in New York, I saw a pair of earrings for sale that I knew I absolutely had to have. The extra money I would have given the beggar lady I used to purchase the earrings. They were lovely ankh earrings. The ankh is the Egyptian (Kemetic) symbol that means "life."

Later that month while preparing for the wedding, I dressed into my attire consisting of beautiful Nigerian Ashoke cloth. As the finishing touch, I positioned the lovely little ankh earrings purchased at the Harlem museum on my lobes and proceeded through the trees in the park to the ceremony.

Surprising, I noticed during the wedding that neither one of the earrings were on my ears. I looked around after the ceremony, but could not seem to locate them any-where. It was rather frustrating, but I couldn't let such a small thing put a damper on my special day so I put it out of my mind.

Mysteriously, later that night when I was taking off my wedding outfit, I found the ankh-meaning-symbol-of-life earrings. They had fallen off my ears, travelled down my bubba (wedding dress top) and had come to rest inside my lappa (skirt). They were safely nestled below my navel. That was the amazing second sign!

The third sign: Jamaica was the perfect setting for our glorious honeymoon. I re-member floating lazily on my back in the lovely pool of an Ocho Rios Hotel, over-looking the Caribbean Sea. The sun caressed my loins under my red, black and green swimsuit. The backdrop of lush green foliage and a variety of vibrant flowers created the most harmoniously serene setting that soothed me to the core of my being. I felt peacefully tranquil, and joyously one with nature.

My new husband and I were famished after our swim and decided to get something to eat. While walking to the restaurant at the intersection of the main road, Kwasi and I came upon an elderly lady sitting by a little stand on the side of the path selling fruit. When we arrived in Jamaica, our goal had been to put as much money as we could directly into the hands of the local people. We purchased about $10 worth of fruit from her, but it wasn't just about the fruit, we really wanted to support her. After leaving, we felt guilty that we hadn't given her enough money and wanted to give her more.

We could not have walked more than 15 feet when we turned back, but she was gone. We walked back to see where she could have gone, but there was no trace of her, the stool she was sitting on, the fruit, or the stand. There were no footprints in the dirt. There was nothing there. Nothing. There is no way she could have gotten up, taken the stand, and the stool, and the fruit. No way at all. But it was all gone.

Looking back, I realized this strange occurrence was sign number three.

I have always felt that the Ausar Auset Society opened the door for my successful pregnancy. I believe that Sekert, the Kemetian deity of divine unfolding, appeared to me in the form of the beggar woman just before our wedding and also as the Jamaican fruit vendor during our honeymoon. I always believed my gifts to these spirit women sealed the deal.

The little ankh earrings nestled in the area of my womb during our wedding ceremony were part of the divine unfolding. According to a sonogram, I likely conceived the very day of our encounter with the disappearing Jamaican fruit vendor, and the same day of my serene float in the waters near the ocean. I did not make any of these connections, however, at the time.

There were more signs that our daughter was a miracle gift from God. Each trimester of my pregnancy a Metu Neter oracle card reading was done and each trimester the reading came up with the same deity, Sekert. Sekert governs destiny, and is described by Shekem Ur Shekhem Dr. Ra Un Nefer Amen, Paramount King of the Ausar Auset Society as follows:

Seker (the 3rd sphere of the Tree of Life) is the divine faculty that is in charge of the life-force, which is the formative base of all things in the world. Although the source of life is infinite, each entity is allowed to share in its infinity through a series of cycles of births. Each entity is thus allotted a finite portion of this life-force at a time, for its adventure in the world. This recycling principle governs the cycles of birth, growth, decay, death, rebirth and so on.

During my first trimester at 12 weeks, I asked the question, "What is the status of my pregnancy?" The reading's answer included the card, Seker tu maat. At my second trimester at 25 weeks, I again asked the question and the status included the card, Seker tu maat. But it also included an indication that some spiritual work needed to be done.

Nana Kwabena, a priest in the Akan tradition who would later become my pastor, strongly suggested I have a Nana Esi bath and wear Nana Esi beads. The beads, he explained, were for Nana Esi's blessings and protection for the unborn baby, myself and husband. Ten spots on my body were anointed with a special medicine. They included the middle of forehead, middle of breasts, side of the elbows, middle of the wrists, base of spine, top of feet near joint, top of ankle on outside and outside of my kneecaps.

For the next seven days I was to anoint these joints with the special mixture of Florida water and medicine given to me, and record all the dreams I had. I was to wear the Nana Esi beads around my neck and the Nana Esi belt around my waist until time for labor and delivery, which I did.

The doctor I chose to deliver my baby was a priest in training at the Ausar Auset Society and was head of the OB-GYN department at a local hospital. I got everything I asked for – a private room and the ability to bring in my spiritual items: blue and white Auset fabric, essential oils, candles, beads, and taped music.

My belly was huge. Sister Aminyah Muhammad, from my natural childbirth class, came to the hospital and sat a while. She was a part of the organization, HABIB – Home and Birth in Bed. Kwasi had wanted me to have a home birth, but a reading we did when I first found out I was pregnant ruled that out.

Shekem't Mut Shat Maat from the Ausar Auset Society was at the hospital with me the entire time, assisting me. We chanted, rubbed my belly and listened to melodic mudrams.[96] I used my arms to dance while sitting up in the bed. The blue and white tie-dyed Auset spiritual cloth hung from the wall within my sight. Another one was draped as a sheet across the hospital bed.

An entire day after my waters broke, it was evident that the pregnancy was not progressing.

Kwasi, looking at the monitor, asks me incredulously:

"You mean you don't feel any pain yet?"

"Nope, not a thing," I replied calmly.

More time went by with nothing progressing. I had never had a cramp in my life, so I was terrified at the thought of pain in actually giving birth. I think menstrual cramps help prepare women for the discomfort of childbirth. Despite having completed a great natural childbirth class, I definitely did not feel prepared.

Then came the clincher. After a day and a half of fruitless, pain free labor, it was determined that too much time had passed since my waters broke. I was informed I would need an emergency Cesarean section. Oh no, I'm thinking. *I didn't prepare for this! A C-Section. That's not natural childbirth!*

I would have to get a needle in my spine or somewhere near the base of my back in preparation for the surgery. I was petrified knowing that if I moved, I could be paralyzed. I didn't move. It was quite evident now why the spiritual reading nine months earlier cautioned against a home delivery. I definitely needed to be in a hospital because I was going to have surgery.

So I was wheeled down to the operating room. Everyone was bustling around preparing for my C-Section. I will never forget the picture of Kwasi with a tear of joy resting on his cheek. He attempted to soothe me while glancing over the surgical sheet tent at the doctor conducting the procedure. I won't forget it because thanks to Shekhem't Mut Shat Maat, the miracle birth was video-taped, capturing key moments. One of the interesting details recorded was the clock on the wall shortly after I gave birth. Months later while watching the video, I realized, *No one is watching the daggone clock. How do we actually know exactly what time my baby is born? Or even more importantly, which day since the surgery started sometime shortly before midnight.*

As I gazed at the doctor and attendants surrounding the hospital bed, patching and sewing me up, my little baby seemed to be all by herself on that little table. Then Kwasi picked up our little bitty bundle and brought her to me. He crooned, "This is your baby girl. She looks just like you." I was completely overcome with indescribable joy and happiness!

The C-Section was the final sign. Because my daughter was not placed in my womb the normal way, of course she could not have been born the normal way. She emerged perfect, with no wrinkles, no misshapen head, etc. I firmly believe she was spiritually placed in my womb.

The beggar woman in Harlem could have been none other than Seker or Sekert, the deity of destiny, often depicted as dragging one leg behind her. To my mind, the woman selling fruit in Ocho Rios was also Sekert. Incredibly, after birth, a Metu Neter reading revealed my daughter's destiny to be none other than Sekert hetep!

I used Shekhem Ur Shekhem's *African Names* book, in conjunction with the Meter Neter oracle cards, to choose my daughter's name. I had been feeling the name, Mariama, for some time and after she was born, the fact that she was born on a Saturday fit perfectly as well. The Akan girl's day name is Ama, which is subsumed within the name, Mariama.

Mariama means "gift from God" and my name, Nkechi, means "God's gift." However, we took our gift from God home from the hospital nameless. Although I was unofficially calling her Mariama, I spent weeks pouring through the African Names book devising combinations of names and meanings. They had to fit the reading revealing her destiny, which was disclosed through a reading as "discipline brings me joy."

I would choose a name combination I liked, then do a reading to see if it was a good fit. Finally, I reached the pot of gold! The deity card "Sekert Hetep" came up with the name combination, Sermeska Mariama. Enough said. Roughly translated, her name means "God's Gift of Discipline Gives Me Joy."

It seems like ages ago when Kwasi drew that prophetic drawing depicting the two of us with a baby. Finally, that vision manifested, and it was all in Divine Order. Unfortunately, however, bringing a beautiful spirit into this world was the only thing in our relationship that seemed in Divine Order. We divorced two years later.

I am convinced that we decided to come back on this Earthly plane at the same time to work out whatever we were supposed to work out with each other. We produced a miracle baby, but missed out on the "harmonizing our relationship" part. Unfortunately, I guess we will have to have a go at it again, the next time around in another incarnation on Earth, or elsewhere.

Chapter Seven
"Every Little Thing is Gonna Be All Right"[97]

Section 1
I Got the Job!

I loved working at the ACLU, but two years after the birth of my daughter in 1994, I realized I needed a change. I did not want to miss special moments in her early life, but legislative advocacy in Washington essentially binds one to a round-the-clock Congressional schedule. So I decided to strive for what I hoped was going to be my career destiny – a tenured professor at Howard University School of Law. I wanted to be able to influence the next generation from the perch of an ivory or, perhaps more appropriately, "ebony" tower.

I saw an ad in the *Legal Times* newspaper for someone to create and build a public service program at Howard Law. Wow, that's my opening, I thought. It wasn't a teaching job, and not even one on the track to tenure, but I was excited for the opportunity to be connected to the law school. I interviewed with the Director of the Clinical Law Center, Professor Homer LaRue, and was hired as Director of what would become known as the Equal Justice Program (EJP).

My vision was to become a professor who inspired students to follow in the esteemed tradition of Howard law predecessors Charles Hamilton Houston, Thurgood Marshall and Goler T. Butcher, all of whom demonstrated the key role academia should play in developing solutions to societal problems, and the special role for Howard as an historically Black institution. Under my aegis, the EJP carried out its mission through five projects: civil/human rights, community outreach, an externship program, a pro bono/public service program, and the public interest resource center.

The Equal Justice Program's Community Outreach program trained law students to serve as legal observers for demonstrations common to our location in the Nation's Capital. Students served as legal observers for historic rallies including the Million Man March, D.C. Statehood demonstrations, Jericho March and Rally in Support of Political Prisoners and Prisoners of War, National Mobilization Against Police Brutality, NAACP Supreme Court Rally, and Millions for Mumia demonstration. My law students also participated in the Volunteer Income Tax Assistance Project (VITA), a product of the American Bar Association and the Internal Revenue Service, assisting low-income taxpayers, the elderly and disabled.

Through the Equal Justice Program, I also directed the Law School's Externship Program and taught the Externship Seminar, which I titled, "Lawyering in the Public Interest." My first interaction with the students seems like it happened yesterday. I vividly remember how excited they were to be at Howard University School of Law, and how eagerly they absorbed every nugget of advice and counsel I had to give.

"Professor Taifa," one student queried. "Can you really do positive things while still in law school?"

I stared right into her eyes and responded affirmatively.

> Can you imagine working on the legal defense of Amnesty International-acclaimed 'prisoners of conscience?' How about mobilizing for divestiture of corporate holdings from apartheid South Africa? Can you picture yourself assisting a public defender with a felony case, or producing substantive memoranda for a legal aid service? Well, I did all of those things on a volunteer basis while still in law school.

"So Professor Taifa, did you have a lot of support?" asked another student.

"I wish," I said as I chuckled while shaking my head.

At that time, there was no popular, well-promoted movement in support of public interest or pro bono work that provided interested students with the types of opportunities, expertise and training we see today. In those days, I was unaware of loan forgiveness programs, if any existed. I knew of no incentives to do public service work other than one's intrinsic altruism and personal sense of commitment. Unfortunately, practicing law in the public interest seemed akin to taking a vow of poverty. Despite any initial desire to assist the underrepresented, struggling lawyers often found the lure of a hefty paycheck too strong to resist.

The students all seemed to listen intently.

"You are blessed today," I continued, "because there is now a large and increasingly sophisticated public interest movement that is generating a wealth of public service resources and opportunities."

"However," I chided emphatically. "If you enjoy being chained to a desk, the practice of law in the public interest is probably not for you. But if you have a passion for the frontlines and don't mind occasional mine fields, now is the time to cultivate contacts in this increasingly competitive field. Taking pro bono placements while still in law school is an excellent way to position yourself no matter what path your law career takes you."

"Professor Taifa, tell us about your public interest law career," a young man in a

Che Guevara tee shirt asked eagerly.

I beamed with delight because I was proud of my employment history. I eagerly answered.

From the National Prison Project to the Women's Legal Defense Fund, from criminal defense to civil litigation, and from the American Civil Liberties Union to the National Conference of Black Lawyers, I have had the pleasure of practicing public interest law throughout my career. Importantly, an integral part of my work has been accomplished with the assistance of volunteer student interns and law clerks. Volunteers have drafted memos for me on everything from the religious protection of sacred sites for Native American peoples, to the disproportionate dumping of hazardous waste in poor communities.

Their efforts helped me research the unwarranted disparity in sentencing between crack and powder cocaine offenses, as well as the debate over reparations for slavery and post-slavery discrimination. Student volunteers have helped lobby members of Congress, acted as decoys in bus and train stations where police were using discriminatory profiles to detain Black travelers, and have served as legal observers during demonstrations.

The students were visibly moved.

"One of these 'assignments' still gives me tremors," I confided to the rapt students. Although I have been arrested in acts of civil disobedience on several occasions, it has never been my intention, much less a requirement of any internship, that students follow in my footsteps to jail."

As students seemed to lean in closer to me, I explained.

One day, I rushed zealously to get to a NAACP/TransAfrica-sponsored demonstration in Lafayette Park in front of the White House. I left hurried instructions for my new ACLU law clerk, a college student, to meet me there. It was his first day on the job. Later, I was shocked to find out he had thought part of his public service to the ACLU was to get arrested with me during the demonstration. I assured him that he didn't have to go to jail that day! Since then, I have carefully ensured that the parameters of public service for students are completely understood.

A student with heavy makeup and perfectly manicured nails timidly raised her hand.

"But Professor Taifa," she grimaced, "I'm gonna have bills. I need to make some money!"

"Students, let there be no mistake about it," I responded. "Public interest work is quite lucrative, not necessarily in the pocketbook, but in the power of knowing that you can actually make a difference," I pointed out.

You may not be able to quantify the impact you are making today, but you are constantly sowing seeds that may come to fruition at a later time. For me, for instance, it was very rewarding to see the political prisoners I had worked to free while in law school finally released from their unjust incarceration. There was also personal satisfaction in witnessing the freedom of Nelson Mandela and the dawn of a new South Africa, issues I also worked on.

A student in the back exasperatedly lamented, "But Professor Taifa, my schedule is too heavy. I really just don't have the time for pro bono service."

My response was firm, yet gentle."You may be surprised how well a community service project can not only fit into your schedule but also enrich your productivity in class. Some organizations may even need legal research or similar projects that can be completed during evenings or weekends."

Public service work also strengthens your resume and shows potential employers that you have legal experience as well as a commitment to justice. Volunteer legal work will expose you to various practice options and help you develop important professional contacts. While still in law school, you can put all your newly learned research, writing, and advocacy skills to work challenging injustice in society and benefiting the community, I counseled.

I paused for effect and continued dramatically.

Students, picture yourself working on the legal defense of death row prisoner Mumia Abu-Jamal; or aiding in the drafting of the new South African constitution; or assisting an HIV-infected woman in writing her will; or drafting memorandums to save affirmative action, the exclusionary rule, or legal aid services from further assault. These are the kinds of experiences you can have, right now, while still in law school.

For me, no matter how busy I am, public service and the practice of law in the public interest is an important part of my life. It has been both rewarding and frustrating, but always fulfilling. It feels great to be on the cutting edge of social change and know I'm actually making a difference in people's lives.

Chapter Seven, Section 2
People's Tribunal Hurricane Katrina

Ten years after presenting the Opening Statement in the Mumia Abu-Jamal Mock Tribunal, I was asked to play a similar role in a national catastrophe of epic proportions. I was invited to serve as a prosecutor for the International Katrina Tribunal in New Orleans, LA. Here are excerpts from the Opening Statement I delivered on August 29, 2007.

May it please the court, members of this esteemed Tribunal of International and U.S.-based jurists, and the stellar team of human and civil rights prosecutors who comprise my co-counsel. I provide this Opening Statement on behalf of the survivors who are the victims of Hurricanes Katrina and Rita.

This is a case about rights and the violation of rights; about obligations and breaches of obligation, about accountability and lack of accountability and lastly, about trust and betrayal of trust. During this Tribunal you will hear from survivors – eyewitnesses who will chronicle for you, in their own words, their suffering and anguish. The testimonies you will hear today are similar to the words spoken by survivors two years ago during an International Commission of Inquiry. At that time some of the following quotes were elicited:

'We were treated as if we were criminals, when all we wanted was to survive.'

'They pointed their guns at us. I didn't look at the National Guard because I know they killed a guy just for looking at them straight in the eyes.'

'We had to get into trucks. We didn't know where they were taking us but we all were separated from our loved ones.'

'Katrina was a man-made disaster, orchestrated by the government. It didn't seem possible that the government would do this to its own people.'

'They were shooting as we ran across the bridge trying to get to dry land, screaming, "you niggahs and monkeys are not gonna get across that bridge," but we ran anyway because we knew if we had to turn around and go back to those rising waters we would die.'

'We didn't get no help from nobody. The real truth is they don't want us back.

'They've wanted to get rid of us for a long time and Katrina gave them the perfect opportunity.'

'They separated families. It was like the slave ships all over again.'

'They carried out a campaign of terror and genocide.'

Although the preceding quotes are chilling, perhaps what summed everything up most poignantly was the oft-repeated phrase, 'they left us here to die. 'They-Left-Us-Here-to-Die.'

You will hear evidence that two years ago, the world witnessed the monumental failure of the U.S. government to protect and respect the lives of people, the majority of whom were African American and poor. Hurricane Katrina indeed, was a natural disaster of proportions heretofore not experienced in the United States. You will hear testimony that Hurricane Katrina was also a man-made disaster involving massive international human rights law violations perpetrated against the people of New Orleans and the Gulf Region. Tragically, the evidence suggests that much of the devastation associated with Katrina could have been avoided.

You will hear charges levied by hurricane survivors against the federal, state, and local government for serious, systemic and ongoing violations of their human rights. These violations are based upon relevant international law rights found in the Universal Declaration of Human Rights, the International Covenant on Civil and Political Rights, the American Convention on Human Rights, the United Nations Guiding Principles on Internal Displacement, and the Convention on the Elimination of All Forms of Discrimination Against Women.

The guarantee of these same rights can also be found in the Convention on the Rights of the Child, the Convention Against Discrimination in Education, the Convention Against Torture and Other Cruel, Inhuman and Degrading Treatment or Punishment, the International Convention on the Elimination of All Forms of Racial Discrimination, and the Convention on the Prevention and Punishment of the Crime of Genocide.

In essence, international human rights law says the following to the United States government: You cannot suspend the grand juries or jury trials of people. You cannot implement shoot on sight orders. You cannot abandon jailed people in waist deep water for days – you will hear that those are violations of the right to liberty and security of the person. They are also violations of the right to be free from torture and cruel, inhumane and degrading treatment; and violations of the right to life, human dignity and recognition as a person.

International law prohibits the U.S. government from misidentifying human remains, which is a violation of rights related to privacy, family life and missing relatives. It outlaws discrimination against internally displaced persons. The same law bans discrimination in the rebuilding process. Those are all violations of the right to return. And the list goes on.

We are here to shed light on difficult questions, and you will hear testimony that will help you formulate answers. Where was the evacuation plan for the hospitals, for the prisons, jails and other vulnerable populations? Why did we see images of dogs being flown first class in chartered planes and buses, while Blacks detained in the Convention Center were packed like human cargo, reminiscent of slave ships? Where was the due process for new arrestees who were held incognito, in a makeshift prison at a Greyhound bus station? Why were those who tried to obtain basic needs such as food or water from nearby stores often identified as 'looters' if they were Black, but as victims or survivors if they were not?

What role does the historical legacy of institutional racism and national oppression play within U.S. society? If a similar disaster were to happen today in another part of the country which primarily impacted the rich and privileged, would the response have been the same as what we saw with Katrina?

Do the residents of the U.S. hurricane-stricken gulf coast deserve the same human rights protections as those living in the tsunami-ravaged Indonesia? Are restitution and reparations due for the grievous injuries sustained by Katrina victims?

Esteemed jurists – you have before you an awesome responsibility. Just as in 1954 when Mamie Till Mobley demanded an open casket for the world to see the image of her 14-year-old son Emmett, savagely mutilated and dumped in Mississippi's Tallahatchie river exactly 50 years ago; this Tribunal will likewise present an open casket for the world to see and hear the testimonies of Katrina's human rights abuses.

'Open it up,' Mamie Till screamed. 'Let the people see what they did to my boy,' she demanded as her son's mangled and battered body was placed on public view. Her decision forced the nation and the world to face in shocked disbelief its horror of racism. 'Open it up,' she demanded. This Tribunal will likewise open up the voluminous body of evidence that occurred here, two years ago, for the world to see and hold those responsible, accountable.

In conclusion, Dr. Martin Luther King once stated that 'the ultimate test of a man is not where he stands in moments of comfort and moments of convenience, but where he stands in moments of challenge and moments of controversy.'

Yes, it may be challenging to some that we are using an international human rights frame through which to present domestic abuses. It may be controversial for some to hear mere whispers that crimes against humanity were perpetrated domestically, or that provisions of genocide could be applicable. But these are not comfortable or convenient times.

Just as Mamie Till Mobley commanded in 1955, there is a time when we must 'Open Up the Casket!' There is a time when we must right the wrong. It is once again time for the world to see and act. That time is now! Moments of national crisis also represent moments of opportunity. Let us rise to the occasion.

On behalf of the survivors who are the victims of Hurricanes Katrina and Rita, I urge that you listen to all of the evidence and return a verdict for justice rooted in international human rights law.

Chapter Seven, Section 3
My Popular Seminars

Teaching always came naturally to me, and my *Racial Disparity in the Criminal Justice System* seminars at Howard University School of Law were always packed. I started teaching this popular seminar in 1995. It was not part of my duties as Director of the Equal Justice Program, and I received no extra renumeration for it. But it was a course I pitched and wanted to teach, and I taught it well. I organized the curriculum around the theme that racism permeates each stage of the criminal punishment process, and the syllabus included readings and analyses exploring the applicable historical data, case law, legislative history and public policy implications of race, crime and punishment in America.

I was in my element teaching this course. We focused on constitutional provisions impacting race and major U.S. legislative and judicial decisions impacting people of color from 1690-1896, including Black codes, rape laws, treaties, Supreme Court cases, and statutes. We covered many of the issues I worked on while at the ACLU, such as racial disparities in pre-arrest and pre-trial proceedings, police misconduct and brutality, and the selective prosecution of targeted groups.

The "war on drugs" was in full swing and we examined its origins and current manifestations, including mandatory minimum sentencing, anti-gang penalties, three-strikes provisions, and the crack/powder cocaine disparity. We addressed the impact of race on the growing prison/industrial complex, including an analysis of prison uprisings such as the 1971 Attica massacre, the reintroduction of chain gangs, and the impact of then-recent legislation severely curtailing prisoner rights litigation. And we focused on the over-representation of Black juveniles in the criminal justice system, the growing issue of Black women in the system, and the impact of increased incarceration of African Americans on the Black family and community.

The seminar also included a critique of the FBI's illegal COINTELPRO campaign against activists in the 60s and 70s and discussion of issues involving political prisoners and the harassment of African American elected officials. Finally, we examined criminal justice issues in the context of international conventions such as the Convention on the Elimination of All Forms of Racial Discrimination and the Convention on the Prevention and Punishment of the Crime of Genocide.

During the Spring of 1997 I also co-taught a seminar on Prisoners Rights with my colleague Jonathan Smith, then Executive Director of D.C. Prisoner Legal Services. I requested to teach this seminar after being approached by several students who were concerned that a seminar offering on prisoner rights would not be taught anymore. Having followed prisoner rights issues throughout my legal career, I was successful in having a proposal to teach the seminar, again gratis, accepted.

This popular seminar addressed issues involving constitutional rights in prison. We also analyzed recently enacted legislation such as the Prison Litigation Reform Act and the emergence of issues such as the HIV-positive prisoner epidemic, the growing corrections/industrial complex and special issues confronting political prisoners.

A highlight of the seminar was to be a field trip to a prison facility. It was a challenge getting the tour scheduled as D.C. prisoners were in the process of being shipped in mass to federal facilities throughout the country, due to the implementation of the D.C. Revitalization Act. Previously, there had rarely been a problem with prison officials authorizing facility tours, but now they feared the possibility of a prison uprising in opposition to the forced transfers.

Unable to tour any of the Lorton facilities, we were fortunate to receive authorization to visit the Correctional Treatment Facility, located adjacent to the D.C. Jail. The tour was substantive and eye-opening, and students had the opportunity to interact with the residents on a one-to-one basis, and made several observations about the facility that happened to be the subject of then-current litigation.

I team-taught the seminar with Jonathan Smith who was an expert in prisoners' rights issues, and provided the class with the "real life" application of the theoretical materials we covered. Years later he would become an assistant Attorney General in the Obama Administration responsible for major consent decrees. His academic contribution to the law school, however, was also gratis.

Chapter Seven, Section 4
How 'Bout a Legislative Clinic?

While at Howard Law, I proposed the creation of a Civil Rights Legislative Clinic. Because of its strategic location in the Nation's Capital, it seemed axiomatic that Howard Law could provide its students with a unique opportunity to learn the practical aspects of the legislative processes of the federal and District governments. The school could also provide hands-on contact with civil rights and public interest advocacy organizations, many of whose national and legislative offices are located in D.C.

I applied in vain on many occasions to be hired as a tenure-track professor and to direct and supervise such a clinic. I already had more scholarship on record than most new professors.

I told the hiring committee that I had law review articles published that researched two issues within the 1994 Crime Bill, titled "Three Strikes and You're Out: Mandatory Life Imprisonment for Third Time Felons," and "Cracked Justice: A Critical Examination of Cocaine Sentencing." I mentioned other publications I authored, including: "Civil Forfeiture vs. Civil Liberties," published by New York Law School, and "Codification or Castration? The Applicability of the International Convention to Eliminate all Forms of Racial Discrimination to the U.S. Criminal Justice System," which was published by the Howard Law Journal. In the end, my many efforts to convince them of my value were futile, and not being hired by Howard Law as a tenure track professor and to create and direct such a clinic remains one of the great disappointments of my career. Fifteen years later the law school did adopt a legislative clinic, which ironically used as its first client, the Justice Roundtable, a coalition I convened.The following year, a Civil Rights Institute was formed, led by a phenomenal colleague, Justin Hansford.

Although I was not afforded the opportunity to join the tenure track at Howard Law, what kept me fueled and inspired to teach were the remarkable students I had the pleasure to teach and interact with over the years. Some of the more memorable included, Niambi Bailey, Opio Sokoni, Meron Wondwosen, Nareissa Smith, Demetria McCain, Andrea Ritchie, Adrion Howell, Ocheyeme Gene Haley, Almo Carter, Motisola Zulu, Talib Karim, Rukia Lumumba, Osa Benson, Dave Jackson, Arthur Sidney, LaShawn Warren, James Carter, Adrian Fenty, Tovah Calderon, Brandi Harden, April Frazier, Aisha Braveboy, Tara Patterson, Carla Bedrosian, Jeff Smith, Omodare Jupiter, Joyce Smith and so many more. They all are now veteran lawyers leading incredible careers as defense attorneys and prosecutors, and working in government, education, employment law, entertainment law, civil and human rights, legal services, law firms, and private practice. I am forever proud I helped to direct and encourage their passions, and those of countless others.

Chapter Seven, Section 5
Doors Close So Others May Open

As much as I admired Howard Law, the "powers that be" didn't seem to return my love, but kept figuratively smacking me in the face. I finally left my formal employ at the law school in 2002, but continued teaching my popular *Racial Disparity in the Criminal Justice System* seminar, this time as a compensated Howard Law adjunct professor.

Everything was going along smoothly until October 14, 2005, which was also the 10-year anniversary of the Million Man March. I was asked by one of my former law students, Opio Sokoni, to co-moderate a Pro-Black Media Forum that he was hosting on media images of the recent Hurricane Katrina. Opio brought together Black writers, activists, media personalities, scholars, and lawyers for this dialogue held in Howard Law's Moot Court Room. The event was broadcast live by C-SPAN, which had a highly visible set up in the back of the auditorium.

Introductory remarks were made by the wide array of panelists. I moderated the first panel, which discussed issues that were not being featured in the mainstream media about Hurricane Katrina. My colleague Opio moderated the second panel that focused on solutions. Everything was going along fine until a panelist took to the podium. He concluded his lengthy remarks with the statement that the only solution he had come to was that "we have to exterminate white people off the face of the planet."

Whoa, that caught me off guard. I was thinking, *Oh my God – is he crazy?! This isn't back room rhetoric amongst Black militants. This isn't barbershop or beauty parlor bombast. This is C-SPAN live TV. At Howard University.*

Because of only mild applause from the audience, the commentator fumed on, "I don't care whether you clap or not, but I'm saying to you that we need to solve this problem because they are going to kill us."

I found myself in a quandary. In a split second I replayed the scenario in my mind, decided not to draw any more attention to the situation, and prayed that the whole fiasco would blow over quickly. I wasn't moderating the forum at the time, was seated at the far end from the podium, so I sat mute as Opio, the segment's moderator, rose to the podium as the individual's harangue concluded.

Wrong decision. Wrong employment move. Even though I was no longer working full time at the University, his diatribe sealed my fate at Howard's Law School. When I received notice to attend a meeting with the law school's Dean the following week, I felt like I was being summoned to the proverbial principal's office.

"But I had nothing to do with what he said," I argued.

"Yes," the Dean agreed. "But we've been getting calls. You were the representative from Howard Law."

I don't recall the exact words he used, but the essence of it was that I should have gone to the mic and officially denounced the tactless person. So I became the scapegoat, and the law school declined to renew my adjunct contract the following semester, citing financial factors.

Ironically, I always counsel my students not to burn their bridges behind them. And here I was, a victim of my own advice. I was so damn pissed. But even more so, I was hurt. This was the institution I loved and in which I had invested so much of my time, energy and enthusiasm, and where I had positively impacted so many lives and futures.

During my full-time position at Howard Law from 1996 to 2002, I served on the law school's Career Services, Alumni and Community Affairs Committee, and on the Board of Directors of a number of organizations, including the D.C. Bar's Public Service Activities Corporation (later renamed D.C. Bar Pro Bono Program), Bureau of Rehabilitation, ACLU of the National Capital Area, the D.C. Prisoner's Legal Services, Inc., and the Washington Council of Lawyers.

I was a member of the National Bar Association, the National Association of Criminal Defense Lawyers and the National Conference of Black Lawyers (NCBL). For years I held leadership positions in NCBL, and from 1994 to 95, I served as co-chair of the D.C. Bar's Criminal Law and Individual Rights Section.

Active in community affairs, I was also chair of the Board of Directors of Roots Public Charter School, chair of the Legislative Commission of the National Coalition of Blacks for Reparations in America, and on the Boards of the Kwanzaa Children's Party, Inc., and the African Freedom Fund Treasury. I was all over the place, and I was in my element.

But a tenure track position at Howard University School of Law was not in the stars for me despite my scholarship, publications, teaching and community service. I was peeved, but kept my chin up. I later realized that it wasn't about my qualifications or lack thereof, they just did not deem me a good fit. That was their prerogative. It was a hard pill to swallow, but a principle of the universe is that when one door closes, another one opens wide. And that is what happened with me.

The Open Society Foundations, the organization of billionaire George Soros, soon made me an offer in 2002 that I could not refuse, and catapulted me back on the front-lines of advocacy for the next sixteen years. In my time with this organization, I would become a catalyst that would help to instrumentally change the narrative on crime and punishment in the United States, and bring about the passage of major pieces of criminal justice reform legislation.

I was back on the frontlines, just where I belonged, where I fit.

Chapter Eight
"I Feel Good, Like I Knew That I Would"[98]

Section 1
Back on the Frontlines

In early 2002, I reached out to Lynthia Gibson-Price, my longtime colleague from my days with both the National Prison Project and the ACLU Legislative Office, to ask if she knew what our old boss, Mort Halperin, was doing. She hesitated for a moment and said, "Nkechi you know I'm working for Mort again now, and he's hiring."

"Oh, really?!" I replied quite excitedly. "I had no idea."

"Mort is now the Washington Office Director of George Soros' Open Society Institute," she explained. "I'm the Office Director. He's already hired Gene."

Clearly, I contacted Lynthia at the right time, and what I feared was possibly too late. I knew about the Open Society, a relatively new philanthropic organization that was making great strides in the area of criminal justice reform. A knot formed in my throat as I recalled that they had twice rejected me for one of their esteemed fellowships. Hearing that Mort was heading up the organization seemed like providence, but I was feeling a bit hesitant.

"So if Gene Guerrero has already been hired to work on criminal justice issues, what am I going to do?"

"Nkechi, go on and call Mort anyway," she urged. "Who knows?"

I didn't need any additional nudging. I read up on what I could, mustered up the courage and called Mort. It turns out that all my anxiety and hesitation was for naught; I got the job. Working for the Open Society Institute was an offer I simply could not refuse, and that is how I entered the world of its founder, billionaire George Soros, proclaimed by *Forbes* Magazine to be the 22nd richest man in the world.

This new job turned out to be the continuation of a phenomenal journey in the realm of advocacy and coalition-building, and a primer to grant-making. Between 2002 through 2018, I would play a pivotal role in ground-breaking legislation: the Second Chance Re-Entry bill, which was signed into law in 2008; the Fair Sentencing Act, which was signed into law in 2010; the strengthening of the First Step Act of 2018; and the institution of an unprecedented Clemency Initiative during the Obama Administration that would lead to the release of over 1,700 over-sentenced people from unjust imprisonment.

All of this began with the formation of the Justice Roundtable in 2002.

I envisioned the concept of the Justice Roundtable, which grew into a coalition of over 100 organizations working together to reform federal criminal justice policies. Organizing the Roundtable, along with my colleague Gene Guerrero, was my first project at the Open Society. We founded the Roundtable to be a catalyst of change, committed to progressive reform of the criminal justice system at the federal level.The Roundtable's goals were to influence public policy by 1) reducing mass incarceration and over-reliance on harsh punishment; 2) eliminating racial disparities and promoting fairness and equity; 3) providing effective alternatives to incarceration and new approaches to addressing crime and drug policy; 4) emphasizing prevention over punishment; 5) successfully reintegrating formerly incarcerated people into society; and, 6) bringing domestic justice policies into conformity with international human rights norms.

The Justice Roundtable successfully coordinated the legislative and advocacy efforts of its participants through working groups, quarterly assembly meetings, a public policy discussion series and, later, a policy website.

Years later, as I reviewed the roster from our first formal Justice Roundtable meeting on October 16, 2002, my eyes rested upon one name in particular, belonging to a soft-spoken, young woman sitting in the back of the room. She was newly graduated from law school and had recently received a Soros Justice Fellowship to work with the NAACP Legal Defense Fund (LDF). LDF deployed her to Tulia, a small town in the panhandle of Texas, to investigate appalling claims of law enforcement and prosecutorial abuse against a Black community.

Twelve years later, this young lawyer would become the top civil rights prosecutor in the U.S. Department of Justice during the Obama Administration, responsible for investigating a wide range of criminal and civil enforcement efforts to ensure equal justice and equal opportunity for all. Her name was Vanita Gupta, and her career was catapulted in a small town in Texas called Tulia.

Chapter Eight, Section 2
Tulia, Tip of the Drug War Iceberg

On the early morning of July 23, 1999, nearly half of the adult African American population of Tulia, TX, was rounded up, arrested and paraded half-dressed through the streets on charges of drug trafficking. The majority of those swept up in the highly publicized, undercover sting operation were impoverished and living in public housing, humble homes, or trailers. The arrests and subsequent convictions resulted in the decimation of entire families, which left dozens of children virtually parentless.

The undercover officer, Tom Coleman, alleged that over an 18-month period, 46 Tulia residents sold him cocaine, all of which was worth less than $200. The first person to be tried, a 57-year-old hog farmer, received a 90-year sentence after being convicted of one count of selling cocaine. Others who went to trial received sentences ranging from 20 to 341 years. After witnessing such extraordinary sentences meted out by the nearly all-White juries, many of the defendants began pleading guilty in exchange for "lighter" sentences ranging from probation to 18 years, despite the fact that no drugs, weapons or large sums of cash were found.

The arrests and convictions were based solely on the uncorroborated allegations of one White narcotics officer with a dubious past, whose modus operandi was to record purported drug buys on his arms and legs. There was no corroboration of his testimonies in the form of a second officer, no audio or video surveillance, no photographs, no wiretaps. The arrests and convictions generated so much attention that Coleman was honored as Lawman of the Year in 1999 by then Texas Attorney General John Cornyn.

Outraged by the Tulia abuses and anxious to highlight the case in Washington, I organized and moderated a high-profile Congressional briefing on May 25, 2003. I was successful in getting Congressman John Conyers, Congressman Charles Rangel, and Congresswoman Sheila Jackson Lee to serve as official hosts of the briefing. We titled the event, "Systemic Injustice in the War on Drugs: A Briefing from the Front-lines of Tulia, Texas and Beyond." Held in one of the Rayburn Congressional Judiciary Committee hearing rooms, the briefing also included a substantive forum with experts.

I strategically positioned the presenters in the stately legislators' chairs, situated in the well of the room.

During the briefing, Vanita explained that the NAACP–LDF got involved two years after the sting operation had actually happened, in November 2001, to coordinate the litigation of the defense appeals. She testified, "It was outrageous that on the word of one undercover narcotics officer, this entire town could be brought down." She continued, "I spent a couple of days down at the Swisher County courthouse basically just collecting and copying documents. I bought a suitcase at Wal-Mart, and stuffed it with maybe thousands of pages of documents. When I came back up to New York, I told the leadership of the Legal Defense Fund that we had to get involved in this case."

She explained that LDF found that all of the trials or pleas were marred by serious due process violations. Her organization found an "indifference on the part of law enforcement to ensure that their undercover agent was credible and trustworthy; that undercover operation protocols were not observed to guarantee the validity of the agent's testimony; and that full disclosure was not made to the defense prior to trial about the character of the government's only witness."

During the forum following our briefing, members of Congress also heard from family members of the unjustly incarcerated from Tulia; an individual directly engaged in advocacy before the Texas Legislature; a partner in a Washington D.C. law firm that provided pro bono assistance in Tulia; criminal justice experts; and, an undercover officer who was a whistleblower in a similar drug task force scandal.

My goal for the briefing and forum was to help illuminate broader issues involving the "war on drugs" and measures that could be utilized to avert corruption and restore public confidence in the criminal justice system. The forum featured the father of one of those unjustly incarcerated. Seated in one of the stately Congressional armchairs at the front of the room, he leaned into the mic and stated:

> My name is Freddie Brookins and I'm pleased to be here today. This gives us an opportunity to voice our opinion and tell what actually happened in Tulia, Texas back in 1999. In '99, many of the residents in Tulia were taken out of their beds in the early morning and then paraded across television screens. I was like most people. The raid was hard for me to believe. I thought they made a mistake. I didn't think the law did things like this. I didn't think things like this happened in this day and time… Listening to the main witness was like a cut out of a movie. It wasn't real. It wasn't really happening. It seemed as if the things that Tom Coleman presented in court couldn't be possible…People testified to Coleman's credibility. They said he was a good man and an upstanding citizen. Yet, he put my child away for 20 years…This is tough. My son has been locked up. He's been locked up on the inside. I've been locked up on the outside. I've been doing time on the outside; it's hard time too.

Seated next to Freddie Brookins was Mattie White Russell, another family member we brought to Washington. A grandmother, four of her children were also swept up in the raid and imprisoned, and as a result she was left to care for her grandchildren. She agreed with Freddie:

> But you know, it's hard for me, too. It's hard to believe that people believed him [Coleman] when he said 'I'm going to write this on my stomach or on my leg.' And this is a town that doesn't really care. But I'm like Freddie. I

was locked up with my kids and I'm still locked up because I'm taking care of two of theirs. They can't see what's going on with their parents.

Congressman Charles Rangel (D-NY) stated, "I tell my White critics here in the Congress that this indictment wasn't against just Black folks. It wasn't against poor folk. It was an indictment against everything this country is supposed to stand for."

Representative Sheila Jackson Lee (D-TX) expressed gratitude that Mattie and Freddie have come to the seat of government and stressed that "you frankly can't give up."

I have somewhat of a bent head, but not a broken spirit. Because sometimes, this hollow place can be very isolating, very stifling, and frustrating is not a strong enough word, but it is important to see those like you to be able to light the fire to press the point. The hearings and committee rooms should not be just for the special interests, but it's got to be for the special people, the special heroes that have suffered and have been penalized and brutalized by a system that does not work.

In the words of Congressman John Conyers (D-MI), "We want hearings because Tulia tells you the whole story about the immorality of drug prosecutions and their relationship to the criminal justice system. You don't need another case. If you didn't hear but one thing about this immoral system, this is it. So it's 'throw down time.'"

The civil rights community also weighed in. Wade Henderson, Executive Director of the Leadership Conference on Civil Rights, added:

The Tulia debacle represents an egregious and compelling example of rampant injustice in our nation's criminal justice system. What happened in Tulia is a stark illustration of the injustices that occur every day in communities across the country that result from racial profiling, unchecked prosecutorial discretion, and the criminal justice system that puts conviction rates ahead of fairness and racial justice…Tulia, Texas is just not in Texas. Tulia is all over and you see it in community after community in the statistics they bear…Tulia is not just a tale of one cop gone bad. It rather is an illustration of an entire criminal justice system that desperately needs reform. And we must all become vigilant in demanding accountability from law enforcement, abolishing the practices of racial profiling, reigning in overzealous prosecutors, ensuring adequate indigent defense, and working toward an end to disparate sentencing.

Vanita shared that she met Mattie and Freddie on her first trip to Tulia. They opened up their doors and told her what happened to their families and to their communities. She marveled that it was "truly a sight to behold that there was not a single African American on the jury." Citing the lack of cross-examination and suppression of evidence, she described the situation as "everything bad that one could imagine taking place in a criminal court."

In August there came a big breakthrough, thanks to Bob Herbert of *The New York Times*. Bob really helped the Legal Defense Fund to bring these cases out to the front. He wrote six columns. In August, he made a trip down and met with Freddie and Mattie and he was on fire... He said, "I will continue to write these columns until this is made right." There was just no stopping him.

Not until August 2003 were all the Tulia defendants pardoned even though the officer had been characterized as "the most devious, non-responsive law enforcement witness this court has witnessed in 25 years on the bench."

To understand what went on in Tulia, one needs to understand the Byrne Grant Program, and the extent to which Byrne JAG-funded drug task forces – federally funded partnerships where local police departments, sheriffs' offices and district attorneys combine efforts to fight the war on drugs – had become a national disgrace.[99] A key factor in the Tulia fiasco was the dearth of federal oversight over the narcotics task force that hired the undercover agent.

A report issued by the Drug Policy Alliance found that the lack of meaningful federal oversight over federal law enforcement grants for drug task forces resulted in the proliferation of corruption and racial disparities. A 2002 report issued by the ACLU of Texas identified numerous scandals involving Byrne-funded narcotics task forces, including tampering with government records, witness tampering, fabricating evidence, stealing of drugs from evidence lockers, selling drugs to children, large-scale racial profiling and unwarranted traffic stops, sexual harassment and other abuses of official capacity.

Federally funded narcotics task forces have also been criticized for focusing their resources on investigations of small-time drug sales that do little to stem the flow of drugs into communities, and that their efforts are disproportionately focused on arresting people of color. Finally, the task forces have been criticized for the use of arrests and forfeitures as outcome measures to judge the success of the task forces, because such goals not only reduce the incentive to find solutions to the drug problem, but actually encourage the kinds of behaviors that resulted in the Tulia scandal. In the words of my colleague Jasmine Tyler, we must "Burn Byrne!"

Chapter Eight, Section 3
Bringing the Human Face to Capitol Hill

The congressional Tulia briefing was not the first time I helped to bring the human face of the "war on drugs," and its real casualties, to Capitol Hill, and it would not be the last.

One of the first people the Justice Roundtable highlighted when we launched in 2002 was Kemba Smith. I first learned about Kemba through a May 1996 feature article in the now-defunct *Emerge Magazine*. The image of a young girl in her high school graduation cap and gown that graced the magazine's cover gripped not only me, but an entire nation. The article's title, "Kemba's Nightmare: A Model Child Becomes Prisoner in Drug Sentencing Frenzy," summed up her ordeal.

I always felt connected to Kemba. She turned herself in to authorities in September 1994, seven months pregnant. At that time my daughter was five months old. Kemba describes her nightmare as follows:

> The prosecutor added extra incentive in negotiating the guilty plea by promising that he would allow me a bond so that I could go home until sentencing to give birth to my son and that I would only receive a two-year sentence. Unfortunately, due to his unethical conduct, after pleading guilty I remained in jail. Minutes after giving birth in a hospital, guarded by two prison officials, the U.S. Marshal Service walked into my room and ordered that I be shackled to the bed, and two days later my son was taken away. I was sent back to a cold jail cell with my breasts gorging and in extreme pain. If my parents had not been able to take and raise my son, my parental rights would have been terminated.

During her many testimonies before Congress, Kemba stressed, "I was not a drug trafficker. I was a college student and became romantically involved with a man who, unbeknownst to me at the time, was the head of a violent four-million-dollar crack cocaine ring, according to the government. The prosecutor stated during my court hearing that I never handled, used or sold any of the drugs involved in the conspiracy. Yet I was sentenced as a first-time nonviolent drug offender to 24.5 years, one for every year of my life."

The Justice Roundtable used Kemba's story to highlight what's been referred to as the "girlfriend problem," the prevalence of minimally-involved women receiving harsh sentences because of their relationship with a partner engaged in drug activity. Kemba served six and a half years of that sentence until her release three days before the Christmas of 2000, when President Bill Clinton commuted her mandatory minimum prison term.

I knew nothing of Kemba in 1994. While I was walking the halls of Congress, very much pregnant and railing against omnibus crime bills, she had recently been sentenced and was just one of thousands of nameless women and men caught up in the system. However, as a result of her parents' endless campaign to bring their daughter home – capturing the support of their Congressman, Bobby Scott, persistently waging awareness campaigns in the news media, in churches, and amongst the criminal justice reform community – she was finally released.

Six and a half years behind bars is a long time to spend in prison, but Kemba has felt she suffers from "survivor's guilt" because of the women she left behind, many of whom had sentences of 10, 15, 20, 25 years and life behind bars without parole. As an advocate for those who remain in prison, Kemba worked closely with our Justice Roundtable coalition in bringing awareness to the plight of women in prisons and the children they left behind.

The Justice Roundtable also brought the daughters of Hamedah Hassan – Ayesha and Kasaundra – to Washington in 2005 to share their mother's story. The chain of events that led to their mother's incarceration began in 1988, when she fled domestic abuse and found shelter in a cousin's home with her children. Their host sold drugs, and Hamedah was convicted of being a part of the operation. She had never been convicted of a crime and had never been found using, possessing or selling drugs. At sentencing, the judge denounced mandatory minimum sentencing, saying, "It is my strongly felt opinion that neither [Hamedah nor her cousin] ought to spend the rest of their days in prison." Yet, she ended up serving 19 years of a 27-year sentence.

While she was still imprisoned, the Justice Roundtable, along with the ACLU, organized a briefing on the destructive impact of mandatory minimum sentencing, featuring Hamedah's two daughters and a short film about her case, *Perversion of Justice*. As the result of the Fair Sentencing Act and changes to the Federal Sentencing Guidelines, Hamedah was released in 2012.

The Justice Roundtable advocates introduced other impacted people to legislators. Eighteen days after he was released from prison, Michael Short testified before Congress about his experience. He told legislators about how, at the age of 21, he received a sentence of almost 20 years for distributing 63 ounces of crack cocaine. He acknowledged that what he had done was wrong, but questioned the logic of mandatory sentences for drug crimes and the senselessness of the crack/powder disparity.

His 2008 appearance before Congress was among the many testimonials that contributed to the 2010 passage of the Fair Sentencing Act.

Clarence Aaron was 24 years old in 1993 when he was sentenced to three life terms for his minor role in a nonviolent drug conspiracy. He had no criminal record. Of all those convicted in the case, Clarence received the stiffest sentence because he refused to plead guilty or testify against others. His case is an example of the inequities and harshness of drug sentencing, and also emblematic of the deficiencies in the pardoning system. An investigation revealed that although the prosecutor and judge in the case recommended his sentence be commuted, in the end it was not. The Justice Roundtable highlighted his case for many years to show the egregiousness of mandatory sentencing laws and to expose critical deficiencies in the pardon system. His sentence was finally commuted during the Clemency Initiative of the Obama Administration.

Karen Garrison, a former cosmetologist, reinvented herself as a staunch justice advocate after her college graduate twin sons, Lawrence and Lamont, were convicted in 1998 of drug conspiracy. The man who named them as members of a conspiracy served an 18-month sentence, reduced from 135 months, for his testimony. Lawrence and Lamont always maintained their innocence, refusing to accept a plea bargain for lighter sentences because it would require them to plead guilty to a crime they did not commit.

They served 11 years and 13 years, respectively, before they were released due to changes in the crack cocaine sentencing guidelines. The family has worked with the Justice Roundtable, testifying before Congress and sharing their story in community forums. Karen, dubbed "Mommie Activist," continues her drumbeat for people still languishing in prison under unduly stringent sentencing laws.

Dorothy Gaines, an Alabama grandmother, speaks ardently on behalf of the many women she left behind in prison who continue to serve excessive terms for low-level drug offenses. When police raided her home in 1993, they found no evidence that she possessed or sold drugs. Unaware that her then-boyfriend was a drug dealer, she was eventually charged with drug conspiracy and sentenced to serve 19 years and seven months. In December 2000, after serving six years, Gaines' sentence was commuted by President Clinton. As a resident of Alabama, Gaines was instrumental in attracting the attention of her senator, Jeff Sessions (R-AL), to these issues. Senator Sessions' efforts ultimately were instrumental in the passage of the Fair Sentencing Act.

Cedric Parker, the brother of Eugenia Jennings, testified eloquently before Congress in 2009 about the impact of the crack/powder cocaine disparity on his sister's life. Eugenia was given a sentence twice the one she would have received for selling powder cocaine because she dealt crack. At the time, Eugenia was facing a second decade in prison. Since her imprisonment, she became sober, an avid student, a supporter of battered women, and a counselor to young people, as well a model prisoner and worker. At the time of Cedric's testimony, Eugenia's three children had only seen her once since her imprisonment. In 2011, Jennings was the first person to receive a commutation by President Obama.

Our Justice Roundtable advocacy also included public engagement. One example was the 2009 premier of a film highlighting the abuses of drug task forces, *American Violet,* starring Nicole Beharie, Alfre Woodard and Charles Dutton. We hosted a screening at D.C.'s E Street Cinema, featuring a talk back afterwards with Regina Kelly, the real person the film was based upon, and actor Tony Goldwyn. Little did I know that a character in the film, Professor Joe Fisher, was based on a real law professor, Mark Osler, who I would meet several years later and become very influential to my advocacy.

Chapter Eight, Section 4
Roots of the Reentry Bill

What became known as the Second Chance Act was architected around the conference table of the Open Society Policy Center, spearheaded by the Reentry Working Group of the Justice Roundtable, under the primary leadership of my colleague, Gene Guerrero. During 2002, focus on the reentry of formerly incarcerated people as a key policy issue was in its embryonic stages. Our New York office was funding large think tanks to study the issue.

There were organizations around our Justice Roundtable conference table that had been around my previous coalition tables, such as The Sentencing Project, Criminal Justice Policy Foundation, National Association of Criminal Defense Lawyers, Families Against Mandatory Minimums, American Bar Association, ACLU, NAACP, Leadership Conference on Civil Rights, United Methodist Church, CURE, and others. New coalition partners joined in, such as the Legal Action Center, National Association of Social Workers, and the Therapeutic Communities of America, along with conservative allies.

Few advocates even realized that the people most impacted were relatively absent from the tables that were debating their futures. Not only were people directly impacted missing, even people who looked like those people were scarce. Often, I would be the only or one of the very few, melanin-enriched people in the room. Something was drastically wrong with that picture, and I vowed that around the Justice Roundtable, that would change. And over time, it did. Indeed, one of my colleagues often states that the Justice Roundtable is the "most racially diverse and inclusive coalition in Washington."

Work around reentry was the first major piece of legislation advanced by the Justice Roundtable coalition. I'll never forget the impetus. I was always very active with the Congressional Black Caucus' annual legislative convening, attending the workshops and oft-times serving as a panelist or moderator. It was 2003, and I was exhausted from the myriad of workshops I was involved with that year.

I begged my co-worker, Gene Guerrero, to attend a Saturday workshop on my behalf, hosted by Chicago Congressman Danny Davis on the issue of reentry of formerly

incarcerated people. Although Gene reluctantly agreed, he emerged from that event fired up. His attendance that Saturday morning resulted in his spearheading the Justice Roundtable's Reentry Working Group, and his open-mindedness to engaging Republican colleagues led to an alliance with Pat Nolan, the former head of the California State Assembly who had recently emerged from serving time in prison from a sting operation and was working for Chuck Colson's Prison Fellowship organization. And the rest is history.

Gene successfully mobilized both progressives and conservatives to come to the same table to strategize and lobby in support of the passage of reentry legislation. After the course of several years, the bill passed both the House and the Senate and was signed into law by President George W. Bush in April 2008.

The Second Chance Reentry Act would have been unthinkable just a few years earlier. Although "tough on crime" was still in vogue, a new day was dawning, and a new narrative about criminal justice reform was taking shape.

I remember sitting in the Senate Judiciary Committee's hearing room during the 114th Congress some eight years later, witnessing the marking up of a bill titled the

Sentencing Reform and Corrections Act. Granted, it was not the bill I would have written, as the reforms, while laudable, did not go far enough, but I wholeheartedly supported it. In fact, I tweeted that the bill had a magical, Goldilocks type of allure. "Not too hard on crime, not too soft, but just right to pass in this Congress at this time."

It was a carefully-negotiated bipartisan compromise bill which sought to reduce some mandatory minimums, broaden the safety valve, make the Fair Sentencing Act and other sentencing provisions retroactive, expand compassionate release, allow for juvenile sealing and expungement, juvenile parole, and limit juvenile solitary confinement.

Three years earlier, the passage of this type of legislation out of committee would have been unheard of. And five years earlier it would not have even passed the laugh test. What brought about the openness to this new narrative? I submit, it was the union of strange bedfellows.

A case in point. After work hours one evening, I did something I did not want to do. I drove out to Arlington, VA, to hear a man who was the former New York City Chief of Police, and the former Commissioner of the New York Department of Corrections. It was a man who at one point was nominated to be the Director of the Department of Homeland Security. Why in the world would I give up my precious evening with my family for this conservative prick? I went because he had recently emerged from six years of incarceration after being convicted of fraud, and from everything I had heard, he was saying all the right things.

He spoke of his concerns about mandatory minimum sentencing, stating that there is too much mass incarceration, over-criminalization, and racial disparities. He expressed concerns with collateral consequences, the need for second chances, and that the box should be banned on employment applications. I was taken aback. His speech was something I could have written!

I went out to Arlington that evening because I wanted to hear him firsthand. I wanted to hear him because, on my way to his presentation, I tweeted, "On way to event in VA featuring Bernard Kerik, past head of NY DOC, spent 6 years in prison for fraud and now talks of cj reform. Hope he's sincere."

I immediately received a reply tweet from twitter handle 'Doing Time With Bernie,' that blasted, "He's anything but sincere." Someone else tweeted, "He once accused the NAACP and ACLU of being un-American and communistic," and that he is "one mean-spirited racist." Someone else said, "he's a media hound, dances to the tune of the highest bidder."

Hmmm, I observed after entering the room. He was indeed flanked by two movie-looking cameras. But everything he was saying was right on time. Although once "tough on crime," Bernie Kerik now seemed the epitome of "smart on crime."

This new bipartisan criminal justice reform movement was becoming very intriguing to me. It presented the curious if not befuddling dichotomy of, per se, the great abolitionist Frederick Douglass literally being the hero of someone like me as well as the ultra-conservative Charles Koch.

Unfortunately, I've observed more times than I can count, that many conservatives only appear to recognize that the system is broken and needs fixing after they get caught up in it. After they have passed the laws they now seek to change, they oft-times have the epiphany. After they have manipulated public opinion and rode the "soft on crime" mantra into the sunset, many find religion. Yet and still, they are critical allies. Why? Because when they finally 'get it', their awakening shatters the stereotype of who is in prison, and for what, and provides critical cover for legislative change.

And so it was that the Justice Roundtable partnered with Chuck Colson, who had spent time in prison for his role in the Watergate scandal. We partnered with Pat Nolan, as stated earlier. We also partnered with Craig DeRoche, former Republican speaker of the Michigan House of Representatives, and current head of Justice Fellowship, a former alcoholic who had been arrested several times for drunk driving.

We developed relationships with Mark Holden, General Counsel of Koch Industries, who decades earlier had served as a prison guard. Progressive groups coalesced with conservative organizations, and reform began to get traction. We found that many of those who had fallen from grace and glory, who emanated from the other side of the aisle, were key if not crucial to helping push legislative reform of the criminal punishment system over the finish line.

They were helping to illuminate what the progressive community has known for years - that sending people to prison and keeping them there for an unconscionable lengthy time, does not make us safer, does not deter future crimes, and does not promote successful reintegration back into our communities. Conservatives and Libertarians are providing the cover now to find better, more cost-effective ways to push the envelope to achieve change.

Although my primary focus has been on sentencing reform, in reflecting on the multitude of police killings across the country, it appears gravely evident that victims of police violence don't get to the sentencing phase of the criminal justice process. They don't get to the courtroom and, reminiscent of motorist Sandra Bland, are out of luck even if they get to the police station. Victims of police violence, disproportionately Black, never get on the path to justice; they only get to the morgue. This state of affairs must change.

The Second Chance Act passed with strong bipartisan support in both houses of Congress and became law in 2008. It authorized $165 million in federal funding for reentry programs. Between 2008 and 2012, over 300 government agencies and nonprofit organizations in 48 states received funding under the Second Chance Act. The Act not only reduced prison costs and improved the lives of people who have been ill-served by the system, it also represented a changed conversation about society's obligations to help formerly incarcerated people transition back into their communities. The Second Chance Act failed to address, however, the myriad of collateral consequences to a criminal conviction. And so, the struggle continues.

Chapter Eight, Section 5
Behind the Cycle

The Open Society Washington Office, under my leadership and direction, hosted a national summit to advance an integrative approach to justice reform. I titled the convening, *Behind the Cycle*, and it was held December 4-6, 2008, at the Bethesda Marriott Hotel. The convening was the culmination of a two-year Behind the Cycle Project that created space for advocates, researchers, service providers and academics who work in different areas of expertise, to collaborate on the linkages that fuel America's cycle of incarceration.

We identified multidisciplinary strategies to abate the disproportionate numbers of poor and people of color entering into and cycling through the juvenile and criminal justice systems. Project consultant Catherine Beane and myself organized the first gathering of its kind, which brought together 300 participants chosen from various disciplines to address collaborative ways to strengthen communities, impact policy decisions, and stop the cycle of incarceration.

The slam dunk convening included a reception with opening remarks by Susan Taylor, former editor-in-chief of *Essence Magazine* who was now the founder of the National CARES Mentoring Movement; Patrice Gaines, author and prize-winning former *Washington Post* reporter who was also a survivor of abuse and incarceration, and the co-founder of the Brown Angel Center; and, John H. Jackson, president and CEO of the Schott Foundation for Public Education.

The next day's Roundtable Discussion was exceptionally impressive, due primarily to the skillful moderation by Professor Charles Ogletree, Director of the Charles Hamilton Houston Institute for Race and Justice at Harvard University. I chose a panel of 14 people to deepen our understanding of the complex linkages behind the cycle of incarceration which are often the root causes of delinquent and criminal behavior.

Using a "big picture" case scenario, Professor Ogletree engaged the panel in a conversation to connect the dots and explore the intersections of race, poverty and the social issues which fuel the cycle of incarceration. The discussants provided insight and shared solutions from their varied perspectives of policies, programs and services that positively influence the life outcomes of at-risk youth and adults.

Congressmen Bobby Scott (D-VA), sponsor of the Youth PROMISE Act, and Danny Davis (D-IL), sponsor of the Responsible Fatherhood/Healthy Families Act, both provided updates from the Hill.

Looking back, I am shocked that out of the 300 participants and 53 speakers, I could only identify two speakers who were formerly incarcerated – journalist Patrice Gaines, who spoke at the opening reception, and Dr. Divine Pryor, who was part of the Roundtable Discussion. There were, however, a number of formerly incarcerated people in attendance at the convening.

Thankfully, there has been a sea change since that 2008 convening with respect to the presence and leadership of formerly incarcerated and directly impacted people and organizations on justice issues. It has been exhilarating watching the growth and learning from the expertise of people with direct lived experiences, and our Washington-based advocacy has been greatly enriched as a result.

Regrettably, I was unable to keep the Behind the Cycle concept sustained within the Open Society Foundations. Although grateful for the opportunity to host the convening, to my chagrin, the continuation of the initiative was deemed "too big and too bold" for our organizational focus at the time.

Chapter Eight, Section 6
A Husband from the Classifieds?

"Girl, just what are you doing?!" I demanded of my friend Kianga.

"Looking to meet a man," she replied nonchalantly.

Lawd have mercy, I thought. In the *Washington Post* classifieds? I literally thought she had lost her mind.

She was a professional Black woman, a dentist in fact, and a person whom I had always held in high regard. I couldn't believe that she was actually pouring through the classified section looking for a man. Despite my protestations of how idiotic this all seemed, somehow the seed to do such a thing became planted in my mind.

Maybe there is someone out there for me, but for some reason that perfect brother has not yet crossed my path, I thought to myself. This was before the existence of online dating sites such as Black People Meet, Christian Social Mingle, Match.com, Black Cupid, etc. *The Washington Post* was in its early days of listing personal classified advertisements, or personal ads. So, along with my dentist girlfriend, I scoured the classifieds. I stepped out on faith, praying that the man I found would not be an ax murderer. I drafted the following ad to be included in the *Washington Post* Personals Plus, July 26, 1998 publication. Under the "Women Seeking Men" category, I offered:

"AFROCENTRIC DBPF, 43, ISO positive BM who enjoys poetry, jazz, movies and cultural events (DC). Phone 21446."

The third person who responded sounded interesting. He said he was a drummer, didn't smoke or drink, and had an African name. We decided to meet in a public place *– just in case he was an ax murderer –* and chose the Cheesecake Factory on Wisconsin Avenue in Northwest D.C.

As he walked toward me, I thought, Hmmm, he's an OK looking brother with locs, tall, thin. As we conversed, I was getting a little agitated with his subject-verb agreement, but still I thought, *This could possibly work.*

He ordered buffalo wings; I ordered a quesadilla. We started talking about "The Struggle." I was relieved to learn that we knew several people in common, people that I deeply respected. He was a really low-key guy, very much the opposite of my "center of the stage-type" personality. We were deep in conversation, talking about our lives, when I stated proudly, "So I worked on cases like Sundiata Acoli, you know – Assata Shakur's co-defendant."

He looked blank.

"Assata," I repeated. "Assata Shakur."

Another blank stare. Oh Lord, I'm thinking. My voice rose in a mixture of astonishment and utter disbelief.

"You do know who Assata Shakur is, don't you!?"

"Uhh," he finally replied. "Yeah, I think I've heard of her."

Well, I was ready to walk right out of that restaurant. Oh my God, how could I possibly be involved in a relationship with a man who had never even heard of Assata Shakur – or, in his words, who "thinks" he may have heard of her?

Then I slowed down and realized that my world of revolution, struggle, political prisoners, and reparations was not necessarily the world of every conscious Black person. *Could I be happy in such a relationship*, I wondered? In my younger years, the answer would have probably been a resounding "No!" However, I had recently passed the 40-year threshold and other priorities seemed more important.

Priorities like having a man who respects you and your views; a man who does not beat you or cuss you out. I decided that if a man is willing to support your endeavors, then maybe he doesn't have to know who Assata Shakur is. That first date at the Cheesecake Factory blossomed into many more and his not knowing who Assata was became a distant memory. This was a man who drove all the way across town to take my toddler daughter for visits with her birth father. This was a man who didn't mind grocery shopping, or going to track meets. So maybe he doesn't have to know about the Genocide Convention, or the Meter Neter. As long as he respects my political views, and doesn't seek to limit my revolutionary fervor, why not?

Six years after I submitted that ad, we got married in an outdoor ceremony in my backyard, branded "sacred garden" for the special occasion. Dakarai, my new husband-to-be, had supreme gardening skills and landscaped a perfect yard for the ceremony, complete with beautiful flowerbeds and tropical plants. The Chens, our next-door neighbors at the time, allowed us to use their yard for our reception, and we creatively combined our backyards, erected a tent, and prepared for a multitude of guests.

The affair was truly amazing, and we were spiritually blessed with a shower of light mist during the ceremony. It was just enough to cool off the scorching hot summer day, but not enough to cause everyone to bolt and go inside for shelter. It

did not really rain until the reception, but by that time we were all safely nestled under the large tent in the adjacent yard.

Dakarai was a very lucky man. First of all, he had me, but beyond that he has been fortunate to have "visitations" that have resulted in money. One time in particular, his oldest brother, who passed years ago, visited him in a dream giving him a message that resulted in lottery winnings from which he purchased the Ford Explorer SUV he was driving when we met.

Leading up to our wedding, my fiancé had been playing the numbers assiduously all week, but because of all the stress in preparing for the big event, he neglected to play on the very day of the wedding. And, of course, the number came out – a four way. He was convinced that the ancestors were giving us a wedding gift, and had he played, we would have cleared over $100,000. He was devastated, and although not a player, I was too.

Amazingly but not surprisingly, the ancestors were still with us. Several days later we received a "consolation" lottery winning of $1,500 from a chance tip given to him by a friend of his father, who had passed several years earlier. We added the winnings to the funds for our honeymoon. It was our first-ever cruise; the ship left from New Orleans, luckily one year before the devastating Hurricane Katrina and the resulting flooding.

Another time, we were watching a television program on the History Channel. It spoke of a spy program the U.S. military had used in the past to determine if some type of intelligence advantage could be gained through a practice called "remote view." It was a type of extrasensory perception similar to clairvoyance, and we decided to experiment.

Dakarai told me to think of a word or name, and he would try to guess it. Being a lawyer and having worked at Howard University School of Law, the name I chose was Charles Hamilton Houston, a former Howard Law School Dean, and the legal giant and mastermind of the strategy that led to the Supreme Court's *Brown v. Board of Education* school desegregation decision. Dakarai closed his eyes, relaxed himself, and went into meditation. Suddenly he blurted out, "Houston."

I nearly had a heart attack. How in the world was he able to guess that?!! I knew he had never heard of Charles Hamilton Houston, which he confirmed. He said that a distinct voice that he did not recognize, whispered "Houston" in his right ear. What that said to me was that whoever or whatever whispered in his ear did not know who Charles Hamilton Houston was either. You see, for some unknown reason, anyone who says his name always says all three names together – Charles. Hamilton. Houston.

He's hardly ever called Charles and never Houston but always *Charles Hamilton Houston*. So clearly, the entity saw I had written down the name, and it whispered the last name, Houston, to my husband. This has also happened on other occasions. Dakarai says although he has experienced dreams and impressions, this was the first time he heard a voice.

***

During much of the early years of our marriage, Dakarai and I entered into the world of multi-level marketing (MLM), also known as network marketing, something I never thought I would ever become involved with. Actually I really did not even know what MLM was and found myself having to have a "coming to terms" with the industry.

In the past, I had always run away from business opportunities. For example, when purchasing skin care products in college during the 1970s, I was frequently advised by the seller, "Nkechi, you know you have the opportunity to build a business."

'No,' I always stubbornly replied. I just want to buy the eyeliner.' I was always skeptical of "those companies." I thought they were all just schemes and scams.

I later learned, however, that the network marketing business model was one in which I was already quite skilled – relationships. Letting others know of a good book to read, a good movie to watch, or a good lawyer to hire. The difference, however, was that I never got compensated for my referrals. What this new business model did, I soon learned, was simply pay people for their referrals to a great product.

Surely not rocket science, I surmised. A trip into any bank today confirms the widespread practice of referral marketing. So why had I and so many others been so skittish? It was because of the thought of people "getting something for nothing." And that is a problem when it happens.

There are millions of people taken advantage of each year by illegal schemes and scams and, at the same time, millions of people who miss out on legitimate opportunities each year because they think they are schemes and scams. I found out that in the world of network marketing, unlike the realities of corporate America, everyone starts on an even playing field. It is often joked that one can excel in this industry, regardless of whether you are "straight out of Yale or just out of jail."

I have always said that there are three types of people in the world. Those who make things happen. Those who watch things happen. And those who missed the boat and then grumble, 'what happened'? I never wanted the third type to be my story. I always prided myself as someone who made things happen.

So when the opportunity for a home-based network marketing business presented itself to me from a credible colleague – again, my dentist friend Kianga – I decided to take a second look. My philosophy has been that if you want a doctor, don't rely on the advice of a lawyer. And if you want a prosperous financial future, don't talk to Ray Ray who hasn't paid you back from last week!

I dug into the books. Some of the texts I relied on over time included *Rich Dad, Poor Dad*, by Robert Kiyosaki; *Think and Grow Rich* by Napoleon Hill; *From the Trash Man to the Cash Man*, by Myron Golden; *The African American Entrepreneur – Then and Now*, by Sherman Rogers; *Acres of Diamonds*, by Russell Conwell; and *The Richest Man in Babylon*, by George Clason. These and other books taught me about financial principals, wealth-building, mindset, abundance, and prosperity.

On May 12, 2006 Dakarai and I held the first of countless get-together dinner meeting/presentations at our home. We reached out to friends and colleagues, inviting them with the question: 'If there was a way you could earn an extra stream of income, part-time, working from the comfort of your home, would it be worth 45 minutes of your time?' Our presentations were riveting, usually consisting of commentary such as the following:

'Have you ever dreamed of owning your own business, being your own boss and in control of your own time? Have you read the authors who say owning your own business is the smart success strategy? Have you been searching for the right product, the right industry, the right thing? Well, we believe this is it, and you are in the right place at the right time!'

'I'm a lawyer. My sponsor is a dentist. Her sponsor is an OB-GYN. We have on our team doctors, teachers, musicians, painters, social workers, postal workers, retired persons and those who are unemployed. Those of us who work a J.O.B., however, don't get paid unless we are billing attorney hours, fixing teeth, seeing patients, painting houses, or playing drums. Prior to launching our home-based biz, my husband and I had no Plan B, no residual income. All that has changed now.'

"What does your circle look like?" I would ask my guests during presentations. "Are there financially independent people in it? Are there prosperity-minded people in it? Or are there only broke people in it?"

I stressed that if they have four broke friends, chances are they will be number 5. "If you want to be prosperous," I emphasized to our future team members, hungry for information, "You must see the opportunity, seize the opportunity, make your decision without engaging in the paralysis of analysis, and receive your blessing."

The best part of the presentation for me, and my primary raison d'etre for becoming a home-based business owner – is that it is the best defense to paying more taxes, period.

This is an "anyways business," I continuously asserted.

I was going to use my cell phone, anyway. I was going to turn on the computer, anyway. I was going to use cable service, anyway. I was going to go to that restaurant, anyway. I was going to travel, anyway. So I might as well do these things in the context of a home based-business, turn expenses into legitimate business tax deductions, and reap the benefits.

And I brought my love for my heroine into my presentations.

'Can you imagine what type of entrepreneur Harriet Tubman would have made today? She was someone who had a goal, was consistent, and persistent against all odds. She was someone who did not just think of herself, but reached back time and time again to help others. Someone who refused to let naysayers jeopardize the collective mission. You see, Harriet definitely had a prosperity mentality. She focused on the opportunity, not the obstacle. It's all a matter of focus because in every situation there are both obstacles and opportunities. Which one do you usually see? Start seeing and focusing on the opportunity and it will lead you to prosperity.'

My husband Dakarai and I totally rocked our new home-based network marketing business. We valued our product and were consummate connoisseurs of it. We loved the company's founders and learned a lot. We built a monumental team and provided leadership and guidance. We attended huge conventions, took fabulous trips and received numerous awards. We earned a $10,000 bonus in our first year. This was on top of countless $1000 bonuses, regular checks and residual income. The times were exhilarating and we were on a whirlwind.

We were blessed to work our home-based business strong for over ten years. We still own the business and still believe in the concept, but moved on from daily leadership as our marriage deteriorated. But yes, we do, however, still receive residual checks!

My third husband may not have been well-versed in the history of revolutionary struggles, but he allowed me to be me. However, despite issues that caused us to ultimately amicably separate, we had a decent relationship that I don't regret.

Throughout my life I have had my share of platonic male friends, boyfriends, "booty calls" and husbands. I've had great times, and I've made grave mistakes. Although I have always believed in, and still do, the institution of marriage, I've decided to just enjoy life with no expectations. And ladies, I must admit being enthusiastically intrigued when I discovered that the great Harriet Tubman, at nearly 60 years of age, married a man 22 years younger than she! As Jesse always says, "keep hope alive!"

Chapter Eight, Section 7
"I Feel Good" Obama

On January 20, 2009, the first Black President of the United States was sworn in. I was asked to provide remarks shortly thereafter at a conference hosted by a Rites of Passage organization on what his election meant for Black people. There would likely be people in the audience who had never voted in a Presidential election, discounting the ballot in Malcolm X's famous "Ballot or the Bullet" speech. I recognized that there may also be people there who enthusiastically vote.

I penned my remarks the night of Obama's inauguration and delivered them the following morning to a packed audience of youth and elders adorned in colorful African garb. The crowd seemed curious, if not eager, to hear my point of view on the historic election. I began with fervor:

In the lyrics of James Brown, 'I feel good, dadadadadada! Like I knew that I would, dadadadadda.!' Well, that's how I feel and millions of others feel the same way regarding the election of Barack Hussein Obama as the 44th President of the United States. This 'feel good' sensation is important, necessary and therapeutic. I mean, I did things I had never done in my life to ensure his campaign would be successful. For the first time I canvassed for a United States President. I went down into the boon docks of Virginia to knock on doors. I donated money to the Presidential campaign and even purchased items, despite them having the red, white and blue U.S. flag on them, waving in the background.

Me. Nkechi Taifa. Revolutionary Black Nationalist freedom fighter! Me. One of the founders of the late 20th century reparations movement in this country. Me. Staunch advocate for the release of political prisoners and prisoners of war in this country. Me. Me. Me. So, why do I support this presidency?

Because it feels good. And after 54 years on this earthly plane, I needed something to feel good about. I needed at least the illusion of victory, and it was handed down on a silver platter. Obama conducted himself like an average, ordinary non-pretentious, non-egotistical Black man. It was a bonus that he had a magnificent Black wife and well-behaved, adorable Black children. I was impressed that Obama believed in community organizing, attended a radical Black church, and walked in shoes with worn soles.

'Will his Presidency make a difference?' I wondered. 'Probably not,' I surmised. You see, despite his attributes, appeal, intelligence, and good intentions, he will nevertheless still be the President of the United Snakes. And what does that mean? It means that he is now President of the American Empire. The position itself is an institution, and he will be the head of that institution. Can he, alone, change it? Absolutely and unequivocally, no!

In fact, if there was any inkling that he would be able to change the fundamental nature of this society, he would have never been elected. That is clear, and many conscious Black people understand that. Which is why many of us were able to vote for him with a clear conscience. We could vote for him although our heroine, Cynthia McKinney, was on the Presidential nomination ticket. We could vote for him despite his repudiation of the views of Minister Farrakhan and his denunciation of his former pastor, Rev. Jeremiah Wright. I cast my vote for Barack Obama despite his pronouncements that reparations are not what the Black community needs, and despite other issues on which he and I are in disagreement.

Many of us understand the complexity of embracing Obama, as it is akin to interviewing for a job 'in the system.' Would you go to that job interview stating that this particular company owes you billions of dollars in reparations? Would you go to that job interview revealing that this particular company is illegally holding dozens of your friends as prisoners of war? Would you go to that job interview saying that your goal is to burn down the factory and rebuild it from the ground up? Absolutely not, not if you are serious about getting the position.

Well, I submit this circumstance to be the same with Barack Hussein Obama. We don't really know what is in his mind. He may say and actually believe that Black folk are not entitled to reparations; however, his minister – the very one he has since disavowed – was in fact the keynote speaker at the National Coalition of Blacks for Reparations in America's convention before the Obama presidential campaign. He may say and actually believe that he knows nothing about the Nation of Islam, but I know that he lives right down the street from Minister Louis Farrakhan.

You see, Barack Obama stands on the shoulders of and is riding on the backs of millions of our ancestors who sacrificed their lives for change. I'm sure he knows that. He is standing on the shoulders of those who perished on the Middle Passage; those who staged insurrections on slave ships. He is riding on the backs of David Walker, Gabriel Prosser, Denmark Vesey, Toussaint L'Ouverture, Dessalines, Harriet Tubman, Ida B. Wells-Barnett, Fannie Lou Hamer, Marcus Garvey, Malcolm X, Martin Luther King, George Jackson, Rosa Parks, just to name a few.

Our Chief Executive is standing on the shoulders of our ancestors in a land where 63% of the people are White (an all-time low) and want him to align himself with their dominant view. Will he make a difference? I don't know. As my colleague Richard Muhammad recommended I say to you, and I will say it because I agree 100%: the presidency of Barack Obama cannot make up for over 400 years of brutal oppression. It can not make up for White supremacy or sadistic torture, or institutional racism. Irrespective of the intellect, morals and strong family values the Obama family bring to the White House, there is still a war going on in America. He may be handsome and Michelle may be fine, but there is still a war going on in America. As Dr. Frances Cress Welsing ominously reminds us, 'There is still white world supremacy.'

Will his election make a difference? Hmmm, perhaps, but the onus is on us not to give up the fight. We can't give him a free ride, and we must hold his feet to the fire. We must demand accountability and take off the rose-colored glasses. We must remember he's only a man – not a magician, not God, and certainly not Jesus. We must continually commit and recommit ourselves to the paradigm of re-Afrikanization.

The election of Barack Obama reminds me of a story I once heard Brother Chokwe Lumumba embellish upon. He told me he actually heard it from another brother named Willie Rose. I will continue the tradition and pass it down to you. Malcolm X always talked about two types of enslaved people on the plantation – the house slave and the field slave. Most of us are familiar with that speech. In sum, Brother Malcolm told us that the house slave lived up in the big house – with Massa. (Actually, he lived up in the attic or the basement.) He ate the same food Massa ate (or at least the crumbs Massa left), but he was satisfied with that. If Massa got sick, he'd say, 'What's the matter boss, we sick?' If Massa's house caught fire, he fought harder than Massa to put it out.

Now Malcolm compared him to the field slave who worked in the fields from 'can't see in the morning til can't see at night.' He lived in a shack, if that, and wore gunny sacks for clothes. When Massa got sick, the field slave prayed he wouldn't recover. When Massa's house caught fire, the field slave prayed for a strong wind.

However, Chokwe tells us that Malcolm didn't mention another enslaved person who was out there on that planation: the yard hand. The yard hand came from the field, but succeeded in getting away from it. The yard hand didn't live up there in the big house, but he didn't live that far from it. He was close enough to look in, sometimes got so close he could sneak right in. Now he didn't live too far from the field either. He could hear the whip of the lash and remembered its bitter sting.

The yard hand could see what was happening in the big house and he could see what was happening in the field. You see, because of his unique position, he often had a choice as to what his position was going to be. Was he going to work in the interests of his people, or work against their interests?

I always tell my law students and young Black professionals that the choice the yard hand had yesterday is the exact same choice we have today. And I submit, it is the same choice Barack and Michelle have today. They have the choice to work against the best interests of our people, or the choice to actively promote justice. The choice to move from 'Yes We Can' to, in the words of Michael Eric Dyson, 'Now We Must.' The choice to listen to the rhythmic breath of our ancestors, over and above the loud drone of the empire.

We all have the choice to remember the sting of the lash and to take the power to do something about it. We can choose to eat Massa's food, but also make sure no one else goes hungry. We can choose to live up in Massa's house, but make sure that everyone else has a house too. Of course, we also have the choice to pray for that strong wind, if necessary.

The election of Barack Obama has brought us time and breathing space. Time for this generation to, in the words of Frantz Fanon, 'discover its mission, fulfill it, or betray it.'

During this time it's OK to feel good, da-da-da-da-da-da. Let's savor the moment and with renewed determination, dedication and hard work, help him make a difference.

Chapter Nine
"Fight the Power"[100]

Section 1
Crack the Disparity!

In 2005, on the eve of the 20th anniversary of the 1986 crack law, I revitalized and broadened the crack disparity coalition I created during the previous decade. Once again, our mission was to advocate for change collectively. Now, under the aegis of the Justice Roundtable, my goal was to strategically use the 20-year anniversary of the law's passage as a catalyst to encourage renewed public and legislative discussion of the issue.

Our new "Crack the Disparity" coalition's rallying cry was strong and succinct: "Twenty years of discriminatory, crack cocaine sentencing is enough. The studies are completed. The research is compelling. The analysis is sound. Now is the time to mend this crack in our system of justice."

We planned to publicly launch the campaign at the beginning of January 2006. Unsure of the reception of our campaign on the Hill, we discussed requesting a hearing before the Inter-American Commission on Human Rights (IACHR) to emphasize the crack disparity as the most egregious example of mandatory minimum sentences meted out in U.S. courts.

The idea for an international effort came to me quite serendipitously. One balmy day in October 2005, during a long leisurely walk from my office, I bumped into Chicago attorney Stan Willis, a colleague from my work with the National Conference of Black Lawyers.

"Hey Stan, my brother. What you doing here in D.C.?"

"Nkechi, I'm about to speak at a press conference to provide testimony before the Inter-American Commission on Human Rights on the Burge Chicago police station torture issue."

"Oh yeah wow, what's happening with that case?"

The Burge debacle was a case I was familiar with, having highlighted it as part of my curriculum while teaching my "Racial Disparity in the Criminal Justice System" seminar at Howard Law. It was a case where evidence was uncovered that Chicago police officers, seeking to extract confessions of African American suspects in custody, routinely tortured them through beatings, electrocution and strangulation.

"Well Sis, we've lost faith," Stan lamented. "Here we are now in 2005. We've got over 20 years of evidence, and absolutely nothing has been done to prosecute. We're moving to a different level now. We've got a replica of the box that we're gonna present to the press."

He was speaking of the crude wooden box wired to a cattle prod-type device that police hooked to the genitals of men they were "interviewing."

"So where are you going again?" I asked.

"The Inter-American Commission on Human Rights. On F Street," he responded.

I was too embarrassed to tell Stan that I didn't have a clue as to what this Commission was. I had frankly never even heard of it before. So here was an international body, in my own backyard, that I was, essentially, ignorant of.

Although I was not at all familiar with this Inter-American Commission headquartered in Washington, I was intrigued and my mind started racing. I thought, *If they could get a thematic hearing on police torture, perhaps we could get one on the crack disparity issue.*

Not too long after my chance encounter with Stan, I noticed that a representative from the Inter-American Commission would be speaking at an upcoming conference of the U.S. Human Rights Network in Atlanta. The Network was headed up by my colleague Ajamu Baraka, who would later become the Green Party's Vice Presidential candidate after the Obama era.

I decided to travel to Atlanta to attend the conference. During lunch, I strategically situated myself in the seat next to Brian Tittimore, the staff attorney for the IACHR who was featured at the conference. I peppered him with questions and he graciously provided answers. He explained that the Inter-American Commission on Human Rights was an autonomous organ of the Organization of American States (OAS), whose members are elected by the OAS General Assembly. One of its main functions is to address the complaints or petitions received from individuals, groups of individuals, or organizations that allege human rights violations committed in OAS member countries.

Conveniently, the Justice Roundtable's Human Rights Working Group was chaired by Margaret Huang who happened to be an expert on the workings of the Inter-American Commission, as well as other international human rights instruments. Margaret guided us step by step through the process of filing a petition before the Commission. Because of her brilliant guidance, the Commission accepted the Justice

Roundtable's request and convened an historic thematic hearing on March 3, 2006. Our goal was to raise international attention to the fact that the crack cocaine disparity was the most egregious example of mandatory minimum sentencing in the U.S. criminal justice system.

As chair of the Justice Roundtable, I was thrilled to moderate the discussion featuring an illustrious panel of witnesses. Included was the Honorable Patricia Wald, former Chief Judge of the U.S. Court of Appeals for the District of Columbia Circuit and judge on the International Criminal Tribunal for the Former Yugoslavia; Professor Charles Ogletree, founder of Harvard Law School's Institute on Race and Justice; Attorney Gay McDougall, executive director of Global Rights and the first United Nations Independent Expert on Minority Issues; and, Kemba Smith, who provided her personal story as a directly impacted person.

The witnesses testified that mandatory minimum sentences – prison terms predetermined by Congress and automatically levied primarily for drug and gun crimes – violate protected human rights found in the American Declaration on the Rights and Duties of Man, and other international instruments. Witnesses cited the wildly disparate sentences between crack and powder cocaine as the most flagrant example of how mandatory minimums have a racially discriminatory impact. The undeniable reality is that harsh sentences for crack cocaine convictions fall disproportionately on African Americans.

Perhaps the most poignant testimony of the proceeding during the Commission's 124th Period of Sessions, were the closing words of Judge Wald. She concluded:

> Unduly long and punitive sentences are counterproductive, and candidly many of our mandatory minimums approach the cruel and unusual level as compared to other countries as well as to our own past practices. On a personal note, let me say that on the Yugoslavia War Crimes Tribunal I was saddened to see that the sentences imposed on war crimes perpetrators responsible for the deaths and suffering of hundreds of innocent civilians often did not come near those imposed in my own country for dealing in a few bags of illegal drugs. These are genuine human rights concerns that I believe merit your interest and attention.

This hearing helped to rally renewed public attention to the long-standing problem and re-galvanized the advocacy community. However, this was 2006 and the 108th Congress boasted a majority of Republicans in both the House and the Senate, under President George W. Bush. Although what became known as the Second Chance re-entry bill was making its way through Congress, it was nevertheless a hostile legislative environment for sentencing reform. Our newly re-established coalition engaged in many brainstorming sessions on the most effective ways to reframe the issue.

We determined in this "tough on crime" environment, that it would be more efficacious to stress the themes of punishment and the importance of law enforcement to pursue high-level drug traffickers. This would take undue focus off of those involved at low levels. We knew we were in for a protracted struggle. We had laid critical groundwork in previous years on the moral theme of the issue, and brought attention to the grave injustice of the gross racial disparities as a result of it. It was critical that the needle now move on the Hill.

Our coalition partner, Eric Sterling, drafted a bill, the Cocaine Kingpin Punishment Act. This proposal couched our message for legislative reform in language that would resonate with conservatives and the law enforcement community. The bill's focus was on large-scale traffickers as opposed to bit players in the drug trade. Its dissemination on the Hill had the desired effect, inspiring Senator Biden to introduce the Drug Sentencing Reform and Cocaine Kingpin Trafficking Act of 2007.

Senator Biden's bill came the closest to rational reform of cocaine penalties. However, I will always acknowledge Senator Jeff Sessions for taking the first step in the Senate towards legislative reform on this issue. His bill would narrow the gap between crack and powder cocaine to a 20:1 quantity ratio. But it also decreased the amount of powder cocaine that would trigger a sentence, although evidence showed that the penalties for powder cocaine were already tough enough.

Our fear all along was that to remedy the issue, the conservative's call would be to raise the quantity levels for powder cocaine to the crack cocaine level. Our coalition remained united that this was non-negotiable. I also commend Senator Orrin Hatch (R-UT) for introducing legislation to reduce the federal crack cocaine disparity without a shift in the penalty for powder cocaine, which would eliminate the mandatory minimum sentence for simple possession of crack cocaine and bring it in line with simple possession of any other drug.

On the House side, Rep. Charles Rangel's Crack-Cocaine Equitable Sentencing Act had been consistently introduced into each Congress since the days of our advocacy the previous decade. It was now joined by a bill introduced by Rep. Sheila Jackson Lee (D-TX) as a companion bill to Senator Biden's crack legislation. The Fairness in Cocaine Sentencing Act of 2008, introduced by Rep. Bobby Scott (D-VA), went further than reform of the crack laws to include elimination of the cocaine mandatory minimum statute as a whole.

Rep. Maxine Waters (D-CA) highlighted the harms of mandatory minimums during the annual Congressional Black Caucus legislative weekend year after year. She audaciously called for the removal of mandatory minimum sentences from federal law with her bill, The Major Drug Trafficking Prosecution Act. Republican Representatives Mike Castle (R-DE) and Ron Paul (R-TX) also vocally endorsed crack cocaine reform.

Our Crack the Disparity coalition fervently supported those bills in the House and Senate that called for the complete elimination of the disparity and, of course, of all mandatory minimum drug sentences.

We organized sign-on letters to Congress and Congressional briefings. Coalition members drafted reports, testified before the U.S. Sentencing Commission, lobbied Congress, and submitted amicus (friend of the court) briefs in support of Supreme Court cases.

Again, one of our coalition's most pivotal contributions towards getting the law changed was bringing the human face to Capitol Hill. These were people impacted by these egregious sentences. They included Cedric Parker, the brother of Eugenia Jennings who testified before the Senate Judiciary Committee in 2009. His sister would become the first person to receive a sentence reduction through clemency from President Obama two-and-a-half years later.

We were eager to bring Willie Mays Aikens to Washington to testify before Congress. His lawyer was Margaret Love, the former pardon attorney under President Bill Clinton and part of our coalition. Aikens was a baseball legend who had been recently released after serving 14 years of a 21 year sentence. He made baseball history when he became the first player to hit two home runs twice  in the 1980 World Series. Years later his baseball career sunk as the result of a long-standing, untreated cocaine addiction. Eventually, it led to an extreme mandatory minimum sentence for selling drugs to a female undercover agent who had purposely befriended him for that purpose.

She repeatedly begged him to bring her cocaine and to "cook" the powder cocaine into crack. As a result, Aikens was arrested and charged pursuant to the harsher crack penalties. Because of the more stringent sentencing penalties for crack, his sentence for selling 2.2 ounces of crack cocaine was treated as though it was equivalent to selling 15 pounds of powder cocaine! He had just been released from prison in June of 2008 as the result of the Sentencing Commission's adjustment to the crack cocaine sentencing guidelines. Our coalition used his story to underscore the cruelty of mandatory minimum crack cocaine sentencing and the racial disparities between crack and powder cocaine.

Chapter Nine, Section 2
Junk Food Justice

Another significant feature of our Crack the Disparity coalition's public education campaign was to depict drug quantities with visual analogies. For example, five grams of crack cocaine, the equivalent weight of five packets of artificial sweetener or a couple of peanuts, yielded a mandatory minimum sentence of five years in prison. Fifty grams of crack cocaine, comparable to the weight of an ordinary candy bar, mandated a ten-year sentence. One third of all federal cocaine cases involved an average of 52 grams, while only 7 percent of federal cocaine cases were directed at high-level traffickers.

To drive this point home, rather than don t-shirts or hats to visualize our message, our coalition engaged in a different type of creative show-and-tell. We delivered candy bars, sugar packets, and peanuts to each member of the Senate and House Judiciary Committees, to remind Congress that absurdly minuscule quantities of crack cocaine yield unnecessarily extreme sentences.

We graphically illustrated that, despite its rhetoric, Congress was not being "tough on crime" with these punitive sentences. We emphasized that two-thirds of the federal cocaine cases were being brought against those at the bottom of the distribution chain. Eric Sterling, the former Hill staffer who was now our coalition member, once stated disdainfully, "These are candy bar crack cases, the criminal justice equivalent to junk food, and the federal courts and prisons have become obese with these peanut prosecutions."

In a meeting with a key conservative congressional staffer the ACLU's Jesselyn McCurdy explained, "The proper federal role in the nation's anti-drug effort must be focused on kingpins – those international and national level traffickers who smuggle drugs into the country by the hundreds or thousands of pounds. If the Department of Justice is not focused on these highest level cases, and it has not been, then these cases are not being prosecuted."

I then emphasized to the staffer, "Peanut prosecutions in federal court of candy bar weight crack cases are not tough on crime. If there is to be strong and effective federal drug enforcement, then Congress must, at a minimum, fix the crack/powder disparity, and mandate to the Justice Department that high-level trafficking cases are to be the new norm for federal court prosecutions."

Our arguments succeeded in garnering significant conservative and law enforcement support. Conservative allies for reform provided additional cover for Republican members of Congress to do the right thing. They included the National District Attorney's Association, National Association of Police Organizations, Federal Law Enforcement Officers Association, International Union of Police Associations, Federal Prison Council, AFGE, AFL-CIO, and Grover Norquist's Americans for Tax Reform. We also received help from David Keene's American Conservative Union, Ward Connerly's American Civil Rights Institute, former 'drug czar' Asa Hutchinson, Pat Nolan from Prison Fellowship, Citizenlink, Focus on the Family, and the National Association of Evangelicals, amongst others.

Hearings were held in both the House and the Senate. Police and prosecutors testified for reform. President Obama and Vice President Biden, both on the campaign trail and in the White House, called for change and the complete elimination of the disparity. In addition to Congressional bills, attention to reform cocaine sentencing gained momentum, from the United States Sentencing Commission and the Department of Justice, to the United States Supreme Court. Many, many windows of opportunity opened. We were so close to triumph, but yet, still so very far away.

If there was ever a moment when change was on the horizon regarding the crack disparity issue, I knew that now was that moment. There had never been as much momentum involving different key players focused on this issue. It was an exciting and exhilarating time to be in the forefront of crack cocaine reform. However, as I cautioned to a newspaper reporter, "It is still critical to remember that these changes represent only incremental progress in the effort to reform the federal crack cocaine law. The Supreme Court's allowance of judicial discretion and the Sentencing Commission's guideline changes will not eliminate or even significantly alleviate the very long mandatory minimum sentences that many people are serving for crack cocaine offenses. The ball is now in Congress's court. Congress must act to eliminate the statutory 100 to 1 disparity." Echoing the coalition's rally cry, I emphatically concluded, "Now is the time to mend this crack in our system of justice!"

Chapter Nine, Section 3
'We're Going To Do This Crack Thing, Wade'

On July 16, 2009, during Supreme Court nominee Sonia Sotomayor's confirmation hearing before the Senate Judiciary Committee, Senator Jeff Sessions leaned over to Wade Henderson, then president and CEO of the Leadership Conference on Civil Rights. He greeted him before the civil rights leader's testimony and casually remarked, "Mr. Henderson, it's good to work with you. Senator Leahy and I are talking during these hearings. We're going to do that crack cocaine thing that you and I have talked about before." After an awkward pause, Wade laughed and graciously responded, "Thank you Senator, I appreciate that."

The Senate gallery erupted with giggles and snickers. I was only half-watching the otherwise monotonous hearing on C-SPAN from my office television monitor when the levity broke.

After Sessions' bombshell declaration traversed the internet and YouTube, Wade publicly clarified, "Please trust me on this: Sessions wasn't talking about doing anything with me and Senate Judiciary Committee Chairman Leahy that we wouldn't want the world to watch." He continued soberly, "When Sessions, a conservative Republican from the Deep South has the courage to talk common sense about crack, then so should other Senators and Representatives from both parties and every part of this country."

But it was a chance meeting in the Congressional gym's locker room months later, in March 2010, when a landmark deal was brokered that finally broke through the legislative logjam. Senator Durbin characterized it as a "miracle." He explained that the legislation was at an impasse until he saw Sessions one morning in the gym. "We both showered, we're putting our clothes on, about to leave," he explained. "I said, 'Jeff, give me a number. If you can't do one-to-one and I won't go for 100-to-one, what is it?' It was 18. I can't tell you why, but it was 18. We agreed."

Scary sausage-making! Another number arbitrarily plucked out of a hat, yet infinitely better than the original 100-to-1 ratio. Magic number ratios have circulated in the past promoting ratios of 10-to-1, 20-to-1, and 5-to-1. But alas, it was the random 18-to-1 that got traction in the Congressional locker room that day.

The 18-to-1 bill passed the Senate unanimously that same day. The bipartisan compromise would shave nearly 30 months off of sentences and impact about 3,000 cases a year, at a savings of $42 million between 2010 and 2015. It was a compromise that would completely eliminate the disparity for simple possession of crack cocaine, and reduce the disparity from 100-to-1 to 18-to-1 for distribution.

Was the compromise imperfect? Absolutely. Was there still injustice? Unquestionably. Had the timing been slow? Incredibly. However, when I candidly asked myself if this was the moment for reform we had been awaiting for so many years – my honest answer could be none other than a resounding: yes.

I said "yes" to that question because never in the 24-year history of this travesty of injustice, had there been agreement on both sides of the aisle. It was July and, as was the case in 1994, we were again on the verge of midterm elections. Rather than waiting to see who could be "tougher than thou" on crime, it appeared as if the sentiment finally was, "Let's be smart on crime."

As an advocate, was the correct stance the complete elimination of the disparity? My answer, of course, is yes. Should we continue to fight for it? Absolutely. Should we have waited for the perfect scenario to appear? To that my position was, no.

This issue had been on the table for nearly 25 years. So many doors had shut in our faces and so many more people since that time had been arrested and were languishing in prison. When I first started advocacy on this issue in 1993, I was pregnant, walking the halls of Congress and testifying before the U.S. Sentencing Commission. I did not know her at the time, but Kemba Smith, who later became the poster child for the movement against mandatory minimum sentences and the crack/powder disparity issue, was likewise pregnant. She, however, was facing a 24-year sentence for crack cocaine conspiracy. Now, after nearly 20 years of work, my daughter and her son were in their 16th years of life. My position had to be that we had waited long enough for some type of change to occur.

As an advocate, I found myself in a bittersweet moment. Bitter, because the complete elimination of the disparity was what I knew to be just and right, but was not part of the bill that seemed destined to pass. Sweet, because this was the first time in 24 years that we appeared on the verge of very real change. Bipartisan change was finally about to be implemented on a criminal justice issue that would completely eliminate a mandatory minimum sentence and significantly lower another one.

I argued to wavering members of the coalition. "I totally agree that the complete elimination of the disparity is the only defensible solution. But this moment must not pass without action that will significantly impact what has been the status quo for nearly a quarter of a century."

So while touting the 2010 bill as a first step, our coalition united around the bipartisan compromise which became known as the Fair Sentencing Act. On August 3, 2010, President Obama signed the Act into law, reducing the sentencing disparity between powder and crack cocaine from 100-to-1 to 18-to-1. The Act represented a crucial step toward federal sentencing that's fair and effective, instead of political and punitive. Subsequently, the U.S. Sentencing Commission adjusted its guidelines to conform to the new law and made the adjustment retroactive. Two years later the Supreme Court ruled that the law would apply to defendants who were sentenced after the law was enacted, even if their offense occurred beforehand.

Let there be no doubt about it. The passage of the Second Chance and Fair Sentencing Acts did not occur in a vacuum. They were largely the result of strategic advocacy by Justice Roundtable working groups, which successfully focused the attention of legislators, the media, and the public on the importance of reentry and sentencing issues.

The Fair Sentencing Act's signing ceremony was low key, involving only members of Congress. I was displeased that the advocates, myself included, who worked so very hard on the issue for so many years, were not even invited to the White House to witness the historic signing. There was, however, a pretty nifty reception at the Department of Justice where Attorney General Holder thanked us for our advocacy and posed for pictures with us.

Although we did not succeed in completely eliminating the disparity, very real people are no doubt quite appreciative for the opportunity to have years shaved off of their disparately lengthy sentences. Despite this historic progress by Congress and advancements from the Sentencing Commission, the Department of Justice and the Supreme Court, the fight for fairness, justice and confidence in the nation's federal drug sentencing policies was not over. Little did I know that I would once again soon become a catalyst in another equally important effort.

Chapter Nine, Section 4
Clemency: An Inside Scoop[101]

The Fair Sentencing Act was signed into law in 2010. I had worked on the issue for 17 long years, overlapping my work with three different employers – the ACLU Washington Legislative Office, the Howard University School of Law and the Open Society Policy Center.[102] Although the Fair Sentencing Act reduced the disparity in penalty between crack and powder cocaine offenses, the law was prospective only, not applying to people already sentenced at the time of its passage. Strategically, as progressive advocates, we kept this issue of retroactivity off the table; it would have been legislative suicide to seek to have it attached to the bipartisan bill with the best chance of passage.

The lack of retroactivity, however, was fundamentally unfair – sentences should not be based on a fluke, one somehow lucky enough to have committed a drug crime after August 3, 2010, the effective date of the Act, as opposed to a mere day before. If the disparity is wrong today, it was wrong yesterday. It was only fair that the new law should apply retroactively, particularly since it was the egregiousness of the sentences of people already incarcerated that inspired the change in the law. Now that the bill had passed, and the storm had blown over, I knew there had to be a solution to this nonsensical conundrum. Always on a quest for justice, I scrambled to come up with a remedy.

"I have it!" I shrieked as I breathlessly blurted my master plan to colleagues. "Mass clemency for those who did not benefit from the Fair Sentencing Act!"

"Nkechi, don't be ridiculous," a close colleague chided.

"Be realistic, that will never happen," another admonished.

Although this proposed remedy was shot down by some coalition members as unrealistic, I knew I was on the right track. I just needed to find the right mechanism and fashion a winning narrative that would provide critical cover in a politically volatile criminal punishment regime.

Then someone handed me an article co-written by a law professor who was not familiar to me, Mark Osler. My eyes got big and my brain started racing.

This is really it, I confidently proclaimed to myself as I rifled through the pages. This is it, and hallelujah, it's coming from a White former-prosecutor-turned-professor who established the first law school clemency clinic in the country. Perfect. The article talked about nearly 14,000 people convicted of anti-drug offenses whose sentences were commuted through a federal clemency commission established by President Gerald Ford in the wake of the Viet Nam War.

The article also described President Jimmy Carter's amnesty for draft dodgers that followed. I was obsessed as I scrutinized this possible precedent from the past. In the clemency commission approach, each case was individually reviewed, a remedy that was not seen as the proverbial "get out of jail free card," and a strategy which would alleviate current fears of releasing those who could pose a threat to public safety. It sounded like a plausible model to replicate, and I was excited.

I needed a platform to introduce Professor Osler's Ford Clemency Commission model as a serious pursuit, especially since my "mass clemency" brainchild idea failed to pass the laugh test, even amongst some of my progressive peers. As I usually do when stuck and need to generate attention to an issue and garner buy-in from colleagues, I contemplated an educational policy event.

This approach worked at the early stages of the crack disparity campaign which I led in 1993 while at the ACLU, when a then-nascent C-SPAN televised our day-long symposium and helped thrust the issue into the national consciousness. It was likewise successful as I sought to revive the campaign in 2006 with an historic thematic hearing before the Inter-American Commission on Human Rights.

I teamed up with Kanya Bennett, a former Congressional Black Caucus Fellow who had recently joined the staff of the American Constitution Society for Law and Policy. We organized a prestigious breakfast forum in the Congressional Rayburn House Office Building on May 10, 2012, a platform through which I hoped we could normalize a Ford-style clemency commission approach.

This catalytic event, *Re-Imagining the Constitutional Pardon Power, Does the President Have a Role in Making Drug Sentencing Fairer*, posed several pivotal questions: Whether the pardon power should be used as a tool for balancing unfair sentencing laws in the criminal justice system? Should clemency in this context become customary? Is there a viable pardon process that can be used? If the pardon power is exercised regularly, how do we ensure fair and nondiscriminatory procedures? Are governors setting an example at the state level for how pardon powers should be used?

I strategically placed Professor Mark Osler, whom I hoped to be the savior of the clemency expansion concept, as part of a slate of experts convened to consider these questions.

To my relief, the briefing was a slam dunk. In addition to Osler, panelists and keynoters included former Obama White House Counsel, Greg Craig, who called for reform of the clemency process during his tenure; former Maryland Governor Robert Ehrlich, who used his clemency power on a customary basis in his state; and, former Clinton Administration Pardon Attorney, Margaret Love, who authored an authoritative text on the reinvigoration of this executive power.

Also joining the briefing was *Pro Publica's* Senior Reporter Dafna Lindsey, who had recently uncovered evidence of dysfunction and discrimination at the Office of the Pardon Attorney. And to round out the briefing, I included American University constitutional scholar Professor Jeffrey Crouch; my "ride or die" partner in crime, Jesselyn McCurdy from the ACLU; and, Cedric Parker, the brother of Eugenia Jennings – his sister being the only person at that time who had been granted clemency by President Obama.

Although Kanya and I had no idea what might happen, we stepped out, as my colleague Dr. Ron Daniels of the Institute of the Black World 21st Century says, on "guts and faith." I pulled out all stops to popularize the idea of using a Ford-style clemency board as a remedy for relief for those not impacted by the new crack law. Mark Osler was, indeed, my savior. Being a Washington insider with critical contacts, I also had something he was missing, and needed.

Mark and I made a great and diverse team. Several times earlier I had spoken with Tino Cuellar, Special Assistant to the President for Justice and Regulatory Policy, about criminal justice policy reform. He left the White House before I had the opportunity to discuss this emerging prospect for reform. Tino was replaced by Tonya Robinson, an African American attorney who reminded me that we originally met when she was a new staffer with Senator Biden years earlier while I was working on the crack issue during my time at the ACLU.

I introduced Mark to Tonya and the three of us had several meetings or, in White House parlance, "listening sessions." Tonya was a great listener, very polite, and seemingly interested in our appeals but, characteristic of White House staff, totally discrete and noncommittal. It was frustrating. We essentially handed the Administration a model toolkit for execution of a clemency process, complete with a sample Executive Order and a Presidential Proclamation Mark drafted.

However, we could get no hint, signal or other intelligence from our courteous but cautious White House official. We did, however, glean that concern about the cost of implementing such a board may be a stickler. President Ford was not confronted with that concern; he had discretionary funds which obviated the need for Congressional approval. President Obama, on the other hand, already battling Republicans in Congress, would likely have an insurmountable barrier getting a commission approved that would cut short drug sentences, no matter how meritorious the case.

By now, coalition partners of the Justice Roundtable were firmly on board with a Ford-style clemency review commission concept. It made sense, and the coalition initiated a broad-based sign-on letter, demonstrating widespread support for the concept. I organized several meetings at the White House for Justice Roundtable working group leaders to meet Tonya and formally present our clemency review board sign-on letter and educate her to the working group priorities. The meetings were good, but it was unclear whether we were making any headway. Our White House listening sessions, nevertheless, continued.

With a foot now in Washington, Mark initiated other high-level meetings even, I understand, surreptitiously leaving a copy of the voluminous Ford Clemency Board report manual in the office of Vice President Biden. Tonya left the White House in 2014, replaced by Roy Austin, Deputy Assistant to the President for Urban Affairs, Justice and Opportunity, who I interacted with on a variety of issues until the end of the Obama Administration.

In the realm of clemency, it seemed as if the entreaties of Mark and myself were falling on deaf ears, and precious time was ticking as people continued to languish unjustly in prison under an outdated and disgraced law. And then it happened: a break.

Chapter Nine, Section 5
Commutations, The Vision Unfolds

In December 2013, President Obama commuted the sentences of eight people serving harsh prison terms on crack cocaine convictions. This was momentous, however the eight commutations represented only the tip of the iceberg of cases left behind when the Fair Sentencing Act became law.

The Justice Roundtable coalition applauded President Obama for using his clemency power to achieve the important public policy goal of bringing attention to those still imprisoned from a policy nearly universally discredited as unfair, inconsistent, and fiscally unsound. However, because of the sheer volume of the cases and the impracticality of the current manner of processing, we again strongly urged the President to establish a review board to vet the old crack cocaine cases languishing in the beleaguered Office of the Pardon Attorney, so it could make appropriate recommendations for clemency.

Clarence Aaron, whose name the Justice Roundtable had elevated for years and was the star of Dafna Lindsay's *Pro Publica* exposé, was one of the eight people serving lengthy mandatory punishments for drug offenses who had their sentence commutated by President Obama that December. Norman Brown, who would later dine with President Obama, was another. Now, instead of dying in prison, they and six others had a second chance for a productive life.

In an interview, I stressed a broader approach. "The Obama administration has recognized that we over-incarcerate, over-punish, and essentially throw away the key," I reflected. "I am indeed ecstatic with these eight commutations, but a more direct path to correct the flaws of drug law sentencing is through a systematic exercise of the clemency power, similar to the drug and anti-war commutations of the past century." I concluded by asserting, "President Obama should follow the path established by Presidents Kennedy, Ford, Carter and Clinton who, with the stroke of their pens, sought to right historical wrongs through widespread clemency."

Two months later, in February 2014, President Obama's Deputy Attorney General James Cole announced a groundbreaking clemency initiative to adjust certain outdated sentences of deserving candidates, using the President's power to commute or shorten prison terms. "For our criminal justice system to be effective, it needs to not only be fair; but it also must be perceived as being fair," Cole stated. "Older, stringent punishments that are out of line with sentences imposed under today's laws erode people's confidence in our criminal justice system, and I am confident that this initiative will go far to promote the most fundamental of American ideals – equal justice under law."

The cornerstone of the initiative were candidates sentenced under archaic laws that had since been overturned and were no longer seen as appropriate. This included people who did not benefit from the reduction in law around crack cocaine because it was not retroactive, as well as those unable to benefit from other major changes in sentencing policy over the past several decades.

This was a major and welcomed expansion from the approach limited to crack cases I was advocating in support of, and an inspiring reminder to me to never limit potential remedies. Although we handed Tonya the fruit of our advocacy on this issue on a silver platter, briefed Roy, met with other officials, and educated the media, Professor Osler and I never had a clue as to whether the concept of a clemency commission was ever taken seriously. I cannot prove that this new clemency initiative was the Administration's response to our advocacy, but in my mind, how could it have been otherwise?

Criteria for the cases, however, were limited to consideration of candidates who had served at least ten years, were low level and non-violent, and had a clean prison record with no significant gang-related ties. Rather than implementing a Ford-style review board or commission, the Department of Justice appealed to the legal community to assist in the identification and vetting of petitions, and identified five organizations – National Association of Criminal Defense Lawyers, American Bar Association, American Civil Liberties Union, Federal Public Defenders and Families Against Mandatory Minimums – to coordinate the screening of candidates and the training of those interested in preparing commutation petitions. I was thrilled when an African American senior attorney from Georgia, Cynthia Roseberry, was hired as Executive Director of the five-member organization coalition, named the Clemency Project 2014.

Over 35,000 prisoners ultimately answered the call for pro bono representation for relief from their unjust sentences. Despite its limitations, with his historic clemency initiative, President Obama did exactly what our breakfast briefing two years earlier advocated: he reimagined the policy discussion around widespread incarceration and the proper role the Office of the President could play to alleviate harsh punishments via clemency, to bring balance to a justice system that for decades had meted out extraordinarily lengthy sentences that often had not fit the crime. The executive focus he initiated on classes of people adversely impacted by unduly harsh sentencing policies injected urgency into the national discourse over mass incarceration.

With the Clemency Project 2014 in full swing, I felt it would bring value to the movement if the human faces of clemency were highlighted and lifted up. In 2015, I reached out to my White House colleagues, Roy Austin and Stephanie Young, to gauge their interest in co-sponsoring an event to honor President Obama's Clemency

Initiative. I suggested it be titled, "Redemption, Reconciliation and Reentry: Honoring President Obama's Clemency Initiative." I recommended March 31, 2016, because that date would coincide with a national convening Mark Osler was hosting in Washington, D.C., of organizations and law school clinics involved in clemency efforts.

I told them the purpose of the event would be to honor the White House's Clemency Initiative and the people who had been released. I wanted to uplift their stories as well as the stories of those assisting them to reintegrate into society, such as family members, housing providers, employers, faith advisors, mentors, etc. I pledged that the Open Society Foundations would fly in targeted commutation recipients to share their journeys since release. I told them I had reserved a room at the National Press Club building for such an event, but would love to partner with the White House and hold the event in the South Court Auditorium on the grounds of the White House, if possible.

I recommended that the commutation recipients we bring to Washington have the opportunity to share their narratives, along with remarks by President Obama, Valerie Jarrett, White House Counsel Neil Eggleston, Pardon Attorney Deborah Leff, and Attorney General Loretta Lynch, among others. I stressed that it would be good if there were an opportunity for commutation recipients to be flanked by President Obama as he executes a mock or real signing of the letters awardees personally received from him. Finally, I stressed that the Justice Roundtable coalition would do the necessary footwork to make the event a success for the Administration.

The White House, being forever secretive and non-communicative, would not give me a definitive answer, causing me concern. I knew we had to identify candidates, book airfare, block hotel rooms, and everything else associated with coordinating a large event. I was frustrated.

My husband and I were blessed to attend the Obama's annual Christmas Party at the White House. Before leaving I spotted Ashley Allison, deputy director in the White House's Office of Public Engagement. After catching her attention and engaging in small talk, I repeated my spiel on the importance of a high-level clemency gathering at the White House, and asked about the status of my proposal. Ashley, with true White House guardedness, merely stated that it was being considered, but I was encouraged by her huge smile and the twinkle in her eye.

It was hard to determine who would be the White House person to make such a colossal undertaking happen, until Elias Alcantara came to my attention. Elias was Senior Associate Director in the Office of Intergovernmental Affairs. He and I began to exchange emails, a firm date was established, and the pivotal event was shaping up.

Although the final program differed somewhat from my original conceptualization, it was a dream come true. The White House titled the March 31, 2016 event "Life After Clemency," and my assistant, Jasmine Mickens, and I proceeded with the mammoth task of coordinating the travel and logistics for invited attendees as well as interfacing with the Federal Bureau of Prisons to insure permission for those on parole to travel.

My only strong request was that the White House coordinate with the Secret Service to either abandon its policy of requiring red badges for those deemed a security risk (i.e., which included anyone with a criminal conviction), or to adopt a policy for that day requiring everyone to don the red badge, thereby eliminating any distinction between the formerly incarcerated and never incarcerated. The request was granted.

I worked closely with Elias to insure the success of the White House Clemency Summit. At some point, it was clear to me that something secretive was going to happen during this process, but I had no clue what it was. Unbeknownst to me, I helped facilitate a secret luncheon for clemency recipients President Obama and his senior advisor Valerie Jarrett were planning at D.C.'s Busboys and Poets, an upscale restaurant owned by entrepreneur Andy Shallal, who had a positive history of hiring formerly incarcerated people.

Because of all the secrecy, I had presumed there was going to be a meeting with President Obama, but I thought it was going to be in the Oval Office. Never in my wildest dreams would I have imagined the creative way in which this historic meeting would occur. Although disappointed because there was no indication that I was to be included in whatever was being planned, I did my best to satisfy the White House's desires. Elias asked which clemency recipients the Open Society Foundations would be flying in for the "Life After Clemency" event. I gave him some of the names we were exploring.

Elias sounded happy when I named Ramona Brant. His reaction was the same with my recommendations of Norman Brown and Kemba Smith. He asked if Angie Jenkins was on the list.

I gulped. "Yes, I think she is."

Angie was one of the names Clinton-era commutation recipient Amy Povah had previously given me as a possible person to bring to Washington, but Angie lived in Oregon and getting her to D.C. sounded like it might be a logistical nightmare. When Elias mentioned her name, I knew I had to make the trip happen. He also asked about George W. Bush-era commutee Phillip Emmert, to which I said I could make that happen too. The same with Clinton commutee, Serena Nunn. The four of them joined

Norman Brown and Michael Short, who were local, and Kemba Smith, who was already confirmed to come to town.

Elias' instructions were definitive. "Make sure they are in D.C. by the morning of March 30th. Make sure they know what White House security entrance to go in. Make sure they are on time."

I went to the airport to pick up Angie Jenkins the evening before. I will never forget the amazed look on her face when she approached my makeshift sign with her name on it. We hugged. She was so very thrilled and excited. After being incarcerated for nearly 18 years, this was her very first flight and it was indeed a logistical nightmare to get her from the West coast to a layover half-way across the country, and then on to Washington, D.C. But she weathered the storm admirably.

Upon entering her plush hotel room, Angie just kept twirling around the room, repeating over and over, "I feel just like Cinderella. I feel just like Cinderella!"

My husband was the designated driver to pick up Ramona Brant and Serena Nunn, the last commutees to arrive, both arriving late the following morning. He had instructions to drop the women off at the White House security guard's entrance on 17th Street. Ramona's flight, however, was delayed.

Little did I know that the five commutation recipients were already in the White House Roosevelt Room. President Obama had just surprised them, bursting open the door with the greeting, "How's everyone doing?" And then, after the shock and amazement wore off, he continued, "I have a little spare time, so let's go out to eat!"

Elias called me to ask for the driver's phone number, which I gave. Rather than take them to the guard's entrance, the driver was instructed to transport Ramona and Serena to the Busboys and Poets restaurant on 14th Street, Northwest. My husband (the driver) told me later, "Busboys and Poets? I thought that was strange, but of course I didn't question the White House."

Now it would have been great if my hubby had called to give me the heads up that there was a change in the drop-off logistics instructions. I might have "just happened" to saunter over to 14th and V Street for lunch at the opportune time but, alas, he did not.

The seven who were selected by the President to join him for a private discussion at Busboys and Poets had a unique and once-in-a-lifetime opportunity to engage in dialogue with the country's Chief Executive.

Norman Brown walked out of prison in 2015, after being granted clemency by President Obama. Norman is not a super predator.[103] He is a grateful, enthusiastic, hard-working man who spent over two decades of his life behind bars. He is a man whose mother, father and grandmother all passed during his incarceration. He is a man who left behind an infant daughter when he was locked up. He is a man dedicated to reaching back and helping those still in prison, equally deserving of clemency, and equally deserving of the benefit of a change in laws that allow people to be ware-housed without a second look.

President Obama queried the seven and asked whether they felt they were the exception, whether they were that different. They all answered emphatically, "No."

"We left behind people like us who are as deserving or better," Norman said. The diners emphasized that they were far from unique, but representative of thousands of others who likewise deserve a second chance.

Valerie Jarrett, who was present in both the Roosevelt Room and at the lunch meeting, described the experience at the "Life After Clemency" White House event the following day: "They told their stories with grace and honesty. There was not a dry eye in the room." That same afternoon came the announcement of an additional 61 commutations by President Obama. I was thrilled, yet bittersweet as a name I was constantly seeking was not on the list.

Because the March 31st White House convening was invitation-only and closed to the press, the Justice Roundtable hosted a wraparound series of events to allow for fuller participation and permit the media an opportunity to interview and interact with the formerly incarcerated people who had been granted clemency, as well as with other formerly incarcerated people, and family members of those still behind bars.

We hosted a fabulous welcome reception the evening of March 30th. Formerly incarcerated people and family members of those hoping to be released made critical connections with the Washington advocacy community and White House staff. Andrea James wowed a packed audience in the South Court Auditorium earlier that day in an armchair discussion with Valerie Jarrett as part of a "Women and the Criminal Justice System" convening.

I met Andrea in 2013 at a forum sponsored by the Institute of the Black World (IBW) 21st Century that was part of a Drug Policy Alliance conference in Colorado. I was already familiar with her book, *Upper Bunkies Unite*, but when she burst into the IBW session, with children, fundraising dish towels and potholders in tow, I knew that this sister was about business. We established a warm relationship, and she brought her sisterhood crew to the Washington convenings held March 30-31, 2016. She was in the process of building what would become a powerful organization, the National Council for Incarcerated and Formerly Incarcerated Women and Girls.

The Justice Roundtable hosted a *Conversations on Justice* event the morning of the White House's "Life After Clemency" convening. This affair featured formerly incarcerated Shaka Senghor, author of the newly released memoir, *Writing My Wrongs*. Van Jones, CNN political commentator and founder of the organization, #Cut50 introduced Shaka, who had recently appeared on Oprah Winfrey's Super Soul Sunday show.

The Roundtable's finale was a special, invitation-only banquet dinner directly after the White House convening, hosted by Google and compliments of my long-time colleague, Malika Saada Saar. This was her first criminal justice gala event at Google after recently being hired to lead the tech company's civil and human rights policy agenda. The genius of these Justice Roundtable-hosted, wraparound events is that they brought together people from different locales across the country into one space. These events were often the catalyst for critical relationship-building that seeded and sprouted initiatives that bear fruit today.

The Presidential commutation recipients we convened in Washington to participate in the two days of historic clemency activity represented several Presidential Administrations. The sentences of Clarence Aaron, Ramona Brant, Norman Brown, Eugene Haywood, Jason Hernandez, Angie Jenkins, Sharanda Jones, Rickey McCall, Alton Mills, Rudolph Norris, Shauna Barry-Scott and Reynolds Wintersmith were all commuted by President Obama.

The sentences of Phillip Emmert and John Forte were commuted by President George W. Bush. And the prison terms of Dorothy Gaines, Serena Nunn, Amy Povah, Michael Short, and Kemba Smith were commuted by President Clinton. Roach Brown's blessing came from President Gerald Ford.

Family members of commutation applicants were there awaiting decision by the President. Those who joined our activities included Beth Curtis, whose brother was serving a life sentence for pot; Tretessa Johnson and Catina Scales, daughters of Alice Marie Johnson who was serving a life without parole sentence for drug conspiracy; Jasmine Mickens, whose brother was imprisoned; Venessa Rosa, whose sister received clemency that weekend; Anthony, Ebony and Miko Underwood, whose father was serving life without parole for drug conspiracy; Rudy Valdez, whose sister was serving life without parole and later produced a film about time on the outside, *The Sentence*; and Miquelle West, who sought to generate attention on behalf of her imprisoned mom, Michelle West.

On that beautiful March afternoon, the group strolled leisurely down the street from the Open Society Foundations' office on Pennsylvania Avenue N.W. to the White House security gate. You could feel the exhilaration and anticipation in the air. People gathered who never thought they would again experience life outside of prison, and who were now walking alongside advocates whose life's work had been about ensuring this very freedom.

Adult children of incarcerated parents patiently waited in the White House security line with the anxious hope that someone would hear their pleas for mercy for their loved ones. Film crews followed clusters of people, documenting their commentaries and movements. Little did anyone know that Tretessa and Catina's mother, Alice Marie Johnson, serving a life without parole sentence, would be coming home within two years, the result of intervention by celebrity Kim Kardashian who took her plea for clemency to President Trump.

It was indeed an historic convening inside the South Court Auditorium on the grounds of the White House, which provided a collaborative environment for not only commutation recipients but also for so many others. Formerly incarcerated people, senior Administration officials, academicians, private sector stakeholders, and the advocacy community all came together to discuss ways to improve paths to reentry for the formerly incarcerated and help improve their lives upon returning to their communities.

Elias Alcantara was the master of ceremonies for an afternoon chock full of featured speakers that included White House Counsel Neil Eggleston, Deputy Attorney General Sally Yates, Assistant Attorney General Karol Mason, Clemency Project 2014 Director Cynthia Roseberry, Professor Mark Osler and Professor Mike Romano.

Perhaps the highlight of the day was the panel moderated by Deputy Assistant to the President, Roy Austin, which featured commutation recipients Ramona Brant, Norman Brown, Rudolph Norris, and Shauna Barry-Scott. They shared moving stories of the difficulties they faced securing housing and employment, re-establishing relationships with loved ones, often after decades of separation, and having to learn to maneuver technological advances such as mobile phones, the internet, ATMs and self-flushing toilets. Valerie Jarrett's moving remarks during the event stressed the importance of personal stories, where she reminded us, "that's how change happens in this country."

The "Life After Clemency" convening began with Elias inviting all those who had received a commutation of sentence to stand and be acknowledged. The room erupted in thunderous applause, and the event ended with an outstanding performance by Fugees producer and rapper, John Forte, who himself received clemency in 2008 from President George W. Bush.

I was once asked by someone if I were to do it all over again, what would I have done differently. My response, "I would have adhered to my initial vision and had President Obama come out on stage, seated behind a desk, with formerly incarcerated people that he granted commutation to, stand surrounding him as he began the signing of thousands of clemency petitions. And I would have opened the White House 'Life After Clemency' convening up to the media so that its significance would be forever enshrined in the nation's consciousness."

Chapter Nine, Section 6
Redemption, Mercy and a Slam Dunk RadioThon

Rhozier "Roach" Brown, an icon in the Washington, D.C. community, is the epitome of redemption and mercy. He is someone who made a mistake, was given a second chance, and when he made a mistake again, he was given a third chance. Because of the chances he was given, the community has been richer as a result.

He heartily greets everyone with the phrase, "Merry Christmas," regardless of the season or time of year. As he explains, "It reminds me of all the good and bad things that have happened in my life around the holidays." It was Christmastime in 1975 when President Ford commuted his 20-year-to-life sentence to 30 years, making him immediately eligible for parole.

Roach, who grew up poor in the alleys of D.C. with no plumbing or electricity, once explained to me that he received his nickname as a young boy because he had a reputation of being "so stubborn and hard to get rid of." And it was this tenacity that ultimately resulted in the commutation of his life sentence.

In prison, as part of his transformation from drug addict to community activist, Roach founded the Inner Voices, a theater troupe which performed plays he had written about the horror and humor of prison life. His work with the Inner Voices garnered so much goodwill and trust that the men were granted furloughs to leave the Lorton Reformatory over 1,500 times to perform throughout the country.

The company even came to the attention of the U.S. Senator from Massachusetts, Ed Brooke, a Black Republican who befriended the prison play-wright, and assisted him in getting clemency from President Ford. Roach Brown, however, was no angel

– he'd been convicted of murder in a robbery gone bad, sold drugs to an undercover agent and, most shamefully, embezzled $45,000 that was to go to a children's charity. Since the commutation of his sentence in 1975, and despite these other crimes which landed him back in prison before his final release, he made invaluable contributions to the community during his releases. He has testified before Congress; directed a performance by the Inner Voices for members of the Senate; served as a special Mayoral assistant; won acclaim at the New York, Sundance and Cannes Film Festivals; produced a television news show and radio show that he still hosts today; designed a drug prevention program for the Embassy of Ghana; registered formerly incarcerated people to vote; and, helped to feed thousands of needy D.C. residents throughout the years on Christmas Day.

Although they knew about Roach Brown and the fact that he had been granted clemency by President Ford, I understood, yet disagreed with why President Obama likely declined to include him as part of his historic Busboys and Poets luncheon. Roach was the opposite of squeaky clean. He had been a heroin addict, and later a crack addict. But, more egregiously, he had been convicted of a violent crime – murder. He had also engaged in fraud.

But, if we are to really significantly reduce the prison population and end mass incarceration, we all must find the courage to move beyond the mantra of the first-time, non-violent drug offender. Including Roach in the lineup of Presidential clemency recipients would not only have included another presidency, it would have also demonstrated that America is not afraid of what traditionally has been deemed the "harder cases," and that change is possible.

As convener of the Justice Roundtable Coalition, I teamed up with Roach Brown, host of WPFW-FM's *Crossroads* radio show, to co-host the first ever National Clemency and Criminal Justice Reform Radiothon. This half-day show was broadcast on the 45th anniversary of the unceremonious declaration by then-President Richard Nixon of drug abuse as public enemy #1. Shortly after this June 18, 1971 proclamation, the media popularized the term, the "War on Drugs." We now know that this war on drugs was a stratagem for criminalizing Black people and critics of the Viet Nam war and has today resulted in the mass incarceration of over two million people.

The purpose of our Justice Radiothon was two-fold: 1) to spotlight and give voice to the men, women and families who had been impacted by mass incarceration, and 2) to examine various strategies in the criminal justice reform toolbox that could be used to provide relief, including executive clemency, legislative reform, compassionate release, judicial second look mechanisms, and reentry.

For the past 45 years, the media had played a huge role in fanning the flames of the horrific war on drugs. We challenged the media and policymakers to listen to the featured speakers in the Radiothon and use the personal stories and educational information as an important part of narrative change, with the goal of reuniting families and strengthening communities.

Clemency expert Mark Osler participated throughout the day with us in the studio. Veteran WPFW anchors Askia Muhammad and Gloria Minott added their special flavor. This first-ever, six-hour radio focus on clemency and criminal justice reform was chock full of change-makers. Judiciary Committee ranking member Rep. John Conyers called in to make remarks, and D.C.'s Congresswoman Eleanor Holmes Norton dropped by the radio station to announce her bill calling on the President to delegate clemency authority for D.C. prisoners to the District's Mayor, as D.C. has no governor to play that critical role.

Celebrities MC Hammer, Keith Sweat, Adam Rodriguez, Lamman Rucker and Maria McDonald called in to stress the need for sentencing reform and executive clemency.

Calls came in from commutation recipients Norman Brown, Kemba Smith, Amy Povah, Jason Hernandez, Ramona Brant, Shauna Berry-Scott and Sharanda Jones, who joined scores of other formerly incarcerated women and men such as Andrea James, Weldon Angelos, Yango Sawyer, Glenn Martin, Teresa Hodge, Topeka Sam,

and Phyllis Johnson in demanding criminal justice reform.

Alice Marie Johnson, Craig Cesal, Tyrie Bell, Eric Wilson, Ian Shepherd and others called in directly from prison. Family members Ebony and Anthony Underwood, Miquelle West, Tony Lewis, Deborah Cain, Erica Wilson, and Ms. Clementine brought attention to their loved ones languishing behind bars.

Civil rights leaders Wade Henderson (Leadership Conference), Sherrilyn Ifill (NAACP-LDF), Dorian Spence (Lawyers Committee for Civil Rights Under Law), and Sara Totonchi (Southern Center for Human Rights) lent their voices and the power of their organizations.

The voices of the #Cut50 crew, including Shaka Senghor, Matt Haney and Jessica Jackson, were heard. Conservative and Libertarian allies Mark Holden (Koch), Craig DeRoche (Prison Fellowship), and John Malcolm (Heritage) joined in, as did Utah Judge Mark Bennett. Attorneys MiAngel Cody, Rachel Barkow, Kendall Minter, Cynthia Roseberry, Vicki Casanova Willis, Brittany Byrd, Soffiyah Elijah, and Damon Hewitt weighed in. Criminal justice advocates Marc Mauer, Norman Reimer, Marc Schindler, Angelyn Frazer-Giles, Jesselyn McCurdy, Jasmine Tyler, Todd Cox, Karen Garrison and others lent their expertise.

And faith leaders Aundreia Alexander (National Council of Churches) and Kara Gotsch (Interfaith Criminal Justice Coalition) joined those representing special issues to educate the public, such as Meghan Maury (LGBTQ), Dara Baldwin (disability), and Maritza Perez and Jasmine Mickens (crimmigration).[104] Ron Hampton and Damon Jones made their voices heard, representing the views of progressive law enforcement.

The programming reached such a high level of attention that #JusticeRadiothon trended on Twitter, reaching the number two spot in top tags that day. The one bill cited over and over for immediate passage was the Sentencing Reform and Corrections Act (SRCA) pending in the Senate. This was legislation that I worked fervently to pass, along with advocates in the Justice Roundtable.

The need for the President to grant more commutations was also a frequent focus of comments during the Radiothon. Disappointedly, I was unable to interest the White House in officially calling into the Justice Radiothon that day. It was a missed opportunity. The Radiothon gave voice to men, women and families who had been impacted by mass incarceration, and all vowed to step up the pace in support of criminal justice reform.

My work in support of clemency was not an amorphous quest. I had "skin in the game," and, in the words of Equal Justice Initiative founder Bryan Stevenson, I was very "proximate" to the cause. In addition to generally advocating for clemency, engaging in strategic grant making and initiating programs to increase awareness amongst stakeholders and the public at large, I too had answered the call for lawyers to represent clients without fee in their pursuit of executive clemency.

I became the pro bono clemency attorney for two clients, and part of the pro bono advocacy team seeking a posthumous pardon for a third. However, despite my strenuous and passionate work on clemency, I was so very disappointed and frustrated that my advocacy failed to translate into success for my own clients.

Chapter Ten
"Tears of a Clown"[105]

Section 1
Underwood Should Be Home by Now

Somewhere around 1999 I had just finished speaking at an event hosted by the Institute of the Black World 21st Century at Brooklyn's House of the Lord Church, when a young sister approached me about her father's case. Her name was Ebony Underwood. She was a Skadden Arps fellow interested in attending law school. I listened as well as one possibly could while hungry and in a crowded church basement standing in line for a plate of chicken wings and potato salad.

She sounded so sincere talking about her father, the love of her life, who was in prison on a drug charge. The story sounded so compelling, yet so complicated. After I returned to D.C., we emailed back and forth several times and then life took over again. All I recall is feeling so helpless that I could not assist in her quest for justice for her dad. It would be another twelve years before I would again hear the name William Underwood.

An attractive and elegant woman approached me at a forum on mandatory minimum sentences hosted by Congresswoman Maxine Waters during the 2010 Congressional Black Caucus (CBC) Legislative Weekend. She spoke of a friend of hers who she described as being in legal limbo. After trading contact information, I kept seeing Facebook messages pop up in my feed that read, "Underwood should be home by now."

I'm thinking, *What is this? Must be some kid named Underwood who had perhaps stayed out too late and was now lost.* But I kept seeing it and finally clicked the link. It was not a child at all but, rather, an aging man who had been incarcerated since the late 80s. And then I remembered the young sister I met years earlier at the House of the Lord Church.

I looked up the profile of the woman who had approached me during the CBC legislative weekend. It was Maria McDonald, a former model and actress. As I perused her name over the internet, I thought to myself, *Why would someone who has graced the pages of Essence, Vogue and Bazaar, been in movies with Denzel Washington, and appeared on Miami Vice, One Life to Live, and Saturday Night Live, be interested in mandatory minimum sentences?*

The answer came as no surprise. Maria later told me she had been stunned by the discovery that William Underwood, an old friend of hers, had been incarcerated for over 20 years on federal mandatory minimum drug conspiracy charges. She described him as an extraordinary person in the music industry, responsible for discovering, promoting, and managing the careers of several artists during the 1980s.

She said that when she discussed Underwood's plight with her girlfriends in the fashion world, she found that many of them also had loved ones warehoused in prisons under excessively harsh mandatory minimum drug sentencing laws. She started an organization, Cover Girls for Change, and became an ardent advocate for the cause.

Again, I became quite proximate, and got to know the Underwood family – first the eldest, Anthony, who was 18 when his father was arrested. Then Ebony, who I had previously met in New York, their sister Miko, and then the youngest, Justin, who was only five-years old when he traumatically witnessed their father being arrested. I invited Mr. Underwood's now-grown children to come to Washington on numerous occasions, to Justice Roundtable assemblies, to the White House, Department of Justice, Congress, advocacy meetings, and vigils.

It was another four years before the Obama Clemency Initiative was born, but as soon as the Initiative was announced, I felt that their father's case was the type of case that commutation was made for. His was a case for mercy, justice, sentence correction and a second chance. His 1990 conviction was his first and only felony conviction. The law that he was convicted under had changed and, if sentenced today, he likely would not have received a life sentence without the possibility of parole. Despite being incarcerated for over a quarter of a century, he maintained a pristine institutional record. Any tie he had to any type of criminal activity was buried in the distant past.

As an elder, Mr. Underwood had been a mentor and positive influence to many youth in prison. He was a changed man with adult children and grandchildren who had never seen him outside prison walls. He deeply regretted the negative impact the behavior in his prior life has had. However, despite having completed a concurrent twenty-year sentence, the life without parole ruling had, essentially, condemned him to die in prison.

Because Mr. Underwood had once been affiliated with a gang and had a conviction which included violence, he did not fit within the strict contours of the Clemency Initiative's mandate, so, like many other attorneys with similar cases, I represented him outside of that process.

I prepared an impressive clemency package, including letters representing a groundswell of support for his immediate release from members of the community, professionals in the music and entertainment industries, scholars, civil rights and conservative leaders and formerly incarcerated mentees. NBA Hall of Famer Earl "The Pearl" Monroe, who knew Mr. Underwood during the 1980s and witnessed his concern and generosity to the needs of youth, stated, "I think Mr. Underwood has served a significant part of his life rehabilitating himself for the better and needs to be with his family, his friends and others who have been deprived of his presence for so long."

Actor Adam Rodriguez from the hit television series, *CSI Miami* and *Empire* wrote, "In the twenty-plus years that I have known him, I have seen a man who has made every effort possible to maintain a strong relationship with his children…I hope you will grant this family, my friends, a chance to pick up their dad/granddad and experience the joy of bringing him to a place they can all call home again."

Rhythm and Blues sensation Johnny Gill wrote, "For over 30 years I have been a successful artist and am now a proud owner of a music label. This is a testament of me getting educated early on from Bill. People often use the words, genius and brilliant, to describe someone…Bill, however, is beyond brilliant and a genius…I would love to have the opportunity to have Bill as part of my advisory team. It would not only provide him with stability, but his guidance and creative genius would be an asset to my company." Maria McDonald poignantly appealed to President Obama, "When does punishment become abuse? When does abuse become inhumane and holocaustic? When is enough, enough?"

Perhaps the most heartfelt appeals for release came from his children, now adults, with children of their own. His eldest son Anthony, wrote:

> President Obama I'm not going to tell you about what type of man my father is because there are letters…speaking to that…instead what I am going to tell you is how a beautiful young woman did a photo shoot – at the young age of 4 and began an 8-year relationship with Nickelodeon. At the age of 8 she starred with the late Gregory Hines, Vanessa Williams, Patti LaBelle, Tom Joyner, and the late Eartha Kitt…At age 11 she starred as Lil' Inez in the first national tour of the musical, "Hairspray"… while maintaining an "A" average in school…she was given free vocal lessons by the great Seth Riggs…because of her 7 octave range. Then sadly, at age 16, she started to…show signs of mental illness, which ultimately led to her abuse of drugs and alcohol. The "her" I have been referring to is my daughter – my father's only granddaughter…I know in my heart if my Dad was home, my daughter would soon be on the road to recovery. So forget about the legal aspect, the humane aspect and the fairness. I'm asking you as one father to another, please grant my Dad clemency so I can save my daughter.

William Underwood's eldest daughter, Ebony, wrote:

> Although he did not have the ability to attend any of our school graduations, visit us in our own homes or witness the births of our children, he remains a committed father. For example…the day after I delivered my son, my Dad had a big beautiful bouquet of flowers sent to my hospital room with a special note. I cried. He sends birthday cards, Valentine's Day cards, Mother's Day cards and Christmas cards and he calls us almost every day. He has even developed and maintained a solid connection with his grand children despite never once meeting them outside prison walls. He empowers us all to continue to educate ourselves. At times, he even informs us about the latest current events and technology…he is really fascinated with nano technology…President Obama is the only one who can grant my father relief through clemency…Any day our Dad comes home will be Father's Day for us.

Ebony, a filmmaker, produced a video, *Home for Father's Day*, and a website in support of their father. The family generated hash tags and garnered over 71,000 signatures on a Change.org petition. What I thought would be the icing on the cake was the strong support of Senator Cory Booker, who had the opportunity to personally converse at length with William Underwood during a visit at the Fairton, New Jersey Federal Correctional Institution.

"The man that stood before me was an intelligent, capable, dedicated father, and an atoned man," the Senator wrote in an Instagram post after the meeting. "He has accepted responsibility for his crime. America is the land of second chances. It's time we lived up to that and show mercy to a man who has served almost three decades in prison."

Senator Booker and many others, including the African American Mayors' Association, the Executives' Alliance for Boys and Men of Color, conservative and civil rights leaders, scholars, and people in the entertainment industry, continue to deeply support a second chance for William Underwood through clemency or, in the alternative, a release date so that his life sentence does not become a death sentence.

So what was the glitch? Why did William Underwood remain incarcerated at the close of the Obama Administration? Although it's the million-dollar question on the lips of all those denied clemency, the answer in this case is likely the twin evils of the nature of his conviction, coupled with the intransigence of prosecutors to have mercy. Mr. Underwood was charged with conspiracy counts containing homicides for which he received a 20-year concurrent sentence. Importantly, he successfully completed serving that sentence in 2008.

However, he seems to forever be saddled with a continuing criminal enterprise (CCE) conviction – a drug charge that keeps him imprisoned for life. Mr. Underwood has always stated that it was the jury in his case that should have decided when his involvement in the conspiracy ended, not the judge. If his involvement was found to have ended prior to the advent of the U.S. Sentencing Guidelines,[106] pre-Guidelines law would have prevailed, and the district court would have had discretion to impose a prison term between 10 years and life, as opposed to life without parole.

Evidence exists that supports Mr. Underwood's claim that his involvement in the enterprise did not continue beyond the effective date of the Federal Sentencing Guidelines and, as such, the jury should have had the opportunity to consider this evidence.

For example, his lack of criminal activity was even noted by a Federal Bureau of Investigation document dated April 21, 1986, under the subject line "William R. Underwood," stating…"(d)ue to the lack of current updated information concerning subject's alleged activities, this case is being closed at this time."

Mr. Underwood was nevertheless arrested two-and-a-half years later and charged with a continuing leadership role in a narcotics conspiracy, despite his assertions that he was engaged in a legitimate full-time career in the music industry. Ironically, had Underwood only been convicted of the specific counts involving violence, he would be a free man today. It is the CCE count that has kept him behind bars.

"President Obama," I argued in the clemency papers. "You have commuted the sentences of at least 14 people with the same CCE conviction. They were given a second chance to reunite with their families and rebuild their lives; Mr. Underwood should as well."

Despite the constant lip service to the contrary, I have come to the painful realization that violence and claims of public safety are really not the issue. For if that were true, prosecutors would not so readily make deals with violent and dangerous people, letting them back into communities in exchange for them providing information on others.

I conceded in the clemency papers that the charges of Bill Underwood's conviction were serious and a lengthy prison term was likely warranted. But I argued that the sentence he received on Count 4, life without the possibility of parole, was not warranted and would most likely not have been imposed had he been tried just a bit earlier or years later. "Ironically," I stated, "Even foreign nationals convicted in the United States under the Foreign Narcotics Kingpin Designation Act have a limit of a maximum 30-year prison term as opposed to life without parole."

The clemency petition stressed his continued incarceration in federal prisons under antiquated laws, and his squeaky clean institutional record as a model prisoner. "Mr. President," I concluded, "We implore you to take a look at the attached clemency petition and memorandum and, with justice, mercy and compassion, use your Constitutional power to set William R. Underwood free and actualize the dreams, hopes and prayers of his children and grandchildren."

Despite the compelling merits of the case, my submission, proximity to White House staff and related advocacy, my appeals on behalf of William Underwood fell on deaf ears. Although it has been stated that the President reviews every clemency petition, I don't even know if the petition actually got to his desk. Or, as rumor alleges, whether petitions like his are blocked from advancing past the door of the Department of Justice.

Chapter Ten, Section 2
The Voice of Jamaica

Another pro bono clemency client was Mark Myrie, also known as Buju Banton, an internationally acclaimed Grammy Award-winning reggae recording star, pegged as one of the most important musical voices to come out of Jamaica since Bob Marley. His was a music that transcended generations, race and time, maturing from songs that glorified vulgarity and promiscuity to those that offered spiritually uplifting messages of inner peace and social justice.

I incorporated as part of his clemency package letter after letter which spoke of his humbleness, his exemplary reputation and humanitarian work, and his cultural contributions to society. Because of his musical genius, inspirational lyrics and remarkable public service, he became known as the "Voice of Jamaica" with an impact extending to fans all over the world.

His songs resonated with the daily experiences of the Jamaican people and their sufferings and triumphs. In 1992, he broke Bob Marley's record for having the greatest number of hit singles in a year. In February 2011, days after winning a Grammy for Best Reggae Album for his 2010 recording, "Before the Dawn," his spectacular career was cut short upon his conviction on a drug charge that smacked of entrapment.

Despite all the above, I am almost ashamed to admit that I had never heard of him. I've said before that I'm not the hippest person in the world, and definitely not the sharpest knife in the drawer when it comes to popular culture. So how was it that I happened to represent him on his clemency case?

Several years earlier I received a call from Brother Attorney Chokwe Lumumba to see if I could secure a location for a press conference he was holding in D.C.

"Sure, Chokwe, what's the press conference about?"

"Nkechi, I'm representing Buju Banton."

"Who?"

"Buju, he's like a young Bob Marley."

Feeling ignorant, I called my daughter. "Mariama, have you heard of Buju Banton?"

"Of course, Mom. You're so square!"

I secured a viable location at the United Methodist Building, across the street from the Supreme Court. Brother Chokwe, along with Rita Marley's aide, Rosemary Duncan, organized an impressive press conference which included Stephen Marley on the panel, which I also joined. Buju's confidante and singer, Gramps Morgan, spoke on behalf of the brotherhood that all three men shared. He stated, "I'm Gramps and I'm standing  here for him. Next to me is Stephen Marley, the king of reggae's son. He's put up the roof over his head in support of Myrie aka Buju Banton." Also to speak was the Buju Banton Defense Committee led by Brother Aula Sumbry.

Elation was soon followed shortly afterwards by despair. Joyously, Brother Chokwe was elected as Mayor of Jackson, MS, but a year later, prematurely and tragically, he transitioned. In the interim, Buju was represented by Professor Charles Ogletree. It was shortly thereafter that I received a phone call from Rosemary.

"Greetings, Nkechi, can you represent Mark?"

"Rosemary, I'm so sorry, but I'm not in private practice. I do policy advocacy before Congress and the Executive Branch and don't take individual cases."

"Nkechi is there anything you can do? Mark really needs help."

"Well, I have been very involved in issues of clemency. Rosemary, if he is interested, I could consider representing him to see if President Obama would shorten his sentence by granting him clemency."

And that's how I came to put my best effort forward to prepare a clemency package for Buju Banton.

On July 26, 2009, while on an international flight to Miami after completion of a world music tour, my client was befriended by a paid undercover informant seated next to him in first class who captivated him with music connections and promises of huge record deals. They talked incessantly of music, women, movies and family. Continuously plied with alcoholic beverages, my client falsely boasted of experience in the illicit drug trade. He later testified, "I never intended to follow through on any drug buy. I lit the fire and had to feed the fire. I was talking the talk, but I didn't walk the walk. I was boasting a lot, drinking a lot."

Over the next six months, the undercover agent who had been paid over $3 million in taxpayer dollars over the course of his career as a confidential informant, tried unsuccessfully to convince him to purchase cocaine. In the end, Buju never did purchase cocaine, but was convicted of conspiracy based on the actions of others purchasing cocaine in a police-controlled drug warehouse. The first jury was deadlocked 7-5 in favor of his acquittal and ended in a mistrial. In a February 2011 retrial, however, the jury found him guilty, and he was sentenced to ten years in prison.

The Drug Enforcement Agency testified at trial that they investigated him for almost one year and found no evidence of any drug dealings, and the prosecution acknowledged that he put no money in the deal and did not profit from it. So why was he in this situation?

There was buzz that the singer was stressed and vulnerable due to the recent death of his mother. There was buzz that there may have been a vendetta against him as the result of past lyrics. There was buzz that he was entrapped and set up. And, on top of all the buzz, my client's case was tainted by illegal conduct by the jury foreperson, who herself was convicted of contempt of court.

I argued that the interests of justice would not be served by his continued incarceration, which cost U.S. taxpayers nearly $30,000 a year. I begged the President to have mercy and release him so he may resume the financial support of his family, foundation and other beneficiaries, and continue providing musical inspiration to his fans.

I argued that as an extraordinary recording star who made a foolish mistake, he has already paid an enormous price through immense public humiliation, immeasurable loss of pride and income, and complete loss of liberty. And I argued that my client was yet another casualty of the overblown war on drugs whose continued imprisonment would not make society any safer.

Buju Banton was a perfect case for clemency. He maintained a clean institutional record, and there was absolutely no violence or any allegation of any gang activity. But because he exercised his constitutional right to go to trial, he received a sentence nearly triple that of his more culpable co-defendants, who actually consummated the drug deal, both of whom pled guilty and had already been released from either the prison or drug conspiracy charge. Clemency was now the only avenue open to him for relief from his lengthy decade-long sentence as a first-time offender.

Countless letters included as part of his clemency package attested to his reputation of generosity. The letters described him paying school fees, books and buying uniforms for many inner-city children to attend school. They spoke of him playing Santa Claus to children whose parents could not afford to buy them gifts or new clothes for the holiday; and taking kids to the library, pointing out the importance of wisdom gained through education.

Actor Danny Glover, who is also an activist and humanitarian, wrote in support of his clemency petition:

> From the impoverished areas in Port-au-Prince, Haiti to the rural communities of Ghana West Africa, I have witnessed the immense admiration of fans of Buju Banton as they listen, hum and sign along to his spiritually uplifting music. His Grammy-Award winning music addresses every aspect of life and feeds the heart, mind, body and soul bringing a message of hope…Not only is Buju Banton a great musician with a great deal of work ahead of him, he is also a role model, philanthropist and employer whose band members, musicians and destitute people in his community depend on him for their livelihood. Most importantly, he is a family man and father. President Obama, society would not benefit from his incarceration. He has learned a lot from this very difficult experience and is truly remorseful. Since this is his first offense, I earnestly ask of you to grant him pardon

through clemency for early release. I am confident that he will also use this most difficult experience to encourage others to keep out of trouble.

Stephen Marley, son of reggae icon Robert "Bob" Nesta Marley, wrote that Buju, who is like a brother to him, "eats, drinks and sleeps his music," and that he "is one of the few artists that really benefits people of Jamaica. He is a mentor for a lot of youth coming up that aspire to be in the music industry. He's a very spiritual person."

The passionate appeal to the trial judge by The Honorable Ambassador Dudley Thompson, who had served in the Jamaican Senate as a Member of Parliament and as Minister of National Security and Justice prior to his 2012 death, was included in the clemency package. Thompson, known as one of Jamaica's finest lawyers, had stressed that there must be a "clear limit between persecution and prosecution," and that the case "gives a bad face to the fair administration of justice."

Etan Thomas, while playing for the NBA's Atlanta Hawks, described Buju as "an extremely positive inspiration" in his life and "countless people around the world, especially Black men." Thomas continued, "His music helped keep me out of trouble and encouraged me to perform to the best of my ability, no matter the challenge… He is truly a humble man who makes himself accessible to all who reach out to him."

Out of the Obama Administration's over 1700 commutation grants, no mercy had been previously granted to any non-citizen. There may have been reticence towards putting non-citizens in jeopardy of immediate deportation should their sentences be shortened. However, my client was not in the country illegally and very much wanted to return to his native country. Instead, because clemency was denied, he was warehoused 1,000 miles away in a privately-owned prison facility serving a decade-long sentence at an annual cost to taxpayers of over $30,000, while penning lyrics to new songs he likely wouldn't be able to record for years. Is this justice?[107]

Chapter Ten, Section 3
A Necessary Posthumous Pardon

On August 17, 2016, the date that would have been Marcus Garvey's 129th birthday, his son, cardiologist Dr. Julius Garvey, represented the Garvey family, friends and supporters at a press conference to announce the filing of a petition to President Obama to posthumously pardon his father. The petition, filed on behalf of the descendants of Marcus Garvey, was submitted by Anthony Pierce and Melissa Chastang from the law firm of Akin Gump Strauss Hauer and Feld LLP, along with Professors Justin Hansford and Charles Ogletree.

I was proud to work closely with them as part of the leadership team. The petition stated that Marcus Garvey made substantial contributions to civil and human rights movements in the United States and worldwide, was targeted because of his race and political beliefs, received an unfair trial, and was unjustly convicted. We appealed to President Obama to honor Garvey's substantial contributions to society with a posthumous pardon.

Marcus Garvey lives in history as one of the first leaders of the civil and human rights movement in the United States. In the early twentieth century, he was an advocate for the social, political and economic independence for people of African descent around the world. Garvey founded the Universal Negro Improvement Association and African Communities League (UNIA-ACL), which at its height boasted nearly 6 million members in 40 countries. Garvey strongly advocated for the development of economics as a source of Black empowerment. In the words of Dr. Martin Luther King, Jr., "He was the first man on a mass scale and level to give millions of Negroes a sense of dignity and destiny. And make the Negro feel that he was somebody."

Because of these achievements, Marcus Garvey was viewed as a threat to the established order by the U.S. government. Decades before Dr. King would become targeted for his political activism, J. Edgar Hoover led the Bureau of Investigation, the precursor to the Federal Bureau of Investigation, in its surveillance of Mr. Garvey and actively sought to disrupt and destroy the Garvey movement.

In 1923, based on intelligence gathered from undercover agents posing as UNIA supporters, and aided by judicial proceedings that have largely been condemned as factually unsound and politically and racially motivated, Marcus Garvey was convicted of mail fraud and sentenced to the maximum five years in federal prison.

Because my grandfather, like Marcus Garvey, was an immigrant from the Caribbean who moved to Harlem after the turn of the 20th century, was an admirer of the trailblazing leader, and owned stock in Garvey's Black Star Line, it is not only fitting but also personal for me, that the name of Marcus Garvey be cleared and his legacy uplifted.

As early as 1927, the year when his sentence became eligible for commutation, the U.S. Attorney General concluded that the case against Marcus Garvey was unwarranted and untenable, given the weak evidence in the conviction against him. In partial recognition of the unsettling facts underlying the prosecution of the case, President Calvin Coolidge commuted his sentence in November 1927, and Marcus Garvey was deported to Jamaica.

In the decades that have passed, history and society have confirmed Mr. Garvey's unfair conviction was based on racial and political motivations. However, his name is still tarnished by the stigma of his conviction. The Garvey family seeks to amend the historical record to reflect the esteemed nature of their ancestor's contributions to the global community.

The Garvey petition explained that posthumous Presidential pardons have been granted to correct injustices and heal societal divisions by restoring the unjustifiably diminished reputations of historical figures admired by their communities. For example, President Clinton granted the first posthumous pardon in 1999 to Lt. Henry Ossian Flipper, the first African American graduate of West Point and the first African American commissioned officer in the regular United States Army.

Lt. Flipper was charged with embezzlement and dishonorably discharged from the Army after a court martial. Although acquitted of embezzlement, the dishonorable discharge remained until his 1999 pardon. Despite great admiration from the community and the state of his birth, his family still endured the painful stigma of his unjust conviction and unjustifiably tarnished reputation.

Following President Clinton's lead, President Bush granted the second posthumous Presidential pardon to Charles Winters in 2008, for his direct violation of the Neutrality Act of 1939 by smuggling three military planes to the new state of Israel. Israeli Prime Minister Golda Meir honored Winters as an American who helped establish the state of Israel. Based on the changing times and relationship between the United States and Israel, President Bush granted Winters a posthumous pardon.

We strenuously argued that Marcus Garvey should also be granted a posthumous pardon. Like Lt. Flipper, Mr. Garvey was not simply wrongfully convicted–his unjust conviction involved racial and political motivations that deserved rectification and redress. And like Lt. Flipper, Garvey was an exceptional historical figure whose family and community continue to be wronged by the unjustifiable diminishment of his contributions to society wrought through the U.S. criminal justice system.

I felt that Mr. Garvey was an extraordinary candidate for a posthumous pardon. There have been ongoing and concerted efforts to fully clear his name by members of the U.S. Congress, civil society organizations, cities, states, and international groups. From the 99th–111th Congress, members of Congress have introduced resolutions that expressed the sense of the Congress that the President should grant a pardon to Marcus Garvey of crimes for which he was unjustly prosecuted and convicted.

City governments have passed resolutions recognizing the injustice of Mr. Garvey's conviction and seeking to have his name cleared. Communities in the United States and throughout the world have honored him by dedicating monuments and landmarks to his memory. The Government of Jamaica declared Garvey its first National Hero, bestowed the title of the "Right Excellent" to his name, and placed his image on Jamaican currency.

The red, black and green flag of the Garvey movement has become known as the flag of the Pan-African Movement worldwide, and the color scheme is also reflected in the national flags of Kenya, Malawi, and other African nations. The accolades and honors bestowed upon Marcus Garvey demonstrate the esteem in which he is held in the United States and around the world.

More than 90 years after the imposition of his unjust sentence, we argued that it was time to exonerate Marcus Mosiah Garvey and let history reflect the true nature of his legacy. The petition respectfully called upon President Obama, in the tradition of the last two United States Presidents who both issued posthumous pardons to people convicted in harsh political climates, to likewise grant a posthumous pardon to the Honorable Marcus Mosiah Garvey.

A pardon would not only correct a gross injustice and remove the stain of his racially and politically motivated conviction, but it would also restore his legacy to not only his descendants but the global community as well. Our entreaties, however, went unheeded and thus, as always, "The Struggle" continues.

Chapter Ten, Section 4
Rollercoaster Ride

While working on clemency and issues of criminal justice reform during the last term of the Obama Administration, colleagues would often joke that I was at the White House so much that I must have my own room there. To that, I just smile. Don't get me wrong, the perks have been superb.

The most memorable event I was blessed to attend was BET's Love and Happiness: An Obama Celebration. It was an evening concert in a fabulously elegant colossal tent on the South Lawn of the White House, featuring musical guests that included Jill Scott, Common, Usher, Bell Biv DeVoe, The Roots, Janelle Monae, De La Soul, Yolanda Adams and more.

I had the honor of attending many other affairs on the

grounds of the Obama White House, including lavish receptions in the East Wing; the colossal South x South Lawn Festival of Ideas, Art and Action; Black History month events; and the riveting performance by the original cast of the Broadway musical *Hamilton* in the East Room.

In the White House's South Court Auditorium, I had the privilege of watching the new television miniseries *Roots*, and meeting the casts of *Scandal* and *Underground*. My coalition partners and I even got to join a bowling party with White House staff we worked closely with at the Truman Bowling Alley in the bowels of the Executive Office Building.

The quest for justice often required audience with, or being adjacent to, the White House, and it was an exhilarating, once-in-a-lifetime roller coaster ride. But while there were many ups, there most certainly were downs. Words cannot express how deeply disappointed I was that neither William Underwood, Buju Banton, nor Marcus Garvey was granted any relief.

I was most chagrined with Mr. Underwood's denial of clemency. Buju, at least, had a release date within a couple of years upon which he would be deported without opposition to his country of origin. And for Garvey, while a pardon would be memorable, historic and the right thing to do, such clemency would not effectuate his freedom as he is already deceased.

But father and grandfather, William Underwood, in his 6th decade of life, needed that second chance. And I, along with his children and countless others, had worked so very hard to try to bring it about. I say with all honesty and sincerity, if I could do it over again, I would gladly trade all the perks and good times the White House afforded me in exchange for a serious consideration of William Underwood's petition.

I was charged with adrenaline each time another batch of commutations were announced. At the end of his term, President Obama successfully granted commutation of sentence to 1,715 people, (including 504 life sentences) out of over 35,000 petitions, and 212 pardons. Although significant, this number pales compared to the nearly 14,000 grants of clemency by the Ford Administration. I wondered what type of numbers may have ensued had a dedicated staff expert with the issues had, from day one, been able to vet the cases and make recommendations directly to the President, as was the case with the Ford Clemency Review Board.

Miscarriages of justice have been an ever-present feature of the U.S. criminal punishment system, and presidents have always had the Constitutional power to correct injustice and impact future policy through the executive clemency power. The Obama Administration significantly advanced the dialogue about racism and mass incarceration and the necessity to bring justice to a historically flawed criminal punishment system.

We still have, however, a long road to go. It is critical that our approach advance beyond the easy cases and low-hanging fruit and courageously embrace heroic reform. The groundwork has been laid and now is the time to plant more seeds and fertilize the soil that will allow us to go even bolder in future times with executive, legislative and judicial reforms that bring about long-awaited relief.

Epilogue
"To Be Young, Gifted and Black"[108]

Assembled in the Roosevelt Room of the White House near the end of the Obama era, I suppressed a chuckle thinking about that ridiculous red badge while pondering my whirlwind life for over half a century. The journey has carried me many places, involved connectivity with countless people, and been multi-faceted. No matter what

vantage point I found myself – from selling Black Panther papers on the street corner, to getting arrested in support of freedom for Nelson Mandela, to advocating for fairer crack cocaine laws, or representing clients in court – the issue of justice in my life has remained paramount.

Some battles may result in victory, bringing closure to the matter. Other struggles, however, may never get resolved in one's lifetime, necessitating the baton being passed to the next generation. Still other challenges may manifest in different forms. Who would have imagined that the COINTELPRO from the 60s and 70s would resurrect in the new millennium under the latest repressive moniker, "Black Identity Extremist?" Who would have thought the term "white supremacy" would become mainstream language? Who would have predicted the election of a reality TV star as the country's Chief Executive? And who would have guessed that reparations would become a top news item in the media?

I'm no less militant or revolutionary today than I was in my teens and 20's, but my rebelliousness has taken on different expressions as I have navigated my evolutionary path. I now realize that we can confront the injustices and hypocrisies of society and still survive it. We can work inside the system, while struggling against it. We can challenge the dominant culture and remain true to our beliefs, have an African name, keep our hair in its natural state, and still kick ass. And we can still make a difference and have a momentous public impact, despite personal shortcomings. The quest for justice does not require perfection, only dedication to its ideals.

Without question, as both a Black power advocate and as a Black attorney, I have been on the cutting edge of change and impactful in countless peoples' lives, but I have also experienced the challenges, personal frailties and battle scars that define what it is to be human. I am far from the courageous and fearless freedom fighters of the past I idolize. These ancestors, I believe, are looking down upon us, shaking their heads, and wondering if we will fulfill the quests for liberation, peace and justice they so ardently struggled for.

I balk at that thought. I balk, cognizant of my own personal insecurities and the times I have questioned whether I had done enough, compromised too soon, or made the wrong choice.

Far from the superwoman facade I project while leading coalitions or otherwise in front of a microphone, my international adventures are most emblematic of my inadequacies. These forbearers may not have known how terrified I was after mounting the nearly prone camel at the foot of the pyramids as the humped animal's bulky frame slowly rose, boosting my trembling body into the air. They may have had no idea that my feet were frozen on the skimpy-roped 40-mile high canopy walkway, as my gaze plunged hypnotically down into the depths of green foliage of Kakum National Park in Ghana. They may have been clueless to the fact that I was a hot mess, wailing and bawling on the back of an old donkey slowly trekking up the steep jagged mountainside to the Citadel in Haiti.

The ancestors may have been oblivious to the fact that I refused to leave the sanctity of the safari jeep as others marveled amidst the clouds at the pinnacle of the Ngorongoro Crater in northern Tanzania. And they may have been shocked at the realization that I jumped every time I heard the recurrent gunshot blasts in Nigeria's Oyo State, despite knowing the booms were in homage to the orisa, Ogun.

As I reflect back to the multitudes who have inspired me either historically, or those who once walked with me on this earthly plane, I recognize that they too were not perfect; they made mistakes and struggled with conflicts and contradictions just as I had. I am, however, comforted in the realization that they did the best they could with the gifts they were given, and that we must do the same as we strive in our growth toward greater heights.

I still struggle with personal issues and challenges, but try not to allow them to limit my calling in life. I have embraced the maxim that there is no advancement without adversity, no strength without struggle, and no destiny without difficulty. As I continue my sojourn on earth, I am thrilled that pursuits for justice are being taken up by others who are on their own quests in the world. I feel that movements can advance as long as we honor and respect those who came before us, learn from their faults and flaws, and embrace their triumphs.

As a lawyer, I am grateful for the Black Power era in general, and the cultural and revolutionary Black Nationalist Movement, in particular, for the incredible influence they had on my life. These movements, however, have yet to be formally acknowl-

edged, much less embraced, by mainstream society. As such, these legitimate expressions of the self-determination of a people are subject to being lost in the hearts and minds of future generations.

My quest for justice will be satisfied as current and future generations of young, gifted and Black souls audaciously pick up batons in their respective eras, fight for what they hold true, and continue "The Struggle" by any means necessary, arousing the ageless wisdom of the great anti-slavery orator, Frederick Douglass:

> "If there is no struggle, there is no progress. Those who profess to favor freedom and yet deprecate agitation are [those] who want crops without plowing up the ground; they want rain without thunder and lightning. They want the ocean without the awful roar of its many waters. This struggle may be a moral one, or it may be a physical one, and it may be both moral and physical, but it must be a struggle. Power concedes nothing without a demand. It never did and it never will."

One day, I too will gaze down from the ancestral realm, point my ethereal finger and query the next generation, What are you doing to connect the dots between the people, the movements, and the struggles of yesterday, and those of today? What are you doing to continue our collective quest for justice? It is my sincere hope that when that time comes, I will rest in peace and power, knowing that "The Struggle" for justice continues.

###

Endnotes

Preface

[1] Maafa, pronounced, Mah-AH-fah, is a Kiswahili term meaning "terrible occurrence" or "great disaster." It refers to the catastrophe of the millions of kidnapped Africans who perished while bound for enslavement in the Americas during what is commonly called the "Middle Passage." The term's adaptation was coined in 1994 by anthropologist and African Studies scholar Marimba Ani in her book, *Let the Circle be Unbroken: The Implications of African Spirituality in the Diaspora.*

Prologue

[2] Marley, Bob. "Judge Not." Songs of Freedom, Beverley's Records and Tuff Gong, 1962 and 1992, track 1. https://genius.com/Bob-marley-judge-not-lyrics

[3] "Locs" are my preferred term for "dreadlocks," a hairstyle made popular in the modern era by Rastafarians, and created when uncombed hair is allowed to naturally matt and form into fused units, creating rope-like strands.

[4] The New Afrikan Independence Movement refers to those seeking the establishment of an independent Black nation-state in territory currently claimed by the United States. The term was birthed with the establishment of the Provisional Government of the Republic of New Afrika in 1968 and popularized with the ascendancy of the New Afrikan People's Organization and the Malcolm X Grassroots Movement. The New Afrikan Independence Movement evolved after the assassination of Malcolm X, uplifting his assertions of the need for self-determination, land, internationalization and self-defense. The slogan, 'Free the Land' became the rallying cry of people adhering to these principles.

Chapter One

[5] Stairsteps, Five. "O-o-h Child." Stairsteps, Buddah Records, 1970, track 5. https://genius.com/Five-stairsteps-ooh-child-lyrics

[6] The Universal Negro Improvement Association and African Communities League (UNIA-ACL) is a Black Nationalist fraternal organization founded in 1914 by Marcus Mosiah Garvey. It is asserted that at its height the UNIA had over six million dues-paying members.

[7] Kemet is the ancient name for Egypt; thus Kemetians is the ancient name for Egyptians.

[8] I prefer to use a term that speaks to resistance and rebellion such as "uprising," as opposed to the popular term, "riot."

[9] Study conducted by Kiri Downs, a 17-year-old film student in Manhattan's Urban Academy. See "New 'doll test' produces ugly results," by Hazel Trice Edney, September 14, 2006, *The Final Call* newspaper.

[10] In 2018, the "Justice for Victims of Lynching Act," anti-lynching legislation introduced by three Black Senators, unanimously passed the Senate.

Chapter Two

[11] Brown, James. "Say it Loud: I'm Black and I'm Proud." A Soulful Christmas and Say it Loud: I'm Black and I'm Proud, King Records, 1968 and 1969, track 7 and 1. https://genius.com/James-brown-say-it-loud-im-black-and-im-proud-lyrics https://en.wikipedia.org/wiki/Say_It_Loud_%E2%80%93_I%27m_Black_and_I%27m_Proud

[12] SNCC is the abbreviation for the Student Non-Violent Coordinating Committee, later known as the Student National Coordinating Council.

[13] Hand-dancing is an improvisational form of swing style partner dancing that was developed in D.C. in the 1950s and remains a popular local dance style.

[14] A gele is a traditional African headwrap.

[15] The Nguzo Saba (N' gu zo Sah bah) are the Seven Principles of Blackness, a system of values developed by Maulana Ron Karenga and principally used during the Kwanzaa season.

[16] The New Afrikan Creed is a belief system developed and adopted by the Republic of New Afrika at its 1968 Founding Convention.

[17] Gi is short for judoji, the formal Japanese name for the traditional uniform used for judo practice and competition. The same term is used for karate uniforms.

[18] The colors red, black and green were popularized by Marcus Garvey and the UNIA in 1920 as the colors of the flag of African people wherever they may be in the world. Each color has a symbolic meaning: red stands for the blood; black stands for Black people, and green stands for land.

[19] "Legalize it all: How to win the war on drugs," by Dan Baum, *Harper's Magazine*, April 2016.

Chapter Three
[20] Marley, Bob., Wailers, The. "Soul Rebel." Soul Rebels, Trojan Records, 1970, track 1. https://genius.com/The-wailers-soul-rebel-lyrics

[21] I re-worked this poem upon the transition of Nana Baba Agyei Akoto; dedicated it to his memory, and recited it at his 40-Day Rites ceremony.

[22] The Youth Organization for Black Unity was an outgrowth of the Student Organization for Black Unity, formed in 1969 in N.C. to stop the forced integration of Black schools with White students so as to provide an educational environment where Black students would not be made to feel inferior.

[23] The African Liberation Support Committee was an anti-imperialist and anti-racist organization formed in 1972. It sought to unite various organizations and individuals to support the African Liberation Movements in Southern Africa and Guinea-Bissau. They sent over $98,000 to the African Liberation Movements, and were the first organizers of the African Liberation Day demonstrations held in Washington, DC.

[24] The February First Movement was formed in tribute to the student sit-in at the Woolworth's lunch counter on February 1, 1960, one of the sparks to the Civil Rights Movement. It was a Marxist, anti-imperialist student organization.

[25] The All African People's Revolutionary Party was founded by Kwame Nkrumah, president of Ghana, in 1968 and expanded to the U.S. in 1972 by Kwame Ture, formerly known as Stokely Carmichael. Its key concept is that "the total liberation and unification of Africa under an All-African socialist government must be the primary objective of all Black revolutionaries throughout the world."

[26] African Liberation Day in the U.S. was initiated by the All African People's Revolutionary Party under the leadership of Kwame Ture.

[27] Detroit's Shrine of the Black Madonna was founded by Reverend Albert Cleage.

[28] The Orisa are Yoruba entities who reflect manifestations of Oludumare (God). They are often intermediaries between humans and the spirit world.

[29] Lydia Wallace Barashango passed in 2011 at age 64.

[30] See Chapter Four, Section 5, "Free the Land, the RNA-11 and COINTELPRO," pg. 129.

[31] *Roe v. Wade* was a 1973 landmark decision of the U.S. Supreme Court that effectively legalized abortion. The ruling stated that the Constitution protects a pregnant woman's liberty to choose to have an abortion without excessive government restriction.

[32] The Ausar Auset Society is a Pan-African religious organization founded in 1973 by Ra Un Nefer Amen. The Society provides Afrocentric spiritual training to the African American and African diasporic communities.

[33] In spelling the word Afrika, a 'k' is often used by Black nationalists rather than a 'c'. Many indigenous sub-Saharan African languages use a 'k,' as do Dutch, Germanic/northern European languages. When Afrikan languages are written in English, the 'c' is often used. The Republic of New Afrika adopted the 'k' as a statement of self-determination. In the memoir I use "k" and "c" interchangeably, dependent upon the particular reference.

Chapter Four

[34] Cooke, Sam. "A Change is Gonna Come." Ain't That Good News, RCA Victor Records, 1964, track 7. https://genius.com/Sam-cooke-a-change-is-gonna-come-lyrics https://en.wikipedia.org/wiki/Ain%27t_That_Good_News_(album)

[35] In the Kiswahili language Kuumba Weusi translates into "Black creativity."

[36] Notable exceptions include a recently published work, *Free the Land: The Republic of New Afrika and the Pursuit of a Black Nation-State*, by Edward Onaci 2020; *How Social Movements Die*, by Christian Davenport (2015); and *We Will Shoot Back*, by Akinyele Umoja (2013).

[37] See Christian Davenport, *How Social Movements Die: Repression and Demobilization of the Republic of New Africa*, 2015.

[38] This implication is reminiscent of the 1957 statement of a police officer, after witnessing the influence Malcolm X wielded as he effectively dispersed a crowd of 4,000 with a simple hand signal, contemptuously stating, "No one man should have that much power." This was in 1957 after the arrest and beating of Hinton Johnson, a fellow Nation of Islam brother. This was the incident that boosted Malcolm to national prominence and, almost immediately, he was placed under law enforcement surveillance.

[39] Imari Obadele, *War in America: The Malcolm X Doctrine*, 45.

[40] During a controversial and heated conflict over self-determination and community control of public schools in the Ocean Hill-Brownsville neighborhoods of Brooklyn, N.Y., the Republic of New Afrika sought to organize a people's referendum for the community to determine whether it wanted to secede from New York and, although located in the North, become a part of the Republic of New Afrika.

[41] The RNA's national territory consists of the states claimed by the U.S. of Louisiana, Mississippi, Alabama, Georgia and South Carolina.

[42] Sonny Carson was the namesake of the movie, *The Education of Sonny Carson*.

[43] As first Vice President, Gaidi Obadele assumed the presidency after the resignation of Robert Williams.

⁴⁴ The Black Legionnaires was the name of the Republic of New Afrika's military force.

⁴⁵ A July 17, 2010, Facebook post written by a retired Detroit police sergeant alluded to the circumstances of Fuller's murder: "I am not sure now what happened to those terrorists, but I know that one of them got his justice on the end of a butcher knife."

⁴⁶ Chokwe Lumumba was a young law student at the time, who had put his legal studies on hold to come to Mississippi. He would become very prominent in the RNA as a Vice President and Minister of Justice.

⁴⁷ COINTELPRO is the acronym for the FBI's once secret Counterintelligence Program, a series of covert and often illegal projects aimed at surveilling, infiltrating, discrediting and disrupting movements for social change in the U.S.

⁴⁸ This was the same Mark Felt who in 2005 was outed as "Deep Throat," the pseudonym given to the secret informant who provided information in 1972 to a *Washington Post* reporter about key details of the involvement of President Nixon in the Watergate scandal. He had been convicted in 1980 of ordering illegal break-ins of houses of Weather Underground suspects and their families.

⁴⁹ The Republic of New Afrika teaches that all Blacks, descendants of Africans brought to the United States to be enslaved, are citizens of the Republic of New Afrika by birth. "Conscious citizens" are those who are aware of their citizenship in the Black Nation.

⁵⁰ This may have been another reason for Brother Imari's insistence that he was still the legitimate President and not incapacitated. His main political argument during trial and appeal was that he was the popularly elected president (sovereign) of a government and, as such, under Article III of the U.S. Constitution, he should have never been arrested pursuant to the doctrine of sovereign immunity.

⁵¹ BLA is the acronym for the Black Liberation Army.

⁵² In 2009, Chokwe Lumumba was elected to the City Council of Jackson, MS. In 2013 he was elected Mayor. This was nearly the precise strategy blueprinted in the 1967 book by Imari Obadele, *War in America: The Malcolm X Doctrine*. Both Lumumba's City Council and Mayoral victories were powered by the organization he co-founded in 1990, the Malcolm X Grassroots Movement, which served as the mass association and political action wing of the New Afrikan People's Organization (NAPO), established by Lumumba in 1984. NAPO's formation left the PG-RNA free to continue along its governmental course. NAPO emerged as a grassroots organizing tool and brought great value as an additional vehicle in the New Afrikan Independence Movement.

⁵³ Assata Shakur escaped from the Clinton Correctional Facility for Women in New Jersey on November 2, 1979, purportedly with the help of Black Liberation Army members and allies. In 1984 she fled to Cuba and was granted political asylum.

⁵⁴ On October 20, 1981, $1.6 million was expropriated from a Brinks armored truck in Rockland, NY purportedly by members of the Black Liberation Army and White allies. A guard and two policemen were killed. A multi-count indictment that also included the November 2, 1979 liberation of Assata Shakur from prison, was used to prosecute the defendants. Several trials were held, the first in 1983.

⁵⁵ MOVE is the name of a political/religious organization with a back to nature/Black liberation/animal rights-type philosophy. MOVE members vigorously protested the unjust imprisonment of nine of their communal family members during a 1978 siege. On May 13, 1985

Philadelphia police dropped a bomb on the MOVE house. Eleven people were killed in the ensuing fire that was let to burn, including five children. Sixty-one homes in the neighborhood of row houses were destroyed. Ramona Africa, the only adult survivor of the attack, despite being severely burned, was immediately imprisoned, and served seven years on charges of riot and conspiracy. No one in city government was ever criminally charged with the bombing.

[56] The Republic of New Afrika's Independent Black Foreign Policy Statement demanded the release of Black soldiers from U.S. wars against oppressed people and revolutionary forces in Latin America, Asia and Afrika. It also demanded recognition of Prisoner of War status for armed New Afrikan liberation fighters captured in the war between the U.S. and New Afrika.

[57] See Chapter 5 Section 1, "Who'll Pay Reparations on My Soul?" p.171.

[58] Brother Imari stressed in his testimony that the overground neither directs nor controls the underground and, "unless and until they surface we don't even know they exist."

[59] George Jackson was also the catalyst for Angela Davis' ascendancy to the public sphere, as she was implicated in purchasing the firearms his brother, Jonathan, used to demand his freedom and that of the Soledad Brothers as part of the deadly August 7, 1970 Marin County Courthouse takeover. After going underground, Angela was arrested and charged with murder. As the result of massive public support, she was acquitted of all charges. The sole survivor of the August 7th incident, Ruchell Magee, remains incarcerated as of 2019.

[60] This speaking engagement was in 1990. Sundiata Acoli, co-defendant of Assata Shakur, has been incarcerated since 1973. Over the past thirty years some political prisoners have been released pursuant to innocence, parole, or commutation of sentence.

[61] *Badge of the Assassin* was a 1985 police drama telefilm based on a 1979 book of the same name purporting to be an account of the 1971 deaths of two N.Y. police officers by members of the Black Liberation Army.

[62] *The Big Dance* is a reporter's account of the October 20, 1981 Nyack, N.Y. Brinks expropriation, including government accounts of the 1979 liberation of Assata Shakur from a N.J. prison.

[63] Memorandum Opinion and Order, *United States v. Marilyn Buck*, Defendant; *United States v. Mutulu Shakur*, Defendant, 690 F. Supp. 1291 (SDNY 1988).

[64] "President to President on the Question of Human Rights: Imari Abubakari Obadele, President, The Provisional Government, The Republic of New Afrika, Challenges U.S. President Jimmy Carter on Oppression of Blacks, Indians, & Others, Genocide, Slave Labor in Prisons, Prisoner Exchange and the U.S. Silence on the Vicious Anti-Black 'Cointelpro,'" 16 July 1978.

[65] On Tuesday, June 10, 1997, Geronimo walked out of an Orange County jail, freed after over a quarter of a century. Johnnie Cochran, who represented Geronimo during his original trial, called Judge Dickey's decision "one of the greatest moments of my life and the greatest moment of my legal career." Although Los Angeles District Attorney Gil Garcetti appealed the ruling of Judge Dickey granting Geronimo a new trial, the California Court of Appeals on February 16, 1999 unanimously upheld the lower court decision.

[66] The now defunct *Emerge Magazine* had previously featured the case of Geronimo JiJaga Pratt. See Reginald W. Major and Marcia D. Davis, "Prisoner of War," June 1994.

[67] Twenty-five years after the Senate Select Committee on Intelligence's hearing investigating

FBI abuses during COINTELPRO, Congresswoman Cynthia McKinney spearheaded a hearing during the Congressional Black Caucus's Legislative Weekend on the subject on September 14, 2000, titled "Human Rights in the U.S.: The Unfinished Story of Political Prisoners/Victims of COINTELPRO." Both Geronimo and I testified at the historic hearing, along with Laura Whitehorn, Kathleen Cleaver, Michael Tarif Warren, and Bruce Ellison. The proceedings were transcribed and compiled into a pamphlet under the same title. Unfortunately, as of 2019, there has been no congressional follow-up. Clearly, hearings to investigate these damages, and serious campaigns for parole, clemency, and other means of release of political prisoners will be necessary in order to expose and redress COINTELPRO. The political prisoners have spent over three, four and nearly five decades in prison; several have passed, and many have failing health. This makes getting justice for the imprisoned survivors of COINTELPRO all the more urgent.

[68] The village of Imbaseni, near Arusha, Tanzania, is the home of exiled former Chairman of the Kansas City Black Panther Party Pete O'Neal and his wife Charlotte. Pete and Charlotte are co-founders of the United African Alliance Community Center (UAACC). Their story is the subject of a PBS documentary, 'A Panther in Africa,' and I have had the honor of staying with them at their Center during two trips to Tanzania. Adorning the Center are tributes to Geronimo, including "Long Live Geronimo: Service for All People," "In Honor and in Memory of Geronimo JiJaga" and "Geronimo Lives: MAJI Ni UHAI!!"

[69] Imari Abubakari Obadele died on January 18, 2010 at age 79 of a massive stroke. He had suffered for years with emphysema, and often complained that his respiratory issues were greatly exacerbated by his time in jail and years in prison, in oft-times cold, damp conditions, including solitary confinement.

[70] Mayor Chokwe Lumumba died on February 25, 2014 at age 66 in a Jackson, MS hospital from congestive heart failure. Although there was speculation (from myself as well) that his sudden and mysterious death could possibly have been the result of nefarious action, an outside autopsy financed by Minister Louis Farrakhan seems to have satisfied the family and there has since not been vocal accusations of foul play.

[71] Geronimo JiJaga Pratt died on June 3, 2011 at age 63 from a heart attack in Tanzania where he was living.

[72] Kwame Ture, also known as Stokely Carmichael, credited as being the founder of the Black Power movement, died on November 15, 1998 at the age of 57 from prostate cancer. He has been quoted as saying that his cancer "was given to me by forces of American imperialism and others who conspired with them." He claimed that the FBI had infected him with cancer in an assassination attempt.

[73] Reverend Dr. Ishakamusa Barashango died on January 14, 2004 at age 65. Sources have said that he collapsed in the street - cause of death, a massive heart attack.

[74] Kwame K. Afoh, also known as Edell Lydia, died on October 24, 2010 at age 66 from lung cancer. He had been both a Vice President as well as President of the Provisional Government of the Republic of New Afrika, and a founding member of the National Coalition of Blacks for Reparations in America, N'COBRA. After leaving D.C. he moved to Florida, continuing his activism as head of the Pan Afrikan Nationalists of Southern Florida. Brother Kwame was not a smoker.

Chapter Five

[75] Marley, Bob., Wailers, The. "Get Up, Stand Up." Burnin', Island Records and Tuff Gong, 1973, track 1. https://genius.com/Bob-marley-and-the-wailers-get-up-stand-up-lyrics https://en.wikipedia.org/wiki/Get_Up,_Stand_Up

[76] Heron, Scott Gil. "Who'll Pay Reparations on My Soul?" A New Black Poet - Small Talk at

125th and Lenox, Flying Dutchman and RCA Records, 1970, track 13.
https://en.wikipedia.org/wiki/Small_Talk_at_125th_and_Lenox
https://genius.com/Gil-Scott-heron-wholl-pay-reparations-on-my-soul-annotated
Portions of this section were originally published by the author in the ACLU Blog on Juneteenth,
titled, *"Reparations, Has the Time Finally Come?"* June 19, 2019.

[77] The label "Black Identity Extremist" was first exposed to the public from a 2017 internal FBI
memo as the result of a baseless assessment of a small number of isolated incidents involving
people likely to target law enforcement officers. As the result of widespread outcry to the designation, the FBI claimed in August 2019 that it had abandoned use of the label.

[78] *Reparations Yes!* was first published in 1987 by the House of Songhay. The 1993 third revised
edition included the 1988 Civil Liberties Act Public Law 100-383 granting reparations to the Japanese-Americans; H.R. 40, the Commission to Study Reparations Proposals for African Americans Act; and a draft reparations bill.

[79] During the process of distributing information about the RNA's Anti-Depression Program at
the 1972 National Democratic Convention in Miami FL, RNA Southern Region Interior Minister
Ahmed Obafemi and Brother Tarik Sonebeyatta were unjustly arrested by the Secret Service and
subsequently convicted of having concealed weapons in the vehicle in which they had traveled
to Miami.

[80] For a comprehensive history of N'COBRA from its founding in 1987 through 2001, see "The
National Coalition of Blacks for Reparations in America (N'COBRA): Its Creation and Contribution to the Reparations Movement," by Adjoa Aiyetoro, in *Should America Pay? Slavery and
the Raging Debate on Reparations*, Ray Winbush, Ed., pp 209-225.

[81] See "Imari Obadele: The Father of the Modern Reparations Movement," by Robert C. Smith,
June 2000. Africana.com, Inc. www.hartford-hwp.com archives.

[82] "How We Gonna Make the Black Nation Rise," by Brother "D" with Collective Effort, 1980.

[83] Goree Island's "Door of No Return" is 3 km off the coast of Dakar, Senegal. It overlooks the ocean
and refers to what is purported to be the final exit point from which kidnapped African prisoners
of war in that area were ripped from their homeland to be placed in ships destined for enslavement
in the Americas. There are similar "Doors of No Return" in other parts of West Africa, two of the
most prominent tourist sites being that of Elmina Castle and Cape Coast Castle in Ghana.

[84] Al Bronstein worked in the Deep South during the 1960s as a civil rights lawyer, attempting to
protect the rights of Blacks. After the bloody 1971 Attica prison rebellion, he extended his advocacy to the prisoners' rights movement. Bronstein was director of the National Prison Project
(NPP) of the ACLU Foundation for 25 years. Under his leadership the NPP was responsible for
most of the large-scale class action prison reform lawsuits throughout the country, resulting in attention being paid to constitutional rights of the imprisoned.

[85] Judge Harold H. Greene was a refugee from Nazi persecution. After coming to the U.S. and
working at the Department of Justice, he was involved in drafting what became the 1964 Civil
Rights Act and the 1965 Voting Rights Act. Judge Greene presided over the 1984 monumental
break-up of the American Telephone and Telegraph conglomerate. In my humble opinion, the defendants received the luck of the draw in his being assigned to their case.

[86] In the Iran Contra scandal, senior administration officials secretly facilitated the sale of weapons
to Iran, which was the subject of an arms embargo, with the goal of diverting the illegal sales proceeds to fund a contra army in their insurgency against the socialist government of Nicaragua,
actions prohibited by Congress.

Chapter Six

[87] Gaye, Marvin. "What's Going On." What's Going On, Tamla (Motown Records), 1971, track 1. https://genius.com/Marvin-gaye-whats-going-on-lyrics https://en.wikipedia.org/wiki/What%27s_Going_On_(Marvin_Gaye_song)

[88] The current name of the Women's Legal Defense Fund is the National Partnership for Women and Girls.

[89] As of 2019, Mumia Abu-Jamal remains imprisoned, but has been released from death row.

[90] Note – Large portions of this section were previously published by the author as "A Bittersweet Moment in History," *Champion Magazine*, National Association of Criminal Defense Lawyers (May 2010).

[91] Kumbaya, a song of peace meaning "come by here," was popularized during the 60s, and it was recently revealed that its origin was part of the oral tradition of the Gullah Geechee peoples of Southeastern Georgia.

[92] This section is thanks to the copious notes from Sam Mistrano who interned for the author at the ACLU in 1993 during the time of this hearing.

[93] On February 11, 2020, the House Committee on Oversight and Reform debated H.R. 51, The D.C. Admission Act and marked up the proposal to make D.C. the 51st state. It was sent to the House floor for the first time since 1993. At the hearing Rep. Jamie Raskin (D-MD) stated, "We're the only nation on earth where the residents of the capital city are disenfranchised in the national legislature. Can you imagine if the people in Paris, France were disenfranchised in the National Assembly? You would have another French Revolution on your hands." Rep. Norton, the bill's sponsor, stated, "The residents of the District of Columbia do not particularly enjoy paying billions and millions of dollars annually to support the federal government without the representation their taxes have purchased." On June 26, 2020 the House of Representatives successfully passed the D.C. Admission Act by a vote of 232-180, bringing the District closer to becoming the 51st state. Upon passage D.C. Mayor Bowser, quoting Frederick Douglass, stated, "power concedes nothing without a demand. And statehood is our demand."

[94] Sweet Honey in the Rock, "The Ancestor's Breath."

[95] Shekhem Hames Metin is currently known as Shekhem Tepraim Saa.

[96] A mudram is a spiritual chant, sometimes accompanied by a series of movements, that are linked to evoking the spiritual energy and power of a particular deity.

Chapter Seven

[97] Marley, Bob., Wailers, The. "Three Little Birds." Exodus, Tuff Gong, 1977, track 9. https://genius.com/Bob-marley-and-the-wailers-three-little-birds-lyrics https://en.wikipedia.org/wiki/Three_Little_Birds

[98] Brown, James. "I Got You (I Feel Good)." I Got You (I Feel Good), King Records, 1965, track 1. https://genius.com/James-brown-and-the-famous-flames-i-got-you-i-feel-good-lyrics https://en.wikipedia.org/wiki/I_Got_You_(I_Feel_Good)

[99] The Edward Byrne Memorial Justice Assistance Grant Program (JAG) is the leading source of federal justice funding to state and local jurisdictions to assist in preventing or reducing crime and violence. The program is named for NYC police officer Edward Byrne, who was killed in 1988 while protecting a witness who agreed to testify against drug dealers.

Chapter Nine
[100] Enemy, Public. "Fight the Power." Fear of a Black Planet, Def Jam and Columbia Records, 1990, track 20. https://en.wikipedia.org/wiki/Fear_of_a_Black_Planet https://genius.com/Public-enemy-fight-the-power-lyrics

[101] Based on an article by the author, "Clemency: An Inside Story from a Progressive Advocate," Federal Sentencing Reporter, Vol. 29 (2017).

[102] The Open Society Policy Center is the C-4 arm of the Open Society Foundations.

[103] The term "super predator" was used by Hilary Clinton in 1996, referring to violent crime and drug cartels. She insinuated that Black youth were "not just gangs of kids anymore. They are the kinds of kids that are called super predators. No conscience. No empathy…we have to bring them to heel."

[104] "Crimmigration" refers to the intersection between the criminal justice and immigration systems.

Chapter Ten
[105] Robinson, Smokey., Miracles, The. "The Tears of a Clown." Make it Happen, Tamla (Motown Records, 1967, track 6. https://en.wikipedia.org/wiki/The_Tears_of_a_Clown https://genius.com/Smokey-robinson-and-the-miracles-the-tears-of-a-clown-lyrics

[106] The Federal Sentencing Guidelines, which became effective in 1987, establish a series of escalating sentencing ranges based on the circumstances of the offense and the criminal record of the convicted person.

[107] Buju Banton was released from prison on December 8, 2018, returned to Jamaica and resumed his singing career. But issues in his and so many other cases that have led to mass incarceration, such as entrapment, the improper use of confidential informants, and the oppressive "trial penalty" when one exercises the constitutional right to go to trial, remain unresolved.

Epilogue
[108] Simone, Nina. "To Be Young, Gifted and Black." Black Gold, RCA Records, 1970, track 7. https://en.wikipedia.org/wiki/To_Be_Young,_Gifted_and_Black

Description of Pictures in Text

Parting Shots....

PCC Chairperson
Nkechi Taifa

PARTING SHOTS Image List

Page 361
Imhotep Alkebulan, Reco Forbes, General X. Rashid, Masai Ehehosi
Nkechi, Khaleed London • Ahmed Obafemi • Imari Obadele
Jesselyn McCurdy, Sakira Cook, Nkechi, Jasmine Tyler, Kara Gotsch
Nkechi, Daima Abdur-Rasheed, Ayofemi Babatunde, Karim Bilal Haqq

Page 362
Assata Shakur, Imari Obadele, Fela Olatunji
Anthony Underwood, Miko Underwood, MC Hammer, Ebony Underwood, Shaka Senghor
Chokwe Lumumba, Nkechi • Imari Obadele, Nkechi
Chokwe Lumumba, Fulani Sunni Ali
Cynthia Roseberry, LaTosha Brown, Nkechi • Brother, Dhoruba Ben Wahad • Nkechi

Page 363
Minister Louis Farrakhan, security, Nkechi, Baba El Zulu
Wade Henderson, Norman Brown • Attalah Shabazz, Nkechi
Maynard Henry • Kamau Amin • Ta-Nehisi Coates, Nkechi

Page 364
Imamu Kuumba, Akili Ron Anderson, Rabia Rayford • Angela Y. Davis, Nkechi
Alina Kee, Malesha Kee, Akili Peyton, Nkechi, Krystal Kee
Nkechi, Mayor Chokwe Antar Lumumba
Kara Gotsch, Jasmine Tyler, Jesselyn McCurdy, Angelyn Frazer-Giles, Nicole Austin-Hillery
Sundiata Acoli, Mwasi, Torres, Yaya (1978 or 79) • Nkechi, Dakarai Kearney

Page 365
Claudette Muhammad, JoAnn Watson, Nkechi, Julianne Malveaux
Iva Carruthers, Danny Glover, Nkechi, Kamm Howard
Paula Drake, Josephine Caldwell, Nkechi, Roberta Kee
Kokayi Patterson, Imari Obadele, Imani Mahdi • Nkechi, Willie Ricks

Page 366
Paula Drake Family (4 generations) plus cousin Carla Potter
Imani Margerum, Khaleed London, Nkechi, Nathaniel Margerum
Roberta Kee Family (3 generations) • Craig DeRoche, Nkechi, Rep. Bobby Scott
Imari Obadele, Bomani Sekou • Pam Africa, Nkechi, Ramona Africa
Dr. Ron Daniels, Dick Gregory (in background)

Page 367
Charles Ogletree, Kemba Smith, Nkechi, Congressman Bobby Scott • Atty Gen Eric Holder, Nkechi
Rosa Parks, Mariama, Nkechi • Poppa Wells (Anwar Pasha), young John Conyers
Daddy and Nkechi • Alice Marie Johnson, Nkechi
Nkechi at CHR Awards Ceremony

Page 368
Nkechi, Bomani Sekou • Nkechi, Col. Hanif (security)
Njeri Algahanee
Marc Mauer, Nkechi, Monique Dixon, Sakira Cook, Jesselyn McCurdy, Kara Gotsch
Nicole Beharie • Nkechi, Chokwe Lumumba • Nkechi, Pete O'Neal
Vice President Alajo Adegbalola, President Imari Obadele

Page 369
Jesselyn McCurdy • Ngina Milner, Baba Lumumba • Angela Y. Davis, Soffiyah Elijah
Angel Drake, Myan Drake, Paula Drake, Aaliyah Drake, Alyssa Drake, Leilani Drake (standing)
Mariama Taifa-Seitu • President Imari Obadele, security • Nkechi

INDEX

Bell, Tyrie – 330
Bennett, Kanya – 316
Bennett, Judge Mark – 330
Bernal, Dr. Eshe Deborah – VII, 262
Bias, Len – 237
Biden, Senator Joe – 309, 312, 317, 318
Biko, Steve – 199
Bipartisan – 292, 293, 294, 313, 314, 315
Bishop, Maurice – 199
Black American Law Students Association (BALSA; BLSA) – 163, 187
Black Arts Movement – 86
Black Consciousness Movement – 190, 199
Black Cross Nurses – 107
Black Identity Extremist – 108, 347, 356
Black Land Movement – 70, 71, 73, 110
Black Land News Magazine – 71, 72, 73
Black Legionnaires – 125, 127, 353
Black Liberation Army (BLA) – 154, 159, 160, 162, 214, 354
Black Lives Matter – 215, 242
Black Manifesto – 173
Black Man's Development Center – 81
Black Nationalist – XIII, 47, 98 101, 103, 108, 115, 118, 133, 134, 135, 137, 175, 183, 218, 303, 349, 350
Black Panther Party – III, XV, 41, 47, 59, 60, 62, 73, 78, 108, 115, 126, 131, 136, 137, 146, 160, 163, 164, 171, 173, 187, 197, 199, 205, 233, 234, 355
Black Women's United Front – 82, 104
Blakes, Bavu – 181
Blakes, Carol – 181
Blandford, Virginia – 86
Blandon, Oscar Danilo – 248
Bland, Sandra – 293
Blood In My Eye – 157
Booker, Senator Cory – 335
Botha, Pik – 193
Bradford, Lawrence – 51
Brant, Ramona – 322, 323, 325, 329
Braveboy, Aisha – 278
Brewer, Willie Yao – VII, 184
Brinks – 220, 258, 353, 354
Brittain, John – 131
Bronstein, Al – 202, 358
Brookins, Freddie – 284
Browder, Anthony – 84
Brown, Claude – 46, 68
Brown, Gerard – 85
Brown, H. Rap – 47, 76, 123
Brown, Larry – 66
Brown, Nana Kwabena – 71, 111, 166, 256, 264
Brown, Norman – 319, 322, 323, 324, 325, 326, 329
Brown, Oscar Jr. – 97
Brown, Roach – 185, 325, 327, 328
Brown, Sterling – 20, 22
Brown v. Board of Education – 05, 17, 298
Brutus, Dennis – 193
Bryant, Carolyn – 24
Bryant, Roy – 24, 25
Buck, Marilyn – 167, 214, 221, 258 259, 354
Buju Banton Defense Committee – 338
Bukhari, Safiya – VI, 158, 161, 162, 163, 164,359

Burge, John – 199, 306
Burnham, Margaret – 203
Burns, Haywood – 195, 203, 230, 231
Busboys and Poets – 322, 323, 328
Bush, George W. – 291, 308, 322, 325, 327
Butcher, Goler T. – 268
Byrd, Brittany – 330
Byrne Grant Program – 286
#Cut50 – 325, 330
Cain, Deborah – 330
Calderon, Tovah – 278
Caldwell, Donna – VIII, 257
Caldwell, Josephine – 07, 08
Caldwell, St. Elmo – 07, 08
Callender, Lorenzo Lord – 85
Capitol Bombing – XV, 213, 214, 219, 222, 225
Carmichael, Stokely – 134, 351, 355, see also Ture, Kwame
Carter, Almo – 278
Carter Barron Amphitheatre – 224, 225
Carter, James – 278
Carter, Jimmy – 162, 316, 354
Cauchon, Dennis – 239
Center for Black Unity – 81, 110
Cesal, Craig – 330
Changa, Baba – 110
Chastang, Melissa – 341
Chocolate City – 72, 98, 250
Chui, General – 127, 359
Churchill, Ward – 234
Cinque, Joseph – 19
Citizens United for the Rehabilitation of Errants (CURE) – 290
Civil Liberties Redress Act – 176
Civil Rights Movement – 25, 28, 185, 230, 249, 250, 351
Clark Amendment – 192
Clark, John Henrik – 84
Clark, Mark – 78, 131
Cleaver, Kathleen – 355
Clemency Initiative – 281, 289, 319, 320, 321, 333
Clemency Project 2014 – 320, 326
Clementine, Miss – 330
Clinton, Bill – 245, 288, 310
Coates, Paul – VIII, 166, 205
Coates, Ta-Nehisi – 172
Cocaine Kingpin Punishment Act – 309
Cochran, Johnnie – 165, 354
Code Name Zorro – 223
Code of Umoja – 258
Cody, MiAngel – 330
COINTELPRO – 108, 118, 129, 132, 133, 352, 353, 354, 355
Cole, James – 319
Colfax Massacre – 33
Combs, Dr. Walter – 10, 11
Committee in Solidarity with the Peoples of El Salvador (CISPES) – 136
Community Fabric and Gift Shop – 66
Confidential Informant – 339
Congressional Black Caucus – 196, 242, 252, 291, 309, 316, 332, 355